Liberalizing Foreign Trade

Volume 2

Liberalizing Foreign Trade

Edited by
*Demetris Papageorgiou, Michael Michaely, and
Armeane M. Choksi*

Volume 2

The Experience of Korea, the Philippines, and Singapore

KOREA   *Kwang Suk Kim*

THE PHILIPPINES   *Geoffrey Shepherd and Florian Alburo*

SINGAPORE   *Bee-Yan Aw*

Basil Blackwell

First published 1991

HF
1411
. L497
1989
V. 2

Basil Blackwell, Inc.
3 Cambridge Center
Cambridge, Massachusetts 02142, USA

Basil Blackwell Ltd
108 Cowley Road, Oxford, OX4 1JF, UK

British Library Cataloguing in Publication Data
A CIP Catalogue record for this book is available from the British Library.

Library of Congress Cataloging in Publication Data

Liberalizing foreign trade/edited by Demetris Papageorgiou, Michael Michaely, Armeane M. Choksi.
p. cm.
Includes index.
Contents: v. 1. Liberalizing Foreign Trade: The Experience of Argentina, Chile, and Uruguay — v. 2. Liberalizing Foreign Trade: The Experience of Korea, the Philippines, and Singapore — v. 3. Liberalizing Foreign Trade: The Experience of Israel and Yugoslavia — v. 4. Liberalizing Foreign Trade: The Experience of Brazil, Colombia, and Perú — v. 5. Liberalizing Foreign Trade: The Experience of Indonesia, Pakistan, and Sri Lanka — v. 6. Liberalizing Foreign Trade: The Experience of New Zealand, Spain, and Turkey — v. 7. Liberalizing Foreign Trade: Lessons of Experience in the Developing World.
ISBN 0–631–16666–1 (v. 1). ISBN 0–631–16667–X (v.2)
ISBN 0–631–17595–4 (7-volume set)
1. Commercial policy. 2. Free trade. 3. International trade.
I. Papageorgiou, Demetris, 1938–. II. Michaely, Michael, 1928–. III. Choksi, Armeane M., 1944–.
HF 1411.L497 1989
382′.3—dc19   88–37455
                                                                              CIP

Typeset in 10 on 12pt Times
by TecSet Ltd
Printed in Great Britain by T. J. Press Ltd., Padstow

Contents

About the Editors

Demetris Papageorgiou is the Chief of the Country Operations Division in the Brazil Department of the World Bank. He has served as a senior economist in the Country Policy Department and as an economist at the Industry Division of the Development Economics Department.

Michael Michaely is the Lead Economist in the Brazil Department of the World Bank. Previously he was the Aron and Michael Chilewich Professor of International Trade and Dean of the Faculty of Social Sciences at the Hebrew University of Jerusalem. He has published numerous books and articles on international economics.

Armeane M. Choksi is Director of the Brazil Department in the Latin American and Caribbean Region of the World Bank. He is co-editor with Demetris Papageorgiou of *Economic Liberalization in Developing Countries*, and has written on industrial and trade policy.

Editors' Preface

The General Objective

"Protection," said the British statesman Benjamin Disraeli in 1845, "is not a principle, but an expedient," and this pronouncement can serve very well as the text for our study of *trade liberalization*. The benefits of open trading have by now been sufficiently demonstrated and described by economic historians and analysts. In this study, we take them for granted and turn our minds from the "whether" to the "how."

The Delectable Mountains of open trading confront the pilgrim with formidable obstacles and there are many paths to the top. The direct route seldom turns out to be the best in practice. It may bring on rapid exhaustion and early collapse, while a more devious approach, skirting areas of excessive transition costs, may offer the best prospects of long-term survival.

Given the sharp diversity of economic background and experience between different countries, and indeed, between different periods in the same country, we should not expect the most favorable route to turn out the same for each country, except perhaps by accident. There are, however, fundamental principles underlying the diversities and it is our thesis that a survey and analysis of a sufficiently broad spectrum of countries over sufficiently long development periods may serve to uncover them.

With this object in view, we set out to study as many liberalization experiences as possible and aimed at including all liberalizations in developing countries in the post-world war period. However, the actual scope of this study had three limitations. First, we restricted the study to market-based economies. Second, experiences with highly inadequate data had to be excluded. Third, to be an appropriate object of study, an experience had to be of some minimum duration. Applying these criteria, we were left with the study of liberalization experiences in the 19 countries listed at the end of this preface. This volume deals with three of these countries (Korea, the Philippines, and Singapore). Five other volumes contain the rest of the country studies, and the seventh volume presents the synthesis of the country analyses.

Definitions

"Trade liberalization" implies any change which leads a country's trade system toward neutrality in the sense of bringing its economy closer to the situation which would prevail if there were no governmental interference in the trade system. Put in words, the new trade system confers no discernible incentives to either the importable or the exportable activities of the economy.

By "episode" we mean a period long enough to accommodate a significant run of liberalization acts terminating either in a swing away from liberalization or in a period where policy changes one way or another cease to be apparent.

The "episode of liberalization" thus defined is the unit of observation and analysis employed in each of our country studies.

Identification of Liberalization Episodes

There are three main indicators of a move in the direction of neutrality: (a) a change in the price system; (b) a change in the form of intervention; (c) changes in the foreign exchange rate.

Price System

The prices in question are nominal protection rates determining consumption patterns and, more importantly, effective protection rates affecting production activities. Any change which lowered the average level and distribution of rates of protection would count as a move toward neutrality. Typically, such a change would arise from a general reduction in tariffs, but it might also be indicated by the introduction, rather than the removal, of instruments of government intervention, or even, indeed, by the raising rather than the lowering of the incidence of government intervention. An instance of this might be the introduction of export subsidies in a protective regime previously biased against exports and favoring import substitution. Another instance might be the introduction or increase of tariffs on imported raw materials and capital goods in a regime where tariffs have previously escalated over the whole field, with the zero and lower rates applying on these imports.

Form of Intervention

The form of intervention may be affected by a change in the quantitative restriction (QR) system itself or by replacing QRs with tariffs. Although the actual changes might be assigned price *equivalents*, it is not feasible to assign price equivalents to their comprehensive effects. Moreover, the reactions they induce are so different from responses to price signals that they are better treated as a separate category.

The Exchange Rate

A change in the level of a *uniform* rate of exchange, since it does not discriminate between one tradeable activity and another, is not of itself an instrument of intervention. A move from a *multiple* to a uniform rate would, however, be equivalent to a change in intervention through commercial policy instruments; changes in the rate would modify the effect of commercial policy instruments already in being, for example, where QR systems are operated through the exchange control mechanism itself or where tariffs effective at an existing rate become redundant at a higher rate. Failing detailed studies of the impact of exchange rate changes on QRs or tariffs we take as a general rule that a formal and real *devaluation* constitutes a step towards liberalization.

Policies and Results

We do not take the actual degree of openness of the economy as an indicator in itself of a liberalization episode. Liberalization policies may commonly be expected to lead to an increase in the share of external trade but this is not an inevitable result. For instance, if, starting from a state of disequilibrium, liberalization is associated with a formal devaluation imports may actually fall. Therefore attempts to detect liberalization by reference to trade ratios rather than to policy *intentions* would be misleading. Exceptionally, however, the authors of the country studies have used trade performance as an indication of liberalization, particularly where actual changes in imports can be used to measure the degree of relaxation, or otherwise, of QRs.

Measurement of Degrees of Liberalization

In each country study we have attempted to indicate the degree of liberalization progressively attained by assigning to each year a mark for performance on a scale ranging from 1 to 20. A mark of 20 would indicate virtually free trade, or perfect neutrality, a mark of 1 would indicate the highest possible degree of intervention. These indices are subjective and peculiar to each country studied and in no way comparable between countries. They are a rough and ready measure of the progress, or otherwise, of liberalization as perceived by the authors of the country study in question. They reflect, for instance, assessments of nominal and effective rates of protection, the restrictiveness of QRs, and the gap between the formal exchange rate and its equilibrium level.

Analysis of Successful Liberalization Exercises

To arrive at criteria of what makes for success in applying liberalization policies, the following questions might be asked in our studies.

1   What is the appropriate speed and intensity of liberalization?
2   Is it desirable to have a separate policy stage of replacement of nonprice forms of trade restrictions by price measures?
3   Is it desirable to treat productive activities during the process of trade liberalization uniformly or differentially?
4   If uniform treatment is indicated, how should it be formulated?
5   On what pattern of performance of the economy is the fate of liberalization likely to hinge?
6   Is it desirable to have a stage of export promotion? If so, what should its timing be in relationship to import liberalization?
7   What are the appropriate circumstances for the introduction of a liberalization policy?
8   How important are exogenous developments in deciding the sustainability of liberalization?
9   Finally, what *other* policy measures are important, either in their existence or absence, for a successful policy of trade liberalization?

Lurking behind many of these issues are the (potential) probable costs of adjustment of a liberalization policy and, in particular, its possible impact on the employment of labor.

Scope and Intention of our Study

The general purpose of our analysis is to throw up some practical guidance for policymakers and, in particular, for policymakers in developing countries where the economic (and political) climate tends to present the greatest obstacles to successful reform. It is for this reason that (as already explained) we have based our studies on the experience of a wide spread of countries throughout the developing world. All country studies have followed a common pattern of inquiry, with the particular analytical techniques left to the discretion of the individual authors. This approach should yield inferences on the questions raised above in two different ways; via the conclusions reached in the country studies themselves, and via the synthesis of the comparative experience of trade liberalization in these countries.

The presence of a common pattern of inquiry in no way implies that all country studies cover the same questions in a uniform manner. Not all questions are of equal importance in each country and the same quantity and quality of data were not available in all countries. Naturally, the country studies differ on the issues they cover, in the form of the analysis, and in the structure of their presentation.

The country studies are self-contained. Beyond addressing the questions of the project, each study contains sufficient background material on the country's attributes and history of trade policy to be of interest to the general reader.

The 19 countries studied, classified within three major regions, are as follows.

Latin America

Argentina	by Domingo Cavallo and Joaquín Cottani
Brazil	by Donald V. Coes
Chile	by Sergio de la Cuadra and Dominique Hachette
Colombia	by Jorge García García
Peru	by Julio J. Nogués
Uruguay	by Edgardo Favaro and Pablo T. Spiller

Asia and the Pacific

Indonesia	by Mark M. Pitt
Korea	by Kwang Suk Kim
New Zealand	by Anthony C. Rayner and Ralph Lattimore
Pakistan	by Stephen Guisinger and Gerald Scully
Philippines	by Florian Alburo and Geoffrey Shepherd
Singapore	by Bee-Yan Aw
Sri Lanka	by Andrew G. Cuthbertson and Premachandra Athukorala

The Mediterranean

| Greece | by George C. Kottis |
| Israel | by Nadav Halevi and Joseph Baruh |

Portugal   by Jorge B. de Macedo, Cristina Corado, and
              Manuel L. Porto
Spain   by Guillermo de la Dehesa, José Juan Ruiz, and
              Angel Torres
Turkey   by Tercan Baysan and Charles Blitzer
Yugoslavia   by Oli Havrylyshyn

Coordination of the Project

Demetris Papageorgiou, Michael Michaely, and Armeane M. Choksi of
the World Bank's Latin America and Caribbean Region are the directors
of this research project. Participants in the project met frequently to
exchange views. Before the country studies were launched, the common
framework of the study was discussed extensively at a plenary conference.
Another plenary conference was held to discuss early versions of the
completed country studies, as well as some emerging general inferences. In
between, three regional meetings in each region were held to review
phases of the work under way. An external Review Board consisting of
Robert Baldwin (University of Wisconsin), Mario Blejer (International
Monetary Fund), Jacob Frenkel (University of Chicago and Director of
Research, International Monetary Fund), Arnold Harberger (University
of Chicago and University of California–Los Angeles), Richard Snape
(Monash University), Martin Wolf (Chief Economic Leader Writer,
Financial Times) contributed invaluable assistance in the reviewing process
of the country studies and the synthesis volume.

The Series

Korea, the Philippines, and Singapore are presented in this volume. The
series' other publications are the following:
Volume 1: Liberalizing Foreign Trade. The Experience of Argentina,
Chile, and Uruguay;
Volume 3: Liberalizing Foreign Trade. The Experience of Israel and
Yugoslavia;
Volume 4: Liberalizing Foreign Trade. The Experience of Brazil,
Colombia, and Perú;
Volume 5: Liberalizing Foreign Trade. The Experience of Indonesia,
Pakistan, and Sri Lanka;
Volume 6: Liberalizing Foreign Trade. The Experience of New Zealand,
Spain, and Turkey;
Volume 7: Liberalizing Foreign Trade. Lessons of Experience in the
Developing World.

Demetris Papageorgiou, Michael Michaely, Armeane M. Choksi

Part I

Korea

Kwang Suk Kim
Kyung Hee University, Seoul

Contents

List of Figures and Tables

Acknowledgments

This study owes much to the support of the World Bank and the helpful guidance of Armeane M. Choksi, Demetris Papageorgiou, and Michael Michaely, the codirectors of the Bank project on the timing and sequencing of trade liberalization policy. I am particularly grateful to Demetris Papageorgiou of the World Bank for his invaluable advice and counsel during the conduct of this study. He read the entire draft of the study very carefully and made numerous suggestions which greatly improved the end results. I have been greatly helped by all my colleagues and the members of the Panel Committee associated with the Bank project, who gave their useful comments on the early version of this study at the regional conferences organized by the Bank.

I would also like to acknowledge the research assistance provided during various stages of the study by Hae-Chul Choi, Pyong-Sup Yang, and other former graduate students at the Kyung Hee University. Finally, the entire manuscript was edited by Philippa Shepherd. The author alone, however, is responsible for all errors and omissions.

1

Introduction

The Republic of Korea (hereafter referred to as Korea) has achieved rapid industrialization and growth since the early 1960s. Gross national product (GNP) grew at an average annual rate of approximately 8.5 percent from 1962 to 1985, and per capita GNP more than quadrupled from US$493 to US$2,070 in constant 1980 prices. This GNP growth was led by the manufacturing sector, which grew at an average annual rate of 15 percent. The manufacturing sector share in GNP more than doubled, from 14 percent to nearly 30 percent, during the same period, while the agriculture, forestry, and fishery sector's share declined sharply from 37 percent to 14 percent.

Before the 1960s, serious disruptions had slowed economic growth to the point of stagnation. Korea's liberation from Japanese colonial rule at the close of World War II was accompanied by an unexpected partition of the country; the resultant Korean war (1950–3) destroyed nearly half the existing industrial facilities and infrastructures in the south. Massive foreign assistance, particularly from the United States, largely financed post-war reconstruction and stabilization, undertaken immediately after the armistice. Although some success was achieved in stabilizing prices in the late 1950s, GNP grew at an average of only 3.8 percent annually between 1953 and 1962; per capita GNP increased by a mere 1 percent a year.

In 1963, however, Korea reached a turning point in its economic development and since then has generally sustained a high rate of GNP growth (except for the unusual year, 1980, in which the real GNP declined by 6 percent). The sudden increase in output growth is generally ascribed to a change in development strategy in the early 1960s. Undoubtedly, there were other economic and noneconomic influences which cannot be easily quantified; however, the shift from an inward-looking import substitution strategy to an export-oriented development strategy must be accounted a central factor in accelerating output growth. Since the shift in development strategy, exports have unquestionably been an engine of growth in Korea.

The total volume of merchandise exports has continuously expanded by about 25 percent annually since 1962, thereby stimulating the growth of the domestic economy. The exports of goods and nonfactor services had jumped from a mere 5 percent of GNP in 1962 to 38 percent by the middle of the 1980s.

Despite the rapid growth of exports, the country's current balance on goods and services was almost invariably in deficit until 1985 (although the size of the deficit generally showed a declining trend in relation to the country's total imports of goods and services). The persistent deficit was mainly attributable to the concurrent rapid expansion of imports from a base in the 1960s that was much larger than that of exports. The rapid growth of output created an ever increasing demand for imports. As a result of this precarious balance-of-payments situation, the Korean government's approach to import liberalization was gradual and cautious even after export trade had been liberalized in accordance with the new export orientation.

Conscious efforts to liberalize trade, particularly imports, began in 1965 when Korea had almost completed the system of incentives consistent with export-oriented industrialization and had gained some confidence in export expansion. The first episode of trade liberalization, characterized by the loosening of quantitative restrictions (QRs) on imports, continued until 1967. Thereafter, however, the liberalization effort was virtually in abeyance for a decade, as a result, among other reasons, of an unfavorable balance of payments. The second episode of liberalization, from 1978 to 1979, was characterized by both the loosening of QRs and a reduction of tariff barriers on imports. In this instance, trade liberalization made continuous, though slow, progress thereafter (apart from a temporary halt in 1980). Tables 1.1 and 1.2 summarize Korea's liberalization episodes and their chronology.

The main purpose of this study is to discuss the Korean experience of designing and implementing trade liberalization policies, using the World Bank's *Analytical Framework for Country Studies* as a guideline (see the preface to this volume). The term "trade liberalization" is interpreted here in a broad sense. It encompasses not only the reductions of tariffs and nontariff trade barriers but also the acts that reduced the administrative procedures of importing, export taxes or subsidies, and export quotas or voluntary restraints. It should also include the change from a nonuniform exchange rate system to a uniform rate. The focus of this study is the procedural issues relating to the timing and sequencing of Korea's trade liberalization policies; other policies are studied only when relevant to analyzing issues essential to formulating and implementing liberalization policy. The normative question of whether liberalization is good or bad is therefore not dealt with.

Table 1.1 Summary of Korea's liberalization episodes, 1965–1967 and 1978–1979

Question	1965–7 episode	1978–9 episode
Broad nature	Mainly the loosening of QRs	Loosening of QRs and reduction of tariffs
Size, duration	Large, short	Small and gradual, long
Stages and targets	No clear stages planned, but an increase in liberalization intended	No clear stages, but a gradual liberalization announced
Economic circumstances		
Balance of payments	Improving	Improving
Prices of major exports	Increasing	Recovering
Rate of inflation	High: 14.5 percent	High: 13 percent
Rate of growth	High: 8.5 percent	High: 12 percent
Foreign debts	Small	Large
Structure of protection	Protection highly differentiated by industry	Protection differentiated by industry, but much simpler than in the 1960s
Shocks	None	Second oil shock at end (1979)
Agricultural output	Fluctuating	Good, except for 1978
Political circumstances		
Strong stable government	Yes, but some opposition	Authoritarian government (until Park's assassination in 1979)
Ideological shifts	None	None
Public perception and debate	Moderate	Increased
Administering arm of government	Mainly the Ministry of Commerce and Industry (MCI)	Mainly MCI and the Ministry of Finance
International influence	Influenced by US aid mission	Some indirect pressures from the General Agreement on Tariffs and Trade and the International Monetary Fund
Accompanying policies		
Exchange rate	Crawling peg (small black market)	Pegged by the monetary authority (negligible black market)
Export promotion	Various incentives provided for exports	Export incentives continuously provided
Export taxes	No	No
Monetary policy	High interest rate policy; monetary contraction attempted but failed	High interest rate policy; monetary contraction attempted but failed

Fiscal policy	Balanced budget; government saving increased	Tax revenue increased but deficits continued
Capital movement	Inflows encouraged but outflows almost prohibited	Inflows encouraged, and outflows restricted except for specified investments
Implementation		
Program deviation	Announced programs were fully implemented, but liberalization did not continue after 1967	Announced programs were fully implemented, and a gradual liberalization continued after a halt in 1980
Economic performance		
Employment	Continuously increased	Continuously increased
Inflation	Fluctuated between 7 percent and 9 percent	Accelerated from 9 percent in 1977 to the peak of 39 percent in 1980 owing to a rapid rise in world oil prices; then fell to 5 percent by 1982
Growth	Accelerated to 11 percent and 14 percent in 1968 and 1969 respectively	High growth continued except for 1980 (in which real GNP declined by 6 percent)
Imports and exports	Trade deficits widened	Trade deficits widened until 1980 but continuously narrowed thereafter
Wages	Real wages increased continuously	Real wages fluctuated

Following this introduction, major attributes of the Korean economy are discussed in chapter 2 to sketch in the economic background in which liberalization policies were formulated and implemented. A historical description of the long-term pattern of the country's liberalization policies follows in chapter 3, to identify the liberalization episodes that merit study. The liberalization episodes thus identified are then analyzed in the next two chapters: chapter 4 deals with the broad nature of each liberalization episode, the circumstances under which it took place, the character of accompanying policies, and the implementation of preannounced plans; in chapter 5 an attempt is made to demonstrate the economic impact of each liberalization episode by analyzing the subsequent changes in major economic variables. Chapter 6 deals with the issues involved in determining an appropriate path for a liberalization policy, and presents inferences from the Korean experience.

Table 1.2 Chronology of Korea's liberalization episodes, 1965–1967 and 1978–1979

Dates	Policy change
First episode (1965–7)	
May 1964	Devaluation from 130 won to 256 won to the US dollar
Jan 1965	QRs on imports somewhat loosened
Mar 1965	The adoption of a unitary floating exchange rate system announced
Aug 1965	Exchange rate pegged at 271 won to the US dollar
Sep 1965	Interest rate reform announced; bank deposit and loan rates sharply raised
Dec 1965	Legal reserve requirements raised
Jan–Dec 1965	The government direct controls on prices gradually removed
Jan 1966	The Foreign Capital Inducement Law enacted to streamline the existing laws
Jan 1966	QRs on imports further liberalized
Feb 1966	Legal reserve requirements raised again
Jan 1967	QRs on imports further liberalized
Jan 1967	Managed floating of the domestic currency again allowed
Jul 1967	QRs on imports substantially loosened by reforming the system of trade control
Dec 1967	Tariff reform announced to be effective from Jan 1, 1968
Second episode (1978–9)	
Jul 1977	Value-added tax newly introduced to simplify the structure of indirect taxes
Feb 1978	The Import Liberalization Committee formally established
May 1978	The first step of import liberalization announced
Jun 1978	Interest rates on bank deposits and loans raised substantially
Sep 1978	The second step of import liberalization announced
Oct 1978	A regulation concerning the administration of Korean residents' investment abroad newly instituted
Jan 1979	Tariff reform put into effect: the average rate of legal tariffs reduced from 41.3 percent to 34.4 percent
Jan 1979	The third step of import liberalization announced
Apr 1979	An overall measure for economic stabilization announced, and the direct price controls which had been intensified during 1977–8 began to be dismantled

2

Attributes of the Korean Economy

Population, Labor Force, and Wage Structure

The Republic of Korea is situated in the southern part of the Korean peninsula with a land area of about 98,000 km². The country is quite mountainous; its highland covers over 70 percent of the total land area. Total population in the country exceeded 40 million by the middle of 1984, although its growth rate declined gradually from nearly 3 percent a year in the early 1960s to about 1.6 percent after the mid-1970s. As a result, population density as of 1984 was roughly 408 people per square kilometer, one of the highest in the world.

According to the 1980 population and housing census, approximately 8.4 million people, or 22.3 percent of the population (37.4 million), were living in the capital city of Seoul in that year. Population in Pusan, the second largest city located at the southern end of the peninsula, was approximately 3.2 million, or 8.4 percent of the total population. About 31 percent of the nation's population is therefore concentrated in the two large cities. Other major cities whose population exceeded 500,000 as of 1980 are Taegu (1.6 million), Inchon (1.1 million), Kwangju (0.7 million), and Taejon (0.6 million) (Economic Planning Board (EPB), *Korean Statistical Yearbook*, 1983).

The concentration of population in the major cities partly reflects the regional dispersion of production activities in the country. According to the Economic Planning Board's *Report on Mining and Manufacturing Survey* for 1981, manufacturing output in the two largest cities, Seoul and Pusan, accounted for about 28 percent of the national total in that year. The manufacturing output in four large cities (including Taegu and Inchon in addition to the two largest cities) accounted for about 40 percent of the total. It should be noted that except for Taegu these cities had a quite diversified structure of manufacturing, resembling that for the whole country.

The overall rate of urbanization, measured in terms of the ratio of urban population to the total, has increased rapidly in the last 25 years.

The population of all cities increased from only 28 percent of the nation's population in 1960 to 57 percent by 1980.[1] This indicates a very rapid migration from rural areas to cities, in particular the major cities. The population aged 14 and over increased at an average annual rate of 3.1 percent between 1965 and 1980, which is much higher than the growth rate of the total population, as shown in table 2.1. This reflects the fact that the children born in the post-Korean War baby boom were joining the working-age population in the 1970s. The labor force grew even more rapidly than the working-age population mainly because of increased female participation in the labor force. It increased from approximately 8.8 million in 1965 to 14.5 million in 1980, showing an average growth rate of 3.3 percent.

Table 2.1 Growth of total population, labor force, and employment, 1965–1980

Categories	1965	1980	Average annual growth rate (%)
Total population (mid-year) (thousands)	28,705	38,124	1.9
Population, 14 years old and over. (thousands)	15,937	25,335	3.1
Labor force (thousands)			
Total	8,859	14,454	3.3
Farm	5,236	5,169	– 0.1
Nonfarm	3,623	9,285	6.5
Labor force participation rate[a] (%)	55.6	57.1	–
Employment (thousands)			
Total	8,206	13,706	3.5
Farm	5,071	5,114	0.1
Nonfarm	3,135	8,592	7.0
Unemployment rate (%)	7.4	5.2	– 2.3
Farm	1.8	1.1	– 3.2
Nonfarm	6.9	7.5	0.6

–, not applicable.
[a] Total labor force divided by population aged 14 years or over.
Source: Economic Planning Board, Korea Statistical Yearbook, 1966 and 1983

Total employment increased at an average annual rate of 3.5 percent during the same period, which is slightly higher than the growth rate of the labor force. As a result, national unemployment gradually declined from 7.4 percent of the labor force to 5.2 percent. The increase in the labor force and employment during 1965–80 was almost totally absorbed by the

[1] If the population of small towns (called "Up" in Korean) were included in the urban population, the degree of urbanization would be 66.7 percent in 1980 (see EPB, Korean Statistical Yearbook, 1981, 1983).

nonfarm sector. The labor force in the farm sector even showed a minor decline, while employment in the same sector remained almost unchanged. In contrast, the labor force and employment in the nonfarm sector grew at average annual rates of 6.5 percent and 7.0 percent respectively.

As shown in table 2.2, the average educational levels of both the labor force and employed people rose significantly during 1965–80. For instance, the average number of years of school education for all the male labor force increased from 6.4 to 8.9 during that period, while that for all the female labor force rose from 3.8 to 6.6. The average educational level of those employed in the nonfarm sector has been significantly higher than that of those employed in the farm sector.

Table 2.2 Average educational levels of the labor force and the employed (number of years in school)

	1966			1980		
Categories	Male	Female	Both sexes	Male	Female	Both sexes
Labor force[a]	6.4	3.8	5.6	8.9	6.6	8.1
Employed persons						
Total	6.2	3.7	5.4	8.9	6.4	8.0
Farm	4.4	2.5	3.8	5.9	4.0	5.0
Nonfarm	8.5	5.5	7.6	10.3	8.6	9.8

[a] The educational levels of the labor force are slightly higher than those of total employed persons because the unemployment rate for the urban labor force, who are better educated than the average rural labor force, was significantly higher than that for the rural labor force.
Source: data provided by the Bureau of Statistics, Economic Planning Board

These increases in the average educational levels of the labor force and the employed could well accommodate a rapid change in the occupational structure of employed persons. As shown in table 2.3, the proportion of people employed in agriculture, forestry, and related works, which had accounted for approximately 64 percent of total employed persons in 1965, declined very rapidly in relative terms to reach 32 percent by 1980. In contrast, the share of "production workers, transport equipment operators, and others" increased rapidly from 4.1 percent to 29.1 percent during the same period. The percentage share of both "clerical workers" and "professional, technical, administrative, and managerial workers" in total also showed significant increases. Sales workers and service workers, however, showed only a minor increase in relative terms.

Park (1983) provides the data on nonagricultural workers' wage differentials by occupation and by educational attainment for 1981. First, the study shows that on average the monthly earnings of a male worker are more than double those of a female worker. As expected, the average monthly

Table 2.3 Change in the occupation structure of the workforce between 1965 and 1980

	1965		1980		
Occupation	Number (thousands)	Share (%)	Number (thousands)	Share (%)	Percentage change (1965–80)
Professional, technical, administrative, and managerial	240	3.2	730	5.3	204.2
Clerical	340	4.5	1,266	9.2	272.4
Sales	1,015	13.5	1,983	14.5	95.4
Service	558	7.6	1,085	7.9	94.4
Agricultural, forestry, and related	4,774	63.5	4,438	32.4	– 7.0
Fishermen, hunters, and related	212	2.8	214	1.6	0.9
Production, transport equipment operators, and others	383	5.1	3,990	29.1	941.8
Total	7,522	100.0	13,706	100.0	82.2

Source: EPB, *Korea Statistical Yearbook*, 1967 and 1983

earnings of nonagricultural workers increase as educational attainment rises. For instance, the average wage per college graduate in 1981 was more than double the average wage per high school graduate. For wage differentials by occupation, the monthly earnings of "managers and officials" are highest of all occupations, even exceeding those of "professional and technical workers." On the basis of an average for both male and female workers, the monthly earnings of sales workers, service workers, and production workers were at the bottom of the scale.

Unionized labor accounted for only about 9–11 percent of total employed persons during 1965–80. The number of unions, including establishment unit unions, showed practically no change between 1965 and 1980 (EPB, *Korea Statistical Yearbook*, 1967, 1983). In any case, the unions have not been able to wield much influence over labor–management relations. It should also be noted that the country does not have a system of unemployment insurance. In accordance with the labor law, however, all workers are entitled to severance pay, equivalent to at least one month's wage per year of service, when they voluntarily or involuntarily quit their jobs.

Growth and Structural Change in National Product

As shown in table 2.4, GNP grew relatively slowly immediately after the Korean War, while the population grew very rapidly. For this reason, per

Table 2.4 Growth rates of gross national product, population, and per capita gross national product for Korea, 1953–1982 (constant 1975 prices)

				Annual growth rate (%)		
Year	GNP (billion won)	Mid-year population (thousands)	Per capita GNP (thousand won)	GNP	Population	Per capita GNP
1953	2,205.2	20,239	109.0	—	—	—
1954	2,318.5	20,823	111.3	5.1	2.9	2.1
1955	2,422.6	21,424	113.1	4.5	2.9	1.6
1956	2,389.8	22,042	108.4	− 1.4	2.9	− 4.2
1957	2,570.5	22,677	113.4	7.6	2.9	4.6
1958	2,711.1	23,331	116.2	5.5	2.9	2.5
1959	2,814.9	24,003	117.3	3.8	2.9	0.9
1960	2,845.6	24,695	115.2	1.1	2.9	− 1.8
1961	3,004.6	25,776	116.6	5.6	4.3	1.2
1962	3,071.1	26,513	115.8	2.2	2.9	− 0.7
1963	3,350.7	27,262	122.9	9.1	2.8	6.1
1964	3,671.5	27,984	131.2	9.6	2.6	6.8
1965	3,885.0	28,705	135.3	5.8	2.6	3.1
1966	4,378.5	29,436	148.7	12.7	2.5	9.9
1967	4,669.4	30,131	155.0	6.6	2.4	4.2
1968	5,195.6	30,838	168.5	11.3	2.3	8.7
1969	5,911.4	31,544	187.4	13.8	2.3	11.2
1970	6,363.0	32,241	197.4	7.6	2.2	5.3
1971	6,962.5	32,883	211.7	9.4	2.0	7.2
1972	7,365.6	33,505	219.8	5.8	1.9	3.8
1973	8,463.5	34,103	248.2	14.9	1.8	12.9
1974	9,141.0	34,692	263.5	8.0	1.7	6.2
1975	9,792.9	35,281	277.6	7.1	1.7	5.4
1976	11,275.5	35,849	314.5	15.1	1.6	13.3
1977	13,432.3	36,412	341.4	10.3	1.6	8.6
1978	13,877.1	36,969	375.4	11.6	1.5	10.0
1979	14,759.1	37,534	393.2	6.4	1.5	4.7
1980	13,842.8	38,124	363.1	− 6.2	1.6	− 7.7
1981	14,723.6	38,723	380.2	6.4	1.6	4.7
1982	15,509.0	39,331	394.3	5.3	1.6	3.7
Average growth rate						
1953–62				3.8	3.0	1.0
1962–82				8.4	2.0	6.3

—, not applicable.
Sources: Bank of Korea, National Income in Korea, 1982; EPB, Korea Statistical Yearbook, 1983

capita GNP barely increased during this period. The country experienced a turning point in 1963, however: the annual growth rate of GNP began to accelerate in that year. The growth rate of GNP again slowed down in the 1980s owing to the effects on the domestic economy of the second world oil shock and the consequent worldwide recession. Despite this slowdown

Korea's GNP grew at an average annual rate of 8.4 percent during 1963–82, compared with 3.8 percent during 1954–62, while per capita GNP grew at an average annual rate of 6.3 percent in 1963–82 compared with a mere 1 percent in 1954–62. This rapid growth of per capita GNP was helped by a gradual decline in the growth rate of the population during the later period.

Korea's per capita GNP in 1975 constant prices, which had been at US$225 in 1953, increased to US$239 in 1962, and then jumped to US$815 by 1982. This implies that per capita income increased by a factor of 3.6 over the three decades 1953–82, and by a factor of 3.4 over the last two decades. This acceleration of economic growth rate since the first half of the 1960s is generally attributed to a shift in the country's industrialization strategy from the previous emphasis on import substitution to an emphasis on export promotion.

The rapid growth of the economy since the first half of the 1960s was accompanied by a rapid change in the structure of industry. The Bank of Korea's *National Income Accounts* (1984) show that the value added in the primary sector (including mining) which had accounted for nearly 40 percent of GNP in 1965 declined to 19 percent by 1981. In contrast, value added in the industrial sector, which includes manufacturing, construction, and utilities, rose rapidly from 23 percent to 40 percent. In particular, the manufacturing sector's share in GNP rose very rapidly from 17.9 percent to 29.6 percent. The share of the service sector in the GNP also increased from 37 percent to 45 percent during the same period. Within the service sector, the transportation, storage, and communications sector marked the most rapid rise in its share in GNP, from 4.0 percent to 7.0 percent. From these figures it is clear that natural-resource-based activities have not been important in economic growth in Korea.

The pattern of expenditures on national product changed significantly during 1965–81, as shown in Bank of Korea, *National Income in Korea* (1982, pp. 150–3). Private consumption expenditures in constant prices grew at an average annual rate of 7.4 percent, lower than the growth rate of GNP during the period, and their share in total GNP declined from 81 percent to 67 percent. Government consumption expenditures also showed some decline in relation to GNP, although they grew reasonably quickly. In contrast, gross domestic investment, exports of goods and services, and imports of goods and services, all in 1975 constant prices, grew much more rapidly than GNP, and their shares in GNP substantially increased. In particular, exports of goods and services grew at an average annual rate of 24 percent, exceeding the growth rate of imports (19.5 percent). As a result, the share of exports in GNP increased from 5.7 percent to 48.9 percent during the period, while that of imports rose from 11.8 percent to 54.1 percent. Net factor income from abroad, which had accounted for 0.7 percent of GNP in 1965, declined to −4.4 percent, mainly because of increased interest payments on foreign borrowings in recent years.

Table 2.5 presents trends in the ratios of gross domestic investment and sectoral saving to GNP during the period 1960–82. As indicated in the table, the gross domestic investment which had generally accounted for less than 15 percent of GNP until 1965 (except in 1963) rose to exceed 20 percent from 1966. If the year to year fluctuations in the investment ratio are disregarded, we would say that the investment ratio has continuously increased over time. That is, the three-year average of investment ratio which was 14.8 percent during 1961–3 increased to 24.2 percent during 1971–3 and then to 28.7 percent during 1980–2.

Table 2.5 Trends in the ratios of gross domestic investment and sectoral saving to gross national product, 1960–1982 (percent, based on current price data)

Year	Gross domestic investment = gross savings[a]	Gross domestic saving rate				Foreign saving rate	Statistical discrepancy
		Government	Business	Household	Total[a]		
1960	10.9	− 2.0	5.3	− 2.5	0.8	8.6	1.5
1961	13.2	− 1.8	5.9	− 1.3	2.9	8.6	1.7
1962	12.8	− 1.5	7.1	− 2.3	3.3	10.7	− 1.1
1963	18.1	− 0.4	7.1	2.0	8.7	10.4	− 1.0
1964	14.0	0.5	6.5	1.8	8.7	6.9	− 1.6
1965	15.0	1.7	7.7	− 2.1	7.4	6.4	1.2
1966	21.6	2.8	7.5	1.6	11.8	8.4	1.3
1967	21.9	4.1	7.9	− 0.6	11.4	8.8	1.7
1968	25.9	6.1	7.8	1.1	15.1	11.2	− 0.4
1969	28.8	5.9	7.7	5.2	18.8	10.6	− 0.6
1970	26.8	6.5	7.5	3.4	17.3	9.3	0.2
1971	25.2	5.4	7.5	2.5	15.4	10.7	− 0.8
1972	21.7	3.6	9.1	3.0	15.7	5.2	0.7
1973	25.6	4.2	11.4	7.9	23.5	3.8	− 1.7
1974	31.0	2.3	12.1	6.1	20.5	12.4	− 1.9
1975	29.4	4.0	11.3	3.4	18.6	10.4	0.4
1976	25.5	6.2	10.9	6.0	23.1	2.4	− 0.0
1977	27.3	5.6	10.9	8.6	25.1	0.6	1.6
1978	31.1	6.5	9.9	10.0	26.4	3.3	1.5
1979	35.4	7.2	9.7	9.7	26.6	7.6	1.2
1980	31.5	6.2	8.2	5.5	19.9	10.2	1.4
1981	28.4	6.7	8.3	4.6	19.6	7.9	0.9
1982	26.2	6.7	9.7	5.1	21.5	4.8	− 0.1
Average for period							
1961–3	14.8	− 1.2	6.7	− 0.5	5.0	9.9	− 0.1
1971–3	24.2	4.4	9.3	4.5	18.2	6.6	− 0.6
1980–2	28.7	6.5	8.7	5.1	20.3	7.6	0.7

[a] Totals may not add up because of rounding errors.
Source: Bank of Korea, National Income in Korea, 1982

The increasing level of gross domestic investment was financed by both domestic and foreign savings since domestic saving was not enough to meet the increasing demand for domestic investment. The ratio of foreign saving to GNP showed a wide fluctuation during the period under observation, reflecting changes in the country's balance-of-payments conditions. Disregarding year to year fluctuations, domestic saving showed a continuous rise in relation to GNP. The three-year average rate of domestic saving rose from 5.0 percent of GNP in 1961–3 to 18.2 percent in 1971–3, and again to 20.3 percent by the final period 1980–2. This implies that the continuous rise in the investment ratio during 1960–82 could not have been possible without the gradual increase in domestic saving.

As a result of the rapid increase in domestic investment, both net and gross capital stocks in Korea have grown very rapidly since the early 1960s, as shown in table 2.6. In the table, the annual series of both net and gross capital stocks of the nonresidential business sector are presented for the period 1963–82. The annual series therefore exclude the capital stock of general government and private nonprofit institutions, the "ownership of dwellings" sector, and the "international assets" sector.[2] The annual series of net and gross capital stock data were obtained by linking the annual series of net and gross fixed investment, respectively, with the estimates of net and gross capital stocks for 1977 which are based on a national wealth survey. Net capital stock (excluding construction work in progress) grew at an average annual rate of 13.5 percent during the period under observation, while gross capital stock grew at a slightly lower rate, 11.1 percent. These long-term growth rates of net and gross capital stocks are substantially higher than the growth rate of total employment, and even higher than that of national output, implying that a considerable capital deepening took place during the past two decades of rapid growth.

Exchange Rate Regime, Trade, and Balance of Payments

Korea had maintained a complicated system of multiple exchange rates during the 1950s and the first half of the 1960s until the exchange rate reform of 1964–5 was put into effect. Under the regime of multiple exchange rates, the official rate was almost always overvalued despite large periodic devaluations to offset the progressive inflation of the won. The official exchange rate, however, was not really important during this period, since practically all trade and other commercial activities were conducted at other exchange rates that were significantly higher than the official rate in terms of won per US dollar.

---

[2] The nonresidential business sector consolidates all economic sectors that produce and sell their products on markets but excludes the dwellings sector (see Denison, 1979).

Table 2.6 Aggregate capital-to-labor ratio for nonresidential business (constant 1975 prices)

Year	1	2	3	4	5
	Capital stock[a] (billion won)		Total number of workers (thousands)	Capital-to-labor ratio (thousand won per worker)	
	Net	Gross		Net	Gross
1963	1,868	4,589	7,289	256	630
1964	2,012	4,868	7,400	272	658
1965	2,142	5,149	7,782	275	662
1966	2,440	5,626	7,973	306	706
1967	2,899	6,306	8,230	352	766
1968	3,488	7,174	8,635	404	831
1969	4,174	8,200	8,864	471	925
1970	4,835	9,222	9,141	529	1,009
1971	5,515	10,323	9,445	584	1,093
1972	5,978	11,332	9,924	602	1,142
1973	6,718	12,743	10,482	641	1,216
1974	7,594	14,279	10,899	697	1,310
1975	8,320	15,578	11,117	748	1,401
1976	9,427	17,452	11,810	798	1,478
1977	10,473	19,432	12,140	863	1,601
1978	12,646	22,586	12,636	1,001	1,787
1979	15,183	26,005	12,756	1,190	2,039
1980	17,596	29,396	12,794	1,375	2,298
1981	19,213	31,728	13,030	1,475	2,435
1982	20,645	34,104	13,377	1,543	2,549
Average annual rate of increase (%)					
1963–72	13.8	10.6	3.5	10.0	6.8
1972–82	13.2	11.7	3.0	9.9	8.4
1963–82	13.5	11.1	3.2	9.9	7.6

Column 4 is column 1 divided by column 3; column 5 is column 2 divided by column 3.
[a] The capital stock series excludes construction work in progress.
Source: Kim and Park, 1985

An important step in the unification of the foreign exchange rate as well as in the transition to export-oriented industrialization policy was the exchange rate reform of 1964–5. In May 1964 the government devalued the official exchange rate from 130 won to 256 won per US dollar and announced that the existing fixed exchange rate system would be changed to a system of unitary floating exchange rate. It was not until March 1965 that the government allowed the actual floating of foreign exchange so that the exchange rate might be determined by market forces. After some initial floating, however, the Korean Monetary Authority actually transformed the system of the unitary floating exchange rate into a fixed rate system by directly intervening in the exchange market.

Table 2.7 Nominal and purchasing-power-parity-adjusted effective exchange rates for exports and imports, 1962–1983

	1	2	3	4	5	6	7	8	9
	Nominal exchange rate (won per US$)	Effective rate for		WPI and PPP index (1965 = 100)			PPP-adjusted exchange rate (won per US$)	Effective rate for	
Year	Official rate	Exports[a]	Imports[b]	WPI, Korea	WPI, major trade partners[c]	PPP index	Official rate	Exports	Imports
1962	130.0	141.8	146.2	56.0	97.7	174.5	226.9	247.4	255.5
1963	130.0	177.6	148.2	67.5	98.4	145.8	189.5	258.9	216.1
1964	214.3	263.6	247.0	90.9	98.6	108.5	232.5	286.0	268.0
1965	265.4	275.3	293.1	100.0	100.0	100.0	265.4	275.3	293.1
1966	271.3	283.8	296.4	108.8	102.8	94.5	256.4	268.2	280.1
1967	270.7	290.7	296.2	115.8	103.9	89.6	242.8	260.8	265.7
1968	276.6	294.8	302.5	125.2	105.6	84.3	233.2	248.5	255.0
1969	288.2	306.6	312.7	133.7	108.7	81.3	234.3	249.3	254.2
1970	310.7	331.5	336.4	145.9	112.8	77.3	240.2	256.2	260.0
1971	347.7	370.55	369.5	158.5	115.4	72.8	253.1	269.7	269.0
1972	391.8	404.3	415.2	180.7	126.8	70.2	275.0	283.8	291.5
1973	398.3	407.0	417.7	193.3	155.6	80.5	320.6	327.6	336.2
1974	407.0	415.6	425.5	274.7	188.4	68.6	279.2	285.1	291.9
1975	484.0	496.9	508.9	347.4	197.0	56.7	274.4	281.7	288.5
1976	484.0	496.3	515.4	389.4	206.7	53.1	257.0	263.5	273.7
1977	484.0	493.4	519.7	424.5	226.8	53.4	258.5	263.5	277.5
1978	484.0	495.0	526.9	473.4	266.1	56.2	272.0	278.2	296.1
1979	484.0	495.0	520.0	562.5	284.1	50.5	244.4	250.0	262.6
1980	618.5	639.1	652.9	781.3	323.7	41.4	256.1	264.6	270.3
1981	686.0	701.0	720.1	940.6	343.0	36.5	250.4	255.9	262.8
1982	737.7	740.7	779.5	984.4	323.9	32.9	242.7	243.7	256.5
1983	781.2	781.2	837.1	986.7	341.1	34.6	270.3	270.3	289.6

WPI, wholesale price index; PPP, purchasing power parity.

Column 6 is column 5 divided by column 4; columns 7, 8, and 9 are columns 1, 2, and 3 respectively multiplied by column 6.

[a] Official exchange rate plus the net export subsidies per US dollar of export given in column 6 of table 3.1.

[b] Official exchange rate plus the actual tariffs and tariff equivalents per US dollar of import given in column 4 of Kim (1988, appendix table 1).

[c] An average of WPIs for the United States and Japan, weighted by the average shares of the United States and Japan in Korea's total trade volumes (exports and imports) with the two countries during 1963–80. The Japanese WPI, however, was adjusted by the index of the exchange rate of the yen to the dollar.

Source: Kim (1988, appendix table 1); EPB, *Major Statistics of Korean Economy*, 1984

Between 1968 and 1980 the won gradually depreciated, as shown in table 2.7. The government sometimes left it to the market to determine the exchange rate by avoiding direct intervention, but in most of the period under observation it pegged the rate and then resorted to periodic devaluation, as under the system of fixed exchange rate, in order to offset widening differences in inflation rate between Korea and its major trading partners. As a result, the official exchange rate in 1980 adjusted for purchasing power parity (PPP) turned out to be roughly equivalent to the level in 1965.

In addition, a wide variety of export promotion measures have been used to increase incentives to exporters, while tariffs and nontariff barriers have been used to restrict imports, as will be discussed in chapter 3. Net export subsidies per US dollar of export are therefore estimated and added to the official exchange rate to obtain the annual series of effective exchange rates for exports. Similarly, actual tariffs and tariff equivalents per US dollar of import are estimated and added to the official rate to obtain the effective rate for imports. We should admit, however, that the estimated series of effective exchange rates for exports and imports are not perfect in the sense that they do not consolidate the effects of nontariff barriers on imports and some unquantifiable effects of export incentives on exports.

Despite the limitations of the estimated series of effective exchange rates for exports and imports, they do show that the effective rates were noticeably higher than the official rate during 1962–83. It is also notable that the differences between the official rate and the effective rates gradually narrowed during the period, implying that the importance of subsidies and tariffs decreased over time.

Korea's commodity exports have increased rapidly since the early 1960s, thanks to the government's export promotion policy. The nominal value of commodity exports increased by a factor of about 422 from a meager US$55 million in 1962 to US$23.2 billion in 1983 (a billion is a thousand million throughout). The average annual growth rate of nominal exports during the period turned out to be 33 percent, considerably higher than the growth rate of nominal imports (about 22 percent). Even the real value of commodity exports, discounted for a rise in export unit value index, grew at an average annual rate of about 27 percent during 1962–83, while that of imports grew at 14 percent a year.

The rapid growth of exports was accompanied by a drastic change in the structure of export commodities. As can be seen in table 2.8, Korean exports in 1962 consisted mainly of primary goods such as fish, rice, mineral ores, raw silk, agar-agar, and so on. Manufactured goods comprised slightly less than 20 percent of total commodity exports in that year. By 1980 the manufactured exports comprised 90 percent of total exports which had expanded greatly compared with 1962. Major manufactured

Table 2.8 Exports by commodity group and major commodities (free on board basis) (percent of total exports)

SITC group and commodities		1962	1965	1980
(0)	Food and live animals	39.8	16.1	6.5
	Fish and fish preparations	14.8	10.2	3.5
	Rice	16.2	1.9	0.0
	Dried lever (seaweed)	1.3	1.9	0.0
(1)	Beverages and tobacco	0.2	0.5	0.8
(2)	Crude materials except fuel	35.4	21.2	1.9
	Raw silk	7.3	3.9	0.1
	Iron, tungsten ores, and concentrates	13.1	7.5	0.1
	Agar-agar	2.4	1.3	0.1
(3)–(4)	Mineral fuels; animal and vegetable oils and fats	5.1	1.1	0.3
(5)	Chemicals	1.8	0.2	4.3
	Chemical elements and compounds	0.0	0.1	1.2
	Fertilizers, manufactured	0.0	0.0	2.0
(6)	Manufactured goods classified chiefly by materials	11.3	37.9	35.7
	Plywood	4.2	10.3	1.7
	Textile yarns	0.0	1.3	3.6
	Textile fabrics	3.3	12.8	9.1
	Iron and steel products	0.0	7.3	9.5
(7)	Machinery and transport equipment	2.6	3.1	19.8
	Electrical machinery	n.a.	1.1	10.7
	Transport equipment	n.a.	2.4	5.0
(8)	Miscellaneous manufactures	3.6	19.7	30.2
	Clothing	n.a.	11.8	17.0
	Footwear	n.a.	2.4	5.0
	Wigs and false beards	n.a.	1.3	0.3
(9)	Unclassifiable	0.2	0.1	0.5
Total exports		100.0	100.0	100.0
(In million US$)		(55)	(175)	(17,505)

n.a., not available.
Sources: Bank of Korea, Economic Statistics Yearbook, various years; Bank of Korea, Monthly Economic Statistics, July 1981

exports in 1980 included clothing, textile yarns and fabrics, electrical machinery, iron and steel products, transport equipment (mainly ships), and footwear.

In contrast, the commodity composition of imports did not show such a drastic change in terms of Standard International Trade Classification (SITC) groups. The only observable movement is a jump in the share of mineral fuels in total imports between 1965 and 1980, mainly reflecting the rapid increase in world oil prices since the early 1970s. On changing the commodity classification slightly, however, we observe that, in addition to petroleum, the imports of capital goods and raw materials for exports increased rapidly in relation to total imports during 1965–80 (see EPB, *Major Statistics of Korean Economy*, 1982, pp. 227–8). In particular, the imports of raw materials for exports increased from a mere 2 percent of total imports to 20 percent, reflecting the increasing importance of export activities in Korea. However, the imports of raw materials for domestic use and finished consumer goods declined in relation to total imports.

The rapid growth of imports meant that Korea could not improve her trade balance significantly, despite the more rapid growth of exports from a much smaller base. As shown in table 2.9, trade deficits increased somewhat in absolute level between 1965 and 1983, although there were many fluctuations in the interim years. The net balance on goods and services showed a similar trend during the period. The current balance, which is equivalent to the net balance on goods and services plus net transfer receipts from abroad, also showed a deficit in most of the years under observation, implying that Korea's external debt should have accumulated to a considerable magnitude by the terminal year.

To examine whether or not the balance of payments was really improving during 1960–83, table 2.9 shows both the net goods and services and the current balance in relation to total imports of goods and services. The net goods and services generally show an increasing trend from −69.1 percent of total imports of goods and services in 1960 to −6.7 percent in 1983, if the two unusual periods of the world oil crisis (1974–5 and 1979–80) are excluded. In contrast, the ratio of the current balance to total imports of goods and services declined from a positive 3.7 percent to a negative 32.2 percent between 1960 and 1971, reflecting a gradual reduction in net current transfers from abroad. Since the early 1970s, however, the same ratio has generally moved in parallel with that of net goods and services, although the former has been slightly higher than the latter.

As a result of the continuous deficits in the balance of payments, Korea's foreign debts had accumulated to a little over 40 billion US dollars, around 50 percent of Korea's money GNP, by the end of 1983 (see chapter 5, table 5.7). Korea's external debt in the early 1970s amounted to only 2.2 billion dollars because the country's current account deficits had been largely financed by foreign assistance until the mid-1960s. The foreign debt accumulated very rapidly after 1970, however, since the external deficits were now mainly financed by foreign borrowings.

Because of the accumulation of foreign debts, Korea's burden of foreign debt services has increased in recent years. The foreign debt services, including interest payments on short-term loans, increased from 5 percent of total current receipts of foreign exchange in 1965 to between 19 and 21 percent in the 1980s (see chapter 5, table 5.8).

Table 2.9 Major trends in Korea's balance of payments: current account balances, 1960–1983 (million US dollars)

Year	Trade balance Exports	Imports	Balance	Total imports of goods and services	Net goods and services	Current balance	Ratio to total imports of goods and services (%) Net goods and services	Current balance
1960	33	365	− 332	379	− 262	14	− 69.1	3.7
1964	119	404	− 285	488	− 221	− 26	− 45.3	− 5.3
1965	175	416	− 240	484	− 194	9	− 40.1	1.9
1966	250	680	− 430	777	− 323	− 103	− 41.6	− 13.3
1967	335	909	− 574	1,060	− 417	− 192	− 39.3	− 18.1
1968	486	1,322	− 836	1,546	− 670	− 440	− 43.3	− 28.4
1969	658	1,650	− 992	1,945	− 794	− 549	− 40.8	− 28.2
1970	882	1,804	− 922	2,182	− 803	− 623	− 36.8	− 28.6
1971	1,132	2,178	− 1,046	2,634	− 1,018	− 848	− 38.6	− 34.2
1972	1,676	2,250	− 574	2,768	− 541	− 371	− 19.5	− 13.4
1973	3,271	3,837	− 566	4,620	− 499	− 309	− 10.8	− 6.7
1974	4,515	6,452	− 1,937	7,598	− 2,305	− 2,023	− 30.3	− 26.6
1975	5,003	6,674	− 1,671	7,997	− 2,114	− 1,887	− 26.4	− 23.6
1976	7,815	8,405	− 591	10,120	− 663	− 314	− 6.6	− 3.1
1977	10,047	10,523	− 477	13,284	− 211	12	− 1.6	0.1
1978	12,711	14,491	− 1,781	18,718	− 1,557	− 1,085	− 8.3	− 5.8
1979	14,705	19,100	− 4,396	24,121	− 4,590	− 4,151	− 19.0	− 17.2
1980	17,214	21,598	− 4,384	28,347	− 5,770	− 5,321	− 20.4	− 18.8
1981	20,671	24,299	− 3,628	32,416	− 5,147	− 4,646	− 15.9	− 14.3
1982	20,879	23,474	− 2,594	31,504	− 3,149	− 2,650	− 10.0	− 8.4
1983	23,204	24,904	− 1,700	32,588	− 2,199	− 1,607	− 6.7	− 4.9

Source: Bank of Korea, *Economic Statistics Yearbook*, various issues

Industrial Organization and Other Features of Major Production Activities

No statistics are available for Korea to indicate the degree of foreign ownership of capital in industry. It is generally believed, however, that the degree of foreign ownership of capital is very low in comparison with other developing countries. The reason is that the country has imported foreign capital mainly in the form of repayable loans. The value of foreign investment only accounted for about 5 percent of total foreign capital inflows during the period 1962–83 (Kim, 1988, appendix table 2). This should not be taken to indicate that the government has been discouraging the inflow of foreign investment, however. All kinds of promotional schemes existed but private enterprises simply preferred to import capital in the form of loans.

According to the result of a mining and manufacturing survey conducted in 1975 (Kim, 1988, appendix table 3), over 70 percent of all manufacturing establishments existing in 1975 were relatively young, less than ten years old. These young establishments employed about 63 percent of total manufacturing workers and produced about 55 percent of total manufacturing output in that year. The manufacturing establishments founded before the Korean War were only about 5 percent of the total. Among mining establishments, only 44 percent were young establishments founded after 1965, indicating that the average age of mining establishments was greater than that of manufacturing establishments.

Despite the relative youth of most manufacturing establishments, industrial concentration is very high on the average, reflecting the small size of the domestic market by sector. According to data given in table 2.10, out

Table 2.10 Distribution of manufacturing industries by class of industrial concentration ratio, 1977 and 1981

Class of industrial concentration ratio[a] (%)	Number of industries examined		Share of sales (%)	
	1977	1981	1977	1981
80–100	108 (32.6)	100 (30.7)	33.0	28.1
60–80	77 (23.3)	76 (22.7)	18.7	26.2
40–60	87 (26.3)	80 (24.5)	22.5	21.8
20–40	50 (15.1)	58 (17.5)	21.1	19.3
0–20	9 (2.7)	17 (5.1)	4.7	4.6
Total	331 (100.0)	331 (100.0)	100.0	100.0

[a] The industrial concentration ratio is calculated in terms of the share of the three largest enterprises in each industry's sales at the five-digit level of industrial classification.
Source: Lee, 1984

of 331 manufacturing industries (or subsectors) about 56 percent belonged to the industries in which the industrial concentration ratio, calculated in terms of the share of the three largest firms in each industry's sales, exceeded 60 percent in 1977. The number of industries belonging to the same group of high concentration ratio had declined to 53 percent of the total in 1981. However, the sales of those industries whose concentration ratios exceeded 60 percent increased somewhat, from 52 percent of total manufacturing sales in 1977 to 54 percent in 1981.

Turning to the problem of the variation in the ratio of value added to production by industry, we find that the value added ratios for the agriculture, forestry, and fishery sector and the mining sector were highest in both 1970 and 1980, as shown in the Bank of Korea's *Compilatory Report on 1980 Input–Output Tables* (1983, pp. 113–16). The value added ratio for manufacturing was lowest in the two years if other sectors not elsewhere classified were excluded. On the whole, the value added ratios for almost all industries declined between 1970 and 1980, indicating an increased interdependence among the industries.

The import dependence ratio, which was calculated in terms of the ratio of imported intermediate inputs to domestic production, also varied widely by industry in both 1970 and 1980. As expected, the manufacturing sector showed the highest import dependence ratio, while both the agriculture, forestry, and fishery sector and the mining sector showed the lowest dependence. Within manufacturing, import dependence ratios were particularly high in such industries as wood and its products, chemicals, primary metal products, and metal products and machinery. The import dependence ratios for most of the industries listed in the table increased between 1970 and 1980.

Finally, the net capital-to-labor ratio for the nonresidential business sector, measured in terms of thousand won capital (constant 1975 prices) per worker, increased by a factor of about six, or at an average annual rate of 10 percent, during the last two decades (see table 2.6). The gross capital-to-labor ratio, however, increased only by a factor of about four, or at an average annual rate of 7.6 percent, during the same period. These data suggest that the average capital intensity of Korean industries has increased very rapidly in the course of rapid economic growth.

3

The Pattern of Long-term Policy

Export Liberalization

Practically all foreign trade activities were controlled by the government during the Korean War (1950–3). In particular, exports were strictly controlled because of shortages of basic necessities and raw materials in the war-ridden economy. Although the economy's urgent adjustments to the disrupting effects of the war were almost completed by 1955, Korea did not energetically seek export expansion until the early 1960s.

During the post-war reconstruction period, the official exchange rate consistently overvalued the won despite large periodic devaluations. This overvaluation resulted from a rate of domestic inflation that was much higher than that of major trading partners. In this situation, the government took various *ad hoc* measures to modify excess demand for imports and to offset disincentives to exporters, and these resulted in the emergence of a complicated system of multiple exchange rates. To restrict trade quantitatively, the import and export licensing system was administered on the basis of a semiannual trade program; measures to counteract the export disincentive effects of currency overvaluation included a foreign exchange deposit system, a preferential export system, direct export subsidies, and the export credit system.[1]

The first major step toward unifying the exchange rate was taken in 1961 by twice devaluing the currency. This attempt was doomed to failure, however, because of the expansionary policy of the Park military government who, to mitigate the continuing effects of currency overvaluation, introduced in 1963 a full-scale export–import link system under which the

---

[1] The foreign exchange deposit system was adopted to permit exporters either to use their export earnings for imports or to sell at the market exchange rate. The preferential export system, instituted from 1951–5, provided successful exporters of specified commodities with the import rights to popular items. Direct subsidies were given to exporters of minerals and other selected items in 1955 and again in the first half of the 1960s. Finally the export credit system extended preferential loans to exporters at interest rates lower than the rate on ordinary bank loans.

volume of nonaid imports was limited to the amount of export earnings. The result was a return to the multiple exchange rate system, especially since the market premium rates on export dollars rose rapidly in 1963–4. More significant in the unification of the foreign exchange rate, as well as in the transition to export-oriented industrialization policy, was the exchange rate reform of 1964–5. The government devalued the official exchange rate from 130 won to 256 won per US dollar in May 1964, and changed the existing system of fixed exchange rate to a system of unified floating exchange rate in March 1965. Thereafter, the government has generally allowed the won to depreciate gradually.

From 1961 to 1965 the system of export incentives was greatly expanded. Preferential export credit became an important incentive for exporters since the interest rate reform of 1965 had substantially widened the interest rate differential between export credit and ordinary bank loans. Among the other export incentives provided during this period were (a) tariff exemptions on imports of raw materials for export production (the drawback system), (b) indirect domestic tax exemptions on intermediate inputs used for export production and export sales, (c) direct tax reduction on income earned from exporting (abolished in 1973), (d) wastage allowances for raw materials imported for export production, (e) a system of linking import business to export performance, (f) tariff and indirect tax exemptions for domestic suppliers of intermediate goods used in export production, and (g) accelerated depreciation allowances for fixed assets of major export industries (see Frank et al., 1975, pp. 40–51).

Unlike the many *ad hoc* measures taken earlier, these measures were mainly to ensure that Korean exporters, who must sell their products at world-market prices, could purchase intermediate goods for export production at world-market prices. In other words, the major incentives served primarily to offset the disincentive effect on export that the trade regime would otherwise have created. It is worth noting that these incentives applied to all exporters on a nondiscriminatory basis.

Even after 1965, some adjustments to the export incentive system were made to accommodate changing economic conditions. These adjustments did not significantly change the system, however. It was of fundamental importance that roughly the same level of real exchange rate as in 1965 could be maintained during the period 1966–83 through periodic exchange rate adjustments. Since the official exchange rate was relatively more realistic between 1965 and 1983, the government could gradually reduce the value of export subsidies per US dollar of export.

Various export subsidies during 1958–83, estimated in terms of the number of won per US dollar of export, are summarized in two different concepts of export subsidies in table 3.1. One is the concept of net export subsidies, including only the subsidies that can directly increase the profit margin of exporters. These kinds of export subsidies include the exchange

Table 3.1 Estimates of net and gross export subsidies per dollar of export for Korea, 1958–1983 (annual averages)

Year	1 Official exchange rate (won per US$)	2 Direct cash subsidies	3 Export dollar premium	4 Direct tax reduction	5 Interest rate preference	6 Net export subsidies[a]	7 Indirect tax exemptions	8 Tariff exemptions	9 Gross export subsidies[a]	10 Net export subsidies	11 Gross export subsidies
		Various export subsidies per US dollar of export (won)								Ratio to exchange rate (%)	
1958	50.0	0.0	64.0	—	1.2	65.2	—	—	65.2	130.4	130.4
1959	50.0	0.0	84.7	—	1.3	86.0	—	—	86.0	172.0	172.0
1960	62.5	0.0	83.9	—	1.2	85.1	—	—	85.1	136.2	136.2
1961	127.5	7.5	14.6	—	1.0	23.1	—	—	23.1	18.1	18.1
1962	130.0	10.3	—	0.6	0.9	11.8	5.1	4.7	21.6	9.1	16.6
1963	130.0	4.1	39.8	0.8	2.9	47.6	5.3	6.6	59.5	36.6	48.8
1964	214.3	2.9	39.7	0.7	6.0	49.3	7.6	10.1	67.0	23.0	31.3
1965	265.4	—	—	2.3	7.6	9.9	13.9	15.4	39.2	3.7	14.8
1966	271.3	—	—	2.3	10.3	12.5	17.8	21.3	51.6	4.6	19.0
1967	270.7	—	—	5.2	14.7	20.0	17.8	24.6	62.4	7.4	23.1
1968	276.6	—	—	3.0	15.2	18.2	19.9	39.6	77.7	6.6	28.1
1969	288.2	—	—	3.7	14.7	18.4	27.4	34.3	80.1	6.4	27.8
1970	310.7	—	—	3.5	17.3	20.8	27.0	40.4	88.1	6.7	28.4
1971	347.7	—	—	4.8	18.1	22.8	32.2	48.0	103.0	6.6	29.6
1972	391.8	—	—	1.9	10.5	12.5	26.4	66.3	105.2	3.2	26.9
1973	398.3	—	—	1.4	7.4	8.7	21.0	64.4	94.2	2.2	23.7
1974	407.0	—	—	—	8.6	8.6	22.5	55.1	86.3	2.1	21.2
1975	484.0	—	—	—	12.9	12.9	33.8	34.3	81.0	2.7	16.7
1976	484.0	—	—	—	12.3	12.3	33.6	35.9	81.8	2.5	16.9
1977	484.0	—	—	—	9.4	9.4	53.1	30.6	93.1	1.9	19.2
1978	484.0	—	—	—	11.0	11.0	53.6	30.0	94.6	2.3	19.5
1979	484.0	—	—	—	11.0	11.0	56.6	30.3	97.9	2.3	20.2
1980	618.5	—	—	—	20.6	20.6	74.6	36.4	131.6	3.3	21.3
1981	686.0	—	—	—	15.0	15.0	n.a.	n.a.	n.a.	2.2	n.a.
1982	737.7	—	—	—	3.0	3.0	n.a.	n.a.	n.a.	0.4	n.a.
1983	781.2	—	—	—	0.0	0.0	n.a.	n.a.	n.a.	0.0	n.a.

—, not applicable; n.a. not available.
Column 6 is the sum of columns 2–5; column 9 is the sum of columns 6–8; columns 10 and 11 are columns 6 and 9 respectively divided by column 1.
[a] Totals may not add up because of rounding errors.
Sources: 1962–75, Westphal and Kim, 1977; 1976–8, Nam, 1981; 1979–83, author's estimates

rate premium resulting from multiple exchange rates, direct cash subsidies, direct tax reductions, and interest rate preferences resulting from preferential export credit. The other concept is defined as the gross export subsidies and includes indirect tax exemptions and tariff exemptions (for imports of intermediate goods for export production) in addition to net export subsidies. Indirect tax exemptions and tariff exemptions only allow the exporters to purchase their inputs at world-market prices and export their products at competitive world-market prices. For this reason, they cannot be taken as genuine subsidies to exporters, although they might influence business sector decisions with regard to export versus import substitution. The ratio of net export subsidies to the official exchange rate is shown in table 3.1, column 10, while the ratio of gross subsidies to the exchange rate is presented in column 11. Both ratios showed a drastic decline between 1958 and 1965, although some fluctuations took place in intervening years.

The ratio of net export subsidies to the exchange rate represents a rough measure of the degree of export liberalization[2] in Korea. As already mentioned, net subsidies have been the only trade-distorting measure introduced by the government on the export side. Unlike many resource-rich developing countries, Korea has made no serious efforts to restrict the quantities of exports. Even before the shift of industrialization policy from import substitution to export orientation in the first half of the 1960s, the government did not attempt to restrict exports in the same terms as it did imports (except for the war period). There have been no tariffs on exports in Korea. Even though semiannual and more recently annual trade programs listed export items for restriction, such restrictions were mainly for the orderly marketing of indigenous products by Korean exporters, particularly in connection with the administration of the mandatory and voluntary export quotas imposed on Korea by industrialized countries.

Import Liberalization from Quantitative Restrictions

It was not until 1955 that any significant number of commodity items could be imported without the government's prior approval. As shown in table 3.2, the semiannual trade program announced by the Ministry of Commerce and Industry (MCI) for the first half of 1955 listed a total of 207 commodity items which could be imported. Of this total, 185 were "automatic approval (AA) items" that could be imported without the prior approval of the government, while the remaining 22 were "restricted items" requiring either prior approval or recommendation by the government.

---

[2] Throughout this study, the term "export liberalization" is used to indicate a removal of the direct and indirect subsidies on exports which have been existing in the country.

Table 3.2 Import restrictions by semiannual trade program in Korea, 1955–1967 (number of commodity items)

Period	1 Normal imports	2 Special imports[a]	3 Import permissible	4 Res- tricted	5 Automatic approval (AA)	6 Prohibited	7 Total	8 Index of number of AA items (1987.I = 100)
1955 I			207	22	185	c	207	6.3
II	195	103	298	51	247	c	298	8.4
1956 I	402	156	558	172	386	c	558	13.1
II	937	208	1,145	242	903	c	1,145	30.6
1957 I	1,406	272	1,678	291	1,387	c	1,678	47.0
II	1,633	283	1,916	282	1,634	c	1,916	55.4
1958 I	1,921	322	2,243	410	1,833	c	2,243	62.1
II	1,828	327	2,155	562	1,593	c	2,155	54.0
1959 I	1,951	345	2,296	725	1,571	356	2,652	51.4
II	1,433	379	1,812	622	1,190	297	2,109	40.3
1960 I	1,465	371	1,836	619	1,217	315	2,151	41.3
II	1,491	387	1,878	613	1,265	326	2,204	42.9
1961 I	1,272	309	1,581	35	1,546	305	1,886	52.4
II	—	—	1,132	17	1,015	355	1,487	34.4
1962 I	—	—	1,314	119	1,195	366	1,680	40.5
II	—	—	1,498	121	1,377	433	1,931	46.7
1963 I	—	—	1,489	713	776	442	1,931	26.3
II	—	—	1,033	924	109	414	1,447	3.7
1964 I	—	—	1,124	b	1,124[b]	617	1,741	38.1
II	—	—	496	b	496[b]	631	1,127	16.8
1965 I	—	—	1,558	111	1,447	624	2,182	49.1
II	—	—	1,633	138	1,495	620	2,253	50.7
1966 I	—	—	2,240	136	2,104	583	2,823	71.3
II	—	—	2,446	139	2,307	386	2,832	78.2
1967 I	—	—	3,082	132	2,950	362	3,444	100.0

—, not applicable, I, first half of the year; II, second half of the year.
Column 3 is the sum of columns 1 and 2; column 5 is column 3 minus column 4; column 7 is the sum of columns 3 and 6.
[a] Items which could be imported only with export earnings.
[b] Not broken down between AA items and restricted items.
[c] Not specified
Source: Ministry of Commerce and Industry, *Semi-Annual Trade Programs* (for respective periods)

From the first half of 1955 the government gradually increased the number of import-permissible items until the first half of 1959, as foreign assistance, mainly from the United States, provided enough foreign exchange resources for imports. After the first half of 1959, however, the number of importable items showed a gradual decline until 1961, reflecting a gradual reduction in foreign assistance. During this period of post-war reconstruction the import-permissible items were classified into two categories: "normal import items" which could be imported with any sources of foreign exchange including foreign assistance, and "special import items" which could be financed only by foreign exchange earned from exporting activities.

The number of AA items in the semiannual trade programs did not exactly follow the trends in the total number of import-permissible items including "import restricted items." The degree of import liberalization, measured in terms of the number of AA items, gradually rose from 1955 to the first half of 1958 and then generally showed a declining trend until 1960.

The import control by semiannual trade program during this post-war reconstruction period was carried out not only to improve the country's balance of payments but also to favor import substitution industries. Industrial policy during this period was generally inward looking although the government gave priority to the reconstruction of the infrastructure and factories destroyed by the war. Because the domestic currency was almost always overvalued in the face of rapid domestic inflation, tariffs were not really effective in discouraging imports during this period even though their rates were reasonably high. For this reason, the government relied mainly on the system of semiannual trade programs to control imports quantitatively. However, a complicated system of multiple exchange rates was used to offset some of the disincentive effects on exports of the won overvaluation.

For the period from 1961 to 1964, no discernible trend in the degree of import liberalization from QRs can be identified. The number of AA items fluctuated from 109 to 1,546. This pattern of change in the degree of import liberalization seems mainly to reflect the effects of trial and error in industrial and trade policy on the balance of payments. As is well known by now, this was the transition period in which the previous policy of reconstruction and inward-looking industrialization was shifted to a policy of export-oriented industrialization. In the course of this policy shift, there were some elements of trial and error in the formulation and implementation of related economic policies (see Kim, 1975).

However, import liberalization made consistent progress from the first half of 1965 to the first half of 1967, as is illustrated by the continuous increase in the number of AA items from 1,447 to 2,950 (table 3.2).

An important accentuation of import liberalization took place in the second half of 1967. The government actually reformulated the semiannual trade program for the second half of 1967 in the form of a "negative list system." The semiannual trade program had previously been formulated as a "positive list system," under which only those items listed in the program could be imported (with or without prior government approval, depending upon the classification in the program). Under the new system the trade program listed only those commodity items whose import was prohibited or restricted, implying that all items not listed were AA items. The new negative list system was implemented in the second half of 1967.

The 1967 reform resulted in a drastic increase in the rate of import liberalization measured in terms of the ratio of AA items to total commodity items (SITC basic codes totaling 1,312), as shown in table 3.3.

Table 3.3 Import restrictions by trade program in Korea, 1967–1984 (number of commodity items)

Period (original program)	Prohibited	Restricted	Automatic approval (A)	Total[a] (B)	Rate of import liberalization (%) A/B	Adjusted[b]
1967 I[c]	42	1,114	156	1,312	11.9	11.6
II	118	402	792	1,312	60.4	58.8
1968 I	116	386	810	1,312	61.7	60.0
II	71	479	756	1,312	57.6	56.0
1969 I	71	508	728	1,312	55.5	54.0
II	75	514	723	1,312	55.1	53.6
1970 I	74	530	708	1,312	54.0	52.5
II	73	526	713	1,312	54.3	52.8
1971 I	73	524	715	1,312	54.5	53.0
II	73	518	721	1,312	55.0	53.5
1972 I	73	570	669	1,312	51.0	49.6
II	73	571	668	1,312	50.9	49.5
1973 I	73	569	670	1,312	51.1	49.7
II	73	556	683	1,312	52.1	50.7
1974 I	73	570	669	1,312	51.0	49.6
II	73	574	665	1,312	50.7	49.3
1975 I	71	592	649	1,312	49.5	48.2
II	66	602	644	1,312	49.1	47.8
1976 I	66	584	662	1,312	50.5	49.1
II	64	579	669	1,312	51.0	49.6
1977 I[d]	63	580	669	1,312	51.0	49.6
	(54)	(499)	(544)	(1,097)	(49.6)	–
II	54	496	547	1,097	49.9	49.9
1978	50	458	589	1,097	53.7	53.7
II	–	424	673	1,097	61.3	61.3
1979 I[d]	–	349	748	1,097	68.2	68.2
	–	(335)	(675)	(1,010)	(66.8)	–
II	–	327	683	1,010	67.6	69.1
1980 I	–	312	698	1,010	69.1	70.6
1980 II–	–	312	693	1,010	68.6	70.1
1981 I[d]	–	(2,282)	(5,183)	(7,465)	(69.4)	–
1981 II–1982 I	–	1,886	5,579	7,465	74.7	75.5
1982 II–1983 I	–	1,769	5,791	7,560	76.6	77.4
1983 II–1984 I	–	1,482	6,078	7,560	80.4	81.2
1984 II–1985 I	–	1,203	6,712	7,915	84.5	85.4

–, nil.

[a] The classification of import items was based on SITC basic codes through the first half of 1977, on the four-digit Customs Cooperation Council Nomenclature (CCCN) codes during 1977–80 (the first half of 1980) and on the eight-digit CCCN codes thereafter.

[b] The rate of import liberalization is adjusted to make it comparable over time on the basis of the same system of classification as the four-digit CCCN codes (1,097 items) used during 1977–9 (the first half of 1979).

[c] Original import program based on a "positive list system" is reclassified to make it comparable with the trade program for the following periods which are based on a "negative list system."

[d] Figures in parentheses indicate the number of commodity items based on the new system of classification which was used in the following period.

Source: Ministry of Commerce and Industry

The rate of import liberalization jumped from about 12 percent in the first half of 1967 to 60 percent in the second half. The rate jumped drastically in this way because the items not listed in the previous trade program had all been regarded as restricted.[3] A gradual improvement in Korea's external payment position during 1964–7 made this import liberalization possible. In fact, Korea's foreign exchange reserves accumulated rapidly during this period, owing to a rapid expansion in exports, increases in foreign remittances from Korean workers in Vietnam, and the increased inflow of foreign capital.

Although the government originally announced that it would continuously promote import liberalization, the rate of liberalization did not increase after 1967 but showed a gradual decline between 1968 and 1977. Progress then resumed from the first half of 1978 to the first half of 1979. Again after some retreat and slowdown, import liberalization made steady progress from the second half of 1981.[4]

The trend in import liberalization from QRs from 1955 to 1984 has been briefly discussed. It should be noted that the rate of import liberalization for 1967–84, measured in terms of the ratio of AA items to total commodity items, may overestimate the true degree of import liberalization in Korea. The reason is that not only is the rate calculated in terms of the number of commodities,[5] but also it does not take into account the possible restriction of imports by special laws. In Korea the government retains the power to restrict the import of various commodities in accordance with about 37 different special laws,[6] even if the commodities belong to the category of AA items in the trade program. It was not possible in this study, however, to estimate the true rate of import liberalization which takes into account the additional restrictions by these special laws.

[3] There is some problem of comparison with the previous period not only because the semiannual trade programs for the second half of 1967 and later periods were formulated in the form of the new, negative list system but also because the system of commodity classification changed in the new program. In the trade programs for the previous years no consistent system of commodity classification was used. In the new program the government used the SITC basic codes totaling 1,312 to classify all import and export commodities. In order to compare the new program with that for the previous period, it was necessary to reclassify the commodity items listed in the program for the first half of 1967, and to reformulate the program as one based on the negative list system (see the first row in table 3.3).

[4] The system of commodity classification used in the trade program changed from SITC to the Customs Cooperation Council Nomenclature (CCCN) beginning in the second half of 1977.

[5] If the average rate of AA items to total commodity items is weighted by the value of actual imports, the degree of import liberalization may be overestimated even more.

[6] Such as the Law on Drug Administration, the Law on Narcotics, the Fertilizer Management Law, the Pesticides Control Law, the Law on Food Sanitation, etc.

Evolution of Tariffs

During 1946–9 a uniform tariff rate of 10 percent was imposed by the US military government on all imports except those financed by US assistance. With effect from January 1950, however, a new law on customs duties was enforced by the Korean government to increase tariff revenues and to provide greater protection for domestic industries. The new customs law listed more than a thousand import items and specified the tariff rate applicable to each. The tariff rates ranged from a zero rate on food grains and on noncompetitive equipment and raw material imports to 100 percent on luxurious consumer goods. These rates applied equally to both commercial and aid-financed imports from September 1950.

A minor tariff reform was introduced from early 1952, the main purpose of which was to differentiate the tariff rates further by detailed commodity items and to provide for tariff exemptions on imports of machinery and equipment required for key industries. As shown in table 3.4, the new tariff schedule specified tariff rates ranging from zero to 100 percent on 1,695 commodity items in total. The simple average of the tariff rates was 25.4 percent.

Between 1952 and 1984 there have been eight major tariff reforms. The variance of the tariff rates and a simple average tariff rate after each of the major reforms are presented in table 3.4. The simple average rate gradually increased from 25.4 percent in 1952 to a peak of nearly 40 percent in 1962, and then declined steadily to reach 21.9 percent by 1984. Despite such a change in the simple average rate, the coefficient of variation in tariff rates (obtained by dividing the standard deviation in the tariff rates by the simple average tariff rate) did not change much during the period under observation. This may be attributable to the fact that a "cascade" type structure of tariff rates was maintained throughout the period, despite attempts at reform.

The discussion so far summarizes the evolution of the regular tariff schedule in Korea. We must not overlook the fact that, in addition to these regular tariffs, special tariffs and tariff equivalents were imposed on imports from time to time. Between 1958 and 1961, foreign exchange tax was imposed on all commercial imports. The foreign exchange tax revenue which was about 8 percent of the won value of cost, insurance, and freight (c.i.f.) imports in 1958 jumped to 23–31 percent in 1959–60, but declined sharply to 0.6 percent in 1961 because the tax was discontinued after devaluation in early 1961 (table 3.5).

Special tariffs were also levied on selected import commodities during 1964–73. The special tariffs which were to be levied on top of the regular tariffs were introduced to soak up the excess profits arising from QRs that might accrue to the importers of inessential commodities. The tariffs were

Table 3.4 Simple average tariff rates (regular) and coefficient of variation in tariff rates, 1952–1984 (number of items by tariff rates)

Tariff rate (%)	1952	1957	1962	1968	1973	1977	1979	1984
0	161	55	79	146	215	45	154	84
5	–	1	54	37	103	–	78[a]	136
10	314	217	153	242	417	57	259	336[b]
15	135	178	281	96	115	–	241	118
20	244	153	133	1,070	1,419	1,336	652	960
25	112	73	156	103	43	–	68	8
30	100	78	178	26	345	398	289	264
35	277	101	147	116	32	–	–	–
40	228	122	148	218	284	359	183	297
50	30	128	152	336	377[c]	–	25	58[d]
60	44	99	125	178	240	247	207	–
70	–	–	76	183	46	–	–	–
80	37	42	172	60	222	14	8	2
90	–	–	13	–	–	–	–	12
100	13	22	132	282	96	25	13	8
120	–	–	–	4	–	–	–	–
150	–	–	–	53	17	14	8	–
180–250	–	–	14	–	–	–	–	–
Total number of of items[e]	1,695	1,269	2,013	3,150	3,971	2,495	2,185	2,283
Simple average tariff rate (%)	25.40	30.25	39.87	39.12	31.50	29.72	24.77	21.88
Coefficient of variation	0.70	0.70	0.77	0.71	0.70	0.61	0.69	0.61

–, nil.
[a] Including four items with the tariff rate of 2.5 percent.
[b] Including two items with the tariff rate of 12 percent.
[c] Including four items with the tariff rate of 55 percent.
[d] Including one item with the tariff rate of 45 percent.
[e] Excluding a small number of items for which tariffs are levied on a quantity basis. The government used the commodity classification by CCCN from 1962.
Source: Ministry of Finance, Tariff Schedules of Korea, various years

levied at the rate of either 70 or 90 percent of all profit in excess of the normal profit or of the spread (assumed 30 percent) between the c.i.f. import price of goods plus regular tariffs plus domestic indirect taxes and the estimated resale price of the same goods. These tariffs were actually imposed on the basis of market surveys on domestic wholesale prices of imported items as well as the import prices. The actual collection of the special tariffs generally ranged from 0.8 percent of the total won value of c.i.f. imports to 3.2 percent during 1964–72. It suddenly declined in 1973, because special tariffs were abolished in the early part of that year.

Table 3.5 Estimation of actual tariff rates, including special tariffs and foreign exchange tax, 1958–1983 (million current won)

	1	2	3	4	5	6	7	8	9
	Actual collections of tariffs and equivalents					Actual tariff rates (%)			
Year	General tariffs	Foreign exchange tax	Special tariffs	Total	Imports[a]	General tariffs	Foreign exchange tax	Special tariffs	Total
1958	2,969	1,425	–	4,394	18,910	15.7	7.5	–	23.2
1959	3,559	4,722	–	8,281	15,190	23.4	31.1	–	54.5
1960	5,150	5,046	–	10,196	22,328	23.1	22.6	–	45.7
1961	5,306	251	–	5,557	41,093	12.9	0.6	–	13.5
1962	6,745	79	–	6,824	54,834	12.3	0.1	–	12.4
1963	6,358	–	–	6,358	72,839	8.7	–	–	8.7
1964	6,681	–	1,550	8,231	103,526	6.5	–	1.5	8.0
1965	8,500	–	4,076	12,576	126,091	6.7	–	3.2	10.0
1966	12,225	–	5,410	17,635	194,503	6.3	–	2.8	9.1
1967	17,026	–	8,387	25,413	273,557	6.2	–	3.1	9.3
1968	29,004	–	8,877	37,881	411,806	7.0	–	2.2	9.2
1969	35,669	–	9,055	44,724	555,286	6.4	–	1.6	8.1
1970	39,395	–	11,529	50,924	628,333	6.3	–	1.8	8.1
1971	41,763	–	10,424	52,187	893,792	4.7	–	1.2	5.8
1972	51,101	–	8,005	59,106	1,006,026	5.1	–	0.8	5.9
1973	80,196	–	2,175	82,371	1,685,519	4.8	–	0.1	4.9
1974	126,494	–	204	126,698	3,316,271	3.8	–	0.0	3.8
1975	181,004	–	–	181,004	3,520,810	5.1	–	–	5.1
1976	275,512	–	–	275,512	4,246,422	6.5	–	–	6.5
1977	385,871	–	–	385,871	5,232,282	7.4	–	–	7.4
1978	646,425	–	–	646,425	7,246,400	8.9	–	–	8.9
1979	732,294	–	–	732,294	9,843,882	7.4	–	–	7.4
1980	766,063	–	–	766,063	14,710,292	5.2	–	–	5.2
1981	890,615	–	–	890,615	18,305,045	4.9	–	–	4.9
1982	1,012,564	–	–	1,012,564	18,158,999	5.6	–	–	5.6
1983	1,463,200	–	–	1,463,200	20,835,895	7.0	–	–	7.0

–, nil.
Column 4 is the sum of columns 1–3; columns 6, 7, 8, and 9 are columns 1, 2, 3, and 4 respectively divided by column 5.
[a] Merchandise imports in US dollar terms multiplied by the official exchange rate for the respective years.
Sources: EPB, Major Statistics of Korean Economy, 1983; Choi, 1983; Ministry of Finance, Trade Statistics Yearbook, 1962–9.

Finally, it should be pointed out that although the average legal tariff rate was generally very high, the average actual tariff rate, which was obtained by dividing the actual collections of all tariffs (including foreign exchange tax and special tariffs) by the won value of total c.i.f. imports, turned out to be much lower than the average legal tariff rate, as might be expected. The average actual tariff rate, after some initial increase between 1958 and 1959, generally showed a declining trend from about 55 percent in 1959 to 3.8 percent in 1974. After 1974, however, the average actual rate fluctuated between 4.9 and 8.9 percent. The main reason for the gap between the average legal rate and the average actual rate is that exemptions and reductions of legal tariffs have been granted for many purposes in Korea. For instance, the imports of raw materials for export production which accounted for a large share in the country's imports have been exempted from tariffs. The imports of machinery and equipment for some major industries have also been subject to tariff exemptions (or reductions in some cases).

Index of Trade Liberalization

Table 3.6 estimates an overall index of trade liberalization in Korea for the period 1955–84. As shown, three main factors – export liberalization, the average legal tariff rate, and the degree of QR on imports – are taken into account in the estimation of the overall index.

First, the index of export liberalization was estimated by inverting the ratio, given in table 3.1, of net export subsidies to exchange rate. Thus we can show the degree of export liberalization for the period 1958–84, assuming that the lower the ratio of net export subsidies to exchange rate is, the greater is the degree of export liberalization. For the period 1955–8, it was simply assumed that the index of export liberalization was roughly the same as in 1958–60. The estimated result for the period 1955–84 is presented in table 3.6, column 1.

Second, the degree of import liberalization in terms of tariffs was estimated. To accomplish this, the annual series of average legal tariff rates was calculated by adding the average rates of both foreign exchange tax and special tariffs to the average legal rate of regular tariffs. The average legal rate of regular tariffs for 1955–84 was obtained by weighting legal rates on commodity groups by the value of domestic production in 1975.[7]

The average legal tariff rate, however, may have an upward bias in two respects: this legal rate has been substantially higher than the average actual tariff rate owing to the tariff exemptions and reductions granted for various purposes; in addition, the average legal rate weighted by the value of domestic production may have an upward bias since high protection on a sector tends to raise the nominal value of that sector's production above the level obtainable without such protection. The average legal rate should therefore be taken as an indicator of potential protection, reflecting the upper boundary of Korean tariff protection.

In any case, the annual series of average legal tariff rate is inverted in percentage form in order to show the degree of import liberalization in terms of tariffs (see column 4). This series indicates that the degree of import liberalization rises as the average rate of legal tariffs declines.

---

[7] A simple average tariff rate was first estimated for each of the two-digit CCCN groups (99 groups), and then the simple average rate was weighted by the value of each group's production in 1975 to obtain the average legal rate for all items in the respective years.

Table 3.6 Estimate of overall index of trade liberalization for Korea, 1955–1984 (percent)

	1	2	3	4	5	6	7
Year	Inverted net export subsidy rate[a]	Average rate of legal tariffs		Inverted total tariff rate[d]	Degree of liberalization from QRs[e]	Overall index of liberalization	
		Regular[b]	Total[c]			Weighted average[f]	Index[g]
1955	40.0	27.4	27.4	78.5	1.0	36.0	7
1956	40.0	27.4	27.4	78.5	3.5	37.0	7
1957	40.0	35.4	35.4	73.9	6.4	36.7	7
1958	43.4	35.4	42.9	70.0	6.3	36.5	7
1959	36.2	35.4	66.5	60.1	4.7	30.8	6
1960	42.3	35.4	58.0	63.3	5.0	33.7	7
1961	84.7	35.4	36.0	73.5	4.0	49.1	10
1962	91.7	49.5	49.6	66.8	5.4	49.7	10
1963	73.2	49.5	49.5	68.3	0.4	42.6	9
1964	81.3	49.5	51.0	66.2	2.0	45.1	9
1965	96.4	49.5	52.7	65.5	5.9	50.9	10
1966	95.6	49.5	52.3	65.7	9.1	52.0	10
1967	93.1	49.5	52.6	65.5	58.8	71.1	14
1968	93.8	56.7	58.9	62.9	56.0	69.4	14
1969	94.0	56.7	58.3	63.2	53.6	68.6	14
1970	93.7	56.7	58.5	63.1	52.8	68.2	14
1971	93.8	56.7	57.9	63.3	53.5	68.5	14
1972	96.9	56.7	57.5	63.5	49.5	67.9	14
1973	97.8	48.1	48.2	67.5	50.7	69.9	14
1974	97.9	48.1	48.1	67.5	49.3	69.3	14
1975	97.4	48.1	48.1	67.5	47.8	68.6	14
1976	97.6	48.1	48.1	67.5	49.6	69.4	14
1977	98.1	41.3	41.3	70.8	49.9	70.6	14
1978	97.8	41.3	41.3	70.7	61.3	75.1	15
1979	97.8	34.4	34.4	74.4	69.1	79.3	16
1980	96.8	34.4	34.4	74.4	70.1	79.4	16
1981	97.8	34.4	34.4	74.4	75.5	81.9	16
1982	99.6	34.4	34.4	74.4	77.4	83.2	17
1983	100.0	34.4	34.4	74.4	81.2	84.5	17
1984	100.0	26.7	26.7	78.9	85.4	87.8	18

[a] The reciprocal of one plus the net export subsidy rate given in table 3.1. Figures for 1955–7 are assumed to be roughly equivalent to the levels in 1958–60.
[b] The average rate weighted by the value of production in 1975.
[c] Includes the average foreign exchange tax rate and special tariff rate on imports in addition to the regular tariffs.
[d] The reciprocal of one plus the average total legal tariff rate.
[e] Represents the degree of import liberalization from QRs for the second half of each year in 1955–79, and that for the second half of the year indicated and the first half of the following year for 1980–4.
[f] The average of columns 1, 4, and 5 weighted by 0.3, 0.3, and 0.4 respectively.
[g] Column 6 multiplied by 0.2 and rounded into integers.

Third, turning to the degree of import liberalization from QRs, the adjusted rate of import liberalization given in table 3.3 is applied to the period 1967–84. For the period 1955–67, an index of the number of AA items, with the first half of 1967 (shown in table 3.2) as 100, was used to extrapolate the adjusted rate of import liberalization. The annual series so obtained for the entire period is shown in table 3.6, column 5.

Finally, the index of export liberalization, the figures representing the degree of import liberalization in terms of tariffs, and the figures represent-

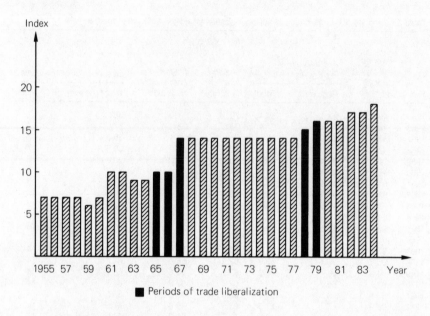

Figure 3.1 Overall index of trade liberalization for Korea, 1955–1984

Source: Table 3.6

ing the degree of import liberalization from QRs are averaged, weighting the three series by 0.3, 0.3, and 0.4, in order to obtain a new index (column 6). This new index is then converted to the "overall index of trade liberalization," which ranges from zero to 20 (column 7). Since a heavier weight is given to the degree of import liberalization from QRs, the overall index seems to reflect the trend in the former. These relative weights of 0.3, 0.3, and 0.4 are based on the author's judgment that in Korea the QRs on imports have been a more binding form of trade control than tariffs have.

The overall index of trade liberalization for Korea is illustrated in figure 3.1. We observe some initial increase in the index in 1961, which is not analyzed as part of the liberalization episodes. This increase in the index simply reflects the effect of a one-shot large devaluation undertaken in that year but does not indicate any conscious effort of the government to liberalize trade, particularly imports. Conscious efforts to liberalize trade were made in Korea, however, during the two periods 1965–7 and 1978–9. Trade liberalization for the first period was not sufficiently successful to assure a continued progress in liberalization. The second period appears to have been rather successful, since trade liberalization continued, albeit slowly, even after 1979.

The Korean government liberalized imports further. The degree of import liberalization from QRs was raised from 85.4 percent in 1984 to 95.2 percent by 1988. The government tariff reform also brought about a gradual reduction in the simple average tariff rate from 22 percent in 1984 to 18 percent by 1988. Therefore, it is estimated that Korea's overall index of trade liberalization reached about 19 by 1988.

4

Announcement and Implementation of Liberalization Policy

On the basis of the long-term policy pattern we identified two episodes, 1965–7 and 1978–9, during which trade liberalization made significant progress.

One apparently "worked" and the other did not: liberalization marked time for ten years after the 1965–7 episode, but progressed steadily after the 1978–9 episode. To understand these two differing outcomes, the broad nature and targets of each must first be assessed, the political and economic circumstances in which they took place delineated, and the accompanying policies evaluated.

Broad Nature and Targets

The First Episode (1965–1967)

Trade liberalization during the first episode mainly resulted from the reduction of QRs on imports, as discussed in chapter 3. Export trade was also somewhat liberalized from 1965 but with negligible impact on the overall index of trade liberalization. A tariff reform following the reduction of QRs reduced the simple average rate of legal tariffs but resulted in a minor increase in the rate when weighted by domestic production. On the whole, however, the trade liberalization for this period cannot be characterized as a simple change from QRs to tariffs, since the loosening of QRs was quite substantial whereas tariffs were only increased by a small margin.

QRs began to be relaxed for imports in 1965 after the exchange rate reform of 1964–5. Since import control by QRs had tightened severely during the previous two years of foreign exchange crisis, the initial loosening in 1965 was not much more than a return to the pre-1963 level of import control. The government did not have any consistent long-term program of import liberalization in 1965; it simply gradually increased the number of AA items in its semiannual trade programs as the country's foreign exchange situation improved after the exchange rate reform. This kind of gradual import liberalization continued until the first half of 1967.

In the middle of 1967, an important step was taken in the direction of import liberalization. For the second half of 1967 the government actually reformulated the semiannual trade program, previously a positive list system, in the form of a negative list system (see chapter 3 for a discussion of the differences between the systems). The government announced that the import liberalization program was promoted with the following general objectives:

1 to strengthen the international competitiveness of domestic industries and increase exports by opening up the domestic economy, which had so far been highly protected, to foreign competition;
2 to protect domestic consumers by increasing the degree of import liberalization;
3 to contribute to the expansion of world trade volume as a member of the International Monetary Fund (IMF) and the General Agreement on Tariffs and Trade (GATT).

In order to prepare an import liberalization program, an *ad hoc* working committee was organized in the MCI in early July 1967. After adopting the negative instead of the positive list system for future trade control, the committee agreed that the following commodity items would be subject to import prohibition or restriction:

1 items already under import restriction in accordance with existing laws;
2 items hazardous to public health;
3 items considered harmful to national security and public safety;
4 items deleterious to sound public morale, or violating social norms;
5 items considered too luxurious in proportion to the country's current stage of economic development.

The committee further decided that import items to be liberalized would be selected according to the following principles:

1 those import items already liberalized from QRs should continue to be liberalized;
2 those items on which basic tariffs exceeded 50 percent should be liberalized;
3 those import items with a ratio of domestic wholesale price to c.i.f. import price exceeding 500 won to the US dollar should be liberalized.

On the basis of these criteria and principles, the committee examined each of the 30,000 commodity items classified in the SITC manual (revised issue). The criteria and principles could not be strictly observed, however, owing mainly to strong pressures from relevant industrial associations and the government agencies dealing with the problems of industrial development. As suggested, the number of AA items was increased substantially by this liberalization program of 1967, thereby greatly contributing to an increase in the overall index of trade liberalization. The real effect of the program on domestic industries, however, was considered to be rather small because items for which imports were expected to increase rapidly under the existing structure of tariffs were not liberalized.

Although the government had announced in mid-1967 that it would continue to promote import liberalization, it was not able to increase the rate of import liberalization measured in terms of the ratio of AA items to total tradeable commodities after the first half of 1968. In response to a deteriorating balance of payments arising from accelerating domestic inflation and increased foreign debt service burdens in that year, the government generally tightened import controls.

The Second Episode (1978–1979)

Trade liberalization remained at a standstill for ten years after 1967. In early 1978, the government resumed efforts to promote trade liberalization, this time concentrating on reducing tariffs as well as loosening QRs. Unlike its predecessor of 1965–7, this episode heralded sustained progress in trade liberalization thereafter (with the exception of 1980, the year of severe recession). The reason for this success may be that, unlike the previous attempt, this effort was characterized by an "advance notice" system, promoting the trade liberalization as a long-run policy (as will be discussed later).

Mainly because of a favorable external environment, Korea's exports had expanded rapidly and her balance of payments had improved substantially in 1976–7. Rapidly growing exports of construction services to Middle Eastern oil-exporting countries in those years helped to improve the country's balance of payments. The rapid improvement in the external balance, however, caused excessive monetary expansion and created a problem in domestic demand management by 1977. It therefore appears that the initial proposal for import liberalization in early 1978 was primarily a response to the problem of excessive monetary expansion.

The Import Liberalization Committee established within the government in February 1978 and chaired by the Vice Minister of Commerce and Industry announced the following objectives for import liberalization:

1 to strengthen the international competitiveness of domestic industries;
2 to alleviate trade restrictions imposed by countries to which Korea exports;
3 to restrict monetary expansion from the foreign sector;
4 to help stabilize domestic prices;

5 to protect domestic consumers;
6 finally, to comply with pressures from international organizations.

The program determined by the committee was as follows: firstly, QRs
on imports should be liberalized, giving priority to items whose domestic
prices far exceeded import prices; secondly, tariffs should initially replace
QRs in protecting the domestic industry, and should then in the long run
be reduced; thirdly, the advance notice system should be adopted to
prepare domestic industries for import liberalization; finally, both semiannual trade programs and trade administration procedures should be
simplified.

On the basis of the committee's recommendation, the government
increased the number of AA items in the semiannual trade programs in
three steps, the first to be effective from May 1978, and the second and
third from September 1878 and January 1979 respectively. The program
gradually increased the number of AA items by 162 on the basis of the
four-digit Customs Cooperation Council Nomenclature (CCCN) classification (table 4.1). As a result, the ratio of AA items to total tradeable items
increased from 53.8 percent in early 1978 (before the first step of
liberalization was put into effect) to 68.6 percent by early 1979.

In selecting the commodity items for import liberalization, the government announced that it gave priorities to the following types: (a) domestic
products already competitive on international markets; (b) items whose
liberalization might contribute to domestic price stabilization; (c) items
domestically produced by monopoly and oligopoly firms; (d) basic raw

Table 4.1 Progress in import liberalization from quantitative restrictions during 1978–1980
(number of items, based on the four-digit Customs Cooperation Council Nomenclature
classification)

Period	Import-prohibited items	Import-restricted items	AA items	Total items	Ratio of AA items to total (%)
First half of 1978	50	456	591	1,097	53.8
Liberalization program					
First step (May 1978)	–	431	666	1,097	60.7
Second step (Sep 1978)	–	385	712	1,097	64.9
Third step (Jan 1979)[a]	–	344	753	1,097	68.6
		(335)	(675)	(1,010)	(66.8)
Second half of 1979	–	327	683	1,010	67.6
First half of 1980	–	318	692	1,010	68.5
Second half of 1980	–	317	693	1,010	68.6

–, nil.
[a] Figures in parentheses indicate the number of items on the basis of the new CCCN classification
which started to be used in the second half of 1979.
Source: Korea Development Institute, 1981, p. 49

materials; and (e) items that could contribute to increasing energy efficiency. It does not seem, however, that these criteria were strictly applied in the selection of AA items during 1978–9.

The government introduced two devices, not employed in the previous episode, to alleviate the impact of import liberalization on domestic industries. One was the system of advance notice by which the list of commodity items for future liberalization could be announced in advance. The other was the system of "observation items," whereby the government could examine the specified import items for possible restrictions when imports increased rapidly after liberalization. When the first step of the import liberalization program was put into effect in May 1978, for instance, the government announced the list of commodity items to be liberalized in 1979–82, as shown in table 4.2. It also specified 28 commodity items out of a total of 75 items liberalized in May 1978 as observation items (based on the four-digit level of CCCN classification).

The relaxation of QRs on imports could not be continued in 1980 owing to balance-of-payments difficulties as well as a severe domestic economic recession. From 1981, however, the government was again able to increase the number of AA items in its trade programs by making use of both the advance notice system and the observation items system. In this way it gradually increased the ratio of AA items to total tradeable items from 68.6 percent in the second half of 1980 to 84.8 percent by the same period of 1984. According to the government plan of import liberalization announced in 1984, this ratio will reach 91.6 percent in 1986 and 95.2 percent by 1988.

Meanwhile, the customs law was revised with effect from January 1, 1979, in order to reduce tariff barriers on imports. As a result of this tariff

Table 4.2 The first step of the liberalization program and the number of items for future liberalization

Items	Four-digit CCCN basis	Above four-digit CCCN basis	Total items
Items liberalized by the first step in May 1978	75	58	133
(Observation items liberalized by the first step)	(28)	(15)	(43)
Total number of items for advance notice	152	36	188
Number of items to be liberalized in 1979–80	63	15	78
Number of items to be liberalized in 1981–2	89	21	110
Total	227	94	321

Source: Korea Development Institute, 1981, p. 47

reform, the average rate of legal tariffs (weighted by 1975 production) declined from 41.3 percent to 34.4 percent. It should be noted, however, that this tariff reform was prepared and carried out separately by the Ministry of Finance (MOF) and was not part of a comprehensive liberalization package. In other words, the loosening of QRs and the tariff reduction were not explicitly planned as a comprehensive package of import liberalization, although the tariff reform actually significantly reduced the average rate of legal tariffs.

The government carried out another tariff reform effective from early 1984. This reform not only reduced the average rate of legal tariffs but also specified the gradual reductions in many tariff rates between 1984 and 1988. In other words, the 1984 reform introduced the system of advance notice for the gradual reduction of tariff protection following the practice used in the liberalization of QRs on imports.

Economic Circumstances

The First Episode

When the first trade liberalization program was introduced in Korea during the 1965–7 period the world economy was enjoying reasonably rapid growth with price stability. The economy of Japan, one of Korea's major trading partners, attained an annual growth rate of about 10 percent in real GNP during the 1960s. The economy of the United States, another major trading partner, also achieved relatively high GNP growth because of military expenditures for the Vietnam War. Real GNP in the United States grew at an average annual rate of 4.6 percent during the 1960s. Other Western industrialized countries were also apparently enjoying a relatively marked growth, as a result of which world trade volume was able to expand at an average annual rate of about 8 percent during this period (see Huh, 1972).

Price levels in industrialized countries were generally stable in the 1960s. The prices of primary commodities in the world market were also relatively stable during this episode compared with the later episode. For this reason, the prices of Korean imports, measured in terms of import unit value index, increased by only 0.4 percent from 1964 to 1967. In contrast, Korea's export unit price index could increase by 18 percent during the same period, thus enabling considerable improvement in the country's terms of trade.

Although interest rates in advanced industrial economies were generally rising in the 1960s, Korea could still borrow from international financial markets at an annual interest rate of 6–7 percent. Foreign long-term capital could easily be imported during the 1960s since Korea did not have much foreign debt until the mid-1960s. The system of government guarantee on foreign loan repayments introduced in 1962 greatly facilitated the import of foreign long-term capital by domestic enterprises. Meanwhile, the interest rate reform of 1965 increased incentives to borrow from abroad by greatly increasing interest rate differentials between domestic and foreign loans.

Owing to this favorable external environment as well as the shift in Korea's industrialization strategy from import substitution to export promotion in the early 1960s, the country's commodity exports were increasing rapidly when the liberalization program was introduced. For instance, commodity exports increased at an average rate of about 40 percent during 1964–7. Despite this rapid growth in exports, the country's trade balance was showing a large deficit, since imports were initially much greater than exports and were also growing rapidly. Balance on goods and services also showed a deficit ranging from approximately US$200 million to US$400 million, or 40–5 percent of the total imports of goods and services, during 1964–7. However, the current account deficits were much lower than the net balance on goods and services since net receipt of foreign transfers was still quite substantial.

Korea's GNP was growing fairly rapidly from 1963, reaching an average annual rate of about 8.5 percent during 1964–7. As a result, total employment increased at an average annual rate of 3.3 percent during the same period. In particular, nonfarm employment expanded by 8.5 percent a year. The nation's unemployment consequently declined from 7.7 percent of the total labor force in 1964 to 6.2 percent in 1967. However, the rate of inflation in Korea, measured in terms of the national wholesale price index, was considerably higher than that in her major trade partners. Although the rate of inflation, which had been as high as 35 percent in 1964, declined to below 10 percent from 1965, the average rate for 1964–7 was still 14.5 percent. In contrast, the average wholesale price index for the United States and Japan, weighted by Korea's trade volume, increased at an average annual rate of only 1.4 percent during the same period.

Turning to Korea's protection regime in 1964–7, it is clear that the levels of protection on domestic industries showed a wide variance. Although multiple exchange rates were now replaced by a unified exchange rate after the reform of 1964–5, a wide variety of export promotion measures was still used to increase incentives to export. On the import side, a highly differentiated structure of tariff rates combined with nontariff barriers provided a differentiated level of protection on domestic industries. The levels of protection, however, varied mainly by type of industries, regardless of the geographic location of the industries concerned. According to a study by Westphal and Kim (1977, pp. 3–9), the effective rates of protection (estimated by the Balassa method) on processed food, beverages and tobacco, construction materials, intermediate products I and nondurable consumer goods were all negative in 1968, but the rates on other industrial groups (mainly agriculture and capital goods industries) were positive, ranging from 3 percent to 164 percent.

The Second Episode

The world economy was fully recovered from a severe recession following the first world oil crisis of 1973–4 when the second liberalization package was introduced in Korea in 1978–9. Both the United States and Japan, the two major trading partners of Korea, achieved a fairly rapid growth of real GNP during 1977–9 after some stagnation and slow growth in the preceding period (1974–6). Growth performance in other Organization for Economic Cooperation and Development (OECD) countries indicated that their economies were also fully recovered from the worldwide recession. The nominal value of world trade expanded at an average rate of nearly 14 percent during 1977–9, owing partly to the worldwide inflation and partly to the increased demand, particularly by oil-exporting countries.

General price levels in Western industrialized countries were much more unstable in the 1970s than in the previous decade. The sharp rises in the international prices of crude oil and other natural resources in 1973–4 set off inflationary trends all over the world. Although the inflationary trends had been largely checked by 1976, the wholesale price index in the United States still increased at an average annual rate of 6.5 percent during 1976–8. The wholesale price index in Japan only increased by 1.4 percent a year during the same period. We should note, however, that the second oil crisis began to set off another round of worldwide inflation and recession in 1979.

Owing to worldwide inflation, the foreign prices of Korean imports measured in terms of unit value index rose by 32 percent during 1976–8. Since the unit value index for exports increased by an even higher rate than that for imports, Korea's terms of trade improved by nearly 10 percent during the same period. This improvement could only partially offset the 36 percent deterioration in Korea's terms of trade recorded during the preceding three years (1973–5).

Interest rates on international financial markets were somewhat higher in the 1977–9 period than in the 1960s, reflecting the higher rate of worldwide inflation in the 1970s. Except for the rise in interest rates, foreign long-term capital was readily available, thanks to the recycling of oil money by Western commercial banks. For this reason, Korea could easily import a large amount of long-term capital for investment in heavy and chemical industries in the late 1970s, even though the country had already accumulated a considerable foreign debt during the first oil crisis of 1974–5.

Between 1975 and 1977, the nominal value of Korean exports increased at an average annual rate of over 40 percent, far exceeding the increasing rate of imports, which was about 25 percent. Korea's trade balance therefore improved greatly and her deficits on goods and services sharply declined from 26 percent of the total imports of goods and services in 1975 to 1.6 percent by 1977. The current account balance, which includes net transfers from abroad, even showed a small amount of surplus for the first time since 1965. The country's balance of payments started to deteriorate again, however, from 1978 because of the more rapid growth of imports than exports. Nevertheless, the drastic improvement in the balance of payments during 1976–7 motivated the government to promote a trade liberalization program beginning in 1978.

Thanks to the worldwide economic recovery from the recession of 1974–5, Korea was able to attain an extremely high rate of economic growth during 1976–8. Korea's real GNP grew at an average annual rate of about 12 percent, much higher than the 7–8 percent growth rate achieved during the preceding two years of worldwide recession. The rapid growth of real GNP in turn resulted in a rapid expansion of employment: total employment grew by nearly 4.5 percent annually. National unemployment declined from 4.1 percent of the total labor force in 1975 to 3.2 percent by 1978. However, the rate of inflation measured in terms of the wholesale price index continued to be considerably higher than for her major trading partners. Though the annual rate of inflation had declined from about 25 percent in 1974–5 to 15 percent in 1976, for the three years 1976–8 it averaged about 13 percent.

The country's protection regimes just before the launching of the second liberalization program in 1978 were ostensibly somewhat more liberalized than those of the mid-1960s. All export subsidies that directly affected the profit margin of the export industry were now abolished except for the preferential interest rate on export credit. On the import side, three tariff reforms undertaken since the mid-1960s significantly reduced not only the simple average rate of tariffs but also the variance of tariff rates. The degree of import liberalization from QRs was around 50 percent in terms of the number of tradeable items in 1977, compared with about 6 percent in 1965.

A study by Nam (1981, pp. 187–211), however, indicates that the average rate of effective protection for all industries (tradeable sectors) in Korea increased to 30.6 percent in 1978, compared with the 11 percent for 1968 estimated in the Westphal and Kim (1977) study. The main reason for the increase was that the protection rate on agriculture increased sharply between the two episodes. Within manufacturing, the effective rates of protection still showed a wide variance by type of industry. In 1978 the effective rates estimated by the Balassa method ranged from a minimum of − 38 percent on intermediate products I to a maximum of 135 percent on transport equipment. As in the 1960s, the protection regimes did not discriminate geographically among industries.

Political Circumstances

The political situation in Korea, of course, changed considerably over the decade between the two episodes. Nevertheless, some relevant political circumstances were similar for both liberalization programs. First the two programs were undertaken by the same authoritarian government under President Park Chung Hee.

In the mid-1960s when the first liberalization program was introduced, Park, who had overthrown the Democratic Party government by a military coup in May 1961 and had ruled the country as head of the military government until 1963, was serving his first term as a civilian president in accordance with the new Constitution approved in late 1963. The new government made clear that it would emphasize economic growth through export-oriented industrialization. Economic growth was apparently regarded as pivotal to legitimizing the new government. Although there were some opposition forces, the political structure under the new government was considered quite stable since it had strong military support.

In fact, the government under Park attempted to achieve political stability by all means available, since it was taken to be indispensable to the government's objective of economic growth. The government tried to achieve political stability by "infrequent change in top government positions, by imposing limitations on civil liberties, and by assuring strong military backing to the government policies" (Mason et al., 1980).

In 1978–9 when the second package of trade liberalization was introduced, Park was still running the government but had had to be helped by the new Yusin (meaning revitalizing reforms) Constitution, enacted in 1972, which gave the president sweeping new powers to rule by emergency decrees. Although he made full use of his emergency powers to repress political opposition, the opposition forces seemed to have grown by this period. Finally, President Park's government came to an end with his assassination in October 1979. One can therefore say that the political structure in 1978–9 was, at least, less stable than in the mid-1960s.

Despite such political vicissitudes, the Korean government has almost always remained strong in the sense of retaining the ability and willingness to carry out its policy decisions. The strong government tradition in Korea is attributable partly to the country's Confucian cultural background and partly to the authoritarian nature of Park's rule. Jones and Sakong (1980, pp. 79–140) once suggested that "Koreans are even better at implementation than at planning" and that this ability essentially stems from the government system which can be characterized as a Myrdalian "hard" state (or "strong state" in Myrdal's terms). (According to Jones and Sakong's definition, a "hard" state is one in which policies are regularly implemented, whereas a "soft" state is one in which policies are often not implemented.) In addition, the government's strong commitment to economic growth has never changed. For this reason, there was no question but that the two trade liberalization programs would be implemented as announced by the government.

The trade liberalization policy announced by the government was not primarily ideologically motivated. Since the country was already pursuing an export-oriented industrialization strategy for economic development, the policy was largely a pragmatic move to gradually open domestic markets to foreign competition.

In Korea, commercial policy was generally considered very important by the public because the economy was highly dependent on external trade. Major commercial policy issues have been regularly discussed at the Monthly Export Promotion Conference (renamed the Monthly Trade Promotion Conference in the early 1970s) since 1966. The conference was usually attended by the President himself, all cabinet members, heads of major financial institutions, business association leaders, and representatives of major export firms. It essentially served as a channel for the President's export promotion drive, and to solve quickly many problems encountered by exporters. However, it seems that the conference increased the general public's concern over trade policy issues, since whatever was discussed was well publicized.

Although the trade liberalization policy proposals were, of course, reported in the conference, they did not become the focus of major discussion. Owing to the Korean tradition of a strong executive branch of government, the trade policy issues were mainly discussed within the bureaucracy. Since the liberalization policy generally involved decisions on conflicting interests of the business sector, however, it usually invited major debates in business circles and the press; thus the policy normally received much attention whenever it was announced.

The administration of QRs is the responsibility of the MCI while tariff administration is that of the MOF. The import liberalization from QRs was therefore usually designed and implemented by the MCI, while the reduction of tariffs was implemented by the MOF. These ministries generally invited the opinions of all concerned agencies of the government when they formulated a liberalization program. It is well known, however, that trade liberalization was favored by the Economic Planning Board and the MOF. Within the MCI, opinions were usually divided: only the Bureau of Trade Administration favored liberalization while all other bureaus dealing with particular industrial sectors were critical. All other ministries took their positions on the basis of whether or not the economic sectors they were dealing with would be adversely affected.

Although the details of liberalization policy were formulated by the government, the direction of the policy was very much influenced by the US government and international organizations. The import liberalization program for the first episode was very much influenced by the US aid mission to Korea, while the program for the later episode was influenced by pressures from GATT and the IMF to increase trade liberalization. The timing of the programs, however, was directly influenced by domestic economic conditions, including the balance of payments, inflationary pressures, and so on.

Accompanying Policies – the First Episode (1965–1967)

Exchange Rate Policy

When the first trade liberalization program was introduced, an exchange rate reform was already virtually completed. The complicated system of multiple exchange rates of the 1950s and the first half of the 1960s was changed to a unitary floating exchange rate by the reform in 1964–5. The reform was not only to unify the exchange rate but also to improve the system of incentives for export-oriented industrialization.

Even after adoption of the new system, however, the Korean Monetary Authority did not allow a clean floating except briefly in the latter half of 1965; in effect, therefore, the Korean Monetary Authority actually transformed the system of unitary floating exchange rate into a fixed rate system, after some initial floating. For this reason, the nominal official exchange rate remained almost constant at around 270 won to the US dollar during 1965–7, as shown in table 4.3. Exports nevertheless increased rapidly since the won had been substantially depreciated in 1964–5. In addition, the inflow of foreign capital was accelerated by the interest rate reform of 1965 which widened interest rate differentials between domestic and foreign loans. Thus foreign exchange availability increased substantially, virtually eliminating any disparity between black-market rate and official rate during this episode.

Nominal effective exchange rates changed little for either exports or imports during 1965–7 (see table 4.3). The effective rate for exports includes the average value of net export subsidies per US dollar of exports for the respective years, while that for imports includes the average value of actual tariffs and their equivalent per US dollar of imports. Real effective exchange rates for exports and imports adjusted by a PPP index, however, showed gradual declines by a small margin, in terms of the number of won to the US dollar, during the same period (see table 2.7).

Table 4.3 Trends in nominal effective exchange rates for exports and imports during the two periods 1964–1970 and 1977–1983 (won per US dollar)

| | 1 | 2 | 3 | 4 | 5 | 6 |
| | | | | Effective rate for | | Ratio of effective |
Date	Official rate	Net export subsidies[a]	Actual tariffs and equivalents[b]	Exports	Imports	export rate to import rate (%)
Dec 1964	255.5	49.3	32.7	304.8	288.2	105.8
Jun 1965	271.1	9.9	27.7	281.0	298.8	94.0
Dec 1965	271.5	9.9	27.7	281.4	299.2	94.1
Jun 1966	270.9	12.5	25.1	283.4	296.0	95.7
Dec 1966	270.9	12.5	25.1	283.4	296.0	95.7
Jun 1967	269.2	20.0	25.5	289.2	294.7	98.1
Dec 1967	274.6	20.0	25.5	294.6	300.1	98.2
Dec 1968	281.5	18.2	25.9	299.7	307.4	97.5
Dec 1969	304.5	18.4	24.5	322.9	329.0	98.1
Dec 1970	316.7	20.8	25.7	337.5	342.4·	98.6
Dec 1977	484.0	9.4	35.7	493.4	519.7	94.9
Jun 1978	484.0	11.0	42.9	495.0	526.9	93.9
Dec 1978	484.0	11.0	42.9	495.0	526.9	93.9
Jun 1979	484.0	11.0	36.0	495.0	520.0	95.2
Dec 1979	484.0	11.0	36.0	495.0	520.0	95.2
Dec 1980	659.9	20.6	34.4	680.5	694.3	98.0
Dec 1981	700.5	15.0	34.1	715.5	734.6	97.4
Dec 1982	748.8	3.0	41.8	751.8	790.6	95.1
Dec 1983	795.3	0.0	55.9	795.3	851.2	93.4

Column 4 is the sum of columns 1 and 2; column 5 is the sum of columns 1 and 3; column 6 is column 4 divided by column 5.
[a] The average value of net export subsidies per US dollar of exports for the respective years, not for the months indicated since such subsidies cannot be estimated by month.
[b] The average value of actual tariffs and tariff equivalents per US dollar of imports for the respective years, not the months indicated.
Source: Bank of Korea, Economic Statistics Yearbook, various issues; Kim, 1988, appendix tables 1 and 8

Export Promotion Policy

Because the price competitiveness of Korean exports increased as a result of the devaluation in 1964, the government began to abolish direct subsidy payments to exporters in 1965. The export–import link system was also eliminated except for a very limited number of unprofitable export items. At the same time, the government not only maintained many of the export promotion measures adopted before 1964 but also introduced some new schemes in 1964–5. The important export incentive schemes introduced through 1965 and implemented in the latter half of the 1960s have already been described in chapter 3. The system of export incentives was so well established by 1965 that it required few additions after that year. It should be noted, however, that the incentive schemes were not introduced as part of the trade liberalization package; indeed, such schemes were probably introduced before the trade liberalization program.

Net export subsidies per US dollar of exports declined from 23 percent of the official exchange rate in 1964 to about 4–7 percent during 1965–7, mainly because of the abolition of the export–import link system. However, they enabled near consistency to be maintained in the nominal effective rate for export in the face of gradual overvaluation of the won in 1965–7 (see table 4.3). As already mentioned, they could not prevent a minor decline in the real effective rate for exports.

The effective exchange rate for exports, including net export subsidies per US dollar of exports, gradually increased from 94 percent of the effective rate for imports in 1965 to 98 percent by the end of 1967. This slightly lower ratio of export rate to import rate seems to result mainly from errors and omissions in the estimation of net export subsidies. Although it is not possible to estimate effective exchange rates for export by type of commodity or sector, we infer that the effective rates did not vary widely by sector. The reason is that each of the export incentive schemes was applied indiscriminately to all exporters who could satisfy certain specified criteria. Further, the net subsidies were only a small proportion of the effective exchange rate for exports.

Monetary Policy

Many changes were made in monetary policy instruments during this first episode of trade liberalization although they were not formally designed as an integral part of the liberalization package. One of the most important was the interest rate reform of September 1965, which sharply raised bank interest rates on both deposits and loans. In fact, the reform raised the maximum interest rate on ordinary bank loans from 16 percent a year to 26 percent, while raising the maximum rate on time deposits from 15 percent to 30 percent. The impact of this reform on financial markets was so great that almost all monetary policy instruments had to be significantly changed after the reform.

First of all, bank deposits, particularly time and savings deposits, increased rapidly following the interest rate reform. The Korean Monetary Authority could therefore improve the techniques of monetary control, as originally planned. It abolished the loan ceiling system and attempted to control the money supply through the indirect techniques of bank reserve manipulations immediately following the reform. In fact, the Authority had to change many policy instruments from early 1966, to experiment wth all the indirect techniques of monetary control available.

As already mentioned, the 1965 reform greatly increased the gap in interest rate between domestic and foreign financial markets. This resulted in accelerated capital inflows, mainly in the form of long-term and short-term foreign loans, which, together with the rapid expansion of Korean exports, caused a rapid accumulation of foreign reserves. To contract the consequent monetary expansion, the Central Bank had not only to increase legal reserve requirements for banking institutions but also to freeze a significant portion of bank reserves by means of forced sales of Stabilization Bonds and compulsory deposits in the Central Bank's Stabilization Account.

The minimum reserve requirements of banking institutions at the time of the interest rate reform in September 1965 were 10 percent on time and savings deposits and 16 percent on demand deposits. These reserve requirements were raised twice between September 1965 and early February 1966. As a result, the reserve requirements as of February 1966 were 20 percent on short-term savings deposits, 15 percent on long-term deposits, and 35 percent on demand deposits. These high levels of legal reserve requirements were maintained until around the end of 1967. On top of these reserve requirements, a marginal requirement of 45–50 percent was also imposed on the increment of bank deposits from October 1, 1966 to April 1, 1967.

However, the Central Bank generally raised its lending rates to restrict its lending. In fact, it succeeded during 1965–7 in restricting its lending to the government, but not to financial institutions. In particular, the Central Bank loans to the National Agricultural Cooperatives Federation (NACF) increased substantially for the operation of the NACF's fertilizer account during this period.

Despite all these efforts to control the reserve base, it increased very rapidly from December 1964 to December 1967, as shown in table 4.4. The rate of increase in the reserve base even accelerated on an annual basis from 18 percent in December 1964 to 100 percent in March 1967. The rate of increase then decelerated between March 1967 and the end of 1970. Owing to this rapid expansion of the reserve base, the money supply increased rapidly. The annual rate of increase in the broadly defined money (M2) was much higher, however, than that in the narrow money (M1), reflecting the fact that time and savings deposits expanded much more rapidly than demand deposits after the interest rate reform of 1965. Domestic credit also expanded very rapidly, as shown in the table.

As already suggested, Korea maintained a very high interest rate between September 1965 and December 1970. Even the real rate of interest after discounting for the rate of domestic inflation ranged from about 10 to 20 percent, as shown in table 4.5. In contrast, the nominal interest rate on foreign borrowings generally ranged from 5 to 9 percent a year during the same period. The real interest rate of foreign borrowings, which is estimated by taking both the annual rate of domestic inflation and the annual change in foreign exchange rate into account, therefore turned out to be negative in many quarters during the 1965–70 period.

Table 4.4 Annual increases in money supply, reserve base, and domestic credit before and after liberalization, 1964–1970 (billion current won)

Date	Money supply M_1		Money supply M_2		Reserve base		Domestic credit	
	Amount	Annual increase[a] (%)	Amount	Annual increase[a] (%)	Amount	Annual increase[a] (%)	Amount	Annual increase[a] (%)
Dec 1964	49	16.7	64	14.8	33	17.9	71	8.8
Mar 1965	51	17.8	66	17.5	29	20.8	79	23.7
Jun 1965	56	24.4	74	25.4	33	22.2	86	27.7
Sep 1965	62	28.1	82	30.2	38	31.0	90	27.4
Dec 1965	66	34.2	97	52.7	48	45.5	100	40.8
Mar 1966	68	34.2	110	66.7	43	48.3	103	30.4
Jun 1966	72	28.0	122	64.9	51	54.5	120	39.5
Sep 1966	78	26.9	139	69.5	60	57.9	121	34.4
Dec 1966	85	29.7	157	61.9	80	66.7	131	31.0
Mar 1967	92	34.4	176	60.0	86	100.0	144	39.8
Jun 1967	101	40.9	201	64.8	83	62.7	169	40.8
Sep 1967	109	39.4	225	61.9	94	56.7	201	66.1
Dec 1967	123	44.5	254	61.8	111	38.8	233	77.9
Jun 1968	140	38.5	325	61.7	140	68.7	310	83.4
Dec 1968	178	44.6	437	72.0	156	40.5	430	84.5
Dec 1969	252	41.6	705	61.3	216	38.5	684	59.1
Dec 1970	308	22.2	898	27.4	300	38.9	865	26.5

[a] Annual percentage increase over the same period of the previous year.
Source: Bank of Korea, Economic Statistics Yearbook (various issues)

Fiscal Policy

The US aid which had financed a significant proportion of government expenditures (including defense outlays) until the early 1960s was declining rapidly whereas government revenue requirements for financing five-year plan projects increased in the mid-1960s. The government therefore concentrated on increasing tax revenue during 1965–70. Since a comprehensive tax reform required time for research and discussion by interested groups, an initial attempt was made to increase tax revenue mainly through administrative improvement without changing tax laws. It was not until early 1968 that the overall tax reforms which generally raised tax rates were put into effect.

While placing emphasis on increasing tax revenues, the government curtailed the rapid growth of current expenditures in order to increase its capital outlays. For this reason, the gross government saving, which had generally been negative in the first half of the 1960s, increased substantially in the second half: from 1.7 percent of GNP in 1965 to 6.5 percent by 1970.

In the meantime, the government adopted a balanced budget policy beginning in 1964. This policy was adopted as part of the government's financial stabilization program to check domestic inflation. It is well reflected in the actual performance of the government budget for 1964–8,

Table 4.5 Nominal and real interest rates on domestic loans compared with those on foreign loans, 1964–1970 and 1977–1983 (percent)

Period	1 Nominal interest rate — Domestic loans[a]	2 Nominal interest rate — Foreign loans[b]	3 Annual change in wholesale price index	4 Annual change in exchange rate	5 Real interest rate — Domestic loans	6 Real interest rate — Foreign loans
Dec 1964	16.0	4.5	27.4	96.5	− 11.4	73.6
Mar 1965	16.0	4.5	15.1	102.3	0.9	91.7
Jun 1965	16.0	4.5	5.9	6.1	10.1	4.7
Sep 1965	26.0	4.5	6.9	6.1	19.1	3.7
Dec 1965	26.0	5.0	7.7	6.3	18.3	3.6
Mar 1966	26.0	5.5	8.1	3.2	17.9	0.6
Jun 1966	26.0	5.8	9.3	− 0.1	16.7	− 3.6
Sep 1966	26.0	6.0	9.4	− 1.1	16.6	− 4.5
Dec 1966	26.0	6.0	8.8	− 0.2	17.2	− 3.0
Mar 1967	26.0	5.5	6.7	− 0.8	19.3	− 2.0
Jun 1967	26.0	5.5	5.3	− 0.6	20.7	− 0.4
Sep 1967	26.0	5.5	5.9	− 0.9	20.1	− 1.3
Dec 1967	26.0	6.0	7.4	1.4	18.6	0
Jun 1968	26.0	6.5	7.7	2.1	18.3	0.9
Dec 1968	25.2	6.8	7.1	2.5	18.1	2.2
Dec 1969	24.0	8.5	7.6	8.2	16.4	9.1
Dec 1970	24.0	6.8	9.2	4.0	14.8	1.6
Dec 1977	16.0	7.8	10.1	0	5.9	− 2.3
Mar 1978	16.0	8.0	10.7	0	5.3	− 2.7
Jun 1978	19.0	8.6	11.7	0	7.3	− 3.1
Sep 1978	19.0	9.4	12.3	0	6.7	− 2.9
Dec 1978	19.0	11.5	12.2	0	6.8	− 0.7
Mar 1979	19.0	11.8	12.4	0	6.6	− 0.6
Jun 1979	19.0	11.7	16.1	0	2.9	− 4.4
Sep 1979	19.0	12.9	28.1	0	− 9.1	− 15.2
Dec 1979	19.0	15.5	23.8	0	− 4.8	− 8.3
Jun 1980	24.0	12.6	41.8	24.6	− 17.8	− 4.6
Dec 1980	20.0	21.0	42.2	36.4	− 22.2	15.2
Dec 1981	17.0	15.8	11.3	6.2	5.7	10.7
Dec 1982	10.0	11.5	2.4	6.9	7.6	16.0
Dec 1983	10.0	11.0	− 0.8	6.2	10.8	18.0

Column 5 is column 1 minus column 3; column 6 is column 2 minus column 3 plus column 4.
[a] Commercial banks' interest rate on ordinary short-term loans (up to a year).
[b] US prime rate.
Sources: Bank of Korea, *Economic Statistics Yearbook*, various issues; US Department of Commerce, *Survey of Current Business*, various issues

Table 4.6 Consolidated central government revenues and expenditures before and after trade liberalization, 1964–1968 and 1977–1981 (percentage ratio to gross national product)

Revenues and expenditures	1964	1965	1966	1967	1968	1977	1978	1979	1980	1981
GNP	100.0	100.0	100.0	100.0	100.0	100.0	100.0	100.0	100.0	100.0
Total revenues and grants	11.0	14.0	15.5	17.0	19.3	15.9	16.4	17.0	17.8	18.2
Current revenues	6.9	9.2	11.0	12.8	16.0	15.8	16.3	16.9	17.7	18.0
Capital revenues and grants	4.1	4.8	4.5	4.2	3.3	0.1	0.1	0.1	0.1	0.2
Total expenditures and net lending	10.6	13.2	16.1	16.9	19.3	17.8	18.2	19.0	20.4	21.6
Current expenditures	8.4	8.7	10.0	10.8	11.6	12.8	13.1	14.3	13.7	13.9
(Direct outlays)	(5.4)	(5.8)	(6.4)	(6.2)	(6.5)	(8.2)	(8.7)	(7.9)	(8.0)	(8.2)
(Subsidies and transfers)	(3.0)	(2.9)	(3.6)	(4.6)	(5.1)	(4.6)	(4.4)	(6.4)	(5.7)	(5.7)
Capital expenditures	1.1	3.5	4.4	4.2	5.4	2.3	2.2	2.3	3.8	3.6
(Direct outlays)	(0.4)	(2.6)	(3.1)	(2.9)	(3.8)	(1.5)	(1.5)	(1.4)	(2.8)	(2.6)
(Capital transfers)	(0.7)	(0.9)	(1.3)	(1.3)	(1.6)	(0.8)	(0.7)	(0.9)	(1.0)	(1.0)
Net lending	1.1	1.0	1.7	1.9	2.3	2.7	2.9	2.4	2.9	4.1
Overall deficit (−) or surplus	0.4	0.9	− 0.6	0.2	0	− 1.9	− 1.8	− 2.0	− 2.6	− 3.4
Financing	− 0.4	− 0.9	0.6	− 0.2	0	1.9	1.8	2.0	− 0.6	3.4
Domestic borrowing	− 0.4	− 0.9	0	− 0.6	− 0.3	0.4	− 0.1	1.1	1.8	2.8
Foreign borrowing	0	0	0.6	0.4	0.3	1.5	1.9	0.9	0.8	0.6

Source: Bank of Korea, *Economic Statistics Yearbook*, various issues

shown in table 4.6. Actual implementation of the central government budget produced a small amount of surplus in all years except 1966. The unusual fiscal deficit for 1966 was only about 0.6 percent of GNP, and was attributable to the government import of long-term foreign public loans for investment projects.

Since the nominal value of total central government expenditures (including net lending) increased much more rapidly than GNP, its ratio to GNP continually rose from 10.6 percent in 1964 and 19.3 percent by 1968 (see table 4.6). Of total government expenditures, the proportion of current expenditures, which was as high as 79 percent in 1964, declined to 66 percent in 1965, and thereafter remained at around 60–4 percent. In contrast, government capital expenditures rose sharply from about 10 percent of total government expenditures in 1964 to 27 percent in 1965, and then remained at 24–7 percent during 1966–8. However, government net lending showed only a minor fluctuation from 8 percent of aggregate government expenditures to 12 percent during 1964–8.

For private investment in specified major industries, the government offered tax concessions in the form of investment tax credit during this period. In other words, for capital investment in such industries as iron and steel, machinery, automobile, shipbuilding, electronics, chemical fertilizer, petrochemicals, power generation, mining, marine product processing, livestock, and agribusiness, and in national land development projects, an amount equivalent to 6 percent of investment could be deducted from corporation or income tax.

Restrictions of International Capital Movements

Until 1968 Korea possessed no legal institution for processing domestic residents' investment abroad. Direct investment in foreign countries was thus effectually prohibited until the end of 1968. With effect from early 1969, however, legal provisions for resident investment abroad were introduced into the country's regulations on foreign exchange control. According to these legal provisions all domestic residents' investment abroad should be reviewed by a special committee and approved by the Minister of Finance.

During the period 1965–7 foreign exchange holdings for resident firms or households were not allowed. In accordance with the foreign exchange control law, all residents received foreign exchange in connection with their export and other activities had to surrender it to a foreign exchange bank in Korea. They were then given foreign exchange certificates, in the amount of foreign exchange they surrendered to the bank, effective for 45 days. The exchange certificates could be used to pay their import bills, or resold on the exchange market within the effective period; they did not provide any automatic right to import license but were simply an instrument of foreign exchange transactions. Furthermore, they had to be sold to a foreign exchange bank in return for domestic currency when the effective period expired.

Except for a few remittances allowed for Korean students studying abroad and for government activities, there was no formal channel for capital outflow from the country. Such tight control of capital outflow might be justified by the significant amount of foreign assistance still being received by Korea at the time.

However, from the early 1960s Korea encouraged inflows of foreign capital in the form of either direct investment or loans. Although all foreign investments to Korea had to be approved by the Minister of Economic Planning, the government provided very generous tax concessions for foreign investors.

The government newly enacted the Foreign Capital Inducement Law in 1966, mainly to revise and streamline the existing legal provisions contained in three different laws: the Law on Promotion of Foreign Capital Inflows, the Law Concerning the Guarantees of Foreign Loan Repayments, and the Special Law Concerning the Imports of Capital Goods by Foreign Long-term Loans. The new law did not significantly change the existing system of administering foreign capital inflows, however.

The new law modified existing provisions mainly by increasing incentives to foreign investors without substantially changing the provisions for the introduction of foreign loans. The imports of foreign loans nevertheless increased very rapidly from 1966, while the inflow of foreign direct investment was not much accelerated. The cause, as suggested earlier, was the large interest rate differential between domestic and foreign financial markets created by the interest rate reform of 1965. The normalization of diplomatic relations between Korea and Japan, signed in June 1965, opened up yet another source of foreign capital.

Domestic Controls

From 1965 the government greatly reduced its direct controls on prices while increasing its efforts to stabilize domestic prices by indirect instruments. The government had relied heavily upon direct control of the prices of daily necessities and other essential goods for domestic price stabilization after the military coup in 1961. The direct control of prices was based on the Law on Temporary Measures for Price Adjustment promulgated in 1961. In 1965, however, the government reduced administrative controls of prices and emphasized the strong implementation of its financial stabilization program, maintaining ceiling prices only on nine items of daily necessities by the end of 1965.

This liberalization from direct price control in 1965 was part of the overall economic liberalization package which included the exchange rate reform of 1964–5, the interest rate reform of 1965, and the trade liberalization program. It reflected a basic change in government policy toward more reliance on the market mechanism for resource allocation. In any case, direct control of prices was not again intensified until 1973, and there was no serious black-market activity during 1965–9. Domestic wholesale prices rose at an average annual rate of only about 8 percent during this time, even though direct control was significantly reduced. One should add that the import liberalization promoted during this period was considered important for domestic price stabilization in two respects: it not only increased the supply of goods but also contributed to reducing monetary expansion from the foreign sector.

During the latter half of the 1960s the government did not intervene in the determination of wages in the private sector, even when wages were increasing very rapidly, as was the case for some categories of skilled workers. A minimum wage had not yet been introduced, since unemployment was still relatively high. Wage levels in these years were mainly determined by market forces.

There were no explicit rules concerning the government's own investment. It seems that the government allocated its investment budget among many competing projects put forward by various ministries by giving priority to the social overhead facilities and large industrial projects that the private sector was reluctant to invest in.

Private investment did not require formal licensing by the government. Private investors were only required to register at a competent ministry and report to the regional branch of the Office of National Taxation (ONT). A firm's request for registration, however, could be delayed or even rejected by the competent ministry for various reasons.

No formal restriction was imposed on any industry's access to capital markets, but it is well known that the export industry and specified major industries received preference in the allocation of loanable funds by financial institutions. Although a special loan program existed for small and medium-size industries, credit control meant that such industries generally could not borrow enough from organized financial markets and had to rely partly on unorganized markets for loans.

All interest rates of financial institutions were determined by the government, regardless of whether they were short term or long term. In particular, during the late 1960s the government usually kept rates for long-term loans much lower than those for short-term loans for the purpose of promoting industrial investment.

Accompanying Policies – the Second Episode (1978–1979)

Exchange Rate Policy

Formally, a unitary floating rate system was continued even during the second trade liberalization episode. However, the official exchange rate was pegged at 484 won to the US dollar by the Korean Monetary Authority during 1976–9 after about 19 percent devaluation in 1975. Despite this exchange rate peg at a constant rate, there was not much disparity between black-market and official exchange rates since foreign exchange became much more readily available during this period.

Nominal effective exchange rates for exports and imports also remained almost unchanged between December 1977 and December 1979 (see table 4.3). PPP-adjusted real effective rates for exports and imports, however, showed some increases in 1978 in terms of the number of won to the US dollar but again declined in 1979 (see table 2.7). The unusual increase in real rates in 1978 was mainly attributable to the more rapid increase in the average wholesale prices of major trading partners (that is, the United States and Japan) than in Korean prices, while the gradual decline in the real rates after 1978 reflected the reverse trend.[1]

In early 1980, however, the government officially devalued the won by about 20 percent, and thereafter allowed the gradual depreciation of the won by refraining from intervention in the exchange market. As a result, the real effective rates for exports and imports increased, with some fluctuations, between December 1979 and December 1983.

Export Promotion Policy

Changes made in export incentives since 1965 have been mainly modifications within the system to accommodate the changing export environment and domestic conditions. In fact, the modifications were mostly directed toward reducing the effective subsidies implicit in the system of incentives.

The government abolished direct tax reduction on income earned from export and other foreign exchange earnings activities with effect from 1973. As a result, although some tax concessions were provided to facilitate the overseas activities of Korean exporters in the same year, net export subsidies per US dollar of exports declined sharply. In 1975 the system of outright tariff exemptions on imports of raw materials for exports was changed to a drawback system, under which exporters were in principle required to pay tariffs on imports but were refunded the

---

[1] In making a weighted average of wholesale price indexes for the United States and Japan, the Japanese price index was adjusted by the index of exchange rate of the yen to the dollar.

payments when exports were actually shipped out. This drawback system was mainly to improve the tariff administration but increased the financial burden of export firms.

Thus, by early 1978 when the second package of trade liberalization was introduced, subsidies implicit in the system of export incentives were significantly reduced compared with the mid-1960s. No additional measures to promote exports, however, were taken during this period. The preferential export credit was therefore the only scheme that continued to provide some net subsidies for exporters.

As shown in table 4.3 the nominal effective exchange rate for exports, which includes net export subsidies on top of the nominal official rate, remained practically unchanged at 493–5 won to the US dollar between December 1977 and December 1979, mainly because the official exchange rate remained unchanged during the period. The effective rate for exports generally ranged from 94 to 95 percent of the effective rate for imports during 1978–9, a ratio similar to that for 1965–6. After 1979, the real effective rate for exports generally showed an increasing trend. The effective export rate jumped from 95 percent of the effective import rate in 1979 to 98 percent in 1980, but then continuously declined to 93 percent by 1983.

Monetary Policy

In 1977, a year before the second package of trade liberalization was introduced, Korea's money supply (M1) expanded by over 40 percent on a year-end basis. As already suggested this rapid expansion was attributable mainly to a rapid accumulation of foreign reserves. Despite this rapid expansion of the money supply, the Korean Monetary Authority did not substantially change its policy instruments during the 1977–9 period.

In June 1978, the Korean Monetary Authority raised interest rates on bank deposits and loans: the interest rate on one-year time deposits was raised from 14.4 percent a year to 18.6 percent, while that on ordinary bank loans moved from 16 percent to 19 percent. These changes in interest rates were mainly to increase public saving in the form of financial assets and to discourage unproductive use of loanable funds.

The legal reserve requirements of deposit money banks, however, were not changed during 1977–9. The ratios of 17 percent on all time and savings deposits and 24 percent on demand deposits, which had been effective since July 1975, continued. However, the Central Bank greatly increased the volume of its Stabilization Bonds issued for open-market operations and short-term treasury bills were also introduced for open-market operations, but the system of requiring banking institutions to deposit a portion of their free reserves in the Central Bank's Stabilization Account was more or less suspended in these years.

The Central Bank's rediscount rates on general bills were adjusted upward in June 1978 to make them consistent with the new interest rates of deposit money banks. The volume of Central Bank lending, however, expanded at an annual rate of about 30 percent between 1977 and 1979. In particular, Central Bank lending to deposit money banks for preferential export loans expanded very rapidly, reflecting the increase in exports.

Because the rapid accumulation of foreign reserves was impeding domestic demand management, the government strictly enforced the regulation of foreign capital. The use of foreign cash loans and supplier's credit to produce domestic operating funds was prohibited in late 1976. Foreign borrowings for the import of machinery and equipment required in the heavy and chemical industries were given special treatment, however.

As shown in table 4.7, the reserve base at the Central Bank increased at an annual rate of over 40 percent in 1977 and in the first nine months of 1978. The increase in reserve base, however, gradually decelerated after September 1978, and even became negative in 1980 and 1981. Following this trend, the narrowly defined money supply (M1), which had increased by over 40 percent in 1977, also showed a decelerating rate of increase after 1977. On a year-end basis, the money supply M1 expanded by about 25 percent in 1978 and 21 percent in 1979. The broad money supply (M2) showed a similar trend, although the annual rate of increase was generally higher than that of the narrow money supply (M1). The annual rate of in-

Table 4.7 Annual increases in money supply, reserve base, and domestic credit before and after liberalization, 1977–1983 (billion current won)

Date	Money supply M_1 Amount	Annual increase[a] (%)	Money supply M_2 Amount	Annual increase[a] (%)	Reserve base Amount	annual increase[a] (%)	Domestic credit Amount	Annual increase[a] (%)
Dec 1977	2,173	40.7	5,874	39.7	2,072	44.1	5,979	23.6
Mar 1978	2,189	35.4	6,293	42.3	2,051	45.3	6,621	32.2
Jun 1978	2,294	32.1	6,580	38.2	2,222	57.1	7,286	38.1
Sep 1978	2,345	17.2	7,118	32.1	2,507	41.4	7,831	36.5
Dec 1978	2,714	24.9	7,929	35.0	2,802	35.2	8,722	45.9
Mar 1979	2,663	21.6	8,190	30.1	2,762	34.7	9,343	41.1
Jun 1979	2,538	10.6	8,311	26.3	2,708	21.9	9,835	35.0
Sep 1979	3,030	28.4	8,992	26.3	3,012	20.1	10,643	35.9
Dec 1979	3,275	20.7	9,878	24.6	3,468	23.8	11,826	35.6
Jun 1980	2,961	16.7	10,663	28.3	2,576	− 4.9	13,870	41.0
Dec 1980	3,807	16.2	12,535	26.9	3,244	− 6.5	16,778	41.9
Dec 1981	3,982	4.6	15,671	25.0	2,802	− 13.6	22,016	31.2
Dec 1982	5,799	45.6	19,904	27.0	3,825	36.5	27,529	25.0
Dec 1983	6,783	17.0	22,938	15.2	4,095	71.0	31,847	15.7

[a] Annual percentage increase over the same period of the previous year.
Source: Bank of Korea, Economic Statistics Yearbook (various issues)

crease in domestic credit was 35 percent or more in 1978–9, but did not follow the patterns of movement in either the reserve base or the money supply.

The interest rate on domestic loans was kept relatively high during 1978–9. The real interest rate on domestic loans, obtained by discounting for the rate of domestic inflation, was around 5–7 percent in 1977–8 and in the first quarter of 1979. It declined, however, to a negative rate in the latter half of 1979 and remained negative until the end of 1980 because the rate of inflation in Korea accelerated during this period.

The nominal interest rate of foreign borrowing gradually increased from around 8 percent in 1977 to 15.5 percent by the end of 1979. It even rose to as high as 21 percent a year in December 1980, after which it gradually declined to reach 11 percent in December 1983. The real interest rate on foreign borrowing stayed negative during 1977–9, but rose to about 15 percent by the end of 1980 and remained high until the end of 1983 (see table 4.5). The real rate on foreign borrowing was therefore significantly higher than that on domestic loans during 1980–3.

Fiscal Policy

As already suggested, the rapid expansion of the money supply resulting from the accumulation of foreign reserves in 1977 made policymakers anxious about the increasing inflationary pressures again building up in the economy. The fiscal authorities were faced with conflicting demands: on the one hand, the government needed to tighten up its budget expenditures to balance the budget; on the other, it was faced with increased demand for public expenditure mainly in connection with promoting the heavy and chemical industries.

In an attempt to solve this problem by increasing tax revenues the government adopted two new taxes: defense surtax and value-added tax. The defense surtax, first levied in 1976, was to finance the increased expenditures required for the modernization of military equipment; the value-added tax, inroduced in the second half of 1977, was to replace the complicated structure of indirect taxes in Korea[2] and at the same time to increase tax revenues. In addition, some tax rate adjustments were made to reduce tax burdens of low and middle income brackets, and to increase tax on capital gains.

Government efforts to increase tax revenues are reflected in the rapid growth of current revenues during 1977–81: they increased from 15.8 percent of GNP in 1977 to 16.9 percent in 1979, and then to 18 percent by 1981 (see table 4.6). Despite this rapid growth of current revenues, consolidated

[2] Eight different types of indirect taxes – business activity tax, commodity tax, textile tax, petroleum tax, electricity and gas tax, travel tax, admission tax, and restaurant tax – were replaced by the value-added tax with a unitary tax rate of 10 percent.

cenral government budget settlements produced a significant amount of deficits in each fiscal year. The budgetary deficits were in the range of 1.8–2.0 percent of GNP in 1977–9 but gradually increased to 3.4 percent by 1981. These deficits were largely financed by borrowings from abroad in 1977–8. From 1979, however, domestic borrowings exceeded borrowings from abroad.

Between 1977 and 1981, the nominal value of total central government expenditures and net lending tripled, thus showing an average annual rate of increase of about 25 percent. This rate of increase was much higher than the annual growth rate of nominal GNP for the same period. As a result, total central government expenditures increased continuously from 17.8 percent of GNP in 1977 to 21.6 percent by 1981. Of these, current expenditures were about 72–5 percent in 1977–9, while capital expenditures and net lending accounted for the remaining 25–8 percent. In 1980–1, however, the total share of current expenditures declined sharply to between 64 and 67 percent, while the share of capital expenditures and net lending increased.

For the private sector's capital investment in such heavy industries as iron and steel, nonferrous metal, machinery, aircraft, shipbuilding, electronics, and chemical fertilizer, the government offered tax concessions in the form of the following three options: (a) full exemption from both income tax and corporation tax for the first three years and 50 percent reductions in the same taxes for the following two years; (b) an amount equivalent to 8 percent of investment deducted from the two taxes in the year of completion; (c) special accelerated depreciation allowances equivalent to double the normal allowance. In addition to the tax concessions, the firms investing in such heavy industries were provided with preferential loans from the Korea Development Bank and other government banks.

Restrictions of International Capital Movements

In October 1978 the government instituted a new regulation concerning the administration of domestic residents' investment abroad. According to this new regulation, residents' investment abroad had to be approved by the Governor of the Central Bank, instead of the Minister of Finance. Criteria for Central Bank approval specified three different categories of industries: "prohibited," "favored," and "restricted;" in screening applications the Central Bank would give priority to those firms investing in "favored" industries abroad.

The new regulation also stipulated that firms approved to make such investments should be (a) those that satisfied business performance criteria established by the Central Bank, (b) those that had been good customers to financial institutions, (c) those that had more than three years of experience in the industries in which they planned to invest, and (d) those head firms with paid-in capital exceeding a minimum specified for each industry.[3] In addition, the resident's investment abroad should in principle be greater than 50 percent equity in the case of a joint venture. The regulation also prescribed that the principal sum of invested capital should be repatriated within ten years, except for investment in real estate.

As in the first episode of liberalization, holdings of foreign exchange and foreign securities by both resident firms and households were continuously restricted. For this reason, any short-term capital outflow could not be made without the approval of the Central Bank and/or the MOF. Even exports on supplier's credit basis which involved a short-term capital loan had to be approved by the Central Bank.

However, foreign investment in Korea was encouraged. The tax and tariff concessions provided for foreign investors since the early 1960s and revised in 1966 were still effective in the latter half of the 1970s. In 1972, the government initiated two lists of industries, one showing the types of industries in which foreign investment was encouraged and the other showing those restricted from foreign investment. In October 1972, for instance, it specified 209 different industries for which foreign investment was encouraged, and 29 for which it was restricted. With the exception of specific export and technology intensive industries, the government generally attempted to restrict foreign share of equity to not more than 50 percent.

All inflows of foreign capital loans had to be approved by the minister responsible for the Economic Planning Board, as in the previous episode. In 1969, however, the government had revised its regulations concerning its guarantee of foreign loan repayments. In other words, it attempted to limit its repayment guarantees to large long-term capital loans for key industries, local governments, and government-invested enterprises. For other cases, its repayment guarantees were to be replaced by the guarantees of commercial banks.

As the country's balance of payments significantly improved in 1977, the government attempted to restrict foreign cash loans and short-term supplier's credit for the purpose of monetary management. Such loans and credit (exceeding US$3 million) as were imported were authorized only for selected major industries[4] and on condition that the maturity term exceeded three and a half years (five years in the case of cash loans) and that interest rates were not higher than the London interbank offering rate (LIBOR) plus 2 percent. Even the introduction of foreign capital loans was

---

[3] That is, W1 billion for forestry, construction, electricity, and gas industries; W500 million for mining, transportation–storage, and other service industries; and W300 million for all other industries.

[4] In general the major industries included the heavy and chemical industries, the power industry, the defense industry, key export industries, government-invested industries, etc.

selectively authorized: import of capital loans by selected major industries could be approved on condition that the maturity term was longer than seven years and that interest rates were lower than LIBOR plus 2 percent.

Such restrictions on both short-term and long-term foreign loans were loosened from early 1980, however, as the country's balance of payments began to feel the negative impact of the second world oil shock.

Domestic Controls

The money supply continued its rapid expansion in 1977 mainly because of the unusual accumulation of foreign reserves. The people's inflationary expectations were also very high, since Korea had experienced a rate of inflation of nearly 20 percent (in terms of the wholesale price index) since 1973. In addition, the adoption of value-added tax in July 1977 was expected to increase the prices of many commodities. The government consequently resorted to direct controls to check price inflation, instead of really trying to reduce demand. In fact, it attempted to attain the two conflicting targets of high growth and price stability simultaneously, simply by relying upon direct control.

The Law on Price Stability and Fair Trade promulgated at the end of 1975 provided the legal base for increased government intervention in commodity markets. In 1976 the government had designated only 148 commodity items produced by monopoly–oligopoly firms for special observation of their prices. In 1977 it announced ceiling prices for 254 commodity items including 157 items produced by monopoly–oligopoly firms and the 97 intermediate product items whose weight in the country's wholesale price index exceeded 0.1 percent. In addition, ceiling consumer (or retail) prices on 45 items of daily necessities were set for the Seoul area. Officials of the ONT and other competent ministries were mobilized to check that ceiling prices were actually observed.

The direct control of commodity prices was not much relaxed in 1978, although some adjustments were made to the list of items subject to such control and to the ceiling prices. While generally keeping direct controls in place, the government attempted to increase the domestic supply of commodities through import liberalization and, in some exceptional instances, by restricting exports. In addition, it took various measures to improve the distribution channels of major commodities, particularly agricultural and fishery products, and to reduce trade margins.

Although the annual rise in the wholesale price index was successfully checked at the government target of around 10 percent in both 1977 and 1978, it seemed that actual price rises far exceeded that level. The rigid price controls meant that many commodities were actually traded at two different prices: the official price for sales to public organizations and for reporting to the government agencies responsible, and an unofficial price for most commercial transactions. In other words, private buyers had to pay large "under-the-table" commissions to suppliers to make up the difference between the official and the market price. Some producers tried to reduce the volume of shipments in anticipation of future rises in their product prices. There were also instances of hoarding, particularly of agricultural commodities.

These undesirable effects of direct price control persuaded the government to dismantle the control gradually in 1979. The sharp rise in world oil prices in that year had in any case made it almost impossible to continue direct control of domestic prices. Consequently, the government allowed increases in many commodity prices and gradually eliminated many commodities from the list of items subject to price control. As a result, only 37 commodity items in total remained on the list by the end of 1979.

Large-scale direct control of prices was not attempted again after 1979. In December 1980, the government promulgated the Law Concerning Monopoly Regulation and Fair Trade, which superseded the previous Law on Price Stability and Fair Trade. The new law was mainly designed to prevent unfair pricing and marketing by large monopoly–oligopoly producers.

In the late 1970s the nominal wages of mining and manufacturing workers increased at an average annual rate of over 30 percent, mainly because of the continuously rising demand for industrial workers, particularly skilled workers, since 1973. The government did not intervene in the labor markets to impose any direct control on wages, however, contenting itself with a very ambiguous guideline that the business sector's annual wage increase should be limited to an expected rate of increase in productivity. Korea did not yet have a minimum wage law, but the government established an informal minimum wage to encourage business firms to raise the lowest level of wages.

As in the late 1960s, no formal restriction was imposed on any particular industry's access to capital markets. Bank interest rates on both short-term and long-term loans, however, continued to be controlled by the Korean Monetary Authority.

Implementation of the Liberalization Policy

As described earlier, Korea's trade liberalization programs were formulated and implemented in two different episodes, the first (1965–7) mainly taking the form of import liberalization from QRs, while the second (1978–9) included both liberalization from QRs and tariff reductions. During the first episode, import liberalization from QRs was implemented gradually in the first two years, and then much more vigorously in 1967 through reform of the system of import controls in 1967. During the second episode, the import liberalization from QRs was implemented in three steps, while tariff reductions became effective from 1979. Although the liberalization came to a temporary halt in 1980 it made uninterrupted progress thereafter, in contrast with the first episode after which liberalization was at a standstill for the following decade.

It has been noted that the program for the first episode was promoted as a short-run policy. No longer-term plan for trade liberalization was announced, except perhaps for a vague statement concerning future direction. For this reason, there could be no distinction between the announced program and the actual implementation, since the government announcement itself represented the implementation of the program.

The program for the second episode involved longer-term planning only in the sense that it included advance notices of import liberalization. Except for these advance notices, therefore, the government-announced program should be taken as implemented. Even in the case of advance notices, the government seems generally to have implemented the pre-announced program in view of the gradual progress in import liberalization from QRs after 1979. However, the tariff reform which became effective from 1979 was carried out not as part of any explicit long-term plan to cut tariffs but as a one-shot program. The indications are therefore that in Korea the liberalization process was neither planned nor implemented in clearly defined stages but was a succession of piecemeal changes.

Korea's import liberalization did not bring about a simple shift from QRs to intervention through tariffs and other price measures. Although the QRs were significantly reduced by the liberalization, tariffs were not raised to replace QRs but were gradually reduced by small margins. Table 4.8 shows the composition of import items liberalized from QRs by type of commodity group. A total of 619 commodity items (on the basis of the four-digit SITC classification) were liberalized from QRs during the first episode. Of this total, manufactured goods other than machinery (SITC groups 6, 8, and 9) accounted for 43 percent, while a broad category of raw materials (SITC groups 2, 3, and 4) accounted for only 21 percent. During the second period, a total of 230 items (on the basis of the four-digit CCCN classification) were liberalized from QRs. The percentage share of manufactured goods other than machinery was high, 63 percent, while that of raw materials was only 14 percent. This indicates that, rather than raising the level of effective protection on Korean industry, import liberalization from QRs contributed to lowering it.

The tariff reform in 1979 was mainly to reduce tariff rates on many items, in particular the prohibitively high rates which had been levied on many luxury items such as liquor, tobacco, and automobiles. Tariff rates were also reduced on such items as agricultural products, raw materials and capital goods for the heavy and chemical industries, machinery and equipment for energy, and other resource development. However, tariff

Table 4.8 Composition of import items liberalized from quantitative restrictions by type of commodity group, 1965–1967 and 1978–1979

Commodity group	Items liberalized during 1965–7		Items liberalized during 1978–9	
	No. of items	Percentage share	No. of items	Percentage share
Food, beverages and tobacco (SITC 0 and 1)	48	7.8	13	5.7
Crude materials, mineral fuels, and animal and vegetable oils and fats (SITC 2, 3, and 4)	132	21.3	32	13.9
Chemicals (SITC 5)	90	14.5	28	12.2
Machinery and transport equipment (SITC 7)	83	13.4	13	5.7
Other manufactured goods and commodities not classifiable (SITC 6, 8, and 9)	266	43.0	144	62.6
Total	619	100.0	230	100.0

Source: Ministry of Commerce and Industry, *Semi-annual (or Annual) Trade Programs* for various periods

rates were raised on those items which had been paying zero tariffs. As a result of this reform, the average rate of legal tariffs weighted by 1975 production declined from 41 percent to 34 percent, and the coefficient of variation in tariff rates also declined from 0.69 to 0.61. We therefore consider that the level of effective protection on Korean industry was significantly reduced by the tariff reform.

5

Economic Performance Following Liberalization

Movements of Major Prices

General Price Level

If the movements of prices in Korea during and following the two episodes of liberalization (1965–7 and 1978–9) are compared, it becomes clear that the rate of inflation was somewhat lower in the first episode than in the second, whichever price index is used for comparison (table 5.1). Further, the rate of inflation did not accelerate following the first episode, while it significantly accelerated during and after the second. The acceleration was not, however, attributable to the liberalization but to the sharp rise in world oil prices, and was largely under control by 1982.

The Real Rate of Foreign Exchange

The real effective exchange rates for both exports and imports declined slightly in terms of the number of won during and immediately following the first liberalization episode. This was mainly due to the slower depreciation of Korean won than the increasing differential in the rate of inflation between Korea and her major trading partners (see table 2.7).

The real rates rose significantly in the first year (1978) of the second episode but declined somewhat in the following year. Although the rates rose again in 1980, the 1980 level could not be maintained in the following two years because the rate of domestic inflation was higher than that of major trading partners. The real rates, however, almost recovered the 1978 level in 1983.[1]

---

[1] The real effective exchange rates for exports and imports by sector for the two periods (1964–70 and 1977–83) are given by Kim (1988, appendix tables 6a and 6b and appendix tables 7a and 7b respectively).

Table 5.1 Movements of general price level in Korea, 1964–1970 and 1977–1983 (index 1965 = 100)

Period	Wholesale price index		GNP deflator[a]		Consumer price index	
	Index	Change[b]	Index	Change[b]	Index	Change[b]
Dec 1964	94.8	27.4	94.0	24.0	94.9	20.9
Mar 1965	97.2	15.2	99.2	19.2	97.4	7.6
Jun 1965	101.0	5.9	102.0	6.3	100.0	8.5
Sep 1965	101.9	6.9	106.3	10.4	101.6	10.2
Dec 1965	102.1	7.7	92.6	− 1.5	100.0	5.4
Mar 1966	105.1	8.1	114.3	15.2	106.7	9.5
Jun 1966	110.4	9.3	115.7	13.4	110.9	10.9
Sep 1966	111.5	9.4	123.7	16.4	115.1	13.3
Dec 1966	111.1	8.8	104.4	12.7	114.2	14.2
Mar 1967	112.1	6.7	129.9	13.6	119.3	11.8
Jun 1967	116.3	5.3	136.5	18.0	121.8	9.8
Sep 1967	118.1	5.9	139.8	13.0	125.2	8.8
Dec 1967	119.3	7.4	121.4	16.3	127.7	11.8
Jun 1968	125.2	7.7	142.6	4.5	134.4	10.3
Dec 1968	127.8	7.1	142.6	17.5	142.0	11.2
Dec 1969	137.5	7.6	173.3	21.5	165.5	16.5
Dec 1970	150.1	9.2	193.2	11.5	189.8	14.7
Dec 1977	440.9	10.0	654.1	13.0	471.2	11.1
Mar 1978	460.4	10.7	729.6	12.9	523.3	17.9
Jun 1978	473.2	11.8	773.6	18.0	539.3	19.0
Sep 1978	485.0	12.3	795.3	19.9	563.6	20.8
Dec 1978	494.8	12.2	800.0	22.3	579.6	23.0
Mar 1979	517.3	12.4	850.1	16.5	604.0	15.4
Jun 1979	549.6	16.1	907.2	17.3	648.5	20.2
Sep 1979	603.4	24.4	944.5	18.8	667.0	18.3
Dec 1979	612.4	23.8	982.8	22.9	690.5	19.1
Jun 1980	779.5	41.8	1,223.7	34.9	822.4	26.8
Dec 1980	871.0	42.2	1,271.4	29.4	911.4	32.0
Dec 1981	969.5	11.3	1,403.6	10.4	1,059.2	16.2
Dec 1982	985.1	1.6	1,453.7	3.7	1,111.3	4.9
Dec 1983	987.5	0.2	1,499.0	3.1	1,133.2	2.0

[a] GNP deflator for the quarter to which the indicated month belongs. The higher rate of increase in the deflator than in the wholesale and consumer price indices may simply reflect that the coverage and calculating method of the deflator are significantly different from those of the latter indices. The deflator is a Paasche type index whereas the wholesale and consumer price indices are the Laspeyers index based on the price survey of selected commodities and services.
[b] Percentage change over the same period of the previous year.
Source: Bank of Korea, Economic Statistics Yearbook, various issues

Real Wages

Table 5.2 presents the monthly real wages of regular employees in mining and manufacturing industries for the two seven-year periods (1964–70 and 1977–83), obtained by deflating monthly nominal wages by the national

Table 5.2 Monthly nominal and real wages of regular employees in mining and manufacturing industries, 1964–1970 and 1977–1983 (thousand won)

Year	Nominal wages			Consumer price index (1965 = 100)	Real wages (1965 prices)			
	Mining	Manufacturing	Average		Mining	Manufacturing	Average wages	Annual increase (%)
1964	5.6	3.9	4.0	87.6	6.4	4.5	4.6	—
1965	7.1	4.6	4.8	100.0	7.1	4.6	4.8	4.3
1966	8.4	5.4	5.7	111.2	7.6	4.9	5.1	6.3
1967	11.0	6.6	7.0	123.2	8.9	5.4	5.7	11.8
1968	12.2	8.4	8.7	136.0	9.0	6.2	6.4	12.3
1969	15.1	11.3	11.6	152.8	9.9	7.4	7.6	18.8
1970	17.5	14.2	14.4	177.6	9.9	8.0	8.1	6.6
1977	93.9	69.2	71.0	459.2	20.4	15.1	15.5	—
1978	127.7	92.9	95.2	525.6	24.3	17.7	18.1	16.8
1979	166.2	119.5	122.3	621.6	26.7	19.2	19.7	8.8
1980	203.3	146.7	150.3	800.0	25.4	18.3	18.8	– 4.6
1981	243.7	176.2	180.7	970.4	25.1	18.2	18.6	– 1.1
1982	268.7	202.1	207.2	1,040.8	25.8	19.4	19.9	7.0
1983	286.4	226.8	231.9	1,076.0	26.6	21.4	21.6	8.5

—, not applicable.
Source: Bank of Korea, Economic Statistics Yearbook (various issues)

consumer price index. The monthly real wages so obtained indicate the trends in industrial wages expressed in terms of workers' purchasing power.

It can be seen from the table that the level of real wages received by each sector's employees increased continuously during the two seven-year-periods, except for the two recession years (1980–1). From 1964 to 1970, monthly real wages for mining and manufacturing enterprises increased at an average annual rate of about 10 percent (in terms of constant 1965 prices), whereas during the 1977–83 period they increased by only about 6 percent annually.

Real Rate of Interest

The real rates of interest on both domestic loans and foreign loans are estimated in table 4.5. As shown, the estimated real rates of interest on domestic loans were negative until the end of 1964, but thereafter became positive and substantial. In fact, the real rates on domestic loans were maintained at a relatively high level from September 1965 to December 1970. During this period the short-term rate was considerably higher than the long-term rate (Bank of Korea, *Economic Statistics Yearbook*, various issues). However, the estimated real rate of interest on foreign loans, which measures the real private cost of such loans, was unusually high between December 1964 and March 1965 owing to the extremely high rate of devaluation experienced in 1964–5. After that, however, it was maintained at a level much lower than that on domestic loans, and was even negative during most of 1966 and 1967.

Even during the 1977–83 period, the real rates of interest on domestic loans were relatively high until March 1979, after which they declined sharply to a negative level. The estimated real private cost of foreign loans, which had been positive during some of the earlier period, became negative during the period from December 1977 to June 1980. In 1981–3, however, the real rate of interest on foreign loans was quite high, ranging from 11 to 18 percent.

External Transactions

Imports

Bank of Korea's *National Income Accounts* (1984) provide data on the aggregate sizes of both imports and exports of goods and services for the two periods (1964–70 and 1977–83) in terms of constant 1980 billion won. It is apparent that the aggregate real imports increased not only in absolute terms but also in terms of their ratio to GNP during both periods. For instance, imports of goods and services, which had been only 9 percent of GNP in 1964, increased to 22.4 percent by 1970. Between 1977 and 1983 they increased from 35.3 percent to 40.8 percent.[2]

The rapid increase in the aggregate import ratio to GNP could not be explained solely by the real effective exchange rate for imports. Using time series data for 1964–83 a simple regression was run relating the aggregate import ratio to the real effective exchange rate. However, the coefficient of determination (R^2) turned out to be almost zero and the regression coefficient was not statistically significant. This kind of regression result is not surprising considering that the import ratio continually expanded while the real exchange rate remained relatively stable. The inference is that the rapid increase in the import ratio is more closely related to the structural change in the economy than the change in relative prices.

Table 5.3 gives the ratio of imports to domestic production of final goods by sector for four selected years: 1966, 1970, 1975, and 1980. Since this kind of information can only be obtained from input–output tables, data are provided only for the years selected in such tables. As shown in the table, the mining sector, which had shown a relatively low ratio of imports to domestic production in 1966, recorded the most rapid increase in the import ratio to domestic production to reach 537 percent by 1980. The general machinery sector also marked a very high ratio of imports to domestic production, reaching 273 percent in 1970 but gradually declining to 115 percent by 1980. Except for these two sectors, electrical machinery,

[2] See Kim (1988, appendix table 4) for the change in the structure of imports by major commodity category during 1964–70 and 1977–83.

Table 5.3 Ratio of imports to domestic production of final goods by sector for selected years (percent)

Sector	1966	1970	1975	1980
Agriculture, forestry, and fishery	2.6	15.8	21.7	21.9
Mining	2.2	76.5	322.8	536.9
Processed food (including tobacco)	3.7	6.1	9.2	7.4
Textile products and apparel	3.5	7.6	5.4	4.0
Lumber and wood products	1.0	1.4	0.5	2.3
Pulp, paper, and allied products	6.3	19.5	19.2	16.9
Chemical and allied products	64.2	46.8	35.5	22.0
Petroleum and coal products	9.2	2.3	9.2	11.4
Nonmetallic mineral products	7.2	5.2	5.4	4.4
Iron and steel	34.7	48.5	32.9	18.6
Nonferrous metal	20.7	50.7	55.8	45.2
Metal products	49.9	55.3	14.4	12.0
General machinery	189.9	273.4	183.0	115.0
Electrical machinery	33.7	63.4	41.7	33.5
Transport equipment	71.9	58.3	63.7	47.6
Other manufacturing	2.2	4.0	8.8	8.6
All services	1.7	0.7	1.4	2.4
Total	7.3	12.5	17.6	16.1

Source: Bank of Korea, Korea's Input–Output Tables, 1966, 1970, 1975, and 1980

transport equipment, chemical products, nonferrous metal, and iron and steel sectors all recorded relatively high ratios of imports to domestic production in the selected years. However, such sectors as all services, lumber and wood products, nonmetallic mineral products, and textile products showed extremely low ratios of imports to domestic production.

Table 5.4 presents the percentage share of the import component in production by sector for selected years. As expected, the two sectors lumber and wood products and petroleum and coal products marked the highest shares of import component in production in the selected years. In contrast, such sectors as agriculture, forestry, and fishery, mining, nonmetallic mineral products, and all services showed extremely low shares of import component in those years. With these exceptions of both extremely high and extremely low shares of import component, all other sectors' import components in production generally ranged from 10 to 40 percent.

Table 5.4 Import component in production by sector for selected years (percent)

Sector	1966	1970	1975	1980
Agriculture, forestry, and fishery	3.1	1.1	2.3	2.2
Mining	0.1	1.6	3.9	0.5
Processed food (including tobacco)	7.1	10.9	18.7	10.2
Textile products and apparel	19.8	19.0	13.5	13.1
Lumber and wood products	43.1	50.8	49.3	53.1
Pulp, paper, and allied products	14.5	18.6	19.9	16.4
Chemical and allied products	24.3	27.1	25.0	19.9
Petroleum and coal products	26.1	34.1	60.6	68.7
Nonmetallic mineral products	6.8	5.0	5.5	5.7
Iron and steel	29.6	36.7	29.6	17.6
Nonferrous metal	18.8	30.5	33.6	39.1
Metal products	27.3	18.5	18.2	15.5
General machinery	16.3	17.9	19.9	18.3
Electrical machinery	17.3	26.7	29.3	23.0
Transport equipment	17.8	24.8	24.8	23.6
Other manufacturing	24.1	21.3	24.0	21.8
All services	3.4	3.3	3.6	6.2
Total	8.3	9.3	13.7	14.2

Source: Bank of Korea, Korea's Input–Output Tables, 1966, 1970, 1975, and 1980

A series of regressions was run by the ordinary least squares method to examine the relationship between the percentage point changes in the ratio of imports to domestic production and the percentage change in real effective exchange rate for imports, and between the percentage point changes in the share of import component in production and the real exchange rate variable.[3] The cross-section data for different periods, consisting of 16 tradeable sectors, were used for the regression analysis. The results are summarized in table 5.5.

It can be seen from the table that the changes in the ratio of imports to domestic production are negatively correlated with the real exchange rate, as expected. However, this relationship between the import ratio and the exchange rate variable was statistically significant only for the two shorter

[3] The real effective exchange rate for imports which was used in the regression analysis is presented by Kim (1988, appendix table 11).

Table 5.5 Results of regression relating changes in the ratio of imports to domestic production and in the import component in production to real effective exchange rates for imports

Dependent variable	Constant	XRM_i	R^2	Time period
(1) MR_i	7.58	− 1.261	0.28	1966–70
	(1.10)	(− 2.35)		
(2) MR_i	22.69	− 1.562	0.25	1975–80
	(1.49)	(− 2.16)		
(3) MR_i	34.31	− 0.217	0.004	1966–80
	(0.64)	(− 0.23)		
(4) MC_i	2.93	− 0.018	0.002	1966–70
	(1.90)	(− 0.15)		
(5) MC_i	− 0.90	− 0.082	0.09	1975–80
	(1.46)	(− 1.20)		
(6) MC_i	9.06	− 0.139	0.16	1966–80
	(1.94)	(− 1.66)		

MR_i, percentage point change in the ratio of imports to domestic production of final goods for the ith sector; MC_i, percentage point change in import component in production for the ith sector; XRM_i, percentage change in the real effective exchange rate of imports for the ith sector; R^2, the coefficient of determination. (Figures in parentheses represent t values).

periods, 1966–70 and 1975–80, and not for the longer period, 1966–80. The regression results for the two shorter periods indicate that the import ratio's elasticity with respect to the real exchange rate was ranging from about − 1.3 to − 1.6. The regression result for the longer period turns out to be statistically insignificant, since in the long run the import ratios are more influenced by changes in industrial structure.

As expected, the relationship between the changes in import component in production and the change in exchange rate were found to be statistically insignificant for all the periods examined. The reason may be that the changes in import component by sector have been determined mainly by production technologies and the country's resource endowments.

Spearman's rank correlation coefficients are also estimated by using the same cross-section data for the three different periods. As with the simple regression results, the rank correlation coefficient between the changes in import ratio and the changes in real exchange rate was statistically significant only for 1966–70 (at − 0.552) and 1975–80 (at − 0.765). The coefficient for the longer period, 1966–80, turned out to be insignificant: − 0.129. The rank correlation between the changes in import component and the changes in real exchange rate were statistically insignificant in all periods, as in the result of simple regressions.

Exports

The aggregate exports of goods and services in constant 1980 prices rose rapidly, far exceeding the growth rate of GNP during the two periods 1964–70 and 1977–83. Accordingly the aggregate exports which had been less than 4 percent of GNP until 1964 increased to 11 percent of GNP in 1970 and then to 39 percent by 1983 (Bank of Korea, *National Income Accounts*, 1984). The rapid growth of exports accompanied a significant change in the structure of exports by major commodity group (Kim, 1988, appendix table 5). As in the case of aggregate import ratio, annual changes in the ratio of aggregate exports to GNP could not be statistically explained by the annual changes in the real effective exchange rate for exports. A statistically significant relation between the two variables could not be found from the time series data for 1964–83.

Table 5.6 shows the ratio of exports to domestic production by sector for selected years. According to this table, the major export sectors that exported more than 10 percent of their domestic production in 1966 were lumber and wood products, mining, miscellaneous manufacturing, textile products and apparel, nonferrous metal, and electrical machinery. In 1975 all sectors other than agriculture, forestry, and fishery, processed foods, paper and allied products, petroleum and coal products, nonferrous metal, and all services exported more than 10 percent of their production. The sectors that exported more than 20 percent of their domestic production in that year included miscellaneous manufacturing (52 percent), lumber and wood products (40 percent), electrical machinery (38 percent), textile products and apparel (36 percent), metal products (29 percent), general machinery (20 percent), and transport equipment (20 percent).

Using the cross-section data for three different periods, regression analysis was conducted to examine the relationship of the sectoral export ratios to real effective exchange rates for exports by sector.[4] The results of regression are shown below.

$$E_i = 4.08 + 0.333 \text{ XRE}_i \qquad R^2 = 0.33$$
$$(2.65) \quad (2.64) \qquad \text{time period 1966–70}$$
$$E_i = -1.60 + 0.185 \text{ XRE}_i \qquad R^2 = 0.25$$
$$(-0.87) \quad (2.17) \qquad \text{time period 1975–80}$$
$$E_i = 2.14 + 0.207 \text{ XRE}_i \qquad R^2 = 0.28$$
$$(0.44) \quad (2.33) \qquad \text{time period 1966–80}$$

where E_i denotes the percentage point change in the ratio of exports to domestic production in the ith sector and XRE_i the percentage change in the real effective exchange rate for exports for the ith sector.

---

[4] See Kim (1988, appendix table 12) for the real exchange rates for exports by sector.

Table 5.6 Ratio of exports to domestic production by sector for selected years (percent)

Sector	1966	1970	1975	1980
Agriculture, forestry, and fishery	1.2	2.6	5.6	5.5
Mining	20.8	19.7	12.3	5.5
Processed food (including tobacco)	5.9	3.7	8.5	3.1
Textile products and apparel	14.9	26.4	36.4	36.1
Lumber and wood products	27.7	36.8	39.9	27.8
Pulp, paper, and allied products	1.3	1.9	5.8	6.2
Chemical and allied products	0.7	3.1	8.1	10.5
Petroleum and coal products	4.6	6.7	5.6	1.2
Nonmetallic mineral products	5.7	3.8	13.3	13.6
Iron and steel	9.1	4.5	15.5	22.1
Nonferrous metal	11.9	11.6	6.2	11.8
Metal products	10.1	13.1	29.0	45.6
General machinery	8.8	5.2	20.1	17.5
Electrical machinery	10.3	22.6	38.1	34.6
Transport equipment	1.6	1.8	29.6	29.4
Other manufacturing	18.1	40.2	51.8	54.6
All services	6.8	4.7	6.7	7.5
Total	6.4	7.4	13.4	13.3

Source: Bank of Korea, Korea's Input–Output Tables, 1966, 1970, 1975, and 1980

All regression coefficients turned out to be statistically significant (as the *t* values in parentheses indicate), even though the coefficient of determination was relatively low in all three cases. These results indicate that the sectoral export ratios were positively correlated with the changes in real effective exchange rates by sector during the periods under observation. The sectoral export ratio's elasticity with respect to the real exchange rate, however, was rather low, ranging from 0.19 to 0.33.

Spearman's rank correlation coefficients were also estimated by using the same cross-section data. The rank correlation coefficients for the three periods 1966–70, 1975–80 and 1966–80 were 0.609, 0.512, and 0.603 respectively. These coefficients are statistically significant and support the regression results described above.

Openness of the Economy

If the aggregate trade ratio to GNP indicates openness of the economy, the Korean economy has increased its openness over time since the mid-1960s. The aggregate ratio of exports plus imports to GNP rose very rapidly from about 13 percent in 1964 to 34 percent in 1970 and then to 80 percent by 1983.

The rapid increase in the aggregate trade ratio resulted, of course, from the relatively more rapid rises in both exports and imports than in GNP. It should be noted, however, that the extremely rapid growth of exports was much more responsible than the growth of imports for such an increase in the aggregate trade ratio. This is explained by the fact that the export ratio increased by a factor of more than ten during 1964–83 whereas the import ratio increased by a factor of only 4.5. Despite the more rapid growth of exports than imports, the import surplus or trade gap could not be completely eliminated during the period, although it generally declined over time.

Balance of Payments Position

Korea's trade balance and the balance on goods and services were in deficit throughout 1964–83, although the size of the deficit varied annually. The current account balance, which includes net unrequited transfers, was also in deficit in all years except 1965 and 1977 (see table 2.9). While the absolute size of the deficit on goods and services fluctuated by year, the ratio of the deficit to total imports of goods and services generally showed a declining trend between 1964 and 1977 if the two unusual years of worldwide recession (1974–5) are excluded. After 1977, however, the same ratio gradually increased to a peak in 1980 and then showed a continuous decline until 1983. The ratio of current account deficits to aggregate imports did not show any discernible trend, mainly because of the effect of the net unrequited transfers on the current balance.

A functional relationship of each of the two ratios to the real effective exchange rate and other variables was investigated through a regression analysis based on time series data for 1964–83. For this analysis it was assumed that each of the two ratios can be explained by the following functional forms:

$$NGS = f(XRM, MSL, Y/N, FD)$$

or

$$BOP = f(XRM, MSL, Y/N, FD)$$

where NGS is the ratio of net goods and services to aggregate imports (of goods and services), BOP is the ratio of current account balance to aggregate imports, XRM is the real effective exchange rate for imports,

MSL is the two-year moving average of percentage change in M1 in year $t - 1$ and year $t - 2$, Y/N is the per capita GNNP in 1975 constant prices (thousand won), and FD is a proxy variable for foreign demand, that is, the average of GNP growth rates in the United States and Japan weighted by Korea's export volumes with the two countries in 1975.

The XRM variable is, of course, assumed to reflect the effect of relative price changes on the balance of payments. The MSL variable is expected to reflect the domestic demand factor, while FD is used as a proxy variable for foreign demand. Finally, the per capita GNP (Y/N) is used on the basis of the "balance-of-payments stages" hypothesis, which assumes that a country goes through a number of distinct balance-of-payments stages as its economy develops, starting as an immature debtor and ending as a mature creditor (see Crowther, 1957, and Halevi, 1971). In any case, the best results of regression that we could obtain by using the Cochrane–Orcutt iterative technique are as follows:

$$NGS = 45.636 + 0.002XRM - 0.423MSL + 0.104Y/N + 1.416FD$$
$$(3.10) \quad (0.19) \quad\quad (-2.00) \quad\quad (2.90) \quad\quad (2.08)$$
$$R^2 = 0.852 \quad\quad\quad\quad\quad\quad \text{Durbin–Watson statistic} = 1.905$$

$$BOP = 17.483 + 0.0003XRM - 0.570MSL + 0.465Y/N + 1.328FD$$
$$(1.25) \quad (0.12) \quad\quad (-2.29) \quad\quad (1.55) \quad\quad (1.49)$$
$$R^2 = 0.618 \quad\quad\quad\quad\quad\quad \text{Durbin–Watson statistic} = 1.589$$

The regression coefficients for all the independent variables had the expected signs and were in general statistically significant, except for the exchange rate variable which turned out to be statistically insignificant in both equations. The reason may be that the real effective exchange rate did not show much variation over the period, while the balance-of-payments deficits fluctuated by year.

External Indebtedness

Table 5.7 presents the aggregate size of Korea's external debts outstanding for the period 1964–83. According to this table, the country's aggregate size of foreign debts, including both long-term and short-term debts, was only around US$200 million in the mid-1960s but increased continuously to reach US$40.1 billion by the end of 1983. In particular, the size of external debts increased nearly ten times in the last decade, from US$4.2 billion in 1973 to US$40.1 billion in 1983.

Of the aggregate external debts outstanding, the proportion of gross short-term debt increased rapidly after 1973: it rose from about 16 percent of the aggregate external debts in 1973 to 35 percent by 1983. The net short-term indebtedness, which is estimated by subtracting the country's foreign exchange reserves from the gross short-term debts, was negative in

Table 5.7 Sizes of long-term and short-term foreign debts outstanding, 1964–1983 (million US dollars)

Year	1 Long-term and medium-term loans	2 Gross short-term loans[a]	3 Gross foreign debts	4 Korea's foreign exchange reserves	5 Net short-term loans
1964	167	10	177	129	− 119
1965	203	3	206	138	− 139
1966	385	7	392	236	− 229
1967	579	66	645	347	− 281
1968	1,110	89	1,199	387	− 298
1969	1,606	194	1,800	549	− 355
1970	1,872	373	2,245	584	− 211
1971	2,443	479	2,922	535	− 55
1972	2,949	640	3,589	694	− 54
1973	3,559	701	4,260	1,034	− 333
1974	4,698	1,239	5,937	1,049	190
1975	6,047	2,409	8,456	1,542	867
1976	7,488	3,045	10,533	2,948	97
1977	8,933	3,715	12,648	4,288	− 573
1978	11,016	3,855	14,871	4,879	− 1,024
1979	13,898	6,602	20,500	5,628	974
1980	16,754	10,611	27,365	6,528	4,083
1981	20,729	11,761	32,490	6,795	4,966
1982	23,099	14,196	37,295	6,890	7,306
1983	26,033	14,061	40,094	6,761	7,300

Column 3 is the sum of columns 1 and 2; column 5 is column 2 minus column 4.
[a] Including foreign banks "A" accounts.
Sources: Kim, 1984; Bank of Korea, *Economic Statistics Yearbook*, 1984

all years until 1973, but thereafter became positive and increased rapidly to reach US$7.3 billion by 1983.

The annual debt service burden of Korea had been increasing gradually since 1964, as shown in table 5.8. It rose from 5 percent of the country's merchandise exports in 1964 to a peak of 32 percent in 1971, but then gradually declined to 15 percent by 1976. After 1976 it rose to reach around 24 percent of total exports by 1983. The annual debt service ratio calculated in terms of the ratio to total foreign exchange receipts also showed a similar pattern of movement, as did the debt service ratio to commodity exports during the same period. The annual debt service ratio to GNP showed an almost continuous rise from 0.2 percent in 1964 to 2.8 percent in 1970 and then to 8.9 percent by 1981. After 1981, however, it showed some decline.

Table 5.8 Trends in Korea's debt service ratio, 1964–1983 (million US dollars)

Year	1 Annual debt services[a]	2 Commodity exports	3 Aggregate foreign exchange receipts	4 Money GNP	5 Commodity exports	6 Foreign exchange receipts	7 GNP
					Debt service ratio (%) to		
1964	6	119	211	2,804	5.0	2.8	0.2
1965	15	175	290	2,968	8.6	5.2	0.5
1966	14	250	455	3,828	5.8	3.1	0.4
1967	35	320	643	4,719	10.9	5.4	0.7
1968	48	455	880	6,088	10.5	5.5	0.8
1969	99	623	1,151	7,080	15.8	8.6	1.4
1970	255	835	1,379	8,988	30.5	18.5	2.8
1971	340	1,068	1,616	9,102	31.8	21.0	3.7
1972	416	1,624	2,227	10,414	25.6	18.7	4.0
1973	609	3,225	4,121	13,531	18.9	14.8	4.5
1974	701	4,460	5,353	18,876	15.7	13.1	3.7
1975	846	5,081	5,884	20,852	16.7	14.4	4.1
1976	1,142	7,715	9,457	28,680	14.8	12.1	4.0
1977	1,557	10,047	13,074	37,429	15.5	11.9	4.2
1978	2,391	12,711	17,161	50,052	18.8	13.9	4.8
1979	3,173	15,056	19,531	64,564	21.1	16.2	4.9
1980	4,234	17,504	22,577	60,008	24.2	18.8	7.1
1981	5,635	21,254	27,269	65,346	26.5	20.7	8.9
1982	5,944	21,853	28,356	69,160	27.2	21.0	8.6
1983	5,826	24,445	30,383	73,262	23.8	19.2	8.0

Columns 5, 6, and 7 are column 1 divided by columns 2, 3, and 4 respectively.
[a] Including interest payments on short-term loans.
Sources: Kim, 1984; Bank of Korea, National Income Accounts, 1984; Economic Statistics Yearbook, 1984

Income and Product

Aggregate Product

Table 5.9 presents quarterly data on real GNP, total employment, and real GNP per worker for the early period (1964–70), while table 5.10 shows the same data for the later period (1977–83). According to these two tables, Korea's GNP grew continuously and rapidly during both periods except for 1980 during which it declined. The annual growth rates of GNP estimated by quarter show a wide fluctuation during the two periods, but give no clear indication of being in any way affected by the trade liberalization programs.

The quarterly GNP per worker shown in the tables should give a rough measure of the country's labor productivity. During the 1964–70 period

Table 5.9 Quarterly data on gross national product, employment, labor productivity, and unemployment, 1964–1970

Period (quarter)	GNP (billion constant 1975 won)		Total employment (thousand persons)		GNP per worker (thousand constant 1975 won)		Total unemployment (thousand persons)		Unemployment rate (%)
	Amount	Change[a]	Number	Change[a]	Amount	Change[a]	Number	Change[a]	
IV 1964	1,764.3	11.5	6,171	− 0.7	285.9	12.3	675	− 4.7	9.9
I 1965	600.4	8.9	7,775	5.1	77.2	3.6	797	0.1	9.3
II 1965	803.0	11.1	9,825	2.4	81.7	8.5	591	− 0.8	5.7
III 1965	690.0	9.0	8,831	1.6	78.1	7.1	604	2.0	6.4
IV 1965	1,791.5	1.5	6,636	7.5	270.2	− 5.5	634	− 6.1	8.7
I 1966	665.4	10.8	7,970	2.5	83.5	8.2	752	− 5.6	8.6
II 1966	955.5	19.0	10,113	2.9	94.5	15.7	596	0.8	5.6
III 1966	793.2	15.0	8,846	0.2	89.7	14.9	608	0.7	6.4
IV 1966	1,964.4	9.7	6,762	1.9	290.5	7.5	638	0.5	8.6
I 1967	754.4	13.4	8,041	0.9	93.8	12.3	683	− 9.2	7.8
II 1967	1,002.0	4.9	10,132	0.2	98.9	4.7	543	− 8.9	5.1
III 1967	899.0	13.3	9,549	7.9	94.1	4.9	536	− 11.8	5.3
IV 1967	2,014.0	2.5	7,145	5.7	281.9	− 2.9	549	− 13.8	7.1
I 1968	853.4	13.1	8,295	3.2	102.9	9.7	674	1.3	7.5
II 1968	1,173.9	17.2	10,618	4.8	110.6	11.8	406	− 25.2	3.7
III 1968	1,058.0	17.7	9,911	3.8	106.8	13.5	445	− 17.0	4.3
IV 1968	2,110.3	4.8	7,799	9.2	270.6	− 4.0	441	− 19.7	5.4
I 1969	975.3	14.3	8,557	3.2	114.0	10.8	656	− 2.7	7.1
II 1969	1,289.3	9.8	10,757	1.3	119.9	8.4	383	− 5.7	3.4
III 1969	1,271.6	20.2	10,267	3.6	123.9	16.0	421	− 5.4	3.9
IV 1969	2,375.3	12.6	8,074	3.5	294.2	8.7	436	1.1	5.1
I 1970	1,038.8	6.5	8,995	5.1	115.5	1.3	583	− 11.1	6.1
II 1970	1,413.7	9.6	10,996	2.2	128.6	7.3	379	− 1.0	3.3
III 1970	1,274.0	0.2	10,670	3.9	119.4	− 3.6	406	− 3.6	3.7
IV 1970	2,636.5	11.0	8,319	3.0	316.9	7.7	448	− 2.8	5.1

a Percentage change over the same period of the previous year.
Sources: Bank of Korea, National Income in Korea, 1982; Bank of Korea, Quarterly GNP, 1984; EPB, Annual Report on the Economically Active Population Survey, various issues

Table 5.10 Quarterly data on gross national product, employment, labor productivity, and unemployment, 1977–1983

Period (quarter)	GNP (billion constant 1975 won)		Total employment (thousand persons)		GNP per worker (thousand constant 1975 won)		Total unemployment (thousand persons)		Unemployment rate (%)
	Amount	Change[a]	Number	Change[a]	Amount	Change[a]	Number	Change[a]	
IV 1977	4,735.1	13.7	11,083	4.6	427.2	8.6	476	1.1	4.1
I 1978	2,575.2	17.1	13,385	6.4	192.4	10.0	501	− 27.4	3.6
II 1978	3,146.8	16.7	14,842	3.1	212.1	17.4	406	− 10.2	2.7
III 1978	3,186.2	13.8	14,082	3.1	226.3	10.4	427	− 0.2	2.9
IV 1978	4,967.9	4.9	11,652	5.1	426.4	− 0.2	431	− 9.5	3.6
I 1979	2,924.4	13.6	13,431	0.3	217.9	13.1	562	12.2	4.0
II 1979	3,438.9	9.2	14,856	0.1	231.5	9.1	537	32.3	3.5
III 1979	3,378.2	6.0	14,374	2.1	235.0	3.8	552	29.3	3.7
IV 1979	5,017.7	1.0	11,993	2.9	418.4	− 0.2	515	19.5	4.1
I 1980	2,893.0	− 1.1	13,876	3.3	208.5	− 4.2	829	47.5	5.7
II 1980	3,228.4	− 6.1	14,758	− 0.7	218.8	− 5.5	672	25.1	4.4
III 1980	3,305.8	− 2.1	14,385	0.1	229.8	− 2.2	692	25.4	4.6
IV 1980	4,415.6	− 12.0	11,894	− 0.8	371.2	− 11.3	802	55.7	6.3
I 1981	2,910.7	0.6	13,871	0.6	209.8	0.6	817	− 1.4	5.6
II 1981	3,344.6	3.6	15,149	2.6	220.8	0.9	610	− 9.2	3.9
III 1981	3,466.0	4.8	14,775	2.7	234.6	2.1	627	− 9.4	4.1
IV 1981	5,002.3	13.3	12,398	4.2	403.5	8.7	591	− 26.3	4.6
I 1982	3,241.6	11.4	14,154	2.0	229.0	9.2	833	2.0	5.6
II 1982	3,788.2	13.3	15,388	1.6	246.2	11.5	602	− 1.3	3.8
III 1982	4,017.0	15.9	15,055	1.9	266.8	13.7	553	− 11.8	3.5
IV 1982	5,084.4	1.6	13,102	5.7	388.1	− 3.8	634	7.3	4.6
I 1983	3,593.4	10.9	14,160	0	253.8	10.8	817	− 1.9	5.5
II 1983	4,148.8	9.5	15,614	1.5	265.7	7.9	537	− 10.8	3.3
III 1983	4,424.1	10.1	15,384	2.2	287.6	7.8	527	− 4.7	3.3
IV 1983	5,503.9	8.3	13,195	0.4	417.1	7.5	591	− 6.8	4.3

[a] Percentage change over the same period of the previous year.
Sources: As table 5.9.

this grew very rapidly in the first three quarters of every year, slipping back in the fourth quarter except for 1969. Even during the 1977–83 period, the GNP per worker increased in all quarters except the four quarters of 1980 and the fourth quarters of 1978 and 1982. The negative growth of labor productivity recorded in many of the fourth quarters reflects a seasonal decline in the annual GNP growth rate related to the conditions of agricultural harvest in Korea.

The total factor productivity of Korea could not be measured by quarter since the calculation of such a productivity index requires quarterly data on capital input and factor shares which are not usually available. The total factor productivity estimate for Korea based on annual data for 1963–82 is therefore quoted from a recent study by Kim and Park (1985). According to their accounting of the sources of economic growth in Korea based on Edward Denison's method (Denison, 1979), total factor productivity (or "output per unit of input" in Denison's terms) grew at an average annual rate of 2.7 percent, thus accounting for about 36 percent of the actual growth rate of national income (7.6 percent) during the period. If the entire 1963–82 period is divided into two subperiods, it is found that the average annual rate of increase in total factor productivity declined sharply from 4.0 percent during 1963–72 to 1.5 percent during 1972–83. The total factor productivity which had accounted for 49 percent of the actual growth rate of national income (8.2 percent) during the early period could explain only 21 percent during the latter period. This, of course, indicates that the increase in total factor input was a more important source of growth in the country than the productivity growth during the latter period.

Production by Sector

Table 5.11 presents the constant price values of domestic production by major sector for selected years, based on Korea's input–output tables. During the period 1966–70, which includes the years of the first trade liberalization, the sectors that recorded especially rapid increase in production were chemical and allied products, electrical machinery, iron and steel, transport equipment, and petroleum and coal products. Only three sectors – agriculture, forestry, and fishery, mining and other manufacturing – showed a rate of growth lower than the average for all sectors (82 percent).

During the period 1975–80, which roughly corresponds with the years of the second liberalization, heavy industries in general recorded a higher rate of increase in production than light industrial sectors. Such heavy industrial sectors as general machinery, electrical machinery, metal products, iron and steel, and nonferrous metal showed particularly high growth, while the lagging sectors included lumber and wood products, petroleum and coal

Table 5.11 Domestic production by major sector for selected years (billion constant 1975 won)

Sector	1966	1970	1975	1980	Percentage change				
					1970 over 1966	1975 over 1970	1980 over 1975	1980 over 1966	
Agriculture, forestry, and fishery	2,165.0	2,597.2	2,987.5	2,845.7	20.0	15.0	− 4.7	31.4	
Mining	114.9	153.7	213.7	214.0	33.8	39.0	0.1	86.2	
Processed food (including tobacco)	406.7	910.7	1,821.4	5,611.4	123.9	100.0	208.1	1,279.7	
Textile products and apparel	288.8	610.9	2,137.4	3,834.5	111.5	249.9	79.4	1,227.7	
Lumber and wood products	69.2	151.7	261.9	364.9	119.2	72.6	39.3	427.3	
Pulp, paper, and allied products	95.7	184.6	326.8	902.9	92.9	77.0	176.3	843.5	
Chemical and allied products	79.0	342.6	1,255.9	2,834.9	333.7	266.6	125.7	3,488.5	
Petroleum and coal products	265.3	707.6	1,013.7	1,659.0	166.7	43.3	63.7	525.3	
Nonmetallic mineral products	71.2	172.3	338.4	791.5	142.0	96.4	133.9	1,011.7	
Iron and steel	65.9	193.5	687.9	2,187.8	193.6	255.5	218.0	3,219.9	
Nonferrous metal	13.5	26.7	90.8	278.7	97.8	240.1	206.9	1,964.4	
Metal products	34.0	61.6	193.6	674.2	81.2	214.3	248.2	1,882.9	
General machinery	30.4	57.3	235.1	1,028.9	88.5	310.3	337.6	3,284.5	
Electrical machinery	25.1	85.0	680.8	2,698.7	238.6	700.9	296.4	10,651.8	
Transport equipment	58.5	158.6	422.2	1,207.1	171.1	166.2	185.9	1,963.4	
Other manufacturing	120.0	218.2	542.5	1,270.7	81.8	148.6	134.2	958.9	
All services	1,510.2	3,238.0	7,781.0	25,711.2	114.4	140.3	230.4	1,602.5	
Total	5,413.4	9,870.2	20,990.6	54,116.1	82.3	112.8	157.8	899.7	

Domestic production in current prices deflated by the wholesale price indices (1975 = 100) for the respective sectors.
Source: Bank of Korea, *Korea's Input–Output Tables*, for respective years

products, and textile products and apparel, in addition to the two primary sectors which had been consistently lagging behind since the earlier period.

The relationship of the change in sectoral production to the change in its effective exchange rate is investigated by two alternative methods. The relationship estimated by a simple regression using the cross-section data for 16 sectors is as follows:

$$X_i = 142.83 + 2.154 XRM_i \qquad R^2 = 0.11$$
$$ (6.78) \quad (1.31) \qquad \text{time period 1966–70}$$
$$X_i = 102.97 + 4.399 \ XRM_i \qquad R^2 = 0.67$$
$$ (5.82) \quad (5.31) \qquad \text{time period 1975–80}$$

where X_i denotes the percentage change in domestic production of the ith sector and XRM_i the percentage change in the real effective exchange rate for imports for the ith sector.

From the above regression results it is found that the increase in domestic production is in general positively correlated with the change in real exchange rate, as expected.[5] It is noted, however, that the regression fit for the earlier period is unusually poor and the regression coefficient for the exchange rate is not statistically significant. In the regression for the later period, the coefficient for the exchange rate variable turned out to be statistically significant. According to this equation, domestic production's elasticity with respect to the real effective exchange rate is about 4.4, which is very high by any standard.

The question then arises why the domestic production became very sensitive to the exchange rate changes during the later as opposed to the earlier period. We offer two plausible reasons: (a) since QRs were a more important tool of import control in the early than in the later period, and the trade ratio (to domestic production) during the early period was still relatively low (less than 20 percent), domestic production could continuously increase regardless of some appreciation in the real effective exchange rates; (b) the percentage changes in real effective exchange rates during the 1966–70 period were generally much lower than during the 1975–80 period and were not high enough to have a significant impact on domestic production.

Table 5.12 gives the labor productivity by sector, measured in terms of domestic production per worker, for the selected years. It is seen that labor productivity increases rapidly in almost every sector during both periods 1966–70 and 1975–80. The sectors that marked particularly high growth of labor productivity during the early period included petroleum and coal products, chemical and allied products, transport equipment, and non-metallic mineral products. In contrast, such sectors as mining, miscella-

---

[5] The regression coefficient did not change significantly whether we used the real effective exchange rate for imports or the rate for exports.

Table 5.12 Production per worker by major sector for selected years (billion constant 1975 won)

Sector	1966	1970	1975	1980	Percentage change			
					1970 over 1966	1975 over 1970	1980 over 1975	1980 over 1966
Agriculture, forestry, and fishery	432	541	658	731	25.2	21.6	11.1	69.2
Mining	1,400	1,410	1,784	1,611	7.1	26.5	− 9.7	15.1
Processed food (including tobacco)	2,233	3,872	5,917	15,842	66.0	52.8	167.7	579.0
Textile products and apparel	1,041	1,644	2,631	4,544	57.9	60.0	72.7	336.5
Lumber and wood products	1,688	2,763	3,971	4,462	63.7	43.7	12.4	164.3
Pulp, paper, and allied products	2,184	3,044	3,736	8,407	39.4	22.7	125.0	284.9
Chemical and allied products	2,251	4,487	8,935	14,815	99.3	99.1	65.8	558.2
Petroleum and coal products	13,605	40,305	48,736	68,895	195.5	20.9	41.4	406.4
Nonmetallic mineral products	1,637	3,050	4,362	7,397	86.3	43.0	69.6	351.9
Iron and steel	5,031	6,593	15,129	32,542	31.0	129.5	115.1	546.8
Nonferrous metal	3,000	4,684	8,518	14,396	56.1	81.9	69.0	379.9
Metal products	1,344	1,806	3,710	8,273	34.4	105.4	123.0	515.6
General machinery	1,246	1,637	3,548	8,079	31.4	116.7	127.7	548.4
Electrical machinery	1,357	2,168	4,696	10,463	59.8	116.6	122.8	671.0
Transport equipment	1,822	3,509	4,472	11,943	92.6	27.4	167.1	555.5
Other manufacturing	1,519	1,717	2,996	4,471	13.0	74.5	49.2	194.3
All services	692	1,041	1,851	4,667	50.4	77.8	152.1	574.4
Total	668	1,071	1,913	4,442	60.3	78.6	132.2	565.0

neous manufacturing, agriculture, forestry, and fishery, general machinery, iron and steel, and paper and allied products showed relatively low rates of increase in labor productivity.

During the later period, only three sectors – processed foods, transport equipment, and all services – recorded a rate of increase in labor productivity higher than the high (132 percent) average for all sectors. Apart from the mining sector, whose labor productivity declined by 10 percent, all sectors attained a positive rate of increase in labor productivity. Rates of increase in labor productivity for such sectors as agriculure, forestry, and fishery, lumber and wood products, petroleum and coal products, miscellaneous manufacturing, and nonferrous metal were significantly lower than for the other sectors, however.

Spearman's rank correlation coefficients are estimated on the basis of the cross-sector data for 16 sectors, in order to examine statistical relationships between domestic production and other related variables. The results are summarized in table 5.13. The correlation coefficients shown above the diagonal in that table are the results based on data for 1966–70, while those below the diagonal are based on data for 1975–80.

Firstly, the rank correlation between the change in domestic production and the change in real exchange rate turned out to be significantly high (0.794) only for the later period, whereas it was not significant for the earlier period. This supports the result of simple regression already discussed.

Secondly, the change in labor productivity is, of course, positively correlated with the change in domestic production, and the size of the rank

Table 5.13 Matrix of Spearman's rank correlation coefficients between domestic production and other related variables

	X	E	X/L	XRM	MR	K/L
X	1.0	− 0.234	0.741	0.332	− 0.469	− 0.432
E	0.385	1.0	0.082	0.609	− 0.313	0.074
X/L	0.803	0.315	1.0	0.391	− 0.724	− 0.056
XRM	0.794	0.512	0.838	1.0	− 0.552	0.026
MR	− 0.776	− 0.579	− 0.715	− 0.765	1.0	0.068
K/L	0.388	0.409	0.168	0.200	− 0.479	1.0

X, percentage changes in domestic production (at constant 1975 prices);
E, percentage point change in the ratio of exports to domestic production;
X/L, percentage change in domestic production per worker (at constant 1975 prices); XRM, percentage change in real effective exchange rate for imports; MR, percentage point change in the ratio of imports to domestic production;
K/L, percentage change in net capital stock per worker (at constant 1975 prices).
The correlation coefficients above the diagonal represent the results based on 1966–70 data, while those below the diagonal are based on data for 1975–80. The coefficients higher than 0.43 are statistically significant at the 90 percent level of confidence.

correlation coefficient between the change in labor productivity and the exchange rate variable turned out to be almost equivalent to that between the domestic production and the exchange rate.

Thirdly, the rank correlation between the change in domestic production or the change in labor productivity and the change in exports was positive, as expected, but statistically insignificant in both periods. It turned out, however, that the rank correlation between the domestic production or the labor productivity variable and the change in the ratio of imports to domestic production was negative and statistically significant, as expected, in both periods. This indicates that, while exports were not the main factor for increasing domestic production (and domestic production per worker), the increase in competing imports contributed to restraining domestic sectors from rapid expansion.

Finally, the rank correlation between the domestic production variable and the change in the capital-to-labor ratio turned out to be only marginally significant but negative for the early period, contrary to our expectation. The same coefficient for the later period is positive but statistically insignificant. For this reason, the correlation between labor productivity and the capital-to-labor ratio was statistically insignificant for both periods. These unexpected results may be attributable to the fact that our sectors are classified too broadly to show the specific characteristics of each industrial sector.

Employment and Unemployment

Aggregate Employment and Unemployment

Aggregate employment increased almost continuously during the two periods (1964–79 and 1977–83), although there were some fluctuations in the annual rate of increase estimated by quarter. Accordingly the aggregate unemployment showed a declining trend during 1964–70, despite the continuous rapid growth of the country's labor force. During 1977–83 the unemployment rate showed an increase in the two recession years of 1979 and 1980, but if these recession years were excluded, the declining trend can be seen to continue even during this later period (see tables 5.9 and 5.10).

The ratio of unemployment to the labor force showed some seasonality by quarter. The unemployment rates for the second and third quarters of each year were generally lower than those for the first and fourth quarters of the same year, mainly because of seasonal changes in agricultural employment. If this seasonal variation is excluded, the unemployment rate shows a continuous decline from almost 10 percent in the fourth quarter of 1964 to 5 percent by the same period of 1970. During the later period it

Table 5.14 Employment by major sector for selected years (thousand people)

Sector	1966	1970	1975	1980	Percentage change			
					1970 over 1966	1975 over 1970	1980 over 1975	1980 over 1966
Agriculture, forestry, and fishery	5,013.0	4,804.0	4,541.2	3,893.5	− 4.2	− 5.5	− 14.3	− 22.3
Mining	82.1	109.0	119.8	132.8	32.8	9.9	10.9	61.8
Processed food (including tobacco)	174.3	235.2	307.8	354.2	34.9	30.9	15.1	103.2
Textile products and apparel	277.4	371.6	812.5	843.9	34.0	118.6	3.9	204.2
Lumber and wood products	41.0	54.9	66.0	81.8	33.9	20.2	23.9	99.5
Pulp, paper, and allied products	43.9	60.7	87.5	107.4	38.3	44.2	22.7	144.6
Chemical and allied products	35.1	76.4	140.6	191.4	117.7	84.0	36.1	445.3
Petroleum and coal products	19.5	17.6	20.9	24.1	− 9.7	18.2	15.9	23.6
Nonmetallic mineral products	43.5	56.5	77.6	107.0	29.9	37.3	37.9	146.0
Iron and steel	13.1	29.4	45.5	67.2	124.4	54.8	47.7	413.0
Nonferrous metal	4.5	5.7	10.7	19.4	26.7	87.7	81.3	331.1
Metal products	25.3	34.1	52.2	81.5	34.8	53.1	56.1	222.1
General machinery	24.4	35.0	66.3	127.4	43.4	89.4	92.2	422.1
Electrical machinery	18.5	39.2	145.0	257.9	111.9	269.9	77.9	1,294.1
Transport equipment	32.1	45.2	94.4	101.1	40.8	108.8	7.1	215.0
Other manufacturing	79.0	127.1	181.1	284.2	60.9	42.5	56.9	259.7
All services	2,180.9	3,111.1	4,204.0	5,509.4	42.7	35.1	31.1	152.6
Total	8,107.6	9,212.5	10,972.8	12,184.0	13.6	19.1	11.0	50.3

Source: Bank of Korea, Korea's Input–Output Tables, for respective years

only fluctuated by year and by quarter, without changing the rate between the beginning and the terminal quarters.

Employment by Sector

Table 5.14 presents sectoral employment data for the years 1966–70 and 1975–80. Sectoral unemployment data are not available in Korea. The table shows that between 1966 and 1970 employment increased in all sectors except agriculture, forestry, and fishery and petroleum and coal products. The sectors in which employment grew particularly rapidly during this early period included iron and steel, chemical and allied products, electrical machinery, and miscellaneous manufacturing.

Between 1975 and 1980, all sectors except agriculture, forestry, and fishery recorded positive rates of increase in employment. The sectors with an especially high rate of employment growth were mainly heavy industries such as general machinery, nonferrous metal, electrical machinery, and metal products. As well as agriculture, forestry, and fishery, sectors such as textile products, mining, transport equipment, processed food, and petroleum and coal products recorded lower rates of employment growth than other sectors.

Using the cross-section data for the different periods, attempts are made to investigate the relationship between changes in employment and changes in the real exchange rate and other variables. As in the analysis of the relationships of domestic production to other variables, two alternative approaches are taken: a simple regression and the rank correlation analysis. The results of simple regression which were found to have some statistical significance are as follows:

$$N_i = 26.56 + 0.803 XRM_i \qquad\qquad R^2 = 0.24$$
$$(3.24) \quad (2.10) \qquad\qquad\qquad \text{time period 1975–80}$$
$$N_i = 113.97 + 3.816 XRM_i \qquad\qquad R^2 = 0.23$$
$$(1.09) \quad (2.04) \qquad\qquad\qquad \text{time period 1966–80}$$

In these regression equations, N_i represents the percentage change in employment of the ith sector and XRM_i the percentage change in real effective exchange rate for imports for the ith sector. It can be seen that the change in sectoral employment was positively correlated with the change in the exchange rate during the two periods 1975–80 and 1966–80. Although the regression coefficients in both equations turned out to be statistically significant, the size of the coefficient has shown too drastic a change between the two periods to be considered reliable. It should be noted, however, that these two regression equations are only the results in which the coefficients turned out to be statistically significant. In the regression result for the earlier period (1966–70), the coefficient for the exchange rate variable was positive, as expected, but was statistically insignificant. The results are quite similar to those already discussed of the regression between the domestic production and the exchange rate variable.

Employment, Production, and Trade

Table 5.15 presents the results of rank correlation estimated between the percentage change in employment and other related variables for the three different periods 1966–70, 1975–80, and 1966–80. As shown in the table, the coefficient of rank correlation between the change in employment and the change in real effective exchange rate was positive as expected but was statistically insignificant for all the periods. The change in employment was also positively correlated with the change in the ratio of export to domestic production but was not statistically significant except for the longer period 1966–80. The rank correlation between the change in employment and the change in the ratio of imports to domestic production produced an insignificantly low coefficient for the early period but significantly large and negative coefficients for the two other periods, as expected.

Table 5.15 Rank correlation coefficients between changes in employment and other related variables

	Related variables			
	XRM	E	MR	X
Changes in employment correlated to other variables, 1966–70	0.235	0.029	0.024	0.429
Changes in employment correlated to other variables, 1975–80	0.368	0.259	− 0.459	0.688
Changes in employment correlated to other variables, 1966–80	0.376	0.626	− 0.588	0.924

XRM, percentage change in the real effective exchange rate of imports; E, percentage point change in the ratio of exports to domestic production; MR, percentage point change in the ratio of imports to domestic production; X, percentage change in domestic production. (The coefficients higher than 0.43 are statistically significant at the 90 percent level.)

The coefficient estimated between the change in employment and the change in domestic production was positive and significantly high for all three periods, as expected. It seems that this significantly positive correlation between the employment and the production variables actually influences the relationships of the change in employment to the changes in both import and export ratios.

Capital and Investment

Aggregate Capital and Investment

The Bank of Korea's *Quarterly GNP* (1984) gives the quarterly data on gross fixed investment for both periods, 1964–70 and 1977–83. During the early period gross fixed investment generally showed a continuous increase, not only in absolute amount but also in terms of its ratio to GNP, although there were a few exceptional quarters. The quarterly ratios of gross fixed investment to GNP showed some seasonality, probably arising from climatic conditions that discourage construction activities during the cold winter. Accordingly, the investment ratio for the fourth quarter of each year was generally much lower than that for the other quarters.

The seasonal influence is evident even during the later period. In addition, gross fixed investment during 1977–83 fluctuated more widely by quarter than during the earlier period. For instance, the absolute value of fixed investment actually declined from the fourth quarter of 1979 to the third quarter of 1981, mainly reflecting the effects on the domestic economy of the second world oil shock and the consequent worldwide recession. In other quarters, it generally showed an increasing trend. As a result, the quarterly ratio of fixed investments to GNP showed a wide fluctuation from a low level of 26 percent to a high of 49 percent during this period.

As a result of this rapid increase in gross fixed investment by quarter, the country's aggregate capital stock, excluding construction work in progress, continuously expanded from 1963 to 1982. As shown in chapter 2, table 2.6, the country's net capital stock increased at an average annual rate of about 13 percent during 1963–72 and 1972–82. However, the country's gross capital stock expanded at an average annual rate of 10.6 percent during 1963–72 but increased at a slightly higher rate of 11.7 percent a year during 1972–82. The average annual growth rate of gross capital stock for the entire period was 11.1 percent, slightly lower than that of net capital stock.

The ratio of capital utilization at this aggregate level is not available in Korea. The same ratio for the manufacturing sector separately is available for 1971–83 (EPB, *Korea Statistical Yearbook*, various issues). The average index of operation ratio for the whole manufacturing sector showed a gradual increase from 90.5 (1980 = 100) in 1971 to 120.0 by 1978. After 1978, however, the index declined to reach 100 by 1980 and remained almost unchanged at around 100 through 1982. It rose again to 109 by 1983.

Table 5.16 Net capital stock by major sector for selected years[a] (billion constant 1975 won)

Sector	1965	1969	1974	1979	Percentage change			
					1970 over 1966	1975 over 1970	1980 over 1975	1980 over 1966
Agriculture, forestry, and fishery	416.3	518.2	748.4	1,568.4[b]	24.5	44.4	109.6	276.7
Mining	17.1	41.7	67.6	144.6	143.9	62.1	113.6	745.6
Processed food (including tobacco)	109.2	183.3	368.8	656.1	67.9	101.2	77.9	500.8
Textile products and apparel	96.5	238.8	598.6	1,098.4	147.5	150.7	83.5	1,038.2
Lumber and wood products	24.9	44.9	92.2	146.4	80.3	105.3	58.8	488.0
Pulp, paper, and allied products	35.7	69.6	138.7	250.7	95.2	99.3	80.7	602.2
Chemical and allied products	76.5	187.1	324.4	536.8	144.6	73.4	65.5	601.7
Petroleum and coal products	24.3	75.0	154.4	164.1	208.6	105.9	6.3	575.3
Nonmetallic mineral products	32.4	152.8	219.0	431.7	371.6	43.3	97.1	1,232.4
Iron and steel	25.3	65.9	300.9	1,377.5	160.5	356.6	357.8	5,344.7
Nonferrous metal	3.9	8.7	20.5	108.6	123.1	135.6	429.8	2,684.6
Metal products	10.6	21.1	67.8	244.7	99.1	221.3	260.9	2,208.5
General machinery	12.4	23.1	76.3	392.4	86.3	230.3	414.3	3,064.5
Electrical machinery	12.1	23.7	136.0	416.5	95.9	473.8	206.3	3,342.1
Transport equipment	34.9	62.0	198.2	527.1	77.7	219.7	165.9	1,410.3
Other manufacturing	19.0	47.7	117.5	301.0	151.1	146.3	156.2	1,484.2
All services	2,000.5	3,478.8	5,447.0	15,080.9[b]	73.9	56.6	176.9	653.9
Total	2,951.6	5,242.6	9,076.3	23,445.6	77.6	73.1	158.3	694.3

[a] The capital stock data originally given in 1977 constant prices were deflated by the price deflator of gross fixed capital formation to obtain the capital stock in 1975 constant prices.
[b] Estimated by adding up the increment of net capital stock during 1978–9 to the net capital stock for 1977 (estimated by Choo).
Source: Choo et al., 1982

Capital and Investment by Sector

Table 5.16 shows net capital stock by major sector for selected years 1965, 1969, 1974, and 1979. These capital stock data are actually the end-of-year figures. It was therefore assumed that the capital stock at the end of the previous year is relevant for domestic production activities in the current year.

Net capital stocks for all major sectors increased fairly rapidly between 1965 and 1979. During 1965–9, which includes the years of the first liberalization, the sectors that recorded especially rapid growth of capital stock were nonmetallic mineral products, petroleum and coal products, iron and steel, and miscellaneous manufacturing. In contrast, such sectors as agriculture, forestry, and fishery, processed food, and all services showed lower rates of increase in their capital stock than the average for all sectors.

During 1974–9, which includes the years of the second liberalization, capital stock expanded quite rapidly in such heavy industrial sectors as general machinery, nonferrous metal, iron and steel, metal products, electrical machinery, and so on. However, the capital stock of the sector "petroleum and coal products" showed the lowest rate of increase. In addition, capital stocks increased relatively slowly for practically all the light industrial sectors, including processed food, lumber and wood products, and pulp, paper and allied products.

Spearman's rank correlation coefficients are estimated by relating the percentage change in net capital stock to the changes in other variables, such as domestic production, employment, and export and import ratios, on the basis of the cross-section data for the three different periods (1966–70, 1975–80, and 1966–80). The results are shown in table 5.17.

As can be seen, it was not possible to obtain any statistically significant coefficients of rank correlation between the change in capital stock and

Table 5.17 Rank correlation coefficients between changes in net capital stock and other related variables

	X	N	E	MR	X/L
Changes in capital stock correlated to other variables, 1966–70	0.262	0.003	0.059	− 0.181	0.079
Changes in capital stock correlated to other variables, 1975–80	0.647	0.574	0.526	− 0.582	0.297
Change in capital stock correlated to other variables, 1966–80	0.694	0.782	0.556	− 0.385	0.391

N, percentage change in employment; X/L, percentage change in domestic production per worker; the definitions of X, E, and MR are the same as in table 5.15.

changes in other variables for the early period (1966–70). For both the 1975–80 and 1966–80 periods, the coefficients of rank correlation estimated between the change in capital stock and the changes in other variables turned out to have the expected signs, and were statistically significant in most cases. For instance, the coefficients between the change in capital stock and the changes in other production-related variables (that is, production, employment, and exports) all turned out to be positive and statistically significant as expected. The change in capital stock was negatively correlated with the change in the ratio of imports to domestic production, since the latter is negatively correlated with the change in domestic production, as already explained.

Then why are the relationships of the change in net capital stock to changes in other production-related variables for the early period statistically insignificant, whereas they are generally significant for the other two periods? It seems that a gestation lag of sectoral investment can at least partly explain the difference. During the 1966–70 period net capital stock increased substantially owing to the rapid growth of fixed investment. But since this early period covers only four years, unlike the other two periods (1975–80 and 1966–80), it is possible that the full impact of the increase in sectoral capital stock could not be felt on each sector's production and other related variables. It should also be remembered that the terminal year, 1970, was an unusual year of recession in the economy.

The coefficients of rank correlation between the change in capital stock and the change in domestic production per worker for the 1975–80 and 1966–80 periods were positive as expected, but were not high enough to claim statistical significance. This seems to indicate that the increase in capital stock has contributed, in general, to increasing that sector's domestic production and employment but not significantly to its labor productivity. The increase in capital stock, however, brought about a substantial increase in sectoral capital intensity (or capital-to-labor ratio) since it was much more rapid than the increase in sectoral employment (Kim, 1988, appendix table 13). The insignificant correlation between the change in capital stock and the change in domestic production per worker therefore explains why the increase in factor intensity could not contribute to increasing labor productivity in many sectors, contrary to our expectation.

Profit Rates by Sector

Table 5.18 gives the ratio of net profits to net worth by major sector for 1964 to 1970, while table 5.19 presents the same ratio for 1975–83. Since the sector classification in that table is not consistent with the 16-sector-level classification of the tradeable sector that we have been using for

Table 5.18 Ratio of net profits to net worth by major sector, 1964–1970 (percent)

Sectors	1964	1965	1966	1967	1968	1969	1970
Mining	18.9	21.8	21.3	8.7	6.3	3.5	6.0
Manufacturing – average	15.0	15.3	16.9	17.0	16.1	13.6	10.7
Food and beverages	29.3	15.1	16.1	12.6	24.4	29.1	19.0
Textiles, wearing apparel, and leather	11.2	13.4	19.8	16.8	12.1	1.9	0.1
(Leather products)	(12.8)	(15.1)	(31.7)	(9.5)	(8.8)	(9.6)	(14.1)
Wood and furniture	33.9	16.1	28.2	20.7	21.3	2.9	− 57.2
Paper, printing, and publishing	12.9	10.9	19.1	14.4	16.7	10.2	7.9
Chemicals, petroleum, coal, rubber and plastics	14.5	18.4	14.7	16.5	15.3	14.7	16.0
(Petroleum and coal products)	(16.8)	(28.0)	(18.8)	(20.7)	(26.3)	(8.6)	(19.7)
(Rubber products)	(23.9)	(20.2)	(16.3)	(11.1)	(13.0)	(9.0)	(− 13.6)
Nonmetallic mineral products	12.5	13.2	15.2	21.8	2.3	8.0	3.8
Basic metal	19.0	12.9	18.9	16.4	16.5	− 13.0	− 2.7
Fabricated metal products, machinery, and equipment	11.6	12.1	15.2	23.9	22.5	26.1	6.5
(General machinery)	(16.1)	(21.5)	(6.2)	(8.9)	(5.5)	(6.8)	(3.2)
(Electrical machinery)	(13.9)	(20.5)	(23.2)	(27.0)	(24.4)	(21.2)	(13.0)
(Transport equipment)	(4.9)	(4.7)	(7.4)	(29.0)	(31.9)	(39.0)	(1.8)
Other manufacturing	–	–	–	–	23.0	34.6	62.9

–, nil.
Source: Bank of Korea, Financial Statements Analysis, various years

analyzing the movements of other variables, it is not possible to relate these sectoral profit rates to changes in other variables.

Table 5.18 indicates that, although the ratio of net profits to net worth for the mining sector was showing a declining trend during 1964–70, the same ratio for the manufacturing sector as a whole remained significantly high, ranging from 11 to 19 percent. Within manufacturing, practically all sectors enjoyed relatively high profit rates during this period, with only a few exceptions in 1969–70. It seems that the manufacturing sector was able to maintain high profit rates because of the rapid growth of net sales during the period.

It can be seen from table 5.19 that the mining and manufacturing sectors' normal profits, which had been generally high in relation to net worth in 1975–8, started to decline in 1979 and became negative in 1980, the year of severe recession.[6] These declines in the profit rates were not directly

[6] The data given in table 5.19 are not directly comparable with those in table 5.18 for two reasons. Firstly, the sector classification in the former table cannot be exactly matched with that in the latter, since the agency collecting the data changed the classification in the early 1970s. Secondly, there was a minor change in the definition of "profit rates" between the two periods. In other words, the term "normal profits" is used to calculate the profit rates for the latter period whereas "net profits" are used for the earlier period. The differences between the normal profits and the net profits are net special gains (nonoperational gains) and corporation taxes, which are included in the former but excluded in the latter.

Table 5.19 Ratio of normal profits to net worth by major sector, 1975–1983 (percent)

Sectors	1975	1977	1978	1979	1980	1981	1982	1983
Mining	20.9	22.7	3.6	– 16.1	– 2.2	2.8	5.7	3.1
Manufacturing – average	16.5	21.3	22.9	15.6	– 1.3	0.1	5.3	15.5
Food and beverages	20.3	40.3	48.5	30.2	16.1	10.4	15.7	22.8
Textiles, wearing apparel, and leather	5.1	8.5	18.3	8.2	– 6.5	4.4	– 0.3	9.1
(Leather products)	(55.6)	(– 10.9)	(– 0.2)	(– 57.7)	(– 5.4)	(18.1)	(8.5)	(13.9)
Wood and furniture	– 8.0	31.3	60.0	6.7	– 118.8	– 1,172.0	– 186.0	40.9
Paper, printing, and publishing	12.6	24.6	25.4	20.6	– 0.8	– 19.3	0.5	18.8
Chemicals, petroleum, coal, rubber, and plastics	28.4	19.3	27.4	26.1	15.5	4.6	12.8	21.4
(Petroleum and coal products)	(34.0)	(– 0.1)	(35.8)	(26.4)	(– 22.6)	(5.1)	(24.4)	(9.7)
(Rubber products)	(38.3)	(25.5)	(40.5)	(30.7)	(39.4)	(26.9)	(20.9)	(23.8)
Nonmetallic mineral products	23.9	25.8	28.3	28.9	11.1	– 2.8	4.4	19.3
Iron and steel	– 1.1	14.4	12.1	8.7	– 6.0	6.8	4.4	11.7
Nonferrous metal	15.4	34.5	48.0	34.1	– 2.1	– 82.3	– 19.3	– 4.6
Fabricated metal products, machinery, and equipment	25.6	25.8	15.9	7.8	– 14.0	– 1.4	3.1	13.3
(General machinery)	(25.5)	(20.4)	(31.7)	(18.1)	(– 53.2)	(– 5.2)	(– 7.9)	(– 9.2)
(Electrical machinery)	(35.1)	(26.3)	(20.4)	(15.2)	(– 4.5)	(14.6)	(13.8)	(28.9)
(Transport equipment)	(13.8)	(24.4)	(6.2)	(– 0.7)	(– 16.6)	(– 8.0)	(3.4)	(13.8)
Other manufacturing	30.4	23.7	13.2	– 2.8	15.0	26.8	35.5	32.2

Source: Bank of Korea, Financial Statements Analysis, various years

Table 5.20 Distribution of national income earned in nonresidential business among input factors in current factor cost, 1961–1982 (billion won)

Year	National income Amount	National income Percentage share	Labor Amount	Labor Percentage share	Structures and equipment Amount	Structures and equipment Percentage share	Inventories Amount	Inventories Percentage share	Land Amount	Land Percentage share
1961	210.5	100.0	130.0	61.76	19.7	9.36	20.7	9.83	40.1	19.05
1962	248.1	100.0	152.6	61.51	25.4	10.24	26.7	10.76	43.4	17.49
1963	377.6	100.0	219.8	58.21	39.0	10.33	38.8	10.28	80.0	21.18
1964	564.6	100.0	328.9	58.25	55.1	9.76	61.3	10.86	119.3	21.13
1965	615.8	100.0	370.2	60.12	70.0	11.37	65.5	10.63	110.1	17.88
1966	774.1	100.0	460.1	59.44	99.5	12.85	85.2	11.01	129.3	16.70
1967	928.6	100.0	560.0	60.30	130.9	14.10	100.0	10.77	137.7	14.83
1968	1,178.3	100.0	706.5	59.96	184.6	15.67	124.6	10.57	162.6	13.80
1969	1,552.9	100.0	977.8	62.97	233.4	15.03	143.6	9.25	198.0	12.75
1970	1,935.0	100.0	1,201.1	62.07	343.2	17.74	173.1	8.94	217.7	11.25
1971	2,398.0	100.0	1,507.1	62.85	394.3	16.44	215.1	8.97	281.5	11.74
1972	2,940.9	100.0	1,798.2	61.15	505.6	17.19	262.6	8.93	374.4	12.73
1973	3,879.6	100.0	2,372.6	61.16	695.9	17.94	305.8	7.88	505.3	13.02
1974	5,533.6	100.0	3,555.5	60.64	1,030.2	18.62	463.9	8.38	684.0	12.36
1975	7,214.0	100.0	4,218.4	58.47	1,377.9	19.10	644.7	8.94	973.0	13.49
1976	9,377.4	100.0	5,295.7	56.48	1,884.9	20.10	889.4	9.48	1,307.4	13.94
1977	11,912.6	100.0	6,755.7	56.72	2,395.7	20.11	1,054.8	8.85	1,706.4	14.32
1978	16,266.0	100.0	9,585.1	58.93	3,246.5	19.96	1,342.2	8.25	2,092.2	12.86
1979	20,476.6	100.0	11,936.2	58.29	4,356.5	21.27	1,682.2	8.22	2,501.7	12.22
1980	23,859.4	100.0	14,223.8	59.62	5,361.1	22.47	2,076.8	8.70	2,197.7	9.21
1981	29,570.7	100.0	16,565.0	56.02	7,178.4	24.27	2,744.0	9.28	3,083.3	10.43
1982	32,652.1	100.0	18,707.5	57.29	8,088.3	24.77	2,627.7	8.05	3,228.6	9.89

National income earned in nonresidential business is equivalent to national income less the income of three small sectors: the "general government, households, and nonprofit institutions," the "ownership of dwellings" sector, and the foreign sector.
Source: Kim and Park, 1985

attributable to the trade liberalization of 1978–9, however, even though they started in 1979. The normal profit rates in almost all sectors were in any case negative in 1980, with the exception of a few sectors such as food and beverages, coal products, rubber products, and nonmetallic mineral products. Between 1980 and 1983, the profit rates of many sectors gradually increased from the negative levels of 1980. By 1983, the average normal profit rate (to net worth) for the manufacturing sector as a whole fully recovered the 1979 level.

Income Distribution and Socioeconomic Attributes

Distribution among Factors of Production

Table 5.20 presents the distribution of national income earned in nonresidential business among the primary factors of production for the period 1961–82. Although national income originating in such small sectors as the "general government, households, and nonprofit institutions," the "ownership of dwellings" sector, and the foreign sector is excluded from the whole economy's national income, the nonresidential business sector's national income covers the bulk of Korea's national income. In fact, national income originating in nonresidential business rose from about 80 percent of the whole economy's national income in 1963 to 94.5 percent by 1982 (Kim and Park, 1985).

According to the table, the labor share in the nonresidential business sector national income fluctuated slightly between a minimum of 58.2 percent and a maximum of 63.0 percent during the period 1961–74, implying a corresponding range for the income share for all types of capital from 37.0 percent of the nonresidential business national income to 41.8 percent. After 1974, however, the labor share became generally lower than in the earlier period: it ranged from a minimum of 56.5 percent to a maximum of 59.6 percent, indicating that the capital share increased in relative terms.

Within the capital share, the share of nonresidential structures and equipment showed an almost continuous rise from 9.4 percent in 1961 to 24.8 percent by 1982, while the shares of both inventories and land generally showed declining trends. This relative increase in the income share of nonresidential structures and equipment reflects the change in the structure of the nation's capital stock over time.

What we may observe from the table is that the trade liberalization programs had little impact on the functional distribution of national income in Korea. During and following the two episodes of trade liberalization, the functional distribution of national income did not show any significant change that could be related to the impact of trade liberalization.

Gainers and Losers

The impact of trade liberalization on consumers' income levels can be estimated if there is evidence that the relative prices of goods and services were significantly changed by liberalization. In the Korean case it is not possible to isolate the price effect of liberalization from the general rises in the prices of goods and services. The extent of losses of quota profits could not be estimated because there is no way to approximate the size of quota profits in Korea. Since many of the QR items had been imported in large quantity even before the liberalization, for export production and for other purposes, with government approval, it is not in fact possible to identify the direct impact of liberalization on commodity imports by detailed commodity item. For these reasons, we simply comment here on who gained and who lost from import liberalization.

Import liberalization from QRs was promoted by the government as a gradual process, in order to minimize adverse impact on domestic industries. The rate of import liberalization, measured in terms of the ratio of AA items to total tradeable items, for commodity items produced by large monopoly–oligopoly firms was lower than that for other items as of the second half of 1982. The average rate of import liberalization for the commodity items produced by monopoly–oligopoly firms was about 45 percent in 1982, compared with the average rate of 77 percent for all tradeable items (see chapter 6, table 6.4). We may therefore say that the large-scale enterprises were the relative gainers while the small-scale enterprises were losers.

Comparing the rate of import liberalization between agricultural and nonagricultural activities, we find that the agricultural sector's rate has been somewhat lower than that for the other sectors. As of 1982, for instance, the rate for the agricultural sector was about 76 percent whereas the rates for the manufacturing sector and the mining sector reached 95 percent and 77 percent respectively. This indicates that the agricultural sector was given slightly higher protection by QRs. However, the legal tariff rates on agricultural products were generally lower than those on other commodity items. It is therefore difficult to judge whether that sector was a gainer or loser from the liberalization.

In Korea, unionized activities accounted for only a small share of all economic activities. There is no indication that the implementation of liberalization programs discriminated against either unionized or non-unionized activities. In addition, there is no reason to expect that some regions were given preference over others in liberalizing trade. Finally, foreign-owned enterprises accounted for too small a proportion of domestic enterprises in Korea to deserve special attention in trade liberalization.

6

Inferences for the Sequencing of Liberalization Policy

Fulfillment of the Announced Schemes

The significant progress in trade liberalization discernible in the two episodes analyzed in this study was the outcome of deliberate government policy. The first episode (1965–7) saw a loosening of QRs, and the second (1978–9) a loosening of QRs accompanied by a reduction in tariffs; both were consciously formulated and implemented with the object of liberalizing trade.

Although a generalized intention to promote trade liberalization in the future was made known, the 1965–7 program was avowedly short term in its aims: it took the form primarily of revision of an existing semiannual trade program. Specific plans were limited to the half-year horizon, so that there was no time lag between announcement and implementation: the two were virtually synonymous and simultaneous.

The second episode involved longer-term planning only in the sense that it instituted a system of advance notices for import liberalization. In all other senses, the announced program and its implementation were once more synonymous. Even the advance notices system presupposed implementation, as evidenced in the gradual progress in liberalization from QRs after 1979.

Against the background of the stated but generalized intention to liberalize trade, the specific moves during the two episodes can thus be characterized as piecemeal and *ad hoc* rather than as stages in a detailed long-term strategy. An instance is the reduction of tariff barriers in 1979, carried out not as part of any explicit long-term plan to reduce such barriers but as a one-shot program.

Thus it would be true to say that all announced schemes were implemented: none were reversed or aborted. This being so, what were the differing circumstances that made trade liberalization sustainable after the second episode whereas it faltered after the first? Reasons must be sought in the performance or movements of major variables before and during each episode.

Table 6.1 shows such movements for the 1965–7 episode, while table 6.2 gives similar data for the 1978–9 episode. The tables demonstrate that the economic climate in which the two liberalization episodes began and took place was generally auspicious. GNP was growing fairly rapidly; as a result, unemployment was gradually declining. More important, the country's balance of payments improved significantly before or at least until the first year of each liberalization episode, mainly because exports were growing more rapidly than imports, net barter terms of trade had improved, and external environments were favorable. Since the 1960s, Korea has experienced a minor current account surplus in only two years: 1965 and 1977, that is, the first year of and the year immediately preceding the liberalization episodes.

Foreign debts outstanding were continuously growing before and during each period of liberalization owing to active domestic investment. During the first episode of liberalization, however, foreign debts were still negligible, while they had increased to a range of US$14 billion to US$21 billion by the second episode. Accordingly, the annual debt service

Table 6.1 Movements of major economic variables before and during the 1965–1967 episode

Variables	1962	1963	1964	1965	1966	1967
Growth rate of GNP (1975 prices, %)	2.2	9.1	9.6	5.8	12.7	6.6
Unemployment rate (%)	n.a.	8.2	7.7	7.4	7.1	6.2
Trade and balance of payments						
Exports (million current US$)	55	87	119	175	250	320
(Annual increase, %)	(34.1)	(58.2)	(36.8)	(47.1)	(42.9)	(28.0)
Imports (million current US$)	422	560	404	463	716	996
(Annual increase, %)	(33.5)	(32.7)	(− 27.8)	(14.6)	(54.2)	(39.1)
Current balance (current million US$)	− 56	− 143	− 26	9	− 103	− 192
Foreign exchange reserves (million US$)	169	131	136	146	245	357
Debt service position						
Total foreign debts (million US$)	89	157	177	206	392	645
(Annual increase, %)		(74.6)	(12.7)	(16.4)	(90.3)	(64.5)
Debt service ratio (%)[a]	0.7	1.0	2.8	5.2	3.1	5.4
Terms-of-trade index (1975 = 100)						
Export unit price index	n.a.	54.5	55.6	57.7	63.0	65.9
Import unit price index	n.a.	45.0	45.5	46.3	45.3	45.7
Terms-of-trade index	n.a.	121.0	122.3	124.7	139.2	144.2
Real effective exchange rate						
Export rate (constant 1965 won per US$)	247.4	258.9	286.0	275.3	268.2	260.8
Import rate (constant 1965 won per US$)	255.5	216.1	268.0	293.1	280.2	265.7
Annual change in wholesale price index (%)	9.3	20.5	34.8	10.0	8.8	6.4
Real interest rate on domestic loans (%)	5.8	− 6.3	− 19.1	12.1	17.1	19.1

n.a., not available.
[a] Debt service ratio to total foreign exchange receipts.

Table 6.2 Movements of major economic variables before and during the 1978–1979 episode

Variables	1975	1976	1977	1978	1979
Growth rate of GNP					
(1975 prices, %)	7.1	15.1	10.3	11.6	6.4
Unemployment rate (%)	4.1	3.9	3.8	3.2	3.8
Trade and balance of payments					
Exports (current billion US$)	5.1	7.7	10.0	12.7	15.1
(Annual increase, %)	(13.9)	(51.8)	(30.2)	(26.5)	(18.4)
Imports (current billion US$)	7.3	8.8	10.8	15.0	20.3
(Annual increase %)	(6.2)	(20.6)	(23.2)	(38.5)	(31.2)
Current balance (current billion US$)	− 1.9	− 0.3	0.0	− 1.1	− 4.2
Foreign exchange reserves					
(billion US$)	1.6	3.0	4.3	4.9	5.7
Debt service position					
Total foreign debts (billion US$)	8.5	10.5	12.6	14.9	20.5
(Annual increase, %)	(42.4)	(24.6)	(20.1)	(17.6)	(37.9)
Debt service ratio[a] (%)	14.1	12.1	11.9	13.9	16.2
Terms-of-trade index (1975 = 100)					
Export unit price index	100.0	111.7	122.3	135.4	161.8
Import unit price index	100.0	98.0	100.2	105.8	129.2
Terms-of-trade index	100.0	114.0	122.0	128.0	125.3
Real effective exchange rate					
Export rate (constant 1965					
won per US$)	281.7	263.5	263.5	278.2	250.0
Import rate (constant 1965					
won per US$)	288.5	273.7	277.5	296.1	262.6
Annual change in wholesale price					
index (%)	26.4	12.2	9.0	11.6	18.8
Real interest rate on domestic					
loans (%)	− 8.7	5.0	7.9	6.5	− 7.2

[a] Debt service ratio to total foreign exchange receipts.

burden was only about 3–5 percent of total current foreign exchange receipts during the first episode but increased to 14–16 percent by the second. No unique movement in the exchange rates is identifiable which might be related to the liberalization episodes. The annual rate of inflation measured by the wholesale price index was declining when the first liberalization package was put into effect, continued to decline until the year before the second episode, and increased thereafter. Real interest rate on domestic bank loans was very high during the first period, was reasonably high (9.5 percent) in the first year of the second episode, and declined to 7.2 percent in the following year.

We can conclude from these movements of major economic variables that both liberalization packages were formulated and implemented at a time when Korea's economic conditions, both internal and external, were very favorable. In fact, there are indications that the two liberalization packages were initially promoted by the government as a means of short-run domestic demand management, that is, to help contract rapid monetary expansion arising from the accumulation of foreign reserves. When the economic environment changed, it became much harder to promote liberalization programs. This was particularly true for the first liberalization episode.

Among many important economic indicators, the balance-of-payments situation seems to dominate decisions on whether to promote trade liberalization. The country's current account deficits, which had begun to gradually increase in 1966, jumped to US$440 million, or 28 percent of aggregate imports (of goods and services), in 1968 and continuously increased thereafter. Under these circumstances, the government suspended trade liberalization efforts, particularly the loosening of QRs on imports, and progress in liberalization consequently ceased after 1967.

In the second liberalization episode, the effort came to a halt in 1980, since current account deficits, which had started to increase in the latter half of 1979, increased sharply to US$5.3 billion (or 19 percent of aggregate imports) in the following year. This sudden deterioration in the balance of payments was, of course, largely attributable to the second oil shock and the consequent recessions in Western industrial countries. However, trade liberalization began to make progress again in 1981, even though the country's current account balance was still in large deficit. Current account deficits declined from their 1980 peak to US$4.6 billion in 1981, but were nevertheless considered to be very high, since the country's external debts had already reached US$27.4 billion by the end of 1980.

We suggest two important reasons why the liberalization continued after a temporary halt in 1980, despite a large balance-of-payments deficit. One is that the system of advance notices instituted in the second episode assured continuous progress in import liberalization as long as the advance notices were implemented as announced by the government. Since the system announces in advance the import items to be liberalized from QRs in the coming four years at the time of the announcement of the current year's liberalization program, the items included in the notice are almost automatically liberalized as scheduled unless really strong opposition is encountered. This made for a continuous progress in liberalization after 1980, because the advance notice items announced in 1978–9 were generally liberalized as announced, though a year behind schedule (because of the temporary halt in 1980).

The other reason is that Korea could no longer ignore the strong external pressures to increase import liberalization, since her export volume increased to over US$20 billion from 1981. In particular, Korea was under strong pressure from the US government to increase the degree of import liberalization because, even though her overall trade balance was still in deficit, her bilateral trade balance with the United States was in Korea's favor. Pressures were also applied by other countries and international organizations. Policymakers in Korea came to realize that continuous promotion of trade liberalization is an almost inevitable condition for expanding exports without concurrently increasing trade frictions with other countries.

Policy Implementation by Sector

In Korea, the overall index of trade liberalization has been mainly influenced by the status of import liberalization since the mid-1960s, because export trade was already liberalized to an almost maximum extent by that time. In measuring import liberalization, we have given more weight to the loosening of QRs than to the reduction of tariffs, because the former has been a more binding form of import control in the country than the latter. In addition, the actual tariff rate (actual tariff collections divided by the won value of total imports) has not changed noticeably since the early 1970s, although the average rate of legal tariffs has been gradually reduced over time. This reflects the fact that tariff exemptions and reductions have been granted not only for imports of intermediate goods for export but for various other purposes as well.

Since the import liberalization from QRs is particularly important in the Korean context, we examine here the status of such liberalization by major industrial group, on the basis of available data (as of the second half of 1982). The status cannot be compared with that in any previous period because data are only available for 1982. For this reason, the discussion based on 1982 data cannot be directly linked to either of the two liberalization episodes but should be considered to deal with the cumulative results of both.

As shown in table 6.3 the average rate of import liberalization from QRs, measured in terms of the ratio of unrestricted items to total tradeable items, was estimated to be 76.8 percent for all tradeable sectors in the second half of 1982. Such rates of import liberalization, however, varied by industrial group. Among the 11 industrial groups shown in the table, the beverages and tobacco sector is given the highest protection as of the second half of 1982. In other words, the import liberalization rate for that sector was 24 percent, the lowest of 11 major industrial groups. Next to this, the liberalization rates for transport equipment, processed foods, consumer durables, and machinery were relatively low, ranging from 41 percent to 63 percent. In contrast, the liberalization rates for construction materials, mining and energy, and intermediate products II were on the high side, exceeding 90 percent.

Table 6.3 Degree of import liberalization from quantitative restrictions by industry group, as of the second half of 1982

Industry group	Total number of items (A)[a]	Number of items liberalized (B)[a]	Liberalization rate (B/A)
Agriculture, forestry, and fishery	443	336	75.8
Mining and energy	168	159	94.5
Primary activities	611	495	80.9
Processed foods	475	238	50.1
Beverages and tobacco	54	13	24.1
Construction materials	131	130	99.2
Intermediate products I	758	646	85.2
Intermediate products II	2,506	2,303	91.9
Nondurable consumer goods	1,479	1,081	73.1
Consumer durables	313	177	56.5
Machinery	985	613	62.6
Transport equipment	212	86	40.6
Total manufacturing	6,913	5,287	76.5
All industries (tradeables)	7,524	5,782	76.8

[a] Based on the eight-digit CCCN classification.
Source: Korea Development Institute, 1982, p. 185

From these observations, it becomes clear that import liberalization made less progress in a broad category of consumption goods, and in machinery and transport equipment. Since the consumption goods included beverages and tobacco, processed foods, and consumer durables, the lower liberalization rates seem to reflect government efforts to restrict imports of inessential consumption goods, on the assumption that such imports would increase conspicuous consumption by high income brackets. The low rates for machinery and transport equipment indicate that these industries were still considered infant industries that required protection. In fact, the Korean government gave substantial preferences to the machinery and transport equipment industries, particularly in the 1970s, in line with its "program for heavy and chemical industry development," which began to be promoted in earnest in 1973. Trade protection was provided for the domestic production of these industries, and also preferential low interest rate loans and tax concessions for investment were available for such industries on a selective basis.

An apparent anomaly, that the liberalization rate for the agriculture, forestry, and fishery sector was nearly as high as the average for all

Table 6.4 Import liberalization from quantitative restrictions of manufactured goods produced by monopoly–oligopoly firms, as of the second half of 1982

Categories	Total tradeable items		Items restricted from import (B)	Liberalization rate (A – B)/A
	Eight-digit KSIC basis[a]	Eight-digit CCCN basis (A)		
Items produced by monopoly–oligopoly firms[b]	48	177	97	45.2
Items produced by other market-dominating firms[c]	18	35	9	74.3
Important items for the national economy, designated by Fair Trade Law	5	69	0	100.0
Subtotal	71	281	106	62.3
All manufacturing	n.a.	6,913	1,627	76.5

n.a., not available.
[a] KSIC, Korean Standard Industrial Classification.
[b] The monopoly and oligopoly firms as designated by the Economic Planning Board. They are defined to include a firm whose domestic supply exceeds a certain minimum amount and accounts for more than 50 percent of total domestic supply of the same commodity (or service), and also three or fewer firms whose market shares occupy more than 70 percent of the same commodity's total domestic supply (but excluding the small firms whose output is less than 5 percent of the total supply).
[c] Designated by the Economic Planning Board as the firms that are not included in the first row but are considered to have some market-dominating power.
Source: Korea Development Institute, 1982, p. 81

tradeable sectors, can be attributed to the special laws controlling imports of major agricultural products in addition to the government's semiannual or (since 1980) annual trade program.

Table 6.4 gives the import liberalization rates for the manufactured goods produced by monopoly and oligopoly firms in Korea. It can be seen from the table that the commodity items produced by the market-dominating firms were more heavily protected by the government than average manufactured goods. In particular, only about 45 percent of the items produced by monopoly–oligopoly firms were liberalized from QRs on imports in the second half of 1982, whereas the ratio for all manufactured products was nearly 77 percent. Since a detailed breakdown of the commodity items produced by such market-dominating firms is not available, we cannot be certain why this was so. We can only speculate that the large monopoly–oligopoly firms were better able than the other groups of firms to influence the policymakers to protect their interests.

Logically, import liberalization of items produced by monopoly–oligopoly firms should be much more significant than that of competitive firms' products, because the former will introduce competition to domestic markets where it has not so far existed. As a result of liberalization, the prices of monopoly–oligopoly items can be reduced to the level of "c.i.f. import price plus tariff levels," thereby reducing potential excess profits which could have been enjoyed by such firms. However, the loosening of QRs on the items produced by competitive firms may not lead to any further reduction in domestic prices as long as the tariffs on imports remain unchanged. Therefore priority should be given to loosening QRs on monopoly–oligopoly items in the promotion of import liberalization. But, as the Korean experience demonstrates, strong pressures from the industrial groups concerned may make it difficult to liberalize such imports.

Pattern of Sector Responses

An effective way of examining the responses of individual sectors over the course of liberalization would be to present the annual time series of major economic variables for the respective sectors. However, since such annual time series are not consistently available by sector, changes in major economic variables for the respective sectors over the whole periods of liberalization are presented in two tables. Table 6.5 shows percentage changes in real effective exchange rates for exports and imports, production, employment, net capital stock, labor productivity, profit rates, exports, and competing imports, all by sector, from 1966 to 1970, which includes the first liberalization episode, while table 6.6 gives the same data for 1975–80, which covers the second episode.

It can be seen from table 6.5 that the real exchange rates for almost all sectors other than light manufacturing declined during 1966–70 in terms of the number of won per US dollar. This simply reflects the higher rates of increase in domestic prices of many sectors than the corresponding foreign producer prices. Despite these declines in exchange rate for many sectors, domestic production increased in all sectors, although at widely varying rates. Employment also increased rapidly in all sectors other than petroleum and coal products and agriculture. Both net capital stock and labor productivity increased in all sectors without exception. Profit rates, however, declined in many sectors owing to the general economic recession in 1970. The ratios of exports to domestic production declined in eight out of a total of 16 sectors and increased in the remaining sectors. In contrast, the ratios of competing imports to domestic production increased in all but three sectors: chemical and allied products, petroleum and coal products, and nonmetallic mineral products.

Table 6.5 Sectoral changes in real effective exchange rates, production, employment, net capital stock, profit rate, exports, and competing imports during 1966–1970 (percent)

Sectors	Real effective exchange rates for Exports	Real effective exchange rates for Imports	Production (1975 prices)	Employment	Net capital stock (1975 prices)	Labor productivity (1975 prices)	Profit rate[a]	Exports[b]	Competing Imports[c]
Agriculture, forestry, and fishery	-24.5	-26.6	20.0	-4.2	24.5	25.2	n.a.	1.4	13.2
Mining	-16.2	-18.6	33.8	32.8	143.9	7.1	-15.3	-1.1	54.3
Processed food	7.0	4.0	123.8	34.9	67.9	66.0	2.9	-2.2	2.4
Textile products and apparel	12.5	9.2	111.5	34.0	147.5	57.9	-19.7	11.5	4.1
Lumber and wood products	15.4	12.1	119.2	33.9	80.3	63.7	85.4	-9.1	0.4
Pulp, paper, and allied products	8.4	5.3	92.9	38.3	95.2	39.4	11.2	-0.6	13.2
Chemical and allied products	9.2	6.0	333.7	117.7	144.6	99.3	1.3	2.4	-17.4
Petroleum and coal products	-3.9	-6.7	166.7	-9.7	208.6	195.5	0.9	2.1	-6.9
Nonmetallic mineral products	-3.1	-5.9	142.0	29.9	371.6	86.3	-11.4	1.9	-2.0
Iron and steel	-12.0	-14.5	193.6	124.4	160.5	31.0	-21.6	-4.6	13.8
Nonferrous metal	-15.8	-18.3	97.8	26.7	123.1	56.1	-8.7	-0.3	30.0
Metal products	-4.9	-7.7	81.2	34.8	99.1	34.4	-3.0	-3.0	5.4
General machinery	-16.3	-18.7	88.5	43.4	86.3	59.8	-10.2	-3.6	83.4
Electrical machinery	-1.7	-4.6	238.6	111.9	95.9	59.8	-5.6	12.3	29.7
Transport equipment	-8.8	-11.4	171.1	40.8	77.7	92.6		0.2	13.6
Other manufacturing	11.9	8.7	8.8	60.9	151.1	13.0	n.a.	22.1	1.8

n.a., not available.

[a] Percentage point change in the ratio of net profits to net worth.
[b] Percentage point change in the ratio of exports to domestic production.
[c] Percentage point change in the ratio of imports to domestic production of final goods.

Source: Kim, 1988, appendix tables 6a and 7a

Table 6.6 Sectoral changes in real effective exchange rates, production, employment, net capital stock, profit rate, exports, and competing imports during 1975–1980 (percent)

Sectors	Real effective exchange rates for		Production (1975 prices)	Employment	Net capital stock (1975 prices)	Labor productivity (1975 prices)	Profit rate[a]	Exports[b]	Competing Imports[c]
	Exports	Imports							
Agriculture, forestry, and fishery	−14.1	−14.5	−4.7	−14.3	109.6	11.1	n.a.	−0.1	0.2
Mining	−4.7	−5.1	0.1	10.9	113.6	−9.7	−23.1	−6.88	214.1
Processed food	35.36	34.8	208.1	15.1	77.9	167.7	−4.2	−5.4	−1.8
Textile products and apparel	28.9	28.5	79.4	3.9	83.5	72.7	−11.6	−0.3	−1.4
Lumber and wood products	11.0	10.6	39.3	23.9	58.8	12.4	−110.8	−12.1	1.8
Pulp, paper, and allied products	62.9	62.3	176.3	22.7	80.7	125.0	−13.4	0.4	−2.3
Chemical and allied products	30.6	30.3	125.7	36.1	65.5	65.8	−12.9	2.4	−13.5
Petroleum and coal products	9.3	8.9	63.7	15.9	6.3	41.4	−56.6	−4.4	2.2
Nonmetallic mineral products	29.0	28.6	133.9	37.9	97.3	69.6	−12.8	0.3	−1.0
Iron and steel	41.5	41.0	218.0	47.7	357.8	115.1	−4.9	6.6	−14.3
Nonferrous metal	40.4	39.8	206.9	81.8	429.8	69.0	−17.5	5.6	10.6
Metal products	51.6	51.0	248.2	56.1	260.9	123.0	−20.9	16.6	2.4
General machinery	42.3	41.7	337.6	92.2	414.3	127.7	−78.7	−2.6	−68.0
Electrical machinery	57.1	56.5	296.4	77.9	206.3	122.8	−39.6	−3.5	−8.2
Transport equipment	60.8	60.2	185.9	7.1	165.9	167.1	−30.4	9.8	−16.1
Other manufacturing	30.7	30.2	134.2	56.9	156.2	49.2	−15.4	2.8	0.2

n.a., not available.
[a] Percentage point change in the ratio of net profits to net worth.
[b] Percentage point change in the ratio of exports to domestic production.
[c] Percentage point change in the ratio of imports to domestic production of final goods.

Source: Kim, 1988, appendix tables 6b and 7b

From 1975 to 1980 the real effective exchange rates for all but two sectors (agriculture, forestry, and fishery and mining) increased, as shown in table 6.6, in contrast with the earlier period. This reflects the fact that the government allowed a relatively more rapid depreciation of the won during this period. Both domestic production and employment increased rapidly in all sectors with the exception of agriculture, forestry, and fishery. As in the previous period, net capital stock and labor productivity also increased rapidly in all but the mining sector, which unusually marked a 10 percent decline in its labor productivity. However, profit rates for all sectors showed a large decline during this period mainly because of the second oil shock and the ensuing worldwide recession of 1979–80. As in the previous period the ratio of exports to domestic production declined in eight out of 16 sectors, mainly reflecting a structural change in Korean industry. The ratio of competing imports to domestic production declined in nine out of a total of 16 tradeable sectors, in contrast with the increase in all but three exceptional sectors during the previous period. The increase in the number of sectors with negative growth of import ratio might be attributable to the relatively more rapid depreciation of the won compared with the earlier period.

These observations of sectoral changes in major economic variables during the two periods seem to suggest that the liberalization programs did not have much impact on domestic industries, at any rate no noticeable negative effects at the level of 16-sector classification. Firstly, employment and domestic production in almost all sectors were unharmed by the liberalizations during both periods. The exceptional decline of employment in the agricultural sector during both periods was more the result of industrial structural transformation than that of trade liberalization, while the employment decline in the petroleum and coal products sector during the earlier period only reflects the substitution of labor by capital, resulting from the relative contraction of the labor-intensive coal subsector within the same sector.

Secondly, the declines in profit rates of many sectors observed during both periods do not seem to be directly influenced by liberalization, since production, employment, and capital stock generally increased over the liberalization episode. As already suggested, they resulted mainly from recession in the last year of each episode (see tables 5.18 and 5.19).

Thirdly, the trade liberalization could have contributed to increasing the ratio of competing imports to domestic production by sector. A comparison of the changes in import ratios with the changes in real effective exchange rates for the two periods, however, indicates that the former has been more influenced by the changes in real effective exchange rates than by import liberalization, at least, at the level of 16-sector classification.

Finally, there is no indication from the above observations on sectoral changes in major economic variables that any particular sector deviates from others sufficiently to require special consideration in future liberalization.

Imports and Unemployment

Although the increase of competing imports can be taken as a major indicator of the extent of liberalization, the changes in sectoral ratios of competing imports to domestic production during the two periods of liberalization could not be directly attributed to the liberalization episodes, as discussed above. At the level of 16-sector classification, the changes in import ratios could be better explained by the changes in real effective exchange rates. In addition, there were no sectoral indicators of trade liberalization to be correlated with the changes in sectoral import ratios.

For this reason, an attempt is made to estimate the actual imports of specific commodity items liberalized from QRs in each episode and to compare them with annual aggregate imports. Table 6.7 presents the estimates of imports of those commodity items liberalized by the first episode over the period 1963–9, while table 6.8 gives similar data on the items liberalized by the second episode over the 1976–81 period.

The two tables show some tendency of those imports liberalized from QRs to accelerate in the same year and the year following the liberalization. Although the imports of items liberalized in the first half of 1978 and in the same period of 1979 did not follow this tendency, the increasing rates of imports of those items liberalized in other periods were generally much higher than the growth rate of aggregate imports in one or both of the first

Table 6.7 Actual imports of commodity items liberalized from quantitative restrictions in 1965–1967 (million current US dollars)

Liberalized commodity items	1963	1964	1965	1966	1967	1968	1969
Items liberalized in the first half of 1965	14.8	16.3 (10.3)	19.5 (19.1)	33.9 (74.4)	53.7 (58.3)	n.a.	n.a.
Items liberalized in the second half of 1965 and the first half of 1966	n.a.	16.3	17.0 (4.3)	34.4 (102.1)	37.8 (9.9)	70.7 (87.2)	n.a.
Items liberalized in the second half of 1966 and the first half of 1967	n.a.	n.a.	6.8	19.5 (187.0)	26.2 (34.0)	44.2 (69.1)	43.4 (− 1.9)
Items liberalized in the second half of 1967	n.a.	n.a.	105.2	179.7 (70.8)	276.0 (53.6)	372.8 (35.1)	449.8 (20.6)
Total commodity imports (c.i.f.)	497.0	364.9 (− 26.6)	415.9 (14.0)	679.9 (63.5)	908.9 (33.7)	1,322.0 (45.5)	1,650.0 (24.8)

n.a., not available.
Figures in parentheses indicate the percentage change over the preceding year.
Source: Ministry of Finance, Trade Statistics Yearbook, various issues

Table 6.8 Actual imports of commodity items liberalized from quantitative restrictions in 1978–1979 (million current US dollars)

Liberalized commodity items	1976	1977	1978	1979	1980	1981
Items liberalized in the first half of 1978	136.9	189.9 (38.7)	243.3 (28.2)	317.4 (30.4)	303.6 (− 4.4)	n.a.
Items liberalized in the second half of 1978	194.3	212.7 (30.1)	373.2 (47.7)	721.1 (93.2)	454.3 (− 37.0)	n.a.
Items liberalized in the second half of 1979	n.a.	552.6	838.2 (51.7)	1,049.1 (25.2)	1,002.0 (− 4.5)	1,027.7 (2.6)
Total commodity imports (c.i.f.)	8,405.1	10,523.1 (25.2)	14,491.4 (37.7)	19,100.1 (31.8)	21,598.1 (13.1)	24,299.1 (10.5)

n.a., not available.
Figures in parentheses indicate the percentage change over the preceding year.
Source: Ministry of Finance, *Trade Statistics Yearbook*, various issues

two years following liberalization. It should be noted, however, that the imports of those items liberalized had been significantly large even before the formal loosening of QRs. The reason is that even the import-restricted items could be imported with government approval for use in export production and other activities.

Since it is clear that the loosening of QRs tends to accelerate the imports of these particular commodity items, in the first two years at least we may expect domestic production, employment, and business ventures to feel some adverse impact. To examine such impact, table 6.9 provides some data on the number of establishments, employment, and production of the manufacturing industries whose products were liberalized from QRs in 1978–9. These data are derived from the results of a mining and manufacturing survey conducted by the Economic Planning Board by matching the commodity classification for trade administration (that is, CCCN codes) with the Korean Standard Industrial Classification (KSIC) codes used in the survey. Similar data for those items liberalized in 1965–7 could not be obtained, mainly because of the lack of detailed industrial survey data for the earlier years.

Contrary to expectation, the data do not provide clear evidence of an adverse impact of import increases on domestic industries over the 1976–80 period. According to the table, the number of establishments producing those import items liberalized in 1978–9 showed a continuous increase except in 1980 when the total number of manufacturing establishments in Korea declined owing to severe recession. There are also no discernible effects of import increases on employment and production during the 1976–80 period.

This negligible impact of import increase on domestic production activities may result from two factors. One is the possibility of measure-

Table 6.9 Number of establishments, employment, and production of the manufacturing industries whose products were liberalized from quantitative restrictions in 1978–1979

	1976	1977	1978	1979	1980
Number of establishments (thousands)					
Items liberalized in the first half of 1978	1.7	1.9 (13.4)	2.4 (22.9)	2.4 (2.9)	n.a.
Items liberalized in the second half of 1978	2.8	2.9 (3.3)	3.2 (11.2)	3.6 (13.9)	n.a.
Items liberalized in the first half of 1979		4.7	5.2 (10.6)	5.7 (10.0)	5.7 (− 0.7)
Total manufacturing establishments	26.6	28.3 (6.5)	31.7 (12.0)	33.6 (5.9)	32.6 (− 0.3)
Employment (thousands)					
Items liberalized in the first half of 1978	179.0	211.3 (18.0)	235.3 (11.3)	231.9 (− 1.4)	n.a.
Items liberalized in the second half of 1978	301.0	313.0 (4.0)	342.8 (9.5)	343.7 (0.3)	n.a.
Items liberalized in the first half of 1979		364.6	412.7 (13.2)	407.9 (− 1.2)	380.8 (− 6.6)
Total manufacturing employment	1,779.0	1,999.8 (11.2)	2,195.0 (9.8)	2,196.0 (0.0)	2,098.9 (− 4.4)
Production (billion current won)					
Items liberalized in the first half of 1978	1,173.0	1,491.6 (27.2)	2,149.7 (44.1)	2,701.9 (25.7)	n.a.
Items liberalized in the second half of 1978	1,334.9	2,168.5 (62.4)	2,564.0 (18.2)	3,130.8 (22.1)	n.a.
Items liberalized in the first half of 1979		2,640.8	3,698.7 (40.1)	4,698.6 (27.2)	5,598.5 (19.2)
Total manufacturing production	11,869.8	15,695.6 (32.2)	21,490.8 (36.9)	27,087.1 (26.0)	36,817.3 (35.9)

n.a., not available.
Figures in parentheses indicate the percentage change over the preceding year.
Source: Economic Planning Board, Report on Mining and Manufacturing Survey, various years

ment error. That is, there could have been some mismatching of the commodity items liberalized from QRs (classified by CCCN) with detailed industrial subsectors based on KSIC since it is almost impossible to make a one-to-one matching between CCCN and KSIC codes. The other factor may simply reflect the success of the Korean government's deliberately gradual and cautious approach to liberalization to minimize adverse impacts on domestic industry.

If the latter hypothesis is correct, the negligible impact would indicate that there could not have been any significant transitory losses due to trade liberalization in Korea. Such losses are in general assumed to equal the reduction in production due to less than full use of resources, but there is no clear evidence of any adverse impact of import increase on domestic production and employment in Korea. However, if there were statistical errors in measurement, it will simply be impossible to estimate short-run losses due to trade liberalization, given the two different systems of commodity and industrial classifications used for the trade administration and the industrial survey respectively.

Impact on the Government Budget

Government revenues would be expected to increase if the liberalization involved a change from QRs to tariffs. If the liberalization was in the form of tariff reductions, the revenues might or might not increase depending upon the effect of tariff reductions on imports. However, government expenditures are expected to increase if liberalization causes unemployment, assuming that there is a system of unemployment compensation in the country concerned.

As already stated, Korea's trade liberalization during the first episode (1965–7) mainly took the form of loosening of QRs. The average rate of legal tariffs weighted by the value of 1975 production therefore did not change much during 1964–7, but showed a minor increase in 1968 from 53 percent to 59 percent and then remained almost unchanged until 1970 (see table 3.6). The actual tariff rate, which was obtained by dividing actual tariff collections by the won value of c.i.f. imports, however, showed an increase from 8 percent to 10 percent between 1964 and 1965 but remained at 8–9 percent until 1970 (see table 3.5). This minor change in actual tariff rate might have resulted from changes in the commodity composition of imports. Since the average rate of legal tariffs did not change much during 1965–7, the loosening of QRs should have increased imports, thereby contributing to increasing government tariff revenues. It is not possible, however, to estimate the exact amount of the increase in government revenues since the increase in imports due to the liberalization is not known.

The second liberalization episode (1978–9), as we have seen, involved both the loosening of QRs and tariff reductions, although the two measures were taken separately by two different ministries (the MCI and the MOF). As a result of the tariff reform in early 1979, the average rate of legal tariffs (weighted by domestic production) declined from 41.3 percent in 1978 to 34.4 percent (see table 3.6). The average rate of actual tariffs also declined from 8.9 to 7.4 percent between the two years. This suggests that imports should have increased as a result of both the loosening of QRs and the tariff reductions. Some increases in government revenues caused by the increased imports, however, should have been offset by the lowering of legal tariffs. Since the effects of the liberalization measures on imports could not be estimated, it is not possible to derive any reliable estimate of the effects on government revenues of the second episode.

However, the government has not yet introduced any system of unemployment compensation in the country. Moreover, there was no clear evidence of an increase in unemployment caused by the trade liberalization which was undertaken during the latter period. This indicates that government expenditures were not directly affected by the two liberalization episodes.

In sum, the liberalization episodes should have definitely caused a net increase in government revenues, thereby contributing to increasing the budgetary surplus in the earlier period and to reducing budgetary deficits in the latter period. They did not, at least, create a new source of budgetary deficits and did not necessitate additional tax collections to meet the new deficits.

Conclusions – Inferences

What light can the Korean experience shed on the timing and sequencing of trade liberalization policies? Some major issues among many that are relevant to this question have emerged from the discussion; inferences from these are analyzed here.

The Approach: One-stage or Multistage?

The Korean experience suggests that a gradual multistage approach to liberalization is preferable to a one-stage liberalization. In a way, the loosening of QRs in 1967 by reforming the system of government trade administration was similar to a one-stage liberalization in the sense that the degree of trade liberalization made a sudden jump by that measure but thereafter made no further progress for a long time. However, the trade liberalization program of 1978–9, which introduced the system of advance notices, was following a gradual multistage approach. As already suggested, the former liberalization efforts faltered after 1967 while the latter made slow but continuous progress even after 1979. Although the gradual multistage approach taken in the promotion of trade liberalization during the later period was not the sole reason for the continuance of the program after 1979, it seems that it definitely conributed to the continuous promotion of liberalization in the 1980s.

One should also consider that given the high levels of protection on domestic industries existing in Korea during the 1960s and 1970s, any substantial trade liberalization by a one-stage approach would have been almost impossible. Strong pressures from political and business groups could have prevented implementation of such a drastic program. If such a program had been carried out by a strong government, many domestic production activities would undoubtedly have been substantially disrupted. It therefore seems that the gradual multistage approach was effectively the only feasible option.

Length of the Process

Once we accept that a gradual approach is preferable to the one-stage liberalization, what should be the appropriate length? In view of the Korean experience of the late 1970s, a period of three to five years is considered the appropriate length of time for the formulation and implementation of a liberalization plan (or program). This does not imply, however, that a country's trade liberalization would be completed by a three-year or a five-year plan for liberalization. The country should actually adopt a system of three- to five-year rolling plans, as practiced in Korea's import liberalization from QRs in the late 1970s and the 1980s. In other words, after reviewing the progress made so far, the government should prepare and announce each year a new five-year liberalization plan, including both the program to be implemented in the first year and advance notices for the following four years, in the light of changing economic and industrial conditions. This system of a rolling plan seems important not only for introducing flexibility to the plan but also for firmly renewing the government commitment for liberalization. Since the advance notices generally provide the business sector with time to prepare for future liberalization, the implementation of an annual liberalization program based on the plan would substantially reduce potential adverse impacts on domestic industries.

Even if the trade liberalization is implemented on the basis of a three- to five-year rolling plan, the appropriate speed of liberalization should be determined by particular conditions prevailing within and outside the respective economy. In effect, there can be no a priori rule about the speed of liberalization. Theoretically, the liberalization should be expedited to the extent that domestic welfare losses due to liberalization-induced unemployment do not exceed the possible welfare gains arising from the availability of lower-priced imports and efficiency gains in domestic industries. In fact, however, the Korean experience suggests that it is not actually feasible to set a rule regarding the speed.

Quantitative Restrictions and Tariffs

A separate stage for replacing QRs by tariffs may be required for smooth progress of trade liberalization. In the 1960s and the 1970s, trade protection by high tariffs in Korea was considered redundant for many commodity groups. For instance, many commodity groups restricted from import by QRs were still subject to a high rate of legal tariffs. For this reason, the loosening of QRs alone would not immediately flood the domestic market with foreign products. It was desirable, however, to loosen QRs first and then to move on to the gradual reduction of tariffs to reduce resistance from industrial sectors and to minimize transitory losses.

Export Promotion

A separate stage of export promotion was almost inevitable in Korea. Since the balance of payments had been in chronic deficit in the early 1960s, Korea had first to promote exports to improve the current account balance in the face of declining foreign assistance. When the country gained some confidence in export expansion and the balance of payments was significantly improved, Korea began to promote the first package of import liberalization in the mid-1960s. It therefore seems that a separate stage of export promotion preceding the implementation of an import liberalization program is desirable in a country like Korea where the balance of payments is in chronic deficit. In any case, some program to increase exports should definitely accompany the promotion of import liberalization since that policy cannot be sustained for long without the growth of exports.

Sectoral Discrimination

When a gradual process of import liberalization is pursued, uniform treatment of all sectors will be almost impracticable, however equitable it may be. Since the status of industrial development and industrial competitiveness are expected to vary widely by sector, uniform treatment may simply eliminate scope even for infant industry protection. In Korea, the government usually preferred to examine the conditions of each industry for discriminatory treatment of sectors. In fact, the Korean government has been very reluctant to relinquish its discretionary power to select favored industries for trade protection. The Korean experience also suggests that the business sector's pressures against liberalization would be much greater when sectors are treated uniformly, because uniform treatment affects all sectors whereas discriminatory treatment reduces the number of sectors adversely affected.

In a nonuniform process of import liberalization, the Korean experience illustrates the difficulty of establishing satisfactory criteria for discrimination among sectors or activities. The Korean government had at least some indicators of each activity's competitiveness, including nominal protection, export and import ratios to domestic production, and so on. It could therefore, in principle, give priority to the import liberalization of those activities which were judged to be reasonably competitive in international markets.

The Korean experience shows that some additional factors should be considered in selecting criteria for sectoral discrimination. First, separate treatment is desirable for the products of the large monopoly and oligopoly firms that can usually mobilize strong pressure on government policy-makers. Except for products designated as those of infant industries, the products of such market-dominating firms should be made the first target of import liberalization. Second, import of intermediate products, capital goods, and essential consumption goods should in general be liberalized before that of inessential or luxury consumption goods (such as cosmetics, liquor, cigarettes). This kind of sequencing of trade liberalization by commodity groups may temporarily increase the effective protection rates on inessential goods relative to those on other goods. Such sequencing seems quite important, however, to assure smooth progress in trade liberalization in the Korean context. The Korean experience indicates that the early import liberalization of luxury goods tended to give a distorted picture of liberalization to the general public who were becoming increasingly conscious of the distributional aspects of government policy. Thus it tended to create public antagonism toward further liberalization.

Circumstances for Introducing Liberalization

The Korean evidence suggests that, for successful introduction of liberalization policy, a country's current balance on external transactions should not be in large deficit and should be expected to improve in the foreseeable future. This suggestion may not apply to other developing countries, since it is not based on an objective macroeconomic reasoning but on actual observations of the decision-making behavior of the Korean government. In any case, the Korean government has not promoted import liberalization actively when the country's balance of payments has been in difficulty. Korea was in a better position to improve her balance of payments when external economic conditions were generally favorable. In this sense, the international economic environment is also important to the introduction of a liberalization policy. In other words, Korea could easily promote trade liberalization when world trade volume was expanding rapidly and when the terms of trade for the country were improving. It should be emphasized that the two liberalization episodes of Korea were both introduced in these kinds of economic circumstances (see discussions in chapter 4 and also the first section of this chapter). In addition, one should note that the existence of a large foreign debt in Korea made the policymakers more cautious than otherwise in promoting trade liberalization in the 1980s. The country could, however, continuously promote the liberalization, since the debt service burden was still within manageable bounds.

Monetary Policy

A liberalization policy can be better sustained when the country in question is implementing an economic stabilization policy than when it is pursuing an expansionary policy. It can actually be implemented as part of an overall economic stabilization policy, as in Korea since 1979. When the country is pursuing an expansionary policy, domestic inflation and the increasing current account deficits resulting from that policy may soon prevent the continuation of the liberalization policy, as was the case in Korea in the late 1960s. The role of exchange rate policy in the promotion of trade liberalization should also be taken into account. That is, the liberalization policy can only be sustained under a realistic effective exchange rate while it cannot be sustained for long under an overvalued rate. Both the discontinuance of Korea's first liberalization program after 1967 and the continuous progress made in the liberalization program after 1979 well support this important link between trade liberalization and the effective exchange rate. Finally, one should add that the realistic exchange rate is more easily maintained under price stability than under inflationary conditions, as is well demonstrated by the Korean experience of the last three decades.

References

Major Statistical Sources

Bank of Korea, *Economic Statistics Yearbook*, various issues.
Bank of Korea, *Financial Statements Analysis*, various issues.
Bank of Korea (1966, 1970, 1975, 1980) *Korea's Input–Output Tables*.
Bank of Korea (1981) *Monthly Economic Statistics*, July.
Bank of Korea (1982) *National Income in Korea*.
Bank of Korea (1982) *Compilatory Report on 1980 Input–Output Tables*.
Bank of Korea (1984) *National Income Accounts*.
Bank of Korea (1984) *Quarterly GNP*.
Economic Planning Board (Korea), *Korea Statistical Yearbook*, various issues.
Economic Planning Board (Korea) (1970, 1983) *Annual Report on the Economically Active Population Survey*.
Economic Planning Board (Korea) (1975, 1977, 1981, 1982, 1983) *Report on Mining and Manufacturing Survey*.
Economic Planning Board (Korea) (1982, 1983, 1984) *Major Statistics of Korean Economy*.
Ministry of Commerce and Industry (Korea), *Semi-annual (or Annual) Trade Program*, various issues.
Ministry of Finance (Korea), *Tariff Schedules of Korea*, various years.
Ministry of Finance (Korea), *Trade Statistics Yearbook*, various issues.
US Department of Commerce, *Survey of Current Business*, various issues.

Other References

Choi, Kwang, ed. (1983) *Facts and Figures on the Public Sector in Korea* (in Korean). Seoul: KDI Press.
Choo, Hak Chung, Yong-suk Kim, and Choo-hyun Yoon (1982) *Estimate of Korea's Industrial Capital Stock for 1960–1977* (in Korean). Seoul: KDI Press.
Crowther, Geoffrey (1957) *Balances and Imbalances of Payments*. Boston, MA: Harvard University, Graduate School of Business Administration.
Denison, Edward F. (1979) *Accounting for Slower Economic Growth: The United States in the 1970's*. Washington, DC: Brookings Institution.
Frank, Charles R. Jr, Kwang Suk Kim, and Larry E. Westphal (1975) *Foreign Trade Regimes and Economic Development: South Korea*. New York: National Bureau of Economic Research.
Halevi, Nadav (1971) "An empirical test of the balance of payments stages hypothesis." *Journal of International Economics*. 1(1), February, 103–17.

Huh, Jai Young, ed. (1972) *World Economic Indicators for Recent Years* (in Korean). Seoul: Konsulpyongnon-sa.

Jones, Lorey P. and Il Sakong (1980) *Government, Business, and Entrepreneurship in Economic Development: the Korean Case.* Cambridge, MA: Harvard University, Council on East Asian Studies.

Kim, In Chul (1984) *Foreign Debt Problems of Developing Countries and Korea's Debt Management* (in Korean). Seoul: KDI Press.

Kim, Kwang Suk (1975) "Outward-looking industrialization strategy: the case of Korea." In Wontack Hong and Anne O. Krueger, eds, *Trade and Development in Korea.* Seoul: KDI Press.

Kim, Kwang Suk (1988) "The timing and sequencing of trade liberalization policy: the case of Korea," unpublished paper. Available from the Brazil Department, World Bank, Washington, DC.

Kim, Kwang Suk and Joon Kyung Park (1985) *Sources of Economic Growth in Korea: 1963–1982.* Seoul: KDI Press.

Korea Development Institute (1981) *Collected Materials on Economic Stabilization Measures (I)* (in Korean). Seoul: KDI Press.

Korea Development Institute (1982) *Basic Issues of Korea's Industrial Policy and Proposals to Reform Supporting Measures* (in Korean). Seoul: KDI Press.

Lee, Kyu Uck, Jai-hyong Lee, and Choo-hoon Kim (1984) "Market structure in the Korean manufacturing industry" (in Korean). *Korea Development Review*, 6(1), March, 19–37.

Mason, Edward S., Mahn, Je Kim, Dwight H. Perkins, Kwang Suk Kim, and David C. Cole (1980) *The Economic and Social Modernization of the Republic of Korea.* Cambridge, MA: Harvard University, Council on East Asian Studies.

Nam, Chong Hyun (1981) "Trade, industrial policies and the structure of protection in Korea." In Wontack Hong and Lawrence B. Krause, eds, *Trade and Growth of the Advanced Developing Countries in the Pacific Basin.* Seoul: KDI Press.

Park, Fun Koo (1983) "Occupational wage differentials in Korea" (in Korean). *Korea Development Review* 5(4), December, 22–48.

Westphal, Larry E. and Kwang Suk Kim (1977) *Industrial Policy and Development in Korea.* Washington, DC: World Bank, Staff Working Paper no. 263.

Part II

The Philippines

Geoffrey Shepherd
University of Sussex, England
The World Bank, Washington, D.C.

Florian Alburo
University of the Philippines
Deputy Minister of Economic Planning, the Philippines

Contents

List of Figures

List of Tables

Acknowledgments

The authors have many people to thank. It is always difficult to reconstruct history, and it could not have been done in this study without the help of the many businessmen, academics, and current and former government officials who were kind enough to talk to us. In addition, we are particularly grateful to the Philippine Institute for Development Studies (PIDS), specifically to Filologo Pante, its President, and to Mario Feranil. They helped set up the study as a genuinely collaborative effort between the World Bank and Filipino researchers, and subsequently provided important intellectual and logistical support, especially in 1985 when most of the fieldwork was carried out. We are also grateful to the moral support provided by Geoffrey Oldham, Director of the Science Policy Research Unit (SPRU, University of Sussex), during the period (up to 1986) when Geoffrey Shepherd was a fellow at the Unit. Aurea Crisostomo, Danny Uy, and Bienvenido Oplas, Jr provided substantial and enthusiastic research assistance. Leila Garcia (PIDS) and Terrie Russell (SPRU) provided much secretarial assistance. We also thank Philippa Shepherd for the editing which helped improve the final manuscript.

1

Introduction

After the Republic of the Philippines achieved independence in 1946, its government instituted, over the space of a few years, a tight control over the allocation of foreign exchange. This substantially increased the level of protection to import-competing activities and introduced a new discrimination against exports. Ever since, the debate on protection and liberalization has continued in the Philippines. There have been two major attempts to liberalize imports: the foreign exchange decontrol of 1960–2, and the import liberalization that began in 1981, was aborted in 1983, but was resumed in 1986. There have also been several measures since the late 1960s to promote nontraditional exports. However, since the successfully executed foreign exchange decontrol, there have been various partial reversals of liberalization policy and one cannot speak of any sustained process of trade liberalization.

Several studies have provided convincing evidence of the resource misallocation costs of the Philippines' protective regime in the 1960s and 1970s. Notable among these are Valdepeñas (1970) on protection and the development of manufacturing, Power and Sicat (1971) on industrialization and trade, Baldwin (1975) on the foreign trade regime, Bautista et al. (1979) on industrial promotion policies, and David (1983) on economic policies and Philippine agriculture. The present study takes these resource misallocation costs as a starting point; the initial assumption of the study is that the considerable protection that some sectors have received in the Philippines has led to costs well in excess of any possible benefits from protection, and that trade liberalization measures will benefit the economy at the very least in the longer run.

The major objective is to study the attempts that have been made in the Philippines to liberalize the trade regime and to see whether these contain any lessons, either for the Philippines or for other countries. Why and how were specific liberalization measures planned? Why and how were they modified or aborted? What kind of short- and medium-term impact did these measures have on the economy?

The study concentrates on the period 1960–83, in particular on three "episodes" of apparent trade liberalization, each terminated by an at least partial reversal of the liberalization measures. The first of these was the foreign exchange control of 1960–2, not completed on the export side until 1965. Substantial foreign exchange controls were completely and quickly abandoned and partially replaced by higher tariffs. This was an unambiguous and fully implemented liberalization episode, partially reversed by some measures introduced towards the end of the decade.

The second "episode" consists of some measures to promote nontraditional exports at the beginning of the 1970s at the same time that a real effective devaluation of the peso was achieved. Nontraditional exports (largely of products assembled from imported inputs) did indeed grow throughout the 1970s. It is questionable how far this was truly a liberalization episode, however, since trade policies do not appear to have been a major factor in this growth. Nonetheless, the episode has generally been perceived in the Philippines as a deliberate strategy that has often gone under the title of "export-oriented industrialization." The episode also contains lessons about the limited effects of export promotion policies when strong import protection policies are not altered. While the export promotion measures remained in force through the 1970s, trade policy became increasingly confused after the mid-1970s as distortions increased among import-substituting activities and traditional exporting activities.

The third and final liberalization episode concerns the so-called Tariff Reform Program: the planned reduction of the level and dispersion of effective protection from tariffs and the elimination of quantitative import restrictions in a phased program beginning in 1981. This program was largely derailed after a massive balance-of-payments crisis in 1983. 1983 marks the end, more or less, of the period covered in this study.

Political and economic crisis in 1983 signaled the beginning of a period of enforced economic austerity and stagnation without parallel in the Philippines' post-war history. The crisis also started a chain of events which led to the end of the 20-year regime of Ferdinand Marcos in early 1986. In 1986 the new government of Corazon Aquino resumed the aborted trade liberalization with a program to eliminate many residual import controls. This latest phase of policy reform falls outside the scope of the present study. Indeed, given the depth of the economic crisis of 1983–4 and the 1986 change in political regime, this most recent phase is probably best viewed as a new episode. Thus, this study cannot draw conclusions about the overall progress of trade liberalization in the 1980s.

Chapter 2 provides a background to the rest of the study by examining some of the political and economic factors that have helped shape Philippine trade policy. These factors include the country's physical endowment and its colonial and more recent history.

In chapter 3 the long-term evolution of Philippine trade policy since independence is analyzed – description being supported with statistics where possible – in order to identify the existence, nature, and timing of specific "episodes" of liberalization (and protection).

In chapters 4–6 we examine the three trade liberalization episodes that more or less opened the decade, respectively, of the 1960s, 1970s, and 1980s. Each chapter describes the economic and political circumstances that precipitated and accompanied the episode, the trade and nontrade policies characterizing the episode, and the short- to medium-term impact of changing trade policies on economic performance. We also examine how each episode came to an end. Appendix 1, "A Summary of the Three Liberalization Episodes," provides a quick reference guide to the content, circumstances, and outcomes of each of these episodes.

In chapter 7 we look at the way the tradeables-producing sectors of the economy have reacted over the post-war period to changing trade policies. Finally, in chapter 8 we summarize some of the main points about the apparent success and failure of each episode, underline the lack of long-term political commitment to trade liberalization policies in the Philippines, and draw some of the inferences for the timing and sequencing of such policies that may be relevant to trade liberalization in other countries.

2

Factors Shaping Trade Policy

Since the decontrol of foreign exchange in the early 1960s Philippine trade policy has been neither the most protectionist nor the most liberal among developing countries. (World Bank, 1987, classifies Philippine trade policy as being on average "moderately inward oriented" between 1963 and 1985.) Nonetheless there was some trade liberalization. Superficially, there was a classic sequence in which the form of protection was changed from nontariff barriers to tariffs in a first stage, exports were promoted in a second, and tariffs were reduced in a third. In spite of this, Philippine governments have shown little political commitment to sustained trade liberalization: each liberalization was substantially reversed.

What are the national characteristics that help explain the particular choice of trade policies in the Philippines? In this chapter we will seek some answers in the structure of the country's economy, its history, and its economic institutions. (On the political, social, and institutional framework, see also Power and Sicat, 1971, chapter 3.) This analysis is tentative and incomplete. For all that, it is important: the lack of progress of trade reform in the Philippines above all reflects national economic and political factors, rather than failures in the design or implementation of trade policy.

The Philippine Economy and its Resources

In the 1950s the Philippine economy was thought to have good development prospects compared with other countries of the region. Between 1950 and 1983 gross domestic product (GDP) (at 1972 prices) grew at 5.8 percent a year, but since population was growing rapidly, GDP per capita grew at only 2.6 percent (data from the National Economic and Development Authority, NEDA). Relative to the other countries of the region (the countries with which the Philippines most readily compares itself) this was a poor performance: from 1965 to 1983 Thailand, Indonesia, and Malaysia achieved gross national product (GNP) growth rates of between 4 and

Table 2.1 The Philippines and its neighbors: some economic development indicators

Country	Population in 1983 (millions)	Area (× 1,000 km²)	GNP per capita in 1983 (US$)	Average annual growth rate 1965–83 (%)	Average annual population growth rates 1973–83 (%)	Secondary enrollment as percentage of age group	Higher education enrollment as percentage of population aged 20–4
						Education enrollment rates, 1982	
Indonesia	156	1,919	560	5.0	2.3	33	4
Philippines	52	300	760	2.9	2.7	64	27
Thailand	49	514	820	4.3	2.3	29	22
Malaysia	15	330	1,860	4.5	2.4	49	5
Korea, Republic of	40	98	2,010	6.7	1.6	89	24
Hong Kong	5	1	6,000	6.2	2.5	67	11
Singapore	3	1	6,620	7.8	1.3	66	11
Middle-income oil importing economies (average)	n.a.	n.a.	1,060	3.5	2.2	48	15

n.a., not available.
Source: World Bank, 1985b, tables 1, 19, 21, and 25

5 percent, while Hong Kong and Singapore exceeded 6 percent (table 2.1). The figure for the Philippines was 2.9 percent. In a broader comparison with developing countries, however, the Philippine growth performance has been above average.

Natural Resources

The Philippines is a large island economy well endowed in natural resources. The mainstay of the economy has remained the primary sector, but the economy is also prone to natural disaster – flood and cyclone – which has its effect both on agriculture and on human lives. Metal mining (principally copper) has also become an important export activity since World War II. The economy remains dependent on energy imports, and efforts to find oil have proven unsuccessful.

Agriculture's share in domestic product has progressively declined (table 2.2). The principal food products are rice, corn, livestock, and fishing. The principal commercial exports are coconut products, sugar, and forest products (see table 2.3 for principal crops produced). The share of rice in agricultural output consistently fell until around 1970. The share of agricultural exports grew strongly until the 1970s when sugar and forest product exports flagged, though this was partly made up for by growing exports of coconut oil.

Table 2.2 Industry distribution of domestic product, 1946–1983 (percent at 1972 prices)

	Agriculture, fishery, and forestry	Mining	Manufacturing	Other industry	Services	Total
Net domestic product						
1946	44.3	–	4.8	11.1	39.8	100.0
1950	38.8	1.0	12.5	8.4	39.3	100.0
1955	37.3	1.2	15.1	5.2	41.3	100.0
1960	34.4	1.3	17.5	4.6	42.2	100.0
1965	34.3	1.2	17.2	5.8	41.5	100.0
1967	33.4	1.3	18.3	5.4	41.6	100.0
Gross domestic product						
1967	30.1	1.5	23.6	5.1	39.7	100.0
1970	29.2	2.2	24.4	4.2	40.1	100.0
1975	26.7	2.1	25.3	6.6	39.2	100.0
1980	25.6	2.4	25.0	8.7	38.3	100.0
1983	24.8	2.0	25.1	8.9	39.2	100.0

–, negligible.
Source: Alburo and Shepherd, 1988, appendix table E.1.1

Table 2.3 Shares of major crops in total gross value of crops, 1950–1980 (percent)

	1950	1960	1970	1980
Crops for the domestic market				
Palay (rice)	51.3	34.8	25.4	22.0
Corn	5.9	7.3	6.5	8.0
Root crops	3.1	4.1	5.0	5.0
Vegetables	0.8	2.2	3.0	3.3
Mangoes	0.8	0.7	1.8	3.2
Coffee	0.3	1.9	2.7	6.9
Other	2.6	4.1	4.9	6.7
Subtotal	64.8	55.1	49.3	55.1
Export crops				
Coconut	17.4	19.1	16.3	22.4
Sugarcane	9.8	17.1	22.1	11.1
Abaca	3.5	2.9	1.3	1.2
Bananas	2.5	1.2	8.1	5.7
Tobacco	1.4	3.6	1.6	0.6
Pineapples	0.6	1.0	1.3	1.9
Subtotal	35.2	44.9	50.7	44.9
Total	100.0	100.0	100.0	100.0

Source: NEDA, *Philippine Statistical Yearbook*, 1985, table 5.1

Crop production was able to benefit both from extensive availability of land and from technical change. From 1950 to 1976 the total area planted more than doubled, averaging a growth of over 3 percent a year (NEDA, 1984, table 5.2). From the late 1970s, however, this area has no longer been growing: the limits of extensive agricultural development appear to have been reached. Since World War II there has been a steady rise in mean yields which accelerated in successive decades. The improvements were more marked in rice and corn than in sugar and coconut and this reflects the effect of new high yielding varieties (HYVs) of seed developed at the International Rice Research Institute, near Manila, in the late 1960s.

Over the last three decades there has been a continuing steep decline in the Philippine terms of trade (figure 2.1). In 1981 the terms of trade stood at 42 percent of their 1955 level, compared with 74 percent for non-oil-exporting developing countries as a whole. The decline over this period reflects the unfavorable evolution of world prices for many of the commodities that the Philippines exports.

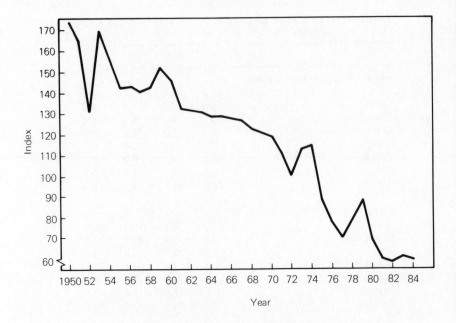

Figure 2.1 Index of terms of trade, 1950–1984 (1972 = 100)

Source: Alburo and Shepherd, 1988, appendix table E.7.3

The Growth of Manufacturing

For the decade of the 1950s foreign exchange shortages resulted in a vigorous process of import substitution and rapid growth in manufacturing industry. Since 1960 this growth has been far lower and manufacturing's share in domestic product has risen only very slowly (table 2.2). According to calculations by Hooley (1985, table 5) total factor productivity in manufacturing as a whole declined in the period 1956–80 by an average 0.5 percent a year. Within this aggregate, labor productivity was rising as a result of substantial substitution of capital for labor. If Hooley's calculation is correct – and such calculations are beset with difficulties (not least because of changes in coverage in the census and survey statistics on which they are based) – it signifies a disastrously poor performance for manufacturing.

Import substitution has been the driving force of Philippine industrialization. The ratio of manufactured imports to manufacturing GDP (all at 1972 prices) fell from 49 percent in 1956 to 21 percent in 1978, though this trend was interrupted in the period 1963–9 (figure 2.2). This process occurred across a broad range of industries. In the 1970s manufactured

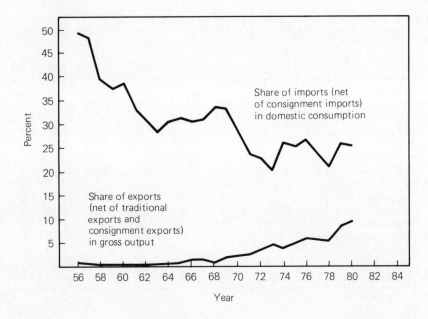

Figure 2.2 Ratios of manufacturing imports and exports to manufacturing product, 1956–1980 (at 1972 prices)

exports (largely clothing, footwear, and electronic components) also became significant, but once account is taken of the large import element in these exports their contribution is seen to be more modest: manufactured exports, net of the imports specifically identifiable as inputs to these exports, grew from a ratio of 1 percent of manufacturing GDP in 1968 to 9 percent in 1980 (see chapter 5). The evidence of high rates of effective protection (see chapter 3) and of stagnation in total factor productivity indicates that import-substituting industrialization has proven extremely costly.

Human Resources

The Philippines, with a population in 1983 of 52 million (table 2.1), is the ninth largest country in the developing world. The population has grown at an average of 2.9 percent a year since 1950 (higher than the average for developing countries as a whole), though the rate has slowed since the early 1970s. The labor force has grown even faster, at 3.3 percent a year from 1957 (the first year for which statistics are available) to 1983 (table 2.4). At the same time there has been considerable rural–urban migration

Table 2.4 Labor force, employment, and wage indicators, 1957–1983

I-n-dicators	1957	1960	1965	1970	1975	1980	1983
1 Labor force							
Participation rate (%)	58	59	58	58	60	63	65
2 Labor force (millions)	8.9	9.9	11.5	11.6	14.3	17.6	20.5
3 Unemployment rate (%)	8.7	6.3	8.2	8.1	4.5	4.3	n.a.
4 Percentage of employed persons wanting additional work	21.0[a]	22.0	27.0	19.0	12.0	n.a.	n.a.
5 Share in labor force (%)							
Agriculture	61	61	57	52	54	51[b]	n.a.
Industry	13	12	12	12	11	12[b]	n.a.
Services	26	27	31	36	35	37[b]	n.a.
6 Index of real wage costs[c] (1972 = 100)							
Agriculture	156	151	116	104	92	81	n.a.
Wage earners	125	127	111	107	65	64	85

n.a., not available.
[a] 1958.
[b] 1978.
[c] Deflated by the general wholesale price index.
Sources: rows 1 and 2, NEDA, Philippine Statistical Yearbook, various years; row 3, Department of Labor, Yearbook of Labor Statistics, various years; row 4, Domingo and Feranil, 1984, table 6.12; row 5, Domingo and Feranil, 1984, table 5.3; row 6, Alburo and Shepherd, 1988, appendix table E.5.7

as the share of services in the labor force has risen at the expense of agriculture.

For a country with a medium level of development – it had a GNP per capita of US$760 in 1983 – the Philippines has surprisingly high educational enrollment rates, levels of life expectancy, and health indicators (World Bank, 1986, tables 27–9).

A particular feature of the Philippine economy has been the abrupt decline in real wages up to 1974. Indeed, separate real wage series both for agricultural laborers and for unskilled (nonagricultural) wage earners indicate a dramatic fall in real wages (figure 2.3). By 1974 real agricultural wages were half their 1958 level, while unskilled wages were half their 1969 level.

Lal (1986) has explained this decline in real wages in terms of the Stolper–Samuelson theorem that protection raises the relative price of the scarce factor. In the Philippines, he argues, land was scarce, labor abundant, and the real devaluations of 1960–2 and the early 1970s reduced the protection, and thus the price, of labor.

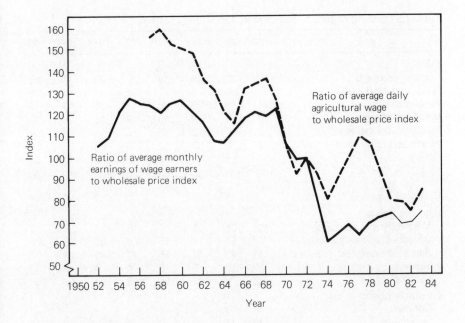

Figure 2.3 Index of real wage costs, 1952–1983 (at 1972 prices; 1972 = 100)

Source: Alburo and Shepherd, 1988, appendix table E.5.7

The Philippines: Land Abundant or Labor Abundant?

In the past the availability of good agricultural land and mineral resources made the Philippines an evidently land-abundant economy, but there are clear signs of change. The limit to extensive agriculture has apparently been reached (even though there is still room for growth in yields). The long-term real decline in commodity export prices has severely reduced the value of the Philippines' natural-resource assets. Meanwhile the population has grown faster than agriculture can absorb it. Finally, real devaluation in the period 1960–74, through its real wage effects, has cheapened the Philippines' human assets.

This shift in relative scarcities has had a dramatic effect on the structure of foreign exchange earnings. Starting in the 1960s, but in particular since the early 1970s, the share of traditional commodity exports has declined sharply in favor of nontraditional manufactured exports (based largely on unskilled labor inputs) and the direct export of labor, mostly to the Middle East. (For the structure of exports see table 2.5.)

Table 2.5 Structure of imports and exports, 1950–1983 (percent)

	1955	1960	1965	1970	1974	1975	1980	1983
Exports								
Coconut products	36	33	34	19	22	20	14	14
Sugar and products	27	25	19	17	28	27	11	6
Forest products	11	18	25	26	12	11	8	7
Mineral products	7	7	9	20	19	15	18	9
Fruit and vegetables	1	5	2	3	3	5	6	4
Abaca and tobacco	8	9	5	3	3	3	2	2
Other[a]	10	4	7	12	12	19	44	56
Total	100	100	100	100	100	100	100	100
Imports								
Producer goods								
Machinery and equipment	11[b]	25	19	19	15	20	16	11
Unprocessed raw materials	5[b]	10	14	15	24	26	29	27
Semiprocessed raw materials	52[b]	42	44	55	47	43	43	50
Supplies	15[b]	10	5	5	6	4	8	7
Subtotal	83[b]	86	82	93	93	92	96	96
Consumer goods								
Durable	1[b]	1	1	1	–	–	–	–
Nondurable	16[b]	13	18	6	7	7	4	4
Subtotal	17[b]	14	19	7	7	8	4	4
Total		100	100	100	100	100	100	100

–, negligible.
[a] Mainly manufactures.
[b] 1957.
Sources: Exports, NEDA, *Philippine Statistical Yearbook*, 1984, table 7.3; imports, Central Bank of the Philippines, *Annual Report*, various years

Historical Influences on Trade Policy

The modern history of the Philippine nation has its origins in the middle to late nineteenth century. In this period of late colonization by the Spanish state (with the help of the Catholic church) a distinctly Philippine middle class was born. It came largely from the mixed race, or mestizo, population that had emerged from the intermarriage of immigrant Spaniards and Chinese with local people (Steinberg, 1986). Social class tended to be based on wealth, and wealth arose largely from commercial activity and from the plantation agriculture (sugar in particular) that developed from the middle of the century.

Toward the end of the century Philippine nationalism developed as a strong political force. It seized its chance in the Spanish–American war of 1898 when the Philippine nationalists threw in their lot with the United States to force the Spanish out of the Philippines. Following a briefly independent Philippine republic, the United States, in a bout of expansionism, became colonial master of its erstwhile ally in 1900. These events of the turn of the century also marked the development of a split in the nationalist movement between those seeking complete independence and those prepared for a greater accommodation with the colonial power.

The American colonization was soon to prove a good deal more politically enlightened than that of its predecessor. Public policies stressed education, health, and the filipinization of local government (Friend, 1986). By 1933 full independence had been scheduled for 1946. American economic policy for the Philippines linked the two countries in a preferential trading relationship in which Philippine sugar and coconut oil received high prices in return for the Philippine import of US manufactures. This close relationship, with its deliberate encouragement of sugar and coconut oil, had several outcomes.

First, it contributed to considerable export-led growth in the first two decades of the twentieth century. Second, the owners of the sugar estates came to spearhead a cohesive political bloc with a particular interest in policies favoring exports. Third, when depression overtook the American economy in the 1930s, US domestic interests opposed to the preferential access of Philippine sugar and coconut oil (and preferential immigration quotas for Filipinos) lobbied for a reduction in preferences and for eventual Philippine independence (Friend, 1986).

In spite of the searing wartime experience – Japan's invasion and occupation of the Philippines (1940–5), collaboration and resistance, war damage, and liberation – much of the pre-war power structure in the Philippines was, surprisingly, left intact after the war (Steinberg, 1986). This political structure and the specific characteristics and arrangements of United States–Philippine relations after independence in 1946 have played a dominant role in the policy debate in the Philippines ever since.

First, the Philippines inherited a constitutional system whose institutions were modeled on those of the United States – an executive president (elected every four years), upper and lower houses of Congress, and a two-party system (of Nacionalistas and Liberals) serving more as electoral coalitions than as repositories of particular philosophies. This political system, which survived until 1972, offered some elements of democratic choice, but it was also well adapted to mediating the interests of various interest groups and elites. (One economic impact of this form of government was, as in many other countries, that the electoral cycle translated into a macroeconomic cycle: public spending increased significantly in the run-up to elections as the government sought to influence voters, and this contributed to fiscal deficits and foreign exchange crises (Baldwin, 1975, pp. 151–2).)

Second, in return for rehabilitation funds, the new Philippine government also agreed in 1946 to a number of economic conditions that limited its economic freedom (see chapter 4). It was not free to alter its exchange rate without US permission. It agreed to a constitutional amendment giving Americans parity rights with domestic investors (while other foreigners faced a more restrictive regime). Mutual trade preferences were to remain, but would be phased out by 1974. Finally, in 1947 the Philippine government agreed to lease military bases to the United States.

The post-war survival of the old Filipino elite, closely tied as it was to US interests, had several effects, sometimes contradictory. It ensured the continuation of a system of capitalism and private ownership and the pursuit (until well into the 1960s) of conservative fiscal and monetary policies. In this system traditional exporters had a large political voice. By the same token the political elite left unsolved many problems of social discontent, particularly those generated by disparities in rural incomes and land holdings. This discontent inspired the rural communist movement of the 1950s, the Huks. This movement was beaten militarily, but at the end of the 1960s a new rural Marxist movement, the New People's Army, was established. It has become extremely powerful in recent years.

Ironically, the inability of the Philippine government independently to alter its exchange rate in the years following 1948 contributed to the *de facto* making of trade policy: the peso became very overvalued, foreign exchange was consequently rationed, and the rationing system was used to promote import-substituting investment (see chapter 4). The protected manufacturing sector that grew up consequently espoused the virtues of protection.

More generally, the continuing close relationship with the United States and the limitations that the economic and military arrangements were seen to place on Philippine sovereignty inevitably fanned the flames of the nationalism that had been smoldering since the turn of the century.

The period of constitutional democracy came to an end in 1972. In this year, in the course of his second term as President – the Constitution did not allow a third – Ferdinand Marcos declared a state of martial law on the grounds of growing civil disorder. At first, the government achieved a measure of popular support and showed signs of using its new-found power to push through various reforms such as rural development, export promotion, and government reorganization. Even if this was not a radically reformist government, it tended to place itself at the more market-oriented end of the debate. By the middle of the decade, however, these intentions were giving way to more immediate political objectives: the economy was increasingly used to consolidate the power of Marcos's political allies by giving them economic privileges. Moreover, the coherence of government economic decision making gradually deteriorated as different factions within government sought to gain the President's ear. (On the Marcos era, see chapter 5).

The post-war period as a whole is characterized for the Philippines by a "love–hate" relationship with the United States that has grown out of the particular colonial experience. This relationship has been the main spur to an intense and continuing post-war debate on the country's external economic options, in particular its policies for import protection, the exchange rate, and foreign investment. It is difficult to classify the protagonists in this debate or the extent to which they belong to particular political parties or factions. Within the traditional political system – this excludes the more radical left, in both its legal and illegal variants – the protagonists can best be characterized as economic nationalists and economic liberals, both before and after martial law.

Economic nationalists have sought varying degrees of protection against foreign imports and foreign investment, and have tended to advocate more interventionist, but not socialist, forms of economic organization. In the area of protection, they share common ground with a more socialist opposition (that tends to be strongest in the universities). Economic nationalist sentiment appears often to have been stronger than liberal sentiment, and there seems to have been an uneasy compromise between the protectionist and interventionist tendencies of the former and the practical need as seen by successive governments for more open international economic relations. This need has grown as the Philippines, since the late 1960s, has increased its level of foreign borrowing and strengthened its relations with the International Monetary Fund (IMF) and the aid agencies, particularly the World Bank.

Markets and Institutions

In principle, successive Philippine governments have been strongly committed to a capitalist system of private ownership (including a relatively modest public sector) and freely functioning markets. In practice, some of the characteristics of Philippine society have combined with substantial intervention in product and financial markets to create uncertain conditions for doing business, that is, an unclear and unpredictable set of property rights. This in turn has led some economic agents to devote substantial efforts to rent seeking – lobbying and the offer of inducements in a political market to gain economic favors. By the same token other economic agents are encouraged to engage in outright illegal activities, such as smuggling, or to operate informally (that is, outside the normal legal framework).

The degree of rent seeking and illegal behavior in the Philippine economy is of course difficult to measure, but it is too important to ignore. Such rent seeking undermines the working of markets by diverting resources from directly productive uses and by substituting political for economic criteria in many allocative decisions. When carried out on a broad society-wide basis, it also greatly weakens the political constituency for making markets work better (and hence for trade liberalization). This by no means suggests that the conditions of doing business that prevail in the Philippines are unique among developing countries. Rather, the openness of Philippine society compared with many others makes it possible for topics such as corruption to be aired as part of the rhetoric of politics. Indeed, if the country has a particular reputation for corruption, it is largely of its own making.

Economic corruption has nonetheless, here as elsewhere, been a vital feature of the economy. Corruption cannot be only, or even principally, associated with the period since 1972, even if the late 1970s and early 1980s do in many ways represent a high point. Economic corruption occurs where public servants illegally accept money or favors in return for using the discretion they possess to provide economic favors. With the revelations and claims that have surfaced about ex-President Marcos's extensive clandestine business interests in the Philippines and his reportedly enormous foreign asset holdings, corruption in the Philippines has become a legitimate topic for international discussion.

A few broad examples can be given. In the 1950s, foreign exchange controls created an overvalued currency and a demand for foreign exchange that exceeded supply (chapter 4). The most visible sign of this – and a clear guide to the value of the "rent" that an allocator of foreign exchange licenses might extract – was the excess of the black-market over the official exchange rate. At its highest, in 1959, the black-market rate was double the official rate – not perhaps excessive by the standards of some countries, but nonetheless a very substantial measure of distortion (Alburo and Shepherd, 1988, appendix table E.6.7). This distortion in the value of foreign exchange led not only to substantial corruption in the allocation of foreign exchange licenses, but also encouraged unrecorded and illegal exports, particularly of coconut products and wood.

Even without distortions in the market for foreign exchange, smuggling has been important in the Philippines, largely because of high import duties. Levels of import duties grew particularly from the 1960s onwards. Some of this smuggling – which has been particularly important in cigarettes, textiles, and electronic goods – has been of the boat-in-the-night variety, facilitated by the country's island geography, but a good deal of the activity is "technical smuggling" where imports are deliberately misclassified to attract lower duties, usually with the connivance of customs officials. (On the incidence of technical smuggling, see Alano, 1984.) Corruption has also reportedly been rife in the area of public contracts. It is always difficult to know where corruption shades off into the more legitimate activities of lobbying to influence government decisions. Certainly a good case can be made for describing as a form of legalized corruption the many government decrees awarding economic privileges to particular individuals and institutions that were made in the Marcos years (see chapter 5).

What are the factors that encourage corruption? In many cases, it is the almost inevitable consequence of interventions that create large price distortions, and hence the possibility of large rents. The undervalued exchange rate of the 1950s and the high tariffs from the 1960s did not result from policies intended to create corruption and smuggling, though this was the almost inevitable consequence. Similarly, until the financial reforms that began in the early 1980s, financial markets have been substantially repressed by controls on interest rates and government direction of credit. Soon after the introduction of martial law the business climate was further politicized by the lucrative profits to be had from direct government favors. Chapter 5 describes the growth of monopoly in agricultural marketing, of import and production monopolies for specific firms, of the influence of public banks in the financial sector, and of public guarantees for private borrowing abroad.

The other side of the coin of specific, discriminatory, and often *ad hoc* intervention in developing countries like the Philippines is the weakness or absence of some of the implicit or explicit institutions which characterize more advanced capitalist economies. Most obviously, what is lacking is an adequate framework for the observation of implicit or explicit contracts that are made at arm's length. This reflects weaknesses in the judicial system and an absence of the kind of business trust that to an extent is taken for granted in more highly developed capitalist systems. The counterpart of this inadequate framework for arm's length contracts is the importance in the Philippines – not unlike other societies at a similar stage of development – of mutual bilateral obligation between close associates. As a Filipino historian has noted:

Filipino relationships with one another are guided by two traditional attitudes: the *pakikisama* and the *utang na loob*. The *pakikisama*, or the sense of deep camaraderie, implies mutual respect and help, while *utang na loob* demands that a man pay his debt of gratitude to a friend or another person who has helped him. Thus, a man is expected to help his neighbor or friend in his hour of need and the latter is expected to repay his debt of gratitude by in turn helping his benefactor. These two attitudes, distorted after World War II, accounted for the graft and corruption that have plagued Filipino society since the end of the war. (Agoncillo, 1969, p. 9)

These personal and bilateral relationships are a mechanism to offset the risks that arise from business, bureaucratic, and political transactions in a modernizing society. They reflect the way that complex societies are required to work in the absence of the institutions (such as an effective legal system, developed insurance markets, or developed social security systems) that characterize more developed societies. The large families (or "clans"), many of which derived their original power from land ownership, stand at the apex of this system of personal relationships (see Doherty, 1982). Thus much economic activity (as well as politics) is effectively cartelized.

In one sense, therefore, "corruption" in some of its manifestations may reflect the way less advanced societies are constrained to work, but in another sense a continuation of such relationships may come to suit the politically dominant forces in a country; that country may then be characterizable as a "rent-seeking society." It can be argued that under-development plus three decades of economic regulation have reinforced just such a society in the Philippines. A combination of personal and bilateral relationships, the "clan" nature of some of the Philippines society, the existence of substantial economic regulation, and the spread of corruption undermine the working of markets and distort the allocation of resources that this would produce. It is likely that the impact of this is strongest in the "modern" sectors of the economy which have been most touched by regulation. However, agricultural markets have also been increasingly affected since the 1970s (see chapter 5).

The Factors Influencing Trade Policy: Some Hypotheses

The brief review of economic structure, history, and institutions undertaken in this chapter leads to some simple propositions about the major factors influencing the formulation of trade policy in the post-war Philippines. Some of these propositions will be further illustrated in the more detailed discussion of liberalization episodes that follows, but by their nature they are unlikely to be "proven."

The key may well lie in the resource base. The country's rich natural resources have supported an export sector capable of generating the surplus to finance the development of a protected import-replacing manufacturing sector. At the same time the country's large population has provided the market for this new sector.

If a protected manufacturing sector is to grow, there is an inevitable political tension between these two sectors since manufacturing is protected (by tariffs and an overvalued exchange rate) at the expense of policies that support exports. This tension developed in the Philippines from the 1950s (see chapter 4, and Power and Sicat, 1971, chapter 3). The tension between exporting and protectionist interests has also been fueled by the broader debate on nationalism in the economic, military, and cultural spheres, itself the product of the Philippines' particular colonial history.

With this underlying political tension between economic interest groups and between philosophies, it is small wonder that there has been no sustained national commitment to trade liberalization. The stalemate also appears to be reinforced by the strong elements of conservatism and rent seeking in Philippine society. The conservatism reflects the broad political continuity, achieved since early in this century, in which political power has remained largely in the hands of a few elite families (although there have been important changes in the structure of the elite, notably the declining power of the sugar bloc and the rise of new groups linked to President Marcos in the 1970s). The rent seeking is largely a product of the substantial market distortions that have developed since World War II.

3

The Long-term Evolution of Trade Policy

In this chapter we provide a brief introductory description of the development of trade policy since independence, we review the available statistical
evidence, and (with the help of a synthetic "index of trade liberalization")
we identify the particular liberalization episodes that will subsequently be
studied.

Key Developments since Independence

As an aid to the exposition here and in subsequent chapters, appendix 2
charts the major changes in trade policy and related policies from 1946 to
1984.

Under its independence settlement with the United States in 1946 the
Philippines continued to cede sovereignty on its exchange rate to the
former colonial power. Forced to live with the now overvalued pre-
war exchange rate of ₱ 2 to the US dollar, the country was obliged to
institute foreign exchange controls from 1949. The system that evolved
tried to ration foreign exchange according to the "essentiality" of the
import. The Philippines regained sovereignty over its exchange rate in
1954, but by this time the foreign exchange control system had acquired a
powerful new rationale – to protect the import-substituting industrial
sector that had sprung up in response to these controls. In the second half
of the 1950s the peso became increasingly overvalued and a series of
countermeasures was introduced, including taxes on foreign exchange and
some incentives to exports.

The government finally decided to undertake a thorough decontrol, in
stages from 1960. The peso would be gradually depreciated through a

multiple exchange rate system in which a progressively larger proportion of foreign exchange transactions would take place at a devalued rate, a process to be completed not later than 1964. In the event, a new administration in 1962 interrupted this gradual process with a float of the peso (which was subsequently pegged at ₱ 3.90 to the US dollar) and the lifting of all foreign exchange controls with the exception of a tax on exports that was not removed until 1965. Since the intention was to counteract overvaluation rather than to remove protection from import-substituting manufacturing, however, import duties were substantially raised in 1962 and subsequent years.

By 1967 a new administration – the first Marcos administration, which came to power in 1966 – had reacted to reemerging balance-of-payments problems by reintroducing some measures to discourage imports. These were followed in 1969 by a partial reintroduction of direct import controls. In early 1970 the peso was further devalued to ₱ 6.40, while many of the controls reintroduced in 1969 were kept in place. In the same year duties on traditional exports were introduced (and were to become a more or less permanent feature). However, several incentives to nontraditional exports were legislated from 1967 to 1973. The subsidy element in these appears to have been modest, but they did make effective provision for exporters to acquire imported inputs at world prices. In 1973 there was a major rationalization of the tariff structure. This did not reduce average levels of production, but it did remove some anomalies, including extensive duty-free privileges (to government, for instance).

From around 1974–5 there were signs of a revival of protection, though the precise course of trade policy is far from clear. Foreign exchange transactions were more closely monitored, while new protective import controls were introduced piecemeal, and substantial import duty concessions (which in many cases probably increased levels of effective protection) were once more accorded to various institutions and activities. Moreover, exchange rate policy after 1974 did not permit sufficient devaluation to neutralize the higher rate of inflation in the Philippines than in its major trading partners.

A major program of tariff reform and liberalization of residual import controls was designed in 1980. Its first stage was implemented in 1981. While the tariff adjustments continued to their planned conclusion in 1985, the removal of import controls started to be partially reversed from 1982. In the economic crisis that developed in the early 1980s and came to a head in 1983 the allocation of foreign exchange came to be fully controlled by the government. With direct import controls reintroduced, many tariffs no longer had a protective effect, and the whole import liberalization program was stalled. (The program was resumed from 1986, but this study does not go beyond 1983.)

Measuring the Evolution of Trade Protection

There are well-known difficulties in interpreting measures of protection. First, protection is often expressed in a single figure – an average. Yet equally important is the dispersion of levels of protection among different types of activity (import-substituting versus exporting activities and activities within these broad groups) or different economic agents (government versus private industry, small versus large firms, and so on). By the same token, different types of protective regime – for instance, tariff protective versus quota protective – will create different kinds of distortions, even where average levels of protection, however measured, may be similar.

Second, there is some arbitrariness in defining protective policies in terms of border measures since nonborder measures, such as subsidies and domestic monopolies, can have equivalent effects. In the following discussion we largely ignore nonborder measures since, with the possible exception of some agricultural products, border measures dominate in the Philippines. However, it is impossible to ignore the vital influence of exchange rates on the level of protection.

Third, the analysis of protection has often been obscured by a confusion between policy effects and some notion of economic efficiency: the fact that, while a policy is ostensibly being quantified, what is often measured, if imperfectly, is some notion of economic efficiency. Estimates of nominal and effective protection using tariffs to derive the difference between domestic and world prices do indeed measure a policy effect, though difficulties in interpretation and measurement arise when there is "water in the tariff," that is, when domestic firms sell at price levels below the world price plus the tariff. Estimates using direct price comparisons, however, measure efficiency as much as they measure policy, especially where domestic competition has removed some of the profits that the tariff might allow.

Finally, in measuring the level of protection at a given point in time, most studies tend to assume, if implicitly, that it is this level of protection that informs the actions of entrepreneurs or investors at this same point in time. In fact, it is equally expectations of future protection, particularly at the time of an investment decision, that affect behavior, but expectations are not easy to measure.

Point Estimates of Tariff- and Tax-based Effective Protection

Several studies of effective protection have been made at a disaggregated level and for different years: for the early 1960s by Valdepeñas (1970); for 1965 by Power and Sicat (1971), an exercise itself largely based on Power (1971); for 1974 by Tan (1979); for 1979, unpublished data supplied by the

Tariff Commission; and for the revised tariff schedules of 1980 and 1985 by Bautista (1981). These exercises all largely derive nominal protection estimates from tariff and tax schedules. (Only Power and Sicat use price comparisons: they compare unit prices from international trade statistics for some products where water in the tariff was presumed.) With the exception of that of Valdepeñas, the exercises all define products according to, and derive domestic cost structures from, input–output tables. Yet the selection of products in the different studies is far from identical.

The primary reliance of these studies on tariff and tax rates to measure nominal protection creates problems, both in interpreting any given study

Table 3.1 Tariff- and tax-based estimates of effective protection, 1965–1983

Estimates	Consumption goods				Intermediate goods			
	1965	1974	1979	1985	1965	1974	1979	1985
Number of items	43	56	69	31	23	35	42	14
Simple mean (%)	57.00	188.02	88.80	43.10	45.48	35.71	46.60	12.63
Standard deviation	236.97	507.77	123.54	48.20	103.22	67.83	42.07	14.31
Coefficient of variation	4.16	2.70	1.39	1.12	2.27	1.30	0.90	1.13
Weighted mean (%)	29.28	163.44	65.58	62.69	7.22	19.94	24.87	7.58
Number of items	24	32	44	30	11	17	13	14
Adjusted for 1965 and 1974								
Number of items	20	20	—	—	14	16	—	—
Simple mean (%)	73.00	89.00	—	—	51.56	32.39	—	—
Standard deviation	203.36	139.44	—	—	130.14	77.17	—	—
Coefficient of variation	2.79	1.57	—	—	2.52	2.38	—	—
Weighted mean (%)	7.05	14.08	—	—	10.03	5.65	—	—
Number of items	11	11	—	—	10	10	—	—
Adjusted for 1974 and 1979								
Number of items	—	49	49	—	—	35	35	—
Simple mean (%)	—	191.30	105.0	—	—	35.71	43.97	—
Standard deviation	—	539.80	140.9	—	—	67.83	41.67	—
Coefficient of variation	—	2.82	1.34	—	—	1.00	0.95	—
Weighted mean (%)	—	48.00	60.69	—	—	18.69	31.64	—
Number of items	—	27	27	—	—	15	15	—

	Inputs into construction				Capital goods			
	1965	1974	1979	1985	1965	1974	1979	1985
Number of items	16	21	22	14	4	7	7	7
Simple mean (%)	80.44	28.00	61.36	24.74	22.00	19.36	67.56	19.61
Standard deviation	102.38	64.82	62.97	26.45	25.73	11.30	83.43	8.50
Coefficient of variation	1.27	1.35	1.03	1.07	1.27	0.57	1.23	0.43
Weighted mean (%)	– 15.05	14.51	6.87	19.92	5.00	17.17	37.61	21.96
Number of items	8	15	15	14	1	7	7	7
Adjustment discarding logging								
Weighted mean (%)	18.46	14.36	43.26	19.92	n.a.	n.a.	n.a.	n.a.
Number of items	7	14	14	14	n.a.	n.a.	n.a.	n.a.

n.a., not applicable.
Sources: for 1965, Power, 1971; for 1974, Bautista et al., 1979; for 1985, Bautista, 1981

and in comparisons over time. Given the rise in tariff rates after 1962 and the importance of nontariff import controls for all the period except 1962–9, there are likely to be many cases where tariff and tax rates inaccurately measure nominal protection.

It is possible to compare samples of common products for any two of the four studies, but these samples turn out to be small as a proportion of the products covered in each study (table 3.1). In fact, the changes over time in average levels of protection are of a different magnitude, and even go in a different direction, depending on whether the basis of the comparison is the aggregate results, an unweighted comparison of a sample for two years, or a weighting of the same sample for the same two years. The same is true for measures of standard deviation and the coefficient of variation. Thus comparability can only be achieved at the expense of representativeness, and these studies allow few reasonable conclusions to be drawn about the evolution of protection.

Of course, these studies were not designed for comparisons over time, except for the Bautista study which tried to gauge the likely effects of the 1981–5 Tariff Reform program. Bautista (1981, table 4) found that tariff- and tax-based effective protection for manufacturing industry would fall from an average of 70 percent in 1980 to 31 percent after the completion of the tariff reform in 1985 and that the average dispersion of tariffs would significantly decrease.

In addition to these four studies, some statistical series give direct and indirect indicators of changing protection over time. These are discussed in the following paragraphs and partly summarized in table 3.2 and several figures.

Time Series for Tariff- and Tax-based Protection, 1949–1980

Baldwin (1975) estimated tariff- and tax-based effective exchange rates and effective rates of protection for the years 1949–71 on the basis of samples of products representing eight major commodity classifications corresponding to exchange control categories of the Central Bank (essential and nonessential producer and consumer goods, etc.). His series of effective exchange rates was updated to 1980 by Senga (1983). We have used this extension of the series, as well as Baldwin's original assumptions and method, to extend the effective protection series to 1980 (for the complete 1949–80 series see Alburo and Shepherd, 1988, appendix table E.6.6; series for some representative product groups are also included in table 3.2 and figure 3.1).

In spite of the narrowness of the product sample in some categories (more so after 1971), the series is useful in tracking the likely evolution of tariff-based protection. The picture that emerges is of consistently negative

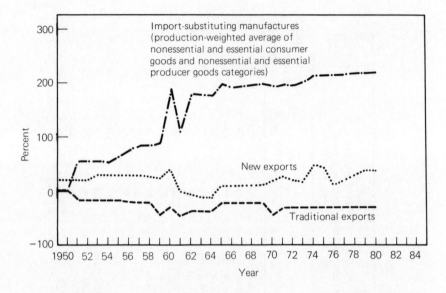

Figure 3.1 Tariff- and tax-based effective rates of protection, 1949–1980

Source: Alburo and Shepherd, 1988, appendix table E.6.6

effective protection for traditional export industries from 1951 onwards. This is more negative in the 1970s (around − 30 percent) than hitherto (typically − 15 to − 30 percent). New export industries have enjoyed positive effective protection (typically around 30 percent), except in the 1960s – particularly in the immediate aftermath of decontrol – when it was lower. (Estimates of effective protection to new exports from 1973 may be too high because they are based on a misinterpreted set of statistics from Rosario Gregorio; see Alburo and Shepherd, 1988, appendix C.) In the import substitution sector protection remained clearly higher for nonessential than essential goods, and there was a larger and steady growth in protection to nonessential and semi-essential categories until the mid-1960s, when this growth slowed down. By the mid-1960s the most protected categories, nonessential consumer and producer goods, had reached levels of tariff-based effective protection of around 350 and 200 percent respectively. The series gives no evidence at all of trade liberalization, though Bautista's study provides good evidence that this trend in tariff- and tax-based effective protection would have been reversed for manufacturing after 1980.

The Tariff Commission has also estimated arithmetic averages of tariffs in manufactures for those post-war years in which major changes in the tariff code took place (see table 3.2, third column). The average rose

Table 3.2 Trade liberalization indicators, 1949–1985

	1	2	3	4	5	6	7	8
	Tariff- and tax-based effective protection (%)		Arithmetic average of tariff on manufactures (%)	Ratio of domestic to world prices (1972 = 100)		Real effective exchange rates (1972 = 100)		Ratio of black-market to official exchange rates
Year	Nonessential consumer goods	Traditional exports		All imports	Manufactures	Imports	Exports	
1949	5	0	n.a.	n.a.	n.a.	n.a.	n.a.	n.a.
1950	5	0	n.a.	196	n.a.	43	74	1.48
1951	114	– 15	n.a.	219	n.a.	44	71	1.50
1952	114	– 15	n.a.	197	n.a.	46	60	1.30
1953	114	– 15	n.a.	195	n.a.	47	77	1.32
1954	110	– 15	n.a.	198	n.a.	46	70	1.36
1955	141	– 16	n.a.	189	n.a.	46	66	1.42
1956	154	– 19	n.a.	202	n.a.	45	64	1.63
1957	179	– 19	36	206	n.a.	45	63	1.73
1958	178	– 20	n.a.	210	n.a.	46	65	1.70
1959	183	– 43	n.a.	224	n.a.	48	72	2.01
1960	349	– 27	n.a.	227	213	47	73	1.29
1961	230	– 45	n.a.	187	180	58	77	1.18
1962	337	– 37	38	135	128	86	101	1.05
1963	332	– 38	n.a.	133	132	86	100	1.01
1964	326	– 38	n.a.	133	134	81	93	1.00

Year	1	2	3	4	5	6	7	8
1965	365	− 22	n.a.	131	136	80	94	1.03
1966	354	− 20	n.a.	129	132	77	97	1.02
1967	357	− 21	n.a.	126	132	75	94	1.05
1968	363	− 22	n.a.	115	145	78	95	1.09
1969	365	− 21	n.a.	117	151	75	90	1.27
1970	354	− 43	n.a.	100	110	100	116	1.12
1971	362	− 33	n.a.	101	98	99	107	1.09
1972	356	− 30	n.a.	100	100	100	100	1.05
1973	402	− 29	44	90	94	112	125	1.06
1974	435	− 28	n.a.	83	111	140	159	1.05
1975	437	− 28	n.a.	90	101	144	125	1.09
1976	437	− 28	n.a.	95	107	134	102	1.06
1977	437	− 28	n.a.	88	110	138	96	1.05
1978	436	− 28	n.a.	91	99	128	99	1.07
1979	434	− 28	42	95	109	122	105	1.08
1980	436	− 28	n.a.	88	122	143	96	1.07
1981	n.a.	n.a.	n.a.	n.a.	n.a.	149	89	1.05
1982	n.a.	n.a.	32	n.a.	n.a.	127	74	1.06
1983	n.a.	n.a.	n.a.	n.a.	n.a.	148	n.a.	1.27
1984	n.a.	n.a.	n.a.	n.a.	n.a.	n.a.	n.a.	n.a.
1985	n.a.	n.a.	n.a.	n.a.	n.a.	n.a.	n.a.	n.a.

n.a., not available.

Sources: columns 1 and 2, Alburo and Shepherd, 1988, appendix table E.6.6; column 3, data supplied by Tariff Commission of the Philippines; columns 4 and 5, Alburo and Shepherd, 1988, appendix table E.6.2; column 6, Alburo and Shepherd, 1988, appendix table E.6.4; column 7, Alburo and Shepherd, 1988, appendix table E.6.5; column 8, Alburo and Shepherd, 1988, appendix table E.6.7

consistently, but not dramatically, from the 1957 reform to a peak in 1973 and declined markedly from 1980 to 1985.

Protection to Agriculture

There are no reliable estimates of changes in effective protection to agriculture over time. David (1983) provides point estimates of price-based effective protection for selected agricultural products for the period around the later 1970s, as well as five-year average rates of nominal protection for 1960–80 (David, 1983, tables 7 and 5). The latter estimates, also based on price comparisons, clearly indicate lower protection in general in the 1970s than in the 1960s, both for import-substituting and export products. For instance, nominal protection for rice averaged 21 percent in the 1960s and 1 percent in the 1970s, and for coconut oil and logs, zero in the 1960s and − 4 and − 29 percent respectively in the 1970s. Our own calculations of annual ratios of domestic to world price indices (Alburo and Shepherd, 1988, appendix tables E.6.2 and E.6.3) tell a similar story for agriculture in the last three decades. (These are not strictly indices of nominal protection since domestic price indices include indirect taxes.)

Indices of Relative Changes in Domestic and International Prices

Philippine trade and price statistics allow a broad comparison of the evolution of domestic and world – or border – price series. Using the prevailing exchange rate at which trade transactions take place – or would probably take place if these transactions were allowed – there are several conventional measures for making numerical comparisons. We use principally two.

The first measure, the ratio of domestic to world price indices (in the same currency) for a given product or group of products, is something like an index of nominal protection coefficients as long as the difference between indirect taxes on domestic products and those on imports does not change over time. As such, this ratio is a proxy for a price-based time series for protection.

The second measure is that of the real effective exchange rate index (REER). The REER is defined in different ways in different studies, most commonly as the comparison of a domestic with a world price series or as the comparison of a nontradeable with a tradeable price series (in a common currency). Either variant can be interpreted as indicating whether domestic costs are getting out of line with international prices, indicating how incentives are moving within an economy as between production of tradeables and nontradeables, or indicating changes in the degree of overvaluation or undervaluation of national currency.

The REER used in this study expresses the ratio of a world price index converted to pesos at the appropriate exchange rate (in the numerator) to a domestic price index (in the denominator). This domestic price index is in most cases the GDP deflator, a proxy for the price of nontradeables in the Philippines. While the ratio of domestic to world price indices may often tell a similar story to the REER – to the extent that the domestic price of a product evolves in line with the price of nontradeables in general – the convention adopted in this study makes one ratio the inverse of the other, the former putting world prices in the denominator, the latter putting them in the numerator.

For an aggregative view of the evolution of relative prices, this chapter presents two ratios of domestic to world prices: the index of implicit import premium (the IIIP) – the ratio of the wholesale price index (WPI) for imports to the index of free-on-board (f.o.b.) import prices – and the ratio of domestic to world prices indices for manufactures (DWM). The IIIP numerator is a base-year-weighted sample of wholesale import prices, while its denominator is the current-year-weighted index for all imports. The DWM similarly uses a base-year-weighted WPI in its numerator, while its denominator is the (current-year-weighted) index of the unit price of all Organization for Economic Cooperation and Development (OECD) manufactured exports (Standard International Trade Classification (SITC) 5–8) to developing countries. Both indices face the problem of noncomparable weighting systems in numerator and denominator, but the DWM faces the additional problem that the basket of products in the two parts of the ratio is likely to be quite different (that is, the Philippines does not produce the same manufactures as those that the OECD exports to developing countries). In fact the OECD price index moved encouragingly closely with the Philippines' own f.o.b. import price index, until the first oil shock at least.

In principle, the IIIP should indicate the net effect of import taxes and import controls in driving a wedge between the world price and the landed price of imports. Power and Sicat (1971, p. 35) used this measure, calling it "a good indicator of trends in the implicit degree of protection provided by the control system." Similarly, the DWM should provide some broad indication of changes in nominal protection to manufacturing.

Not too surprisingly, both indicators move similarly (table 3.2 and figure 3.2). The IIIP rises from the mid-1950s to 1960; Power and Sicat (1971, p. 34) took this as evidence of a tightening of foreign exchange controls after a more lax period in the first half of the decade. After 1960 both indices show a precipitate fall to 1962, strongly suggesting that, when decontrol and devaluation forced a large rise in the world price of imports in pesos, domestic prices of imports and local manufactures did not rise correspondingly (in other words, nominal protection quickly fell). A

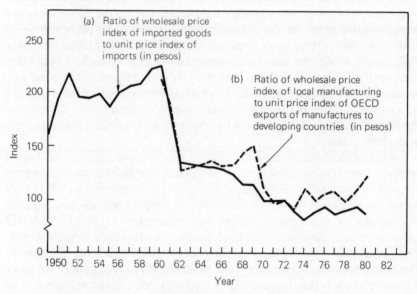

Figure 3.2 Index of implicit import premium (curve a) and ratio of domestic to world prices for manufactures (curve b) for 1949–1980 (1972 = 100)

Source: Alburo and Shepherd, 1988, appendix table E.6.2

similar phenomenon is observable after the 1970 devaluation, though more strikingly for the DWM than for the IIIP.

Less explicable is the dramatic long-term decline in both ratios over the decades since the 1960s, suggesting that the wedge between domestic and world prices has been systematically reduced. This is unexpected and inconsistent with our strong impression that protection was lower in the post-decontrol period than in the 1970s. This may raise questions about the use of these two indicators in the identification of long-term trends in protection. Nonetheless, they are useful where sharp changes are indicated in the shorter term. In chapter 2 it is argued that the fall in these ratios in 1960–2 provides evidence favoring the thesis that decontrol removed a lot of protection in spite of government intentions to counter decontrol with higher tariffs.

Table 3.2 and figure 3.3 also report on REERs for imports and exports (see also Alburo and Shepherd, 1988, appendix tables E.6.4 and E.6.5 for REERs at a more disaggregated level). The import REER rises (depreciates) over the whole period, particularly in 1960–2 and 1969–70, thus indicating progressively more favorable cost conditions for producing tradeables relative to nontradeables. The export REER moves similarly, but only until the middle of the 1970s; after the commodity boom, the adverse movement in export prices leads to a halving (appreciation) of the ratio from 1975 to 1982. In fact, since manufactured exports (gaining an important share of exports after 1974) are underrepresented in the export price index, the fall in the export REER from the mid-1970s is an indicator of the erosion of Philippine comparative advantage in its traditional exports. The import REER in contrast tells virtually the same story as the two ratios of domestic to world prices discussed above.

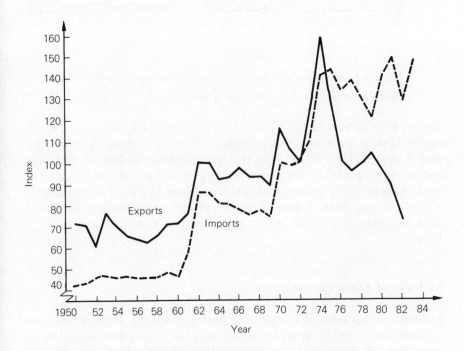

Figure 3.3 Real effective exchange rates for imports and exports, 1950–1983

Source: Alburo and Shepherd, 1988, appendix tables E.6.4 and E.6.5

The Black-market Exchange Rate Premium

The black-market exchange rate premium (the percentage excess of the black-market exchange rate over the official exchange rate) provides a measure of the excess of total demand for foreign exchange over its "legal" supply. In this, restrictions on foreign exchange for current and capital transactions all play a role; the protective effect of exchange controls on commodity imports is thus but a part.

According to table 3.2 and figure 3.4, the black-market premium was around 50 percent in 1950–1, and then fell until 1954. This is consistent with the story told by the IIIP for the same period. After 1954 the premium

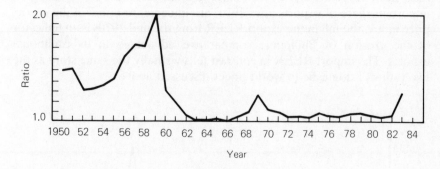

Figure 3.4 Ratio of black-market to official exchange rate, 1980–1983

Source: Alburo and Shepherd, 1988, appendix table E.6.7

steadily rose to around 100 percent by 1959. Then, with decontrol, it fell rapidly to the point where it was virtually eliminated, remaining at no more than 5 percent for 1962–7. With the reintroduction of foreign exchange controls on imports in 1969 it rose to 27 percent, but fell to the 5 percent level again by 1972, tending thereafter to remain at a level slightly higher than in the mid-1960s. It shot up again with the foreign exchange crisis of 1983, reaching 24 percent in October 1983, and remained high through 1984.

An Index of Trade Liberalization

As usual, the statistics do not tell an unambiguous story. The most obvious inconsistency is the tendency of tariff-based and price-based indicators of protection to the import-substituting sector (largely manufacturing) to point in opposite directions for the period as a whole. Certainly the signs are that, after decontrol, tariffs took a large part of the protective burden from import controls. Yet the price-based indicators of protection – which include the protective effects of tariffs – suggest a long-term fall in protection. This apparent fall – suggesting a dramatically improving level of Philippine competitiveness – simply is not consistent with other qualitative and quantitative indicators. The import-substituting sector appears to be still a long way from being world competitive: the negative growth of total factor productivity in manufacturing is one indicator of this.

With all due caveats about the time series data on protection, the index of trade liberalization in figure 3.5 represents our judgment of how aggregate trade policy moved in the three and a half decades since 1949 on a scale from 0 to 20, 0 representing complete illiberality and 20 complete liberality. The judgment is subjective as to the level and slope of the line

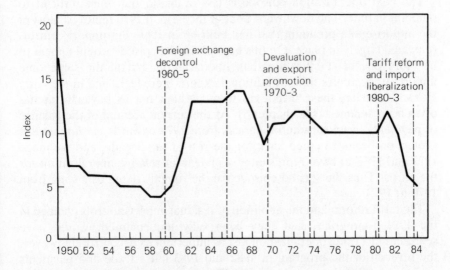

Figure 3.5 Index of the degree of trade liberalization in the Philippines, 1949–1984: 0, least liberalized; 20 most liberalized

drawn. It is based on our interpretation of the likely effects of the policies themselves. Thus, the lower the average rate of protection, the dispersion of the protection between activities, and the extent of distortion in the administration of the protective system (for instance, tariffs versus direct import controls), the higher our index would be. The exercise of drawing the index is useful, not in suggesting a spurious statistical precision, but in crystallizing and expressing clearly the judgments underlying this study on the magnitude of trade liberalization efforts.

The trade liberalization index evolves in a way not unlike the REER for imports, or an inverted version of the ratio of the black-market to the official exchange rate of the IIIP. The index posits the imposition of the foreign exchange control system as the largest single act of protection in post-war Philippine history (the index fell from 17 in 1949 to 7 in 1950) and then reflects a gradual, but far less spectacular, tightening of controls in the 1950s.

Similarly, the import decontrol of 1960–2 is seen as the largest single act of liberalization since the war (the index rising from 4 in 1960 to 13 in 1962). The attainment, by late 1965, of a completely liberal foreign exchange system, but with significant growth in tariffs, represents the high point of post-war liberalization. The episode only comes to an end with the practical reimposition of direct controls in 1968–9 (the index falls from 14 to 9).

The next liberalization episode is less dramatic and more difficult to pinpoint in time. The downward float of the peso in 1970 removed most of the import quota premium that had built up in 1969, but import controls remained largely in place. On this basis alone the episode would appear to be more one of stabilization than liberalization, but at the same time important incentives to nontraditional exports were legislated in the early 1970s. However, these incentives were perhaps not as powerful as has often been assumed (see chapter 5). As the current account of the balance of payments faced substantial deficits from 1974 onwards, *ad hoc* import protection began to creep back for the rest of the decade, and we judge 1972 and 1973 to have represented a plateau of relative liberalization for the 1970s. Thus the second episode can be roughly dated as lasting from 1970 to 1973.

The tariff reform and the abolition of residual import controls planned in the 1981–5 program, had they been fully implemented, would have represented a trade liberalization just as important as decontrol. However, the reversal of the program in 1982 and 1983 left a trade and payments regime as illiberal as in the 1950s. The program was important if only because it began a liberalization process which, after an interruption, has been resumed since 1986.

4

The 1960s: Foreign Exchange Decontrol

The essence of the foreign exchange decontrol of 1960–5 was to use a multiple exchange rate system to carry out a stepwise move from an overvalued exchange rate with severe foreign exchange controls to a new reunified but depreciated exchange rate with no controls on foreign exchange transactions. At the same time tariffs were deliberately raised to compensate for the effects of decontrol on protection. To set the scene for decontrol we need to rehearse the salient features of the control era, 1949–60. This era, and decontrol itself, have been well covered in the literature (Golay, 1961; Hartendorp, 1961; Valdepeñas, 1970; Power and Sicat, 1971; Baldwin, 1975).

1946–1954: Establishing Foreign Exchange Controls

The terms of Philippine economic independence were established in the Philippine Trade Act of April 30, 1946 (also known as the Bell Trade Act) of the US 79th Congress (Valdepeñas, 1970, p. 67; Baldwin, 1975, p. 19). This Act

1 allowed Philippine–US free trade to continue for eight years (until 1954), to be followed by gradual elimination of preferences by 1974,
2 provided for quota arrangements on some Philippine exports to the United States,
3 required the Philippines to maintain free convertibility of the peso at the rate of ₱ 2 per US dollar and not to change this rate without US approval,
4 required free repatriation of the proceeds of US investment in the Philippines,
5 guaranteed access of US nationals to Philippines' natural resources and public utilities on an equal footing with Filipinos, and
6 maintained tight quotas for Filipino emigration to the United States.

The Philippines' obligation to maintain free trade with its dominant trade partner and its lack of sovereignty in exchange rate policy severely circumscribed its control of its external sector. Moreover, the Philippines had maintained its pre-war exchange rate parity in spite of a substantially war-damaged economy and high domestic inflation. Thus the scene was set for 14 years of exchange rate overvaluation and for the development of an industrialization policy which helped create groups with a vested interest in maintaining overvaluation.

The first serious attempt directly to control "luxury" imports – more to make sure "essential" imports were not crowded out than to encourage local manufacture – was implemented in early 1949 (Republic Act RA 330 of August 1948, the Import Control Act). However, the intent of the Act was frustrated by the permissive monetary policy of the election year of 1949 (Baldwin, 1975, pp. 23–6). A new Act to Control Imports in May 1950 (RA 426) moved policy closer to a system of budgeting the available foreign exchange. For the first time, these controls were consciously seen as an instrument to encourage import-substituting investment. In 1951 a 17 percent tax on the sale of foreign exchange for most purposes was introduced (RA 601, March 28, 1951). This *de facto* modification of the import exchange rate was to last, in one form or another and at one rate or another, until the beginning of 1962.

In 1953, as a consequence of extreme public dissatisfaction with the mismanagement and corruption of the Import Control Board (created in 1949), and with the expiry of its enabling legislation, the Central Bank took direct control of import licensing, establishing the classification of each import line according to a hierarchy of essentiality. This classification was to be a key feature of the import system for most of the succeeding two decades. The system was to work with relatively free licensing for "essential" producer and consumer goods, with the remaining foreign exchange allocated on a residual basis according to declining levels of essentiality (semi-essential, nonessential). During the 1950s the Central Bank remained convinced of the virtues of such a system for promoting substitution.

The import allocation system that started in 1949 can be associated with a spurt of import-substituting investment in the early 1950s and substantial manufacturing growth rates thereafter. Of course, such an allocation system could hardly be infallible; it is not surprising that the import-licensing system should have become associated with substantial corruption. The pent-up demand for imports pointed to a significant overvaluation of the peso. To judge from the black-market exchange rate premium, overvaluation climbed slowly from the early 1950s, accelerating from 1955 to the end of the decade (figure 3.4).

1955–1959: Pressures for Reform

On both the import and the export side moves were afoot from the mid-1950s to offset exchange rate overvaluation as the economy's external performance deteriorated.

Control over the Exchange Rate

Under the Laurel–Langley agreement of December 15, 1954, the US and Philippine governments renegotiated their bilateral trade relations. The agreement was not primarily aimed at the decontrol issue, but it did give the Philippine government some of the means for taking action. The agreement allowed the government to regain control over its own exchange rate (Golay, 1961, p. 172), though it was several years before this new power was used.

Tariff Reform

Tariffs played only a minor role in the incentive system of the 1950s, while developments in tariff policy set the scene for the 1960s. In the early 1950s both US official advice (the Economic Survey Mission to the Philippines of 1950) and Central Bank thinking turned to tariff reform as a way of dealing with some of the constraints imposed by the 1946 Bell Trade Act. The first major step came with the Laurel–Langley agreement. This accelerated the schedule of Philippine imposition of duties on US imports: these would pay 25 percent of the tariff in 1956, 50 percent in 1959, 75 percent in 1962, 90 percent in 1965, and 100 percent in 1974.

In 1953 the Tariff Commission had been established with reform of the tariff structure (basically untouched since 1909) as its first major task. The reform was achieved in the new tariff code of 1957 (RA 1937, June 22), though this appears to have been as much the product of Congress as the Tariff Commission, whose initial draft was rejected by the House of Representatives.

The 1909 tariff had been largely designed to raise revenues, with only a few exceptions of modest protective intent. The significantly higher rates in the 1957 reform introduced greater escalation, not only between processing stages but also between items deemed essential and those deemed nonessential (these changes are inferred from data in Valdepeñas, 1970, p. 81). However, given the existence of high quota premia on many imports in the late 1950s and the deliberate correlation of tariff rates under the reform with Central Bank commodity classifications, the immediate effect of the reform was largely to transfer parts of the premia from private to public hands, rather than to increase protection.

The Politics of Decontrol

The issue of decontrol, as part of a broader debate on economic policies, was firmly on the political agenda from the time of the Magsaysay administration (Nacionalista Party) of 1954–7. More immediately decontrol (and its counterpart, the value of the peso) came to be central to a conflict between the (old) agricultural land-owning class and the (new) industrial import substitution class (Golay, 1961, p. 135).

It was, above all, this battle between landowners and industrialists that politicized the issue (and timing) of decontrol and devaluation. Though they were politically strong (particularly in Congress), the exporting interests pushing for decontrol and devaluation – especially the sugar interests – were highly unpopular by virtue of their evident self-interest, their abuse of political power, and their enjoyment of economic privilege (the US sugar quotas, for instance).

In 1955 exporters achieved some compensation for peso overvaluation through the barter law (the No Dollar Import Law, RA 1410, September 10) which allowed certain exports under certain conditions to be bartered for imports. (Frequently, this law may merely have legitimized existing transactions.) Even though the subsequent implementing regulations weakened the incentive, barter exports grew to 10 percent of total exports by 1959. The law was replaced in 1959 by RA 2261 (June 19) which specified more precisely the (largely nontraditional) activities that could engage in barter.

President Magsaysay, lacking his own clear economic philosophy, was host from around 1957 to a "great debate" in which, broadly speaking, the proponents of orthodox conservative macroeconomic policy were allied with the proponents of import controls (and, to an extent, of planning), and pitted against those favoring fiscal and monetary expansion and the abolition of controls. The latter group was strongly associated with the sugar bloc. Magsaysay appeared to listen to one and then the other group alternately. In macroeconomic policy he appeared to favor the expansionary group, but beyond his assent to the 1955 barter law he did not allow any progress in decontrol. (At one point, in 1955, Magsaysay recommended decontrol to the National Economic Council but was immediately forced to retract; see Hartendorp, 1961, p. 42.)

President Garcia (Nacionalista) succeeded Magsaysay as president on the latter's death in 1957 and was subsequently elected for a four-year presidential term at the end of that year. Garcia immediately chose a more economically conservative path than Magsaysay, attempting to stabilize the economy in a series of monetary and fiscal measures in 1957–9. In addition he clearly supported his Central Bank governor, Miguel Cuaderno, in maintaining import controls.

However, in a speech on July 2, 1959, a reluctant President Garcia undertook, in the briefest of terms, to effect a program of decontrol over a four-year period provided that "stabilization measures were to produce the effect of stabilizing the finances of the government" (Baldwin, 1975, p. 48, 46). This change in policy direction represented a compromise with Congress: President Garcia's acceptance of a commitment (if unspecific) to decontrol in return for congressional legislation of the margin fee that he sought as a stabilization measure. (For this Garcia also needed the acquiescence of the US Congress.)

The compromise was reflected in RA 2609 (July 19, 1959) which, in establishing a sales tax on foreign exchange sales, contained a brief injunction to the Monetary Board to carry out a four-year program of decontrol. The foreign exchange sales tax – or "margin fee" – of up to 40 percent that RA 2609 permitted was the culmination of efforts that the Central Bank had been making since 1955. This replaced the 17 percent foreign exchange sales tax, being diminished by 1.7 percentage points a year, which was instituted in 1955.

Other political factors may have helped President Garcia to live with his distaste for decontrol. The public were becoming increasingly outraged at the corruption associated with import controls (Valdepeñas, 1970, p. 40), a sentiment that provided something of a counterweight to disapproval of the sugar bloc. It is likely, too, that the suspicion was growing that exporters were finding ways round peso overvaluation, through legal and illegal barter arrangements and underinvoicing of exports.

There was some bickering between Congress and the Administration when the latter announced its decontrol program in April 1960, but this was more over the scope and pace of reform than its direction: Congress preferred something more sweeping (Hartendorp, 1961, p. 481) (though Hartendorp also suggests that the real problem may have been that Congress felt insufficiently consulted). In spite of these disagreements, once a reluctant administration accepted decontrol, a broad consensus had come into being. The consensus existed despite the obvious pro-control interests of the existing industrial-import-substituting sector – typified by the Philippine Chamber of Commerce – which favored retaining its privileges through an import-licensing system. Clearly, at this time at least, this industrial group did not wield a veto power either with Congress or with the Administration. The powerful American business community, however, favored decontrol (Payer, 1974, p. 62). So did the IMF, but it is not clear that this played a significant role in the decision.

Economic Conditions Preceding Decontrol

The first stage of decontrol came on the heels of a significant improvement in the external balance of the economy, as a result of both international price movements and domestic policies.

The balance of payments deteriorated after 1953 largely because of the expansionary policies of the regime of President Magsaysay. As a result Central Bank reserves fell from 4.7 months of imports of goods and services in 1953 to only one month in 1957. The deflationary policies of the succeeding Garcia administration in 1957–9 significantly improved the balance of payments and kept reserves stable, but still at a very low level (table 4.1).

During the 1950s exports expanded by around 6 percent a year in volume and 5 percent in value (table 4.1 and Alburo and Shepherd, 1988, appendix table E.7.3). In 1958 and 1959 exports expanded at over 10 percent a year by value, partly because of a rapid increase in export prices. This trend continued into 1960. (Using partner-country data instead of Philippine trade data to account for annual variations in the degree of apparent underrecording of Philippine exports, a strong export growth is still evident, at least for 1959 and 1960; see Alburo and Shepherd, 1988, appendix table E.7.4.)

Table 4.1 Indicators of the external sector, 1955–1969 (1962 = 100 for indices)[a]

	Quantum index		Price index (US$)		Index of terms of trade	Current account balance as percentage of GDP	Foreign exchange reserves in equivalent months of imports	External debt as percentage of GDP
Year	Exports	Imports	Exports	Imports				
1955	76	107	94	87	108	− 3.2	2.6	1.8
1956	85	99	96	88	109	− 1.2	2.8	1.9
1957	80	117	97	91	107	− 3.6	1.0	1.9
1958	88	103	101	93	109	− 1.3	1.5	1.7
1959	88	93	109	95	115	0.1	1.6	2.4
1960	94	103	108	97	111	− 1.0	1.8	2.6
1961	91	106	99	98	101	− 1.5	0.7	4.8
1962	100	100	100	100	100	0.4	1.2	6.3
1963	124	98	105	107	99	3.4	1.7	7.3[b]
1964	127	122	104	108	97	1.3	1.5	8.2
1965	131	125	106	109	97	1.9	2.2	10.2
1966	139	133	107	111	96	1.9	1.8	9.8
1967	134	159	109	114	96	− 1.4	1.5	15.2
1968	142	158	116	124	93	− 3.7	1.3	18.3
1969	145	155	116	126	92	− 3.2	1.0	21.7

[a] Indices rebased from 1972 in original source.
[b] After 1963 a different series is used. The 1963 figure for the former series is 5.1 percent.
Sources: Alburo and Shepherd, 1988, appendix tables E.7.1, E.7.2, and E.7.3

According to Philippine statistics (though these may be distorted by the misvaluation of trade) 1957–9 was a period of falling import and rising export prices, with a concomitant marked improvement in the terms of trade. These fell back slightly in 1960, but not below the general level of the second half of the 1950s (table 4.1).

Up to the beginning of decontrol, inflation in the Philippines was negligible (see the GDP implicit price deflator in table 4.2).

What economic factors argued for decontrol, given that the first phase of decontrol occurred in a period of improving external performance? The view adopted in much of the subsequent economic literature is that there was a pressing need to correct for the evident overvaluation of the peso. Power and Sicat (1971, p. 38) have also echoed Fabella's (1964) view that the government had less and less discretion in foreign exchange allocation as more and more foreign exchange became totally committed in advance for the input requirements of producers; the manufacturing sector was becoming starved of inputs and consequently the growth of manufacturing in the late 1950s was depressed.

Table 4.2 Macroeconomic indicators, 1955–1969 (percent)

Year	1 Annual growth of money supply (M1)	2 Annual growth of GNP at 1972 prices	3 Annual change in GDP implicit price deflator	4 Central bank discount rate	5 Required commercial bank reserve ratio for demands deposits (year end)	6 National government budget surplus/deficit as percentage of GDP
1955	9.0	6.4	− 1.5	1.50	18	n.a.
1956	12.2	7.9	3.5	1.50	18	n.a.
1957	6.6	5.3	3.3	4.50	18	− 1.5
1958	8.8	4.0	0.5	4.50	18	− 0.2
1959	6.1	6.2	− 1.6	6.50	21	− 0.9
1960	2.7	1.4	6.8	5.00	18	n.a.
1961	17.1	6.9	2.9	3.00	15	− 1.5
1962	12.9	5.5	1.9	6.00	19	0.3
1963	18.0	6.9	7.9	6.00	19	− 0.6
1964	− 2.7	3.4	7.2	6.00	19	0.1
1965	6.7	5.0	3.2	6.00	10	− 1.3
1966	9.9	4.4	5.8	4.75	10	− 0.6
1967	12.2	4.8	5.3	6.00	16	− 0.8
1968	5.3	5.7	6.0	7.50	16	− 0.8
1969	19.4	5.3	5.8	10.00	16	− 2.8

n.a., not available.

Sources: column 1, NEDA, Philippine Statistical Yearbook, various years; column 2, NEDA, 1978, table 3.3B; column 3, Alburo and Shepherd, 1988, appendix table E.5.1; column 4, IMF, International Financial Statistics, various years; column 5, Central Bank, Statistical Bulletin, 1982; column 6, IMF, International Financial Statistics, various years, and Alburo and Shepherd, 1988, appendix table E.1.1

Nonetheless, the evidence on the overvaluation of the peso is somewhat paradoxical. The 1950s exchange rate was clearly overvalued, as a result of a peso–dollar parity that had remained fixed in spite of rapid inflation in the Philippines during the 1940s. Yet the import REER gently depreciated from 1949 to 1959 (chapter 3, table 3.2 and figure 3.3) because of the abiding stability of prices in the Philippines. However, the export REER appreciated significantly from 1953 to 1957. Moreover, the rise in the black-market exchange rate premium from 1952 onwards (with alacrity after 1955) provides prima facie evidence of increasing overvaluation and foreign exchange shortages at the prevailing exchange rate (table 3.2 and figure 3.4). Clearly, the problem of overvaluation was becoming more severe. Yet, as we have seen, political factors were evidently as important as economic factors in impelling the first phase of decontrol.

1960–1961: the First Phase of Decontrol

The 1960–5 decontrol had two distinct phases. In 1960–1, there was a slow gradual move to a progressively more devalued peso exchange rate via a system of multiple exchange rates, with only a partial relaxation of import controls. This gradual approach was replaced by complete decontrol on the import side, in January 1962, though complete unification of import and export rates was not achieved until 1965. The second phase represented a change of policy accompanying a political change, and the two stages therefore merit separate treatment.

The first of several stages of the 1960–1 phase came about suddenly in April 1960. Congressional and public agitation finally forced the administration to make good its reluctant 1959 commitment to decontrol. Accordingly, the Monetary Board supervising the Central Bank hastily drafted regulations which appeared as Central Bank Circulars 105 and 106 of April 25, 1960. At the same time, the principal author of decontrol, Central Bank governor Miguel Cuaderno, proposed several measures that Congress would need to pass to accompany a proposed gradual four-year decontrol: the barter law of 1959 would become redundant and would need repealing; the margin fee would need to be retained, and exemptions to it eliminated; an export tax of up to 40 percent should be imposed by the end of 1962. Cuaderno also recommended that tariffs on decontrolled items be increased, that the machinery of the Bureau of Customs and Internal Revenue be strengthened, and that a sound fiscal policy be maintained.

Congress acted on none of this, at least initially, and the central feature of decontrol remained the Central Bank's measures to depreciate the peso through a multiple exchange rate system. Through Circular 105 a so-called "free-market" exchange rate was established alongside the "official rate" or par value. This free rate, whose level was not specified in the Circular, was actually a *de facto* depreciated rate set by the Central Bank. Circular 105 also listed which categories of foreign exchange sales and receipts were to be converted at official or free rates, or a mixture of these. At the same time, a Central Bank Decontrol Committee set a free rate at ₱ 3.20, a rate broadly based on the black-market peso rate in Hong Kong (₱ 3.25 at the end of March 1960).

The combination of official and free rates for various transactions led to four different exchange rates. The classification of transactions is most easily seen in table 4.3 which presents the actual exchange rate for different transactions. Gold and tourist receipts were to attract the free rate ₱ 3.20, other exports and invisible receipts a rate of ₱ 2.30, and the more "essential" imports, government expenditure, existing forward exchange contracts and reinsurance premia a rate of ₱ 2.50 (that is, a rate of ₱ 2.00 plus a 25 percent margin fee on foreign exchange sales); all other imports faced a rate of ₱ 4.00 (the free rate plus a 25 percent margin fee).

For imports still subject to the official rate, the Central Bank maintained its traditional system of foreign exchange rationing, though imports in excess of the quota were to be freely importable at the free rate, subject to the new import-licensing conditions that free-rate imports faced. These conditions, the subject of Circular 106, meant that import licenses were still required but would in principle be freely given to new Filipino importers or producers, including corporations with at least 60 percent Filipino equity (subject to a complex set of documentary requirements proving good standing and so on). In addition, producer goods could only be imported for bona fide production, not resale, and the availability of foreign exchange for "unclassified items" – goods that were virtually banned – would continue to be severely restricted. On paper at least this represented an important, if incomplete, dismantling of direct controls.

Concurrently with Circulars 105 and 106 the Central Bank's commodity classification was revised (April 27, 1960). Of 117 changes in classification, the vast majority represented shifts of items – mostly producer goods – from more to less essential categories, thus reducing the number of goods subject to the official exchange rate. Industries prominently affected included auto assembly, consumer durables, clothing, footwear, and textiles.

The intended sequencing of the decontrol that began in April 1960 was established in the broadest of terms – and in one sentence only:

> The percentage of transactions in the free market will be increased gradually each year until all purchase and sale of foreign exchange will be effected in the market not later than 1964 (Circular 105, para. 1).

In September 1960 a minor adjustment to the free-market exchange rate and to the mix of official and free exchange rates for some transactions

Table 4.3 Changes in exchange rates by category of transaction, 1960–1965

Category	Until Apr 24, 1960	From Apr 25, 1960 (Circular 105)	From Sep 12, 1960 (Circular 111)	From Nov 28, 1960 (Circular 117)	From Mar 3, 1961 (Circular 121)	Floating rate end Jan 1962 (Circular 133, Jan 21, 1962)	Supported rate from around Apr 1962	Supported rate from Nov 6, 1965
Foreign exchange receipts								
Exports	2.00	2.30	2.30	2.50[c]	2.75[f]	3.26		
Invisibles								
US government expenditure								3.90
Gold exports		3.20	3.00	3.00	3.00	3.59	3.50[i]	
Tourists							3.90	
Foreign exchange expenditure (excluding rate of premium tax (margin fee))								
Decontrolled items		2.00[b]	2.00[b]	2.00[d]	2.50[g]			
Essential producer goods	2.00							
Essential consumer goods				2.50				
Semi-essential producer goods				2.60				
Semi-essential consumer goods								
Nonessential producer goods		3.20	3.00	3.00	3.00	3.59	3.90	3.90
Nonessential consumer goods								

Item							
Unclassified items							
Government expenditure				2.50 / 2.00[e]			
Contractual obligations prior to April 25, 1960		2.00		2.00			
Reinsurance premia	2.00	3.20	3.00	3.00	3.00		
Import requirements of dollar-earning industries				2.00[h] / 3.00 / 2.75			
Par value of peso	2.00	2.00	2.00	2.00	2.00	2.00	3.90
"Free rate"	—	3.20	3.00	3.00	3.00	—	—
Rate of premium tax ("margin fee") on foreign exchange sales (%)	25[a]	25	25	20	15	—	—

—, not applicable.

[a] Introduced under RA 2609 of July 19, 1959.

[b] Purchases made in excess of exchange license granted are at free rate.

[c] Foreign investment, inward remittances of veterans and Filipino citizens, personal expenses of diplomatic personnel face the free rate (3.00).

[d] Also at the free rate are "special financing items previously approved by the Monetary Bank."

[e] Covers only government expenditure in the fiscal 1960–1 budget.

[f] Includes foreign capital without government approval while the free rate is granted to approved foreign capital, inward remittances of veterans and Filipino citizens, payment by foreign insurance companies of settlements relating to claims after November 28, 1960, personal expenses of diplomats, and certain charitable contributions.

[g] Including newsprint requirements of newspaper publishers.

[h] Existing contractual obligations without foreign exchange contracts but with Monetary Board approval prior to April 25, 1960, and letters of credit opened before April 25, 1961.

[i] In December 1964, exports with a 1962–3 annual average value of US$2 million or less were allowed to convert at the free rate.

Sources: rates from April 25, 1960, to the end of 1961, extracted from various Central Bank Circulars (reprinted in Central Bank of the Philippines, *Annual Report*; other rates, from IMF, *International Financial Statistics*; see also Baldwin, 1975, ch. 3)

(Circular 111) had the effect of a mild revaluation of the exchange rate for imports of less essential items and for exports (table 4.3).

On November 27 of the same year, and earlier than expected because of the favorable results of the first stage, a second stage of the decontrol extended transactions covered by the free rate (Circular 117, November 28, 1960). At the same time, the margin fee fell slightly from 25 to 20 percent. As a result five different exchange rates existed (table 4.3).

Finally, in March 1961 a third stage of decontrol further reduced the disparity between exchange rates (Circular 121, March 3). The Central Bank reported that this move was precipitated by the continuing sluggishness of the export sector and the large losses entailed by the Central Bank's buying pesos at a higher rate than it was selling them (Central Bank of the Philippines, *Annual Report*, 1961, p. 107).

Table 4.4 Trade-weighted average exchange rates for exports and imports, 1959–1963

Date	Exports	Imports (excluding margin fee)
1959	2.00	2.00
1960	2.21	2.05
1961	2.70	2.58
1962	3.43	3.82
1963	3.50	3.85

Source: Alburo and Shepherd, 1988, appendix table E.6.1

The major liberalization characteristics of the 1960–1 phase can be summarized as follows:

1 The phase represented a move toward a real depreciation by first creating a range of effectively devalued rates and then progressively moving more transactions toward the devalued end of the spectrum, in effect beginning to reunify the exchange rate; the movement in trade-weighted average exchange rates is given in table 4.4.
2 On average the depreciation was somewhat stronger on the export than the import side and considerably more modest in 1960 than in 1961.
3 Decontrol must have been considerably eased, for many of those producers previously protected by controls, by the existence of the protective tariff of 1957; moreover, the purpose of phasing decontrol through a program of up to four years was to ease the transition for protected import-substituting industry.
4 The sequencing of the decontrol was established in the broadest possible terms, while the timing and specific contents of the second and third stages to be implemented appear to have been decided on empirical grounds.

Undoubtedly the major nontrade policies that interacted with the decontrol measures were fiscal and monetary policy. Broadly, somewhat expansionary macroeconomic policies were applied in the first phase of decontrol in 1960–1 specifically to ease the adjustment process. Some of the major macroeconomic indicators for the period are presented in table 4.2.

From 1957 to 1959 the Garcia administration had put a high priority on reversing the 1954–6 expansionary policies pursued by President Magsaysay. The Garcia administration raised interest rates and the required level of reserve requirements against deposit liabilities of the banks. It also introduced new taxes on foreign exchange, notably the 25 percent margin fee in 1959.

Shortly after implementing the April 1960 decontrol, the same administration began to change policy in order to ease the adjustment process. The resulting package of reflationary policies, plus a rapid improvement in foreign reserves as exports grew in 1960, worked through to create a marked expansion in the money supply from early 1961. Because 1961 was also an election year, there was the customary explosion of public expenditure which resulted in a budget deficit of 1.5 percent of GDP (table 4.2). The resulting record level reached by the money supply in 1961 (a one-year increase of 17 percent) led to a higher demand for import licenses; in an election year, the Central Bank was obliged to acquiesce. In this second year of decontrol, no one knew how low the peso would fall, and the expansionary policies of the same year reinforced the speculation against the peso that eventually ended the gradualist approach to decontrol.

In 1961 a downturn in the terms of trade, a deteriorating balance of payments, and decreasing reserves together fueled speculation about further decontrol and encouraged illegal exports and anticipatory importing. Thus both external circumstances and domestic policies in 1961 led to the deteriorating economic circumstances that ushered in the second phase of decontrol.

1962–1965: the Second Phase of Decontrol

The US government appears to have played a somewhat more important role in the accelerated second phase of decontrol in 1962. It is said that no Filipino president was ever elected without the support of the US government. For the November 1961 presidential election, Diosdado Macapagal, the Liberal Party candidate, made acceleration of decontrol one of his important planks, but, interestingly, the appeal was more to elimination of graft than the promotion of efficient resource allocation. The Liberal Party, tending marginally more to free trade than the

Nacionalistas, had long had an informal alliance with sugar interests in Congress. It is possible that Macapagal's stance on decontrol may have won him the crucial support of the US government in this election.

The second phase was simple and sweeping where the first had been complex and gradual. In one of his first acts as President, Macapagal (who had appointed a new Central Bank governor) announced on January 21, 1962, almost complete decontrol of foreign exchange and a free float of the peso (Circular 133). The margin fee was abolished, but stringent time deposit conditions for letters of credit were introduced. All restrictions on foreign exchange transactions were removed, with the exception of 20 percent of export receipts which were to be sold to the Central Bank at the "official" rate of ₱ 2 per US dollar. By May 1962 the freely floating rate had settled at around ₱ 3.90, at which level the Central Bank stepped in to support the exchange rate (and continued to do so until February 1970). At this rate the equivalent effect of the 20 percent export retention was an export tax of around 10 percent. The administration also intended Congress to legislate an export tax but was unable to achieve this: first, Macapagal's party had already lost control of Congress in 1960; second, the administration was greatly occupied with other political objectives, in particular getting its ambitious five-year Integrated Socio-Economic Development Program through Congress.

Concurrently with the decontrol, the President used his executive tariff-amending capacity to increase the level of many tariffs, in a deliberate effort to offset the deprotecting effects of decontrol. In the next five years several Executive Orders sustained this upward movement. The rise in tariffs appears substantial (see table 3.2; see also Valdepeñas, 1970, p. 81).

In November 1965 the 20 percent retention on exports was removed, the exchange rate was finally unified, and the official per value of the peso was devalued to its market value of ₱ 3.9.

This second phase of decontrol was represented by the incoming administration as significantly different from the first phase. Yet complete decontrol must have been the ultimate objective of the first phase, even if this was not made explicit. The insistence on differences between the two phases may have been political. However, the comprehensiveness of the decontrol of January 1962 responded to the developing foreign exchange crisis in late 1961. The 1962 phase of decontrol also seems to have been impelled by a continuing outcry against the corruption that was still permitted, under the first phase of decontrol, by the continued existence of import licensing.

In early 1962 the new administration combined its decontrol policy with an about-face in fiscal and monetary policy. Interest rates and reserve requirements were raised, the sale of government bonds – stepped up in 1961 – was reduced in volume, and special time deposits were introduced

on imports. The export retention (the conversion of part of export proceeds at the old exchange rate) was also partly intended as a deflationary measure. Moreover, 1962–4 was a period of budgetary austerity, with surpluses in two of the three years (table 4.2). In spite of these measures, the money supply grew rapidly by historical standards from August 1962 and did not really come under control until 1964, after further deflationary measures had been taken towards the end of 1963.

Fiscal and monetary policy changed yet again in the presidential election year of 1965, heralding the advent of a far more expansionist administration whose policies are briefly discussed at the beginning of chapter 5.

Outside macroeconomic policy, perhaps the major relevant policy initiative of the first half of the 1960s, covering both phases of decontrol, was the legislation of the Basic Industries Act in 1961 (RA 3127). This offered fiscal incentives to industries designated as "basic," and attests to the administration's continuing commitment to the import-substituting sector. But this Act in many ways circumscribed the incentives that industries had enjoyed under the preceding legislation, RA 901 of 1953 (see Power and Sicat, 1971, pp. 83–4).

Decontrol and Protection to Manufacturing

The 1960–5 decontrol is acknowledged in the literature as an extremely important liberalization. The importance of the episode in stimulating traditional exports, even if this stimulation was not seen as lasting, is acknowledged, as too is the fundamental change in the nature of protection for the import-substituting sector. Yet, because tariff protection was rising at a time when import controls were being eliminated the literature is more ambiguous about the overall effect of the measures on protection of the manufacturing sector. For instance, Baldwin (1975) says: "exchange controls were removed, but liberalization in the sense of a significant easing of all controls over imports did not occur" (p. 58), yet he acknowledges "the extent of the economic difficulties that the import-substitution sector did face" (p. 62); Treadgold and Hooley (1967, p. 112) maintain that "although domestic industry was 'squeezed' . . . , it was not squeezed very hard;" Power and Sicat (1971) tend to the view that tariffs succeeded in maintaining the level of protection to manufacturing.

In many ways, not much seemed to change in the structure and behavior of the manufacturing sector in the 1960s, though its rate of growth fell (see below). But did structural change fail to occur because there was little change in protection or in spite of a loss of protection? We argue in this section that, on balance, decontrol had an important net deprotecting effect on manufacturing and reduced the discrimination between manufacturing activities. This occurred in spite of policymakers' intentions to offset import liberalization with higher tariffs.

Before decontrol, manufacturing output was highly protected by controls on "nonessential" imports while producers could import "essential" producer goods fairly easily. This led to high levels of protection. Imports largely did not compete with domestic products, and protection has to be measured by comparing the domestic price of import substitutes and the world price of equivalent products. On the basis of some price comparisons, Baldwin (1975, p. 101) concludes that:

> It is clear . . . that exchange control added greatly to the degree of protection provided by explicit fiscal and monetary measures. In 1959, for example, implicit protection rates of 400 percent were not uncommon for nonessential consumer goods, whereas the average explicit degree of protection in 1959 for this category was around 150 percent. For the essential-consumer-goods group, average implicit and explicit protective rates in the same year were roughly 30 and 5 percent, respectively.

The decontrol and related measures that most affected manufacturing were undertaken in the period 1960–2 with the following major effects on protection.

1 The *de facto* peso devaluation, which had its biggest impact in 1961 and early 1962 and was not substantially eroded by domestic inflation, raised the peso price of imports. This improved the profitability of those producers who had faced import competition, and raised levels of protection for potential import-substitute products. It also increased incentives to exporting.

2 The elimination of import controls over the same period clearly removed the high, often absolute, protection many producers had enjoyed; it also removed barriers to domestic competition arising from producers' unequal access to import licenses.

3 Higher import duties from 1962 tended to raise potential effective protection inasmuch as tariffs on outputs became significantly higher while those on inputs became lower; however, the substantial raising of tariffs, together with the greater domestic competition that came with decontrol, may in some cases have led to tariff redundancy (as Roxas, 1968, suggests).

The effect of devaluation is caught in calculations of the REER. In table 4.5 the REER for imports (row 8) is calculated using the f.o.b. unit price of imports in the numerator and the GDP implicit price deflator (as a proxy for the price of nontradeables) in the denominator. This REER rose (depreciated) substantially in 1961, the second year of the decontrol program, and even more substantially in 1962 when the program was completed on the import side. After 1963 the import REER began to fall slowly but steadily as, under a fixed exchange rate, domestic prices rose faster than world prices.

The best available measure of the effect of decontrol in eliminating foreign exchange control premia is to compare the evolution of the landed (tax- and tariff-inclusive) price (in pesos) of imports with their f.o.b. import price in pesos; this IIIP is reported in row 9 of table 4.5. The measure is not without problems, but is useful for measuring movements in the shorter term (see chapter 3). If neither tax nor tariff levels changed and if there was no foreign exchange premium, the IIIP would stay constant whatever the changes in the exchange rate. This is not the case: it fell in 1961, and even more in 1962, suggesting that the decontrol effects were more powerful in reducing import prices than tariff changes were in raising them. Comparing the relative movements of the WPI for industrial goods and the unit price index of OECD exports of manufactures to developing countries produces an almost identical result (see table 4.5 and figure 3.2).

The ratio of the black-market to the official exchange rate indicates the overall mismatch between total demand for and "legal" supply of foreign exchange (see chapter 3). According to table 4.5, row 7, a large black-market premium was virtually eliminated from 1960 to 1962, though this crept back modestly in the years after 1962. The elimination of this premium is thus consistent with the separate evidence of the IIIP.

Tariff rises in 1962 and thereafter were significant. Estimates of nominal and effective protection, derived from and updating Baldwin's (1975) calculations (see table 3.2 and figure 3.1), clearly show how tariff changes, taken in isolation, increased protection during the 1960s. Baldwin's sample of products is somewhat restricted, but the extent of tariff changes at a more disaggregated level comes out clearly in the work of Valdepeñas (1970, table 6.1), on which some of Baldwin's calculations were based.

If decontrol led to a substantial drop in aggregate protection, there were also important shifts in its distribution. Again, this is not evident from estimates based on tariffs and taxes alone. Baldwin's effective protection calculations indicate that changes in taxes and tariffs served, if anything, to increase the discrimination in favor of essential categories at the expense of nonessential categories and exports (see figure 3.1). However, the value of the implicit import premium was higher for nonessential than essential goods before decontrol, and removal of the premium must have significantly decreased the discrimination. Using data from the WPI, Baldwin showed how the price of those imports most protected before decontrol rose more slowly in 1959–62 than prices for less protected items (Baldwin, 1975, pp. 68 and 100).

Valdepeñas (1970, tables 4.5 and 6.1) provides some evidence of the distribution of nonessential and essential product categories at the two-digit level for manufacturing industry – an indicator of where decontrol

Table 4.5 Indicators of protection, 1958–1967 (1962 = 100 for indices)

Indicators	1958	1959	1960	1961	1962	1963	1964	1965	1966	1967
1 Unit price of imports f.o.b.	48.4	49.6	51.8	66.1	100.0	107.7	109.0	111.0	113.3	116.2
2 Unit price of manufactured exports from OECD countries	n.a.	n.a.	53.7	67.8	100.0	101.1	103.7	104.3	111.0	112.8
3 WPI for imports	75.4	82.3	86.9	91.4	100.0	106.3	107.2	107.7	108.4	108.6
4 WPI of local manufactures for domestic consumption	85.0	86.9	89.0	96.0	100.0	104.6	109.3	111.4	114.9	117.0
5 GDP implicit price index	90.8	89.3	95.4	98.1	100.0	107.9	115.7	119.5	126.4	133.1
6 Nominal wage (urban)	88.9	932.8	98.2	98.6	100.0	101.1	105.6	111.8	123.5	130.5
7 Ratio of black-market to official import exchange rate	1.70	2.01	1.72[a]	1.49[a]	1.02	1.02	1.01	1.04	1.02	1.05
8 REER for imports (row 1/row 5 × 100)	53.0	56.0	54.0	67.0	100.0	100.0	94.0	93.0	90.0	87.0
9 IIP (row 3/row 1 × 100)	156.0	166.0	168.0	138.0	100.0	99.0	98.0	97.0	96.0	93.0
10 Index of nominal protection (row 4/row 2 × 100)	n.a.	n.a.	166.0	142.0	100.0	103.0	105.0	107.0	104.0	104.0

n.a., not available.

[a] These are calculated according to the average exchange rate for imports (2.05 in 1960, 2.58 in 1961). Based on the "official" rate (2) and the most reduced rate (about 3 in both years), the ratio would be as follows: for 1960, official rate 1.77, most devalued rate 1.18; for 1961, official rate 1.92, most devalued rate 1.28.

Sources: Alburo and Shepherd, 1988, appendix table E.5.5: row 2, appendix table E.5.6; rows 3 and 5, appendix table E.5.1: row 4, appendix table E.5.2; row 6, appendix table E.5.7; row 7, appendix table E.6.7; row 8, appendix table E.6.4; indices are rebased from 1972 in the original tables

was likely to be most important – but all sectors contain a mixture of essentials and nonessentials and there are not enough data to provide a convincing quantitative indicator by sector. It is plausible that the decontrol effects were felt most strongly in consumer goods, often with substantial import content and only assembled or finished in the Philippines. Such typical "nonessentials" may be processed foods, beverages, and tobacco products; textiles, clothing, and footwear; and final goods in the paper, chemical, rubber, metal products, electrical goods, and transport equipment industries. These are the kinds of products that more casual commentary has picked up as the "victims" of decontrol.

Economic Performance after Decontrol

The Philippine economy's performance in the wake of decontrol has been analyzed previously by several works, notably Treadgold and Hooley (1967), Power and Sicat (1971), and Baldwin (1975). In this section we examine post-decontrol developments under the headings of prices and wages, external performance, production and employment, investment, and the redistribution of income flows.

Trends in Prices and Wages

Prices had been fairly stable in the 1950s, but began to move upwards in the month following the April 1960 decontrol (table 4.6). From 1960 to 1969 annual inflation averaged between 4 and 5 percent, whether measured by consumer or wholesale prices, and was at its highest in 1963 and 1964. For a devaluation that almost halved the value of the currency between 1960 and 1972 this was surely a modest inflation, but it marked the beginning of a period, which has lasted to the present, in which successive governments have accommodated themselves to a generally increasing rate of inflation.

The WPI for imports rose in 1959–62 by only 22 percent. The 101 percent rise in the f.o.b. peso price of imports in the same period provides prima facie evidence that the loss of import quota premium was large enough to offset most of the devaluation. Similarly, the wholesale price of exports rose by only 22 percent in 1959–62, when the f.o.b. peso export price rose by 57 percent. The higher rise in the f.o.b. than the wholesale price partly reflects the introduction of the export retention in 1962 (equivalent to an export tax a little in excess of 10 percent), but it also supports the contention of Castro (1969, p. 192) that already in 1959 exporters had been finding ways of getting around the control system, for instance through underdeclaring exports and converting some of their foreign exchange earnings at the black-market rate.

Table 4.6 Price indices, 1955–1969 (1962 = 100)

		WPI					
Year	Consumer price index	General	Exports	Imports	Food for export	Local food	Local manufactures
1955	84	77	60	63	54	84	80
1956	87	80	62	69	55	84	83
1957	88	83	65	72	59	90	85
1958	90	86	72	75	62	92	85
1959	88	87	82	82	59	85	87
1960	93	91	80	87	63	91	89
1961	97	95	83	91	76	98	96
1962	100	100	100	100	100	100	100
1963	108	110	120	106	133	114	105
1964	118	115	116	107	116	122	109
1965	121	117	119	108	106	124	111
1966	127	122	121	108	119	137	115
1967	134	126	129	109	109	141	117
1968	137	129	144	108	143	143	120
1969	139	131	141	112	137	144	125

Sources: Alburo and Shepherd, 1988, appendix tables E.5.1 and E.5.2

From 1962 onwards prices rose faster, as measured by the consumer price index (CPI). Until about 1966, rising food prices were principally to blame (table 4.6); within food, prices rose fastest for cereals, particularly rice. Treadgold and Hooley (1967) demonstrate that improving producer prices in export agriculture relative to food crops for domestic consumption drew land resources out of food crops and into export crops. They go on to suggest that, in a post-decontrol situation of excess domestic demand, this excess demand was particularly concentrated in the food sector because of the greater price incentives to export crops. This in turn contributed to the particular inflation in food.

Inflation in food prices notwithstanding, post-decontrol price rises in the Philippines were at first moderate. Another way of looking at the rise in domestic costs and prices compared with international trends is through the REER (table 4.7). The large devaluation-induced rise in REERs occurred in 1961 and 1962 for imports and 1962 for exports, indicating that the first phase of decontrol – particularly the first year, 1960 – had a limited effect on exchange rates. The peak of the real devaluation of the peso did not last beyond 1962 and 1963. After this there was generally an erosion, albeit moderate, in REERs for the rest of the decade, as domestic inflation proceeded faster than international inflation, with no more offsetting exchange rate adjustments and a generally unfavorable trend in world prices for Philippine exports. However, even with a markedly faster

Table 4.7 Real effective exchange rates, 1955–1969
(1962 = 100)

Year	Exports	Imports	Rice	Manufacturing
1955	65	54	n.a.	n.a.
1956	64	53	n.a.	n.a.
1957	62	53	n.a.	n.a.
1958	65	53	n.a.	n.a.
1959	71	56	n.a.	n.a.
1960	72	54	54	56
1961	76	67	66	69
1962	100	100	100	100
1963	99	100	100	94
1964	92	94	95	90
1965	93	93	94	87
1966	96	90	105	88
1967	93	87	103	85
1968	94	90	101	75
1969	89	87	92	71

n.a., not available.
Source: Alburo and Shepherd, 1988, appendix tables E.6.4 and
E.6.5

fall in REERs after 1966, REERs still remained higher, and more apparently favorable to exporting, than in the 1950s.

Agricultural and nonagricultural real wages fell by 10–20 percent around the beginning of the 1960s. (They were to fall even more around the beginning of the 1970s.) The real wage decline appeared to be significantly larger for agricultural workers: from the peak in 1958 to the trough in 1965 agricultural real wages fell by 27 percent, while real wages overall fell by 15 percent over the shorter period 1960–3. (Figure 2.3 reports only on WPI-deflated real wage costs but, during the 1960s at least, CPI-deflated real wages moved in a very similar way.) From the mid-1960s, however, both agricultural and nonagricultural real wages rose significantly, though not to the level they had enjoyed at the end of the 1950s: in 1966–9 agricultural real wages stood at about 90 percent and nonagricultural at about 95 percent of their level at the end of the 1950s.

On a monthly basis real nonagricultural wage costs fells from April 1960 to the end of 1963. The steepest fall was around 10 percent and occurred in the 12 months from October 1962. The first half of 1963 marked the most serious round of labor problems – in particular a dock workers' strike – to hit the Philippines for many years.

In August 1963 minimum wages in agriculture were increased from ₱ 2.50 (established in 1951) to ₱ 3.50 a day, while in April 1965 the nonagricultural minimum wage was increased from ₱ 4 (also established in 1951) to ₱ 6 a day. The rise in the agricultural minimum was unable to halt a slide in nominal agricultural wages that continued into 1965, while the rise in the nonagricultural minimum does not appear to have had a dramatic impact.

Foreign Trade and the Balance of Payments

Both import and export values have been almost permanently, but highly variably, undervalued by Philippine trade statistics in comparison with those of partner countries (see Alburo and Shepherd, 1988, table appendix E.7.4). It is reasonable to assume that import undervaluation is aimed at minimizing payment of import duties, while export undervaluation has to do with export smuggling in view of peso overvaluation (see Baldwin, 1975, pp. 109–110). However, since the degree of export undervaluation is highly variable and does not appear to correlate with the level of currency overvaluation, it is difficult to explain annual variations in export undervaluation.[1] Given these uncertainties, we rely principally on the Philippine statistics.

Exports
Philippine export growth was rapid at the beginning of the 1950s but had slowed down by the middle of the decade (Alburo and Shepherd, 1988, appendix table E.7.3). From 1957 to 1966 the volume of exports once more grew quickly, by more than 6 percent a year, and then slowed down to average only 1.5 percent in 1966–9 (table 4.1). From 1957 to 1960 exports were helped by a rising dollar price (in this period the f.o.b. dollar export index rose by 11 percent, see table 4.1). There was no further growth in export prices until 1967. 1963 was the year of largest reported export growth: volume expanded by 24 percent, though partner-country data suggest that this growth may have been spread more smoothly over 1963 and 1964.

Export growth was dominated by traditional exports but there were some structural changes (see table 2.5). From 1960 to 1965 the share of sugar fell but was compensated for by a rise in log exports. In fact, sugar exports depended largely on US quotas (which had expanded significantly at the beginning of the 1960s). From 1965 to 1970 the share of coconuts in exports fell, while that of copper rose (thanks to new mines coming on stream toward the end of the decade). Throughout the decade, there was a steady shift within coconut product exports from (unprocessed) copra to coconut oil. The share of manufactures in total exports actually fell from

---

[1] Five-year averages of the degree of export undervaluation (from two alternatives series) are compared with equivalent periodic averages for the ratio of the black-market to the official exchange rate in table 4.11. The five-year average was taken to minimize the problem of annual fluctuations in the degree of export undervaluation. Little correlation is evident.

1955 to 1960, from 9 to 3 percent, but it grew steadily, if unspectacularly, in the 1960s to reach 10 percent by 1970.

Imports

After 1957 there was no overall growth trend in import volume until 1964 when, according to national trade statistics, imports grew by 24 percent in one year and then grew steadily until 1967 (table 4.1). In fact, partner-country statistics suggest that the rapid import growth started a year earlier, in 1963 (Alburo and Shepherd, 1988, appendix table E.7.4). Before this, the year of highest import growth since 1957 had been 1961, the second year of decontrol. The period up to mid-1970s was also marked by a steady but modest growth in the dollar price of imports (2.4 percent a year in 1955–65; see table 4.1).

The structure of imports in the 1960s showed some important departures from trends or averages: specifically, an interruption in the post-war trend of import substitution in industrial products, particularly consumer goods, and a temporary growth in the level of food imports in the mid-1960s.

The level of import substitution is best measured by comparing the ratio of imports to the size of the market, or of output. Given the very large changes in relative domestic and world price levels (reflected in the REER), it is important to measure this import ratio in constant prices if possible. This was possible for manufacturing and the economy as a whole, but not for agriculture. The ratio of manufactured imports to the domestic market for manufactures fell from 49 percent in 1956 (in constant prices) to 25 percent in 1980 (table 4.8). But from 1962 or 1963 to 1969 the trend towards import replacement was halted (though not reversed). This phenomenon, common to many manufacturing industries, is discussed further in chapter 7.

The ratio of agricultural imports (SITC 0) to agricultural product in table 4.8 is expressed in current prices. The effective peso devaluation of 1961–2 would tend to increase the current price ratio even if imports and domestic output stayed stationary in real terms. Between 1962 and 1969, when the exchange rate remained stable (except for the end to the export retention in 1965), annual changes in the ratio are more comparable. The agricultural import ratio rose significantly, from 6 percent in 1963 to 11 percent in 1965, and then fell rapidly from 1967 to 1969. By the same token, the share of agricultural products (SITC 0) in total imports rose from 13 percent in 1963 to 20 percent in 1965, falling to 11 percent by 1969 (United Nations, various years).

The hiatus in industrial import penetration and the surge in agricultural imports in the middle of the 1960s are mirrored in statistics on the composition of imports by end-use. The strong post-war trend in the composition of imports has been a falling share of consumer goods, from 17 percent of total imports in 1957 to 4 percent in 1980, in favor of

Table 4.8 Ratios of exports and imports to domestic product, 1955–1980 (percent)

	1	2	3	4	5	6
	Ratio of total trade to total GDP at 1972 prices		Ratio of manufacturing trade to manufacturing gross output at 1972 prices		Ratio of agricultural trade to agricultural GDP at current prices	
Year	Exports	Imports	Exports[a]	Imports[b]	Exports	Imports
1955	22	27	n.a.	n.a.	25	8
1956	18	23	1.4	49	27	6
1957	17	23	1.2	48	29	7
1958	17	22	0.8	39	28	8
1959	16	18	0.9	35	28	4
1960	17	20	0.9	37	31	5
1961	16	20	0.8	33	31	6
1962	18	19	0.9	31	40	7
1963	20	17	0.9	28	45	6
1964	20	20	1.0	31	44	10
1965	22	20	1.3	31	41	11
1966	22	20	1.5	31	42	7
1967	22	23	1.5	31	36	9
1968	22	23	1.3	34	30	6
1969	17	23	2.1	33	24	5
1970	17	20	2.3	28	38	6
1971	17	19	2.5	24	35	7
1972	18	18	3.0	23	33	8
1973	19	18	4.8	20	39	7
1974	16	20	4.2	26	44	8
1975	15	20	5.0	25	34	8
1976	16	19	6.2	27	30	7
1977	18	18	5.8	23	32	6
1978	17	20	5.5	21	27	5
1979	18	22	8.0	26	28	6
1980	19	22	8.6	25	31	7
1981	19	20	n.a.	n.a.	29	7
1982	18	20	n.a.	n.a.	23	7
1983	19	19	n.a.	n.a.	n.a.	n.a.
1984	21	16	n.a.	n.a.	n.a.	n.a.

n.a., not available.
[a] Exports, net of traditional products (food and wood) and net of consignment exports, as a ratio to gross output.
[b] Imports net of consignment imports as a ratio to domestic consumption (gross output – exports and imports).
Sources: columns 1 and 2, Alburo and Shepherd, 1988, appendix table E.1.1 and E.7.2; columns 3 and 4, trade in manufactures in current values, Alburo and Shepherd, 1988, appendix tables E.7.7 and E.7.6, deflated by the second column of appendix table E.5.5; columns 3 and 4 value of output from Alburo and Shepherd, 1988, appendix table E.1.2, deflated by the first column of appendix table E.5.2; columns 5 and 6, exports of coconut products, sugar and sugar products, forest products, and fruit and vegetables, NEDA, *Philippine Statistical Yearbook*, 1976, table 12.4, and 1984, tables 7.3 and 7.5; imports (SITC 0), United Nations, *Yearbook of International Trade Statistics*, various years; domestic product, Alburo and Shepherd, 1988, appendix table E.1.1

unprocessed raw materials and, until the end of the 1960s, machinery and equipment. However, from 1959 to 1965 the share of consumer goods actually rose from 12 to 18 percent before beginning to fall again (Central Bank of the Philippines, *Annual Report*, various years).[2]

The Terms of Trade

From 1955 to 1960 the Philippine terms of trade did not deteriorate; indeed 1959, with a 6 percent improvement, was a bumper year (figure 2.1). In 1961 the terms of trade deteriorated rapidly (by 9 percent) and at a slow and steady annual rate (averaging 1.25 percent) thereafter to 1970. Thus decontrol, particularly in 1961, occurred under conditions of deteriorating international prices for the country.

The Balance of Payments

In every year from 1953 to 1961 except 1959 there were current account deficits. However, the period 1962–5 is exceptional in post-war Philippine history as providing four years of current account surpluses in succession. This clear underlying improvement (in a period of worsening terms of trade) was due not only to improvements in the balance of merchandise trade after 1961, but even more to improvements from 1960 to 1966 on the services account (Alburo and Shepherd, 1988, appendix table E.7.1). This improvement, not obviously attributable to any one item (NEDA, 1976, table 12.1), perhaps indicates that decontrol and devaluation had a positive influence on the balance in tradeable services. (Foreign military aid also grew significantly from 1964 to 1968, probably as a result of the Vietnam War.)

The current account deficits before 1962 were largely financed by drawing down reserves until 1957, and then by an increase in foreign debt. The latter grew particularly quickly in 1961 and 1962 (from a ratio of 2.6 percent of GDP in 1960 to 6.3 percent in 1963, according to one measure; see table 4.1). From 1962 to 1966, when the current account was in surplus, this ratio continued to grow, but much more modestly.

---

[2] Central Bank statistics on imports by exchange control category provide qualified evidence of changes in import composition following decontrol. The categories attracting most stringent import control were nonessential producer and consumer goods and unclassified items. According to Central Bank statistics quoted in Power and Sicat (1971, table 4.3), the share of these categories in total imports was 12 percent in 1959 (13 percent in 1960 when, however, there was a reclassification of products which had the effect of enlarging these categories) and grew to 19 percent by 1963. According to a slightly different Central Bank series (quoted in International Labor Office (ILO), 1974, table 21), the share of these same categories rose from 18 percent in 1960 and peaked at 23 percent in 1965, falling back to 11 percent by 1970. In the mid-1960s, however, it is probable that these categories were dominated by the high level of food imports.

Output, Employment, and Factor Use

The economy grew in the first half of the 1960s at more or less the rate of the preceding five years. Agriculture and manufacturing grew at similar rates in 1960–5, near the average for net domestic product (NDP) as a whole of just under 5 percent a year (table 4.9).

The manufacturing growth rate of 4.5 percent in 1960–5 was in fact the lowest post-war growth rate for manufacturing up to 1980. It was inevitable that the high rates of manufacturing growth in the 1950s could not be kept up once the easier opportunities for import substitution began to be exhausted; this low growth, however, has been generally attributed to decontrol. There is little evidence of important changes in the structure of manufacturing; thus the slowdown in growth was experienced across manufacturing industries.

Table 4.9 Growth rates of domestic product, 1946–1983 (average percent per annum at 1972 prices)

Period	Agriculture	Manufacturing	Services	NDP
1946–50	12.2	47.2	15.6	16.0
1950–5	7.1	12.1	9.0	7.9
1955–60	2.9	7.7	5.1	4.6
1960–5	4.8	4.5	4.5	4.8
1965–70	3.5	6.1	4.8	4.4
1970–5	4.3	6.9	5.7	6.2
1975–80	5.3	6.0	5.7	6.2
1980–3	1.5	2.7	3.5	2.6

Sources: 1946–70, NEDA, 1978, table 3.3.B; 1970–83, data supplied by NEDA, January 1985

Agriculture, however, grew more rapidly in 1960–5 (its domestic product expanding by 4.8 percent per annum) than in 1955–60 (2.9 percent a year). Poor growth in the earlier period largely reflected the failure of the export sector to grow, while the improvement in 1960–5 reflected a spurt in the growth of export crops from 1961 to 1964. Production of export crops then more or less stagnated again until 1969. Power and Sicat (1971, p. 44) have commented that the traditional sector's response to devaluation was "immediate, substantial and short-lived."

There is little evidence of any important shift in the employment structure of the economy in the first half of the 1960s. Nor is there any evidence of changes in the level of open unemployment following decontrol. Open unemployment remained in the area of 7–9 percent in the 1960s (table 4.10). However, underemployment, as measured by the share of the workforce seeking additional work, rose from 22 percent in 1960 to

Table 4.10 Unemployment indicators, 1957–1969 (percent)

	1 *Share of unemployed in labor force (May figures)*	2 *Share of those wanting additional work in total employment*	3 *Share of industrial unemployment in total unemployment*
1957	8.7	n.a.	n.a.
1958	9.1	21	n.a.
1959	7.7	19	n.a.
1960	6.3[a]	22	n.a.
1961	8.6	24	n.a.
1962	9.5[b]	25	n.a.
1963	7.8	31	16
1964	6.4	n.a.	24
1965	8.2	27	28
1966	7.2	25	21
1967	8.2	26	18
1968	9.4	28	17
1969	6.9	23	19

n.a., not available.
[a] October.
[b] April.
Sources: columns 1 and 3, Department of Labor, *Yearbook of Labor Statistics*, various years; column 2, Domingo and Feranil, 1984, table 6.12

31 percent in 1963, and then remained between 25 and 30 percent until 1968. Furthermore, statistics on unemployment by last sector of employment indicate that industry's share rose from 16 percent of total unemployment in 1963 to 28 percent in 1965, and then fell back to 18 percent by 1967 (table 4.10). Thus there is some slender evidence of a transitory rise in unemployment in industry in the middle of the decade.

Power and Sicat (1971, pp. 55–8) and Baldwin (1975, pp. 128–31) have remarked on the capital-using bias of Philippine manufacturing in the 1950s and 1960s. In the 1950s a falling capital-to-output ratio (suggesting growing efficiency in the use of capital) accompanied the trend to increasing capital-to-labor and output-to-labor ratios, while in the early 1960s it seems that there was growing inefficiency in factor use. Hooley (1985), covering the period 1956–80, found that total factor productivity grew from 1957 to 1961 and then failed to grow for several years, actually declining from 1963 to 1965 (figure 4.1). A major element in this was the strong tendency of the capital-to-output ratio to grow in the first half of the 1960s. In the same period, according to Hooley's figures, both output per worker and fixed capital per worker stagnated. It is possible that this

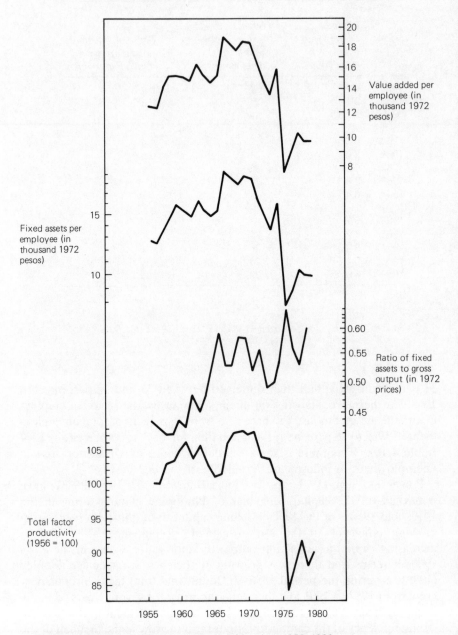

Figure 4.1 Indicators of factor use in manufacturing, 1956–1980

Sources: Alburo and Shepherd, 1988, appendix table E.3.2; Richard Hooley, unpublished data

performance is connected with decontrol, though the very variability of Hooley's figures, which is probably the consequence of the variability of the manufacturing survey figures on which they are based, should lead to caution about his results.

Redistribution of Income Flows

Around the decontrol period income flows were generally redirected from both manufacturing and food production for the domestic market to export activities, principally in agriculture (Treadgold and Hooley, 1967). From 1959 to 1963 the internal terms of trade, as measured by relative move- ments in wholesale prices, shifted markedly in favor of export agriculture at the expense of manufacturing and the rest of agriculture (see table 4.6). This process began as early as 1955 in agriculture, but was fastest from 1960 to 1963. From 1959 to 1963 wholesale prices of local manufactures and of agricultural products for the domestic market grew by around 5 and 6 percent a year, while wholesale prices for agricultural exports grew by 16 percent.

The effect of these relative price changes is reflected in changing rates of profit by sector. Castro (1969, p. 190) reports falling rates of return on net worth in manufacturing after 1959 and growing rates in agriculture and mining (data to 1962 only). Treadgold and Hooley (1967, p. 113) report falling rates of return on sales in manufacturing from 1959 to 1965.

Real investment was somewhat depressed in the early 1960s, largely because investment in durable equipment, which had grown from 3 to 9 percent of NDP (at 1972 prices) from 1952 to 1957, declined from 9 percent in 1959 to 7 percent in 1962 and 1963 (figure 4.2).[3] These figures suggest a slowdown in manufacturing investment, though this is not supported by the investment figures coming from the annual survey of manufactures.[4]

The shift in incomes to the rural elite did not impair the savings performance of the economy. No estimate is available of a savings ratio in constant prices, but a rough assessment can be made by adding the current account balance-of-payments deficit (as a ratio of GDP in constant prices) to the investment ratio. This arithmetic suggests a substantial improvement in the "real" savings ratio from a level of 13–16 percent of GDP in 1959–61 to over 20 percent in 1963–6, falling back to 15 percent by 1969.

---

[3] Power and Sicat (1971, p. 49) report the opposite – a rising share of investment in GDP – but this was based on GDP at current prices. The largest investment item, durable equipment, is extremely import intensive and, for real investment ratios to stay constant, nominal ratios would have had to have risen after decontrol.
[4] Survey data on investment were reworked by Hooley (1985, annex D) into a constant-price series for fixed assets. These show no interruption to growth in the first half of the 1960s.

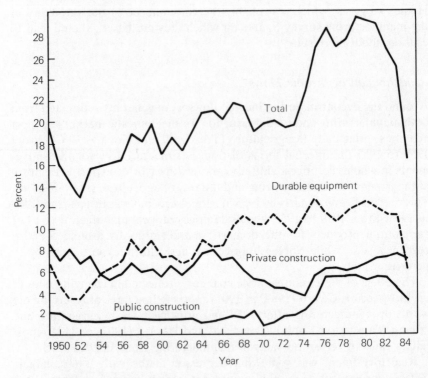

Figure 4.2 Gross domestic capital formation as a percentage of gross domestic product, 1949–1984 (at 1972 prices)

Source: data supplied by NEDA

Thus, as other commentators have noted, it was consumption that appeared to suffer in the wake of decontrol: the share of the national product going to consumption fell, consumer prices – especially for food – rose, and, as noted earlier, the real wage fell in the first few years of the 1960s.

Decontrol: an Evaluation

Decontrol in the early 1960s was undoubtedly the most important single liberalization achieved in post-war Philippine trade policy: an overvalued peso was devalued and the distortions associated with direct controls were eliminated. Yet decontrol proved limited in its effects: it neither set the economy on a path to higher growth, nor was it sustained beyond the end of the decade.

The Implementation of Decontrol

Two points about the implementation of decontrol are noteworthy. A prime objective was to eliminate the foreign exchange bottleneck caused by an overvalued currency, while political reaction against the corruption this bottleneck caused – the "buying" of import rights – was also important in creating the constituency for change.

Second, decontrol was achieved through a phase of gradual reform in 1960–1 which was then replaced by an abrupt reform in 1962. The gradual phase went wrong for several reasons. In 1960 the government deliberately pursued an expansionary macroeconomic policy to ease the pains of decontrol, a policy which became excessively expansionary in 1961 because this was a presidential election year. In addition, export prices and receipts fell steeply in 1961, adding to the pressure on the balance of payments and fueling speculation on the eventual value that a devalued peso would assume. World prices and domestic political conditions were more appropriate for the abrupt completion of decontrol in 1962, and a less expansionary macroeconomic policy was adopted. Both phases of decontrol made an important contribution, and it is perhaps difficult to compare them given changing political and economic conditions. Even so, inasmuch as the short-term disruption to the economy after 1962 appeared minimal, there are reasons for preferring the abrupt rather than the phased approach (see chapter 7).

Decontrol and Economic Growth

The agricultural sector led in the more or less sustained expansion of exports from 1958 to 1966. This export growth, together with a very low growth in imports, was the main element of the economy's success in reestablishing external equilibrium – the current account was in surplus from 1962 to 1965. The expansion of agricultural exports, and hence of output, pre-dated decontrol by several years. The early success of these exports is explained by two features. First – and contrary to the long-term trend – there was a favorable movement in world prices for Philippine exports from 1957 to 1960. Second, from the mid-1950s exporters were able to find ways around the peso overvaluation, partly through the barter laws and partly through smuggling. As the terms of trade resumed their downward trend after 1960, it appears that the effective peso devaluation of 1961 and 1962 took over as the driving force behind exports.

The shift in relative domestic prices in favor of export agriculture and against food production for the domestic market – which occurred largely over the period 1958–66 – was accompanied by a clear switch in land use from domestic to export crops over roughly the same period. This shift had a palpable effect on production shares by the early 1960s and contributed to rising prices of local food for the domestic market. This not only fueled the general inflation, helping to erode the effective devaluation, but also led to large food imports in 1963–5 which helped erode the trade surplus.

Whatever the intentions of its architects, decontrol significantly reduced the level of protection (by eliminating the large quota premium), without by any means eliminating it (since tariffs were increased). If, indeed, protection was thus reduced, a sector that had been artificially boosted by high protection might be expected to contract, or to improve its productivity significantly in reaction to new competitive pressures, or to show a cominbation of these effects. In fact, none of this appears to have happened. The apparent inertness of manufacturing remains a mystery.

There is reasonable evidence of low growth rates in manufacturing in the first half of the 1960s. There was also a clear fall in profit levels in manufacturing, while profits in the export-oriented sectors, agriculture and mining, rose. Finally, there is clear evidence of an interruption – from 1963 to 1968 – of the long-term post-war tendency towards import replacement in manufactured goods. This was only an interruption, however: the level of import substitution stagnated rather than declined. There is some slight evidence that investment in machinery may have fallen off in 1962 and 1963 and that unemployment related to manufacturing job losses may have temporarily increased around 1963–5.

What is surprising is how little structural change appears to have occurred in manufacturing, for instance in shares by industry. However, there are some signs of growing inefficiency in factor use in the first half of the 1960s: Hooley (1985) records a decline in total factor productivity from 1961 to 1965 and a rise from 1966 to 1968. If these measures are reliable, they might suggest (à la Verdoorn's law) that productivity growth correlates with output growth. It is the strongest piece of statistical evidence – supporting the contentions of the industrialists themselves – that, in an immediate sense at least, decontrol was "bad" for industry. The statistical evidence that points in the opposite direction relates to nontraditional manufactured exports which grew from 3 percent of total exports in 1960 to 10 percent in 1970. (For a statistical test confirming the importance of REERs and real wages in the growth of nontraditional exports see chapter 7.)

Decontrol also involved the abolition of most controls on trade in invisibles and appears to have benefited the trade balance in services. A marked improvement from 1960 to 1966 in the trade balance in services was as instrumental in the regaining of external equilibrium as the improvement in merchandise trade.

Decontrol does not appear to have set the Philippine economy firmly on a changed path of higher and more sustained growth (though arguably a continuation of controls would have led to a substantially worse result).

Overall growth rates did not rise – in fact, higher agricultural growth was canceled out by lower industrial growth. The major achievement was the attainment of external equilibrium, but only for the short period of 1962–6.

There are two different explanations, not necessarily mutually exclusive, of why the effects of decontrol were short lived. First, the Treadgold and Hooley thesis is, in effect, that decontrol was self-cancelling because agricultural export expansion both proved inflationary and resulted in greater food imports when it led to the substitution of limited resources within agriculture. In fact this was the diagnosis accepted, implicitly at least, by the new Marcos government which, from 1966, promoted both rural development and nontraditional exports as an answer to the perceived agricultural constraint.

Second, the country's competitive position was steadily eroded after 1963 as domestic prices were allowed to rise faster than world prices, the terms of trade continued to decline, and no exchange rate adjustments were made until 1970, apart from the elimination of the export retention in 1965. While this inflation is not uniquely associated with the Marcos government, it is nonetheless true that more expansionary policies, notably in 1966 and 1967 and the presidential election year of 1969, both led to more inflation and encouraged a large growth in imports.

There is no doubt much truth in both explanations. If so, the former explanation suggests that there were limitations on the economy's supply response to decontrol. This was in part because of limited resources in agriculture, and in part because the manufacturing sector was not sufficiently de-protected to turn to exporting in anything more than a marginal manner. Meanwhile, the latter explanation emphasizes the important interrelationships of trade policy and macroeconomic policy.

Other Effects of Decontrol

Real wages clearly reacted systematically to changes in the role of the tradeables-producing sectors in the economy. Real wages fell around the beginning of the 1960s, recovering, more or less, by the end of the decade. In agriculture, the period of falling real wages, 1958–65, partially pre-dates decontrol but coincides with the switch in land use from domestic to export crops (1958–65), the favorable move in domestic prices for agricultural exports *vis-à-vis* domestic crops (1955–63), the rise in export REERs (1957–62), and the export boom (1957–66). Similarly, the decline in nonagricultural real wages from 1960 to early 1964 corresponds to the period of import decontrol and the associated period of rising REERs (both 1960–2).

Decontrol encouraged inflation both through raising import and export prices and, later, through indirectly inducing rises in food prices. Yet, with such a large nominal devaluation and not the tightest of macroeconomic

Table 4.11 Export undervaluation and the black-market exchange rate premium, 1950–1983

| | Measures of export undervaluation (%) | | |
	Major trading partners	All trading partners	Ratio of black-market to official exchange rate
1950–4	98	n.a.	1.39
1955–60	94	103[a]	1.70
1960–4	94	89	1.11
1965–9	94[b]	86	1.09
1970–4	n.a.	91	1.07
1975–9	n.a.	90	1.07
1980–3	n.a.	87	1.11

n.a., not available.
[a] 1958–9.
[b] 1965–8
Sources: Alburo and Shepherd, 1988, appendix table E.7.4 and E.6.7

policies, inflation – at 5–6 percent a year in the 1960s – was relatively mild. While the nominal devaluation was inflationary, decontrol, by removing the foreign exchange premium on both imports and exports, was also deflationary. Thus a liberalization consisting of the removal of direct controls need not prove too inflationary.

Finally, there is some evidence that decontrol may have been associated with a depressed level of real investment in the first few years of the 1960s. This would not be an unreasonable outcome of decontrol, given the import intensity of much investment and the increased cost of importing. However, there was some evidence of a marked improvement in the domestic savings ratio from 1963 to 1966.

5

The 1970s: Export Promotion and the Growth of Manufactured Exports

Policies for export promotion in the 1970s have their origins in the events that reversed the policies of decontrol in the late 1960s. On the economic front the first Marcos administration, which took office in 1966, pursued a more expansionary macroeconomic policy than the foregoing Macapagal administration. This led to a growing balance-of-payments and debt crisis in 1967–9. By 1969 import controls had been partially reintroduced. The government's subsequent reactions to the crisis, as well as its stance on broader trade and industry policies, were largely conditioned by its perceptions of the decontrol experience. In 1970 the peso was substantially devalued, but most of the newly introduced import controls were retained. Thus most manufacturing activities continued to receive substantial protection, greater on average than in the period 1962–9 but less than before decontrol. At the same time, measures to promote nontraditional exports were introduced, notably in 1970 and 1973. Thus trade policy consisted of steps forward and steps backward. This was by no means an episode of unequivocal trade liberalization.

The period from 1970 to about 1974 was one of economic stabilization combined with direct export promotion. For the rest of the 1970s, the level of protection to import-replacing activities appears to have grown. Yet it was during the second, rather than the first, half of the decade that the composition of exports changed dramatically, as a result of growth in nontraditional manufactured exports and the stagnation of traditional exports. In this chapter we argue that decontrol in the early 1960s, devaluation in 1970, and a remarkable decline in the real wage between 1969 and 1974 laid the basis for this growth in manufactured exports, while the effect of the formal export subsidy measures of the early 1970s was less important.

In the first part of the chapter we review the policies and events in the later years of the 1960s that led to the reintroduction of foreign exchange controls and precipitated the policy changes of the early 1970s. The second part describes the major trade and related policy developments for 1970–4. In the third part the effects of these policies on the development of the economy in this period are examined, while the changing political circumstances during the 1970s and their apparent effects on policy changes after 1974 are discussed in the fourth part. The fifth part briefly looks at economic performance in 1974–80. Finally, we evaluate the growth of nontraditional manufactured exports in the 1970s.

1966–1969: the Partial Reintroduction of Controls

The Marcos government that came to office at the beginning of 1966 began a new era in economic policy. To some extent it turned its back on the experiment in free markets of the decontrol period, yet it did not return to the macroeconomic conservatism nor the tight controls that marked the 1950s. There was a predominating sense of disappointment with decontrol which the new government appeared to share. The first half of the decade was seen as a period of austerity, low industrial growth, and high inflation, especially in food. This inflation had in turn affected incomes and led to labor unrest (particularly in 1963). The Marcos government drew some specific policy lessons from these perceptions. There was a renewed emphasis on rural development, a move towards a moderate degree of industrial planning, a new interest in promoting nontraditional manufactured exports, a belief in the virtues of attracting foreign investment, and a decidedly more expansionary stance on macroeconomic policy.

According to Baldwin (1975, pp. 66–7) the new government's particular emphasis on rural development reflected its view that food inflation in the mid-1960s had prevented decontrol from restoring higher growth rates.

Policies towards Industry

The decontrol experience had engendered a strong feeling that import liberalization had led to a waste of economic resources through, for instance, the development of excess capacity. Such a feeling was of course fostered by the industrialists who were no longer receiving the levels of protection they had enjoyed in the 1950s. The Philippine Chamber of Industry (PCI) was vociferous in representing this group – broadly in the camp of "economic nationalists" – which was successful in pressing for policies to support existing Philippine firms.

Thus the climate was ripe for more interventionist policies, including a modest degree of planning. As a result, a comprehensive set of investment incentives was legislated in 1967 (the Investment Incentives Act, RA 5186), and a Board of Investments (BOI) was established in the same year to administer this. The BOI was empowered to determine areas of investment priority and to regulate direct foreign investments through the criteria set out in RA 5186 and in another act covering foreign investments not entitled to incentives (RA 5455). RA 5186 and RA 5455 attached more restrictive conditions to foreign investment than the government had wanted. These laws also did much to calm the fears of economic nationalists.

The BOI was also empowered in 1970 to control investments in some 30 industries declared to be overcrowded. Many of these industries – textiles for instance – were the avowed "victims" of decontrol. Another important expression of the prevailing reaction against decontrol was a refinancing program for distressed industries established in April 1966 by the Development Bank of the Philippines (DBP) (*Central Bank News Digest*, 1966).

In this atmosphere the constituency for any further import liberalization was small (its nucleus having been formed by a few of the "technocrats," many of them trained in the United States, that Marcos began to appoint to key economic positions). These economic liberals were much less powerful than the business interests favoring continued protection, which had been consolidating their position in Congress. Tariff reform of the protection-reducing variety was simply not on the agenda.

However, the promotion of nontraditional manufactured exports was an objective that everyone, economic nationalists and economic liberals alike, could agree on: it was a liberalizing move which did not disturb the vested interests of the import substitution lobby. The 1967 Investment Incentives Act legislated the first direct export incentives since the effective expiry, after decontrol, of the barter laws of the 1950s. For many, the export success of Korea and Taiwan, countries in the process of overtaking the Philippines, was an auspicious precedent.

The IMF seems to have had a strong influence on trade-related policy from the late 1960s. This agency's argument for floating the peso in early 1970 appears to have been decisive in the debate on the relative merits of devaluation versus multiple exchange rates versus austerity measures. This period also saw, however, the beginning of a closer relationship between the Philippines and international aid donors – led by the World Bank – who were impressed by the administration's development policies (the Consultative Group for the Philippines was formed in 1970).

Macroeconomic Policy

Baldwin (1975, pp. 65–75) describes in detail the monetary and fiscal policies pursued by the Marcos administration up to 1969. From the beginning of 1966 to half-way through 1967 the government made credit liberally available, by reducing interest rates and reserve requirements on special time deposits and other measures (including the DBP refinancing scheme). By 1967, inflation was beginning to grow again and imports grew

Table 5.1 Estimated value of fiscal incentives to nontraditional exports, 1967–1983

	1	2	3	4	5
			Local input-intensive		
	Import-intensive product		product		
Legislation	10% profit margin	20% profit margin	10% profit margin	20% profit margin	Arithmetic average of columns 1–4
Ratio of value of incentives to sales value (%)					
RA 5186 1967	3	3	3	3	3
RA 6135, 1970	3	3	4	9	5
PD 92, 1973	4	9	4	9	6.5
BP 391, 1983	5	7	9	10	8
Ratio of value of incentives to value added (%)					
RA 5186, 1967	10	7	10	7	8.5
RA 6135, 1970	7	5	10	18	10
PD 92, 1973	10	8	10	18	11.5
BP 391, 1983	14	14	27	27	20.5

Average may not compute exactly owing to rounding.
Source: Alburo and Shepherd, 1988, appendix table C.3

by a massive 24 percent in volume in this year, while export volume contracted – for the first time since 1961 – by 4 percent (table 4.1). The government responded by tightening credit once more from mid-1967 and reintroducing some import and foreign exchange controls. For instance, special time deposit requirements against letters of credit were introduced in June 1968.

The year 1969 was a presidential election year. It started with some relaxation of the new foreign exchange controls, but in the run-up to the election both government spending and the money supply increased substantially and, of course, pressure on the balance of payments resumed. In consequence, in June 1969 the government effectively banned the import of all but essential producer and consumer goods and semi-essential and nonessential producer goods, and even put ceilings on the latter (Baldwin, 1975, pp. 69–72).

While the expansionary policies of the Marcos government were clearly crucial in the large balance-of-payments crisis of 1968–9, the crisis did not arise uniquely from developments after 1965. In its last year, the presidential election year of 1965, the Macapagal administration had pursued the traditional expansionary policy (though not as expansionary as in 1969). Also the export success of decontrol appears to have contributed to inflation by "crowding out" the production of food for local consumption. Moreover, the process of inflation, encouraged by devaluation in the early part of the decade and by food prices in the mid-1960s, itself steadily eroded the economy's competitiveness: both export and import REERs fell after 1963 (table 4.6).

1970–1974: Policies for Stabilization and Export Promotion

No coherent trade policy package can be discerned from the complex of differing directions pursued by trade and related policies in the early 1970s.

Exchange Rate Policy

In February 1970, when the peso was floated, it went immediately from ₱ 3.90 to ₱ 5.50 per US dollar and had reached ₱ 6.40 by December 1970 when the authorities agreed to maintain it at that rate. The downward float, accompanied by a conservative macroeconomic policy, in fact constituted an episode of stabilization. It was instigated by the IMF and was the price that the government had to pay for getting a third tranche from the IMF and obtaining the agreement of foreign banks to the rescheduling of the external debt that had grown in the late 1960s.

While some import controls were relaxed following the introduction of the package, controls were retained on certain consumer goods imports and some invisibles. These retentions appear to have been a deliberate reaction of the "excessive" decontrol of 1962. The February 1970 measures also imposed the condition that 80 percent of foreign exchange receipts from leading exports be converted at the old rate. Ostensibly intended to encourage further processing of export goods and to minimize the problems of excess domestic liquidity from increased imports, the real intention of this effective export tax was to spur Congress to legislate formal export taxes, which it did in May of that year (see below).

The Central Bank began to intervene actively to stabilize the exchange rate after 1972 (Pante, 1982). De facto exchange rate policy in the 1970s was that of a "crawling peg" based on the US dollar.

Tariff and Nontariff Barriers to Imports

In 1969 the government had reintroduced import controls on the categories that, by and large, domestic manufacturers tended to produce. The retention of these controls (with some other controls on invisible imports) after the 1970 devaluation contrasts with the complete dismantling of such controls in 1962. After 1970 individual products were occasionally reclassified by the Central Bank between controlled and uncontrolled categories. These reclassifications had little systematic liberalizing or deliberalizing effect.

Ever since the introduction in Congress of a draft omnibus tariff reform bill in 1964, tariff reform had been stalled by the conflict of individual pressure groups represented in Congress. Under the circumstances, reform in individual rates was undertaken through the Presidential prerogative (under various Executive Orders). One of the first economic acts of the government after martial law was declared in September 1972 was a thorough revision of the tariff code under Presidential Decree (PD) 34, of January 1973. This was largely a rationalization of the tariff structure, reducing many columns to only seven (ranging from 10 percent to 100 percent *ad valorem*), and intended to narrow the scope for technical smuggling. It was a positive, if modest, step towards tariff reform: the highest rates (above 100 percent) were reduced, a minimum 10 percent tariff was introduced (eliminating some of the bias toward capital intensity by taxing imported capital goods), and all previous duty exemptions enjoyed by public institutions were removed (Sicat, 1974, p. 56). In contrast, and less publicized, tariff rates were realigned with the Central Bank commodity classification used to control imports in an attempt to make protective instruments more consistent (Tariff Commission of the Philippines, 1976). Beyond the greater consistency in protection, this was not a major tariff reform.

Measures to Promote Nontraditional Exports

The Investment Incentives Act of 1967 (RA 5186) was a landmark piece of legislation seeking to promote industrial planning through fiscal incentives. In addition the Act legislated fiscal incentives for exports of nontraditional goods for the very first time. Apart from enabling exporters to acquire imported inputs at world prices (through a tax credit on import taxes), these incentives provided for some modest subsidy to the use of local raw materials (via tax credits) and to export-related marketing and shipping expenses (through tax deductions).

In 1970 these provisions were augmented by the Export Incentives Act (RA 6135) which legislated incentives for nontraditional exports of goods and services for firms exporting more than 50 percent of their output. It also extended some of the incentives to export traders. A direct subsidy to value added was given under a formula for tax deductions based on the amount of use of direct labor and local raw materials. In November 1972 following some initial congressional legislation of 1969 that was never implemented, provisions to create the first export-processing zone at Mariveles, Bataan, and to subsidize its construction were decreed (PD 66).

In January 1973, PD 92 (amending RAs 5186 and 6135) added to some of the previous incentives. The main feature for exports was to remove the tax deductions for export-related marketing and shipping expenses under RA 5186, but to provide a strong tax deduction incentive for use of local direct labor and raw material than was provided for under RA 6135. In 1973, in addition, the establishment of bonded warehouses was permitted under certain conditions; this applied to larger firms exporting at least 70 percent of their output.

After 1973 export incentives remained virtually unchanged until the wholesale overhaul of fiscal incentives under Parliamentary Law BP 391 of 1983. The new export incentives system as it developed in the 1970s undoubtedly provided effective means for firms to price their imported inputs at or near world prices, but the effect of subsidizing the use of local raw materials or the firm's value added is less clear.

Alburo and Shepherd (1988, appendix C) report on some simple stylized calculations that represent the incidence of certain fiscal incentives on the sales value of exports and on value added (that is, a range of specific cost structures under four major successive measures to promote exports). These calculations include those fiscal incentives that subsidize current costs of production for domestic inputs; they exclude the value of incentives to investment (since domestic investors receive similar concessions), and they exclude tax and tariff concessions on imported current inputs (since such concessions are not a subsidy, but enable inputs to be obtained at world prices). They assume two alternative types of product, one using imported material inputs, the other local material inputs (in each case accounting for about half of the sales value), and two levels of profitability, 10 and 20 percent returns on sales. These options result in four basic cost structures to which the formulae for calculating incentives can be applied. Table 5.1 summarizes the results.

First, the value of incentives tends to increase with the level of profits. Indeed, since the 1967, 1970, and 1973 export incentives take the form of deductions from taxable export income, they depend crucially on profit levels. Moreover, assumptions of 10 and 20 percent returns on sales may be high for the kind of labor intensive assembly activities in garments and electronics that have become the backbone of nontraditional exports.

Second, the value of the incentives has clearly increased over time, tending more or less to double in effective terms, going from 9 percent of value added in 1967 to 12 percent in 1973 and 21 percent in 1983, according to the arithmetic average of the four cost structures.

Third, since 1970 at least, incentives have tended to favor increasingly the use of local, rather than imported, inputs. Indeed, the increase from 1967 to 1983 in the effective subsidy to the low profit import intensive activity – from 10 to 14 percent – was marginal.

Given the assumptions made in these calculations, and offsetting financial costs (in the case of tax credits, for instance) and the costs of bureaucratic procedures, the results are likely to be on the high side. They suggest levels of nominal and effective subsidy for the 1970s that, even under the most favorable cost structure assumptions, were modest compared with probable levels of effective protection or peso overvaluation. In contrast, Tan has calculated an average rate of tariff- and tax-based effective protection of 44 percent for Philippine manufacturing in 1974 and an estimated 34 percent overvaluation of the peso (Tan, 1979, table 4, p. 146).

Nontraditional exports came to be dominated in the 1970s by import intensive activities, in all probability with low margins of profits on sales. These activities were not favored by the structure of export incentives. Many exporting firms have operated from bonded warehouses and have not even been registered with the BOI for incentives. Such exports would not have grown, however, without effective provisions for obtaining imported inputs at world prices.

Even if incentives to value added proved weak in the 1970s, successive legislation nonetheless moved them in the right direction, shifting the bias from import-substituting activities toward the use of imported inputs. The amendments were largely an *ad hoc* form of "fine tuning" coming from the technical and economic analyses of the BOI.

Export Taxes

In May 1970, Congress legislated export (or "stabilization") taxes (under RA 6125) at 4–10 percent on leading export products. These taxes were intended to last only until the end of 1973, but soon after martial law they were made permanent as part of the new tariff code (PD 230). Subsequently some new products were added. In February 1974, an additional premium duty, taxing 20–30 percent of the excess international price above the level at this date, was introduced for 15 products (Executive Order 425). Both the basic export tax and the premium duty have been varied over time for different products following international price trends and domestic conditions in the industry.

Export taxes have been applied ostensibly to stabilize prices, generate government revenue, encourage further processing, and safeguard domestic supply. They have not been justified as a means of influencing the country's terms of trade: for the Philippines' leading exports its only dominant share in world trade is in coconut products, but substitutability of these with other vegetable oil products is high. While the export tax has to an extent been used since 1974 to stabilize prices received by exporters, nonetheless it became a permanent feature of commercial policy in a decade when terms-of-trade movements continued to be extremely adverse. In general terms, therefore, export tax and export promotion policies combined from the early 1970s to create a bias against traditional exports (mostly agricultural and mining) in favor of nontraditional exports (mostly manufactured).

Policies toward Agriculture

Since the 1930s the government has intervened in the sugar market to administer the US sugar quota. Until the end of the US Sugar Agreement in 1973, the United States was virtually the only export market for Philippine sugar, and exporters enjoyed prices well above world levels. Even so, failures to fulfill quotas were the norm. The ending of the agreement thus removed price support from the industry.

Outside sugar, the major intervention in agriculture before the 1970s, apart from general tariff and tax policies, was the government's monopoly on international trade in rice and corn since the 1950s. In general the government has imported only as necessary to assure supply and stabilize prices. In 1972 this monopoly was broadened to cover all grains; most importantly, the government then controlled wheat imports. In 1981 the foreign trade monopoly was extended to all food crops, and the government, in addition to controlling prices, also went into food marketing, in direct competition with the private sector.

From 1973 to 1982 copra farmers were levied (at the equivalent of a 20 percent export tax) for the Coconut Consumer's Stabilization Fund (CCSF). Policy trends in coconut and sugar are further discussed below in the section on martial law.

Since 1975, in theory at least, there has been an increasingly stringent ban on log exports, for conservation reasons.

In agriculture policy measures, including the export tax, have generally created disincentives for exports. For cereal production the trend is less obvious. There was considerable public expenditure on rural development, particularly in aid of food production, in the first Marcos administration (1966–70) and again in the first flush of martial law from 1973. This push for food self-sufficiency at times constituted an important subsidy to agriculture, even offsetting in some cases – most notably irrigated rice – the disincentive of high cost inputs.

Other Policies

Three important areas of policy related to trade policy should be mentioned. First, macroeconomic measures were a key part of the 1970 stabilization package. Second, the manufacturing export sector benefited from a relatively liberal regime on capital movements. Third, elements of planning were used from the late 1960s in support of existing producers in the import-substituting manufacturing sector.

Macroeconomic Policy

In 1970–2 a tight fiscal and monetary policy was pursued, but by 1972 there were clear signs of expansion: growth in the money supply and of the budget deficit (table 5.2). Inflation became endemic in 1973 and 1974 (18 and 31 percent respectively). These were the two years when international inflation grew – the US dollar price for Philippine imports more than doubled in 1972–4 (Alburo and Shepherd, 1988, appendix table E.7.3) – but they were also the years in which a more expansionary domestic policy was pursued.

Restrictions on Capital Movements

Since decontrol the Philippines has followed a more liberal policy on capital movements except at times of balance-of-payments crisis. However, in the 1970s it continued to restrict direct foreign investment to minority participation, except in the case of activities defined as "pioneer" under incentives legislation and in the case of certain wholly export-oriented operations (such as export-processing zones).

Table 5.2 Macroeconomic indicators, 1967–1980 (percent)

	1	2	3	4	5
Year	Annual growth of month supply (M1)	Annual growth of GNP at 1972 prices	Annual change of GDP implicit deflator	Central Bank discount rate	National government budget surplus as percentage of GDP
1967	12.2	4.8	5.3	6.0	− 0.8
1968	5.3	5.5	6.1	7.5	− 0.8
1969	19.4	5.2	5.8	10.0	− 2.8
1970	− 1.2	3.9	14.8	10.0	0.1
1971	10.3	6.5	14.1	10.0	− 0.4
1972	24.9	5.4	7.0	10.0	− 1.8
1973	12.3	9.3	18.1	10.0	2.9
1974	24.0	5.6	31.0	6.0	2.4
1975	14.5	6.0	8.2	6.0	− 0.8
1976	17.1	7.2	9.4	6.0	− 1.7
1977	23.7	6.3	7.4	6.0	− 1.7
1978	13.4	5.8	9.2	4.0	− 1.2
1979	11.2	6.9	15.2	11.0	− 0.2
1980	19.6	5.0	15.5	n.a.	− 1.3

n.a., not available.

Sources: column 1, NEDA, *Philippine Statistical Yearbook*, various years; column 2, data supplied by NEDA, January 1985 estimates; column 3, Alburo and Shepherd, 1988, appendix table E.5.1; columns 4 and 5, IMF, *International Financial Statistics*, various issues

Domestic Controls

The incentives legislation of 1967 and 1970 and the creation of the BOI in 1967 laid the basis for stronger government controls in industrial (and agro-industrial) investment. Until the partial abandonment of this system in the early 1980s the government, through its control on imports of capital goods, had a powerful weapon to control new entry (and to protect existing inefficient investments).

1970–1974: a Successful Stabilization of the Economy

The External Sector

In the four years following the 1970 devaluation (that is, through 1973), exports grew substantially. Some of this growth occurred as large investments made in the later 1960s, particularly in copper mining, banana plantations, and sugar milling, came on stream; this particular export growth might be better ascribed to decontrol in the early 1960s than to the 1970s devaluation.

Exports grew by 14 percent in volume for 1969–70 (table 5.3). Some of this growth was more apparent than real, as some smuggled exports reverted to official channels. Nonetheless, since export volume grew 6–7 percent in the following two years while the terms of trade declined from 1969 to 1972, there is obvious evidence of a real devaluation effect. In 1973, however, exports were only able to expand by 8 percent in volume in spite of a 57 percent rise in their prices in the first year of the 1973–4 world commodity boom. The country's export price index further expanded by 48 percent in 1974, yet export volume fell by 11 percent, largely as a result of an enormous decline in copra exports. There was little systematic change in the structure of exports from 1970 to 1974 (table 2.5). The big four product groups – sugar, coconut, wood, and copper concentrates – more or less maintained their share (around three quarters of the total) while miscellaneous exports – mostly nontraditional manufactures – grew from 12 to 16 percent.

The drop in import quantity in 1970 to 6 percent below the 1969 level probably reflected anticipatory stockbuilding as the peso became progressively overvalued in the period before the devaluation. In fact import volumes were generally stagnant until 1974, when volume and dollar prices grew substantially (dollar inflation having seriously set in the year before). The period saw no significant change in the producer-good-dominated structure of imports.

The rapidly deteriorating terms of trade, which fell by 18 percent in 1969–72, saw a partial, but temporary, reversal with the commodity boom of 1973–4 (table 5.3).

Table 5.3 Indicators of the external sector, 1967–1980

	1	2	3	4	5	6	7	8	9
	Quantum index		Price index (US$)			Current account balance as percentage of GDP	Foreign exchange reserves in equivalent months of imports	External debt as percentage of GDP	Share of manufactures in total exports[a] (%)
Year	Exports	Imports	Exports	Imports	Terms of trade				
1967	71	102	103	81	127	−1.4	1.5	15	n.a.
1968	75	101	109	89	123	−3.7	1.3	18	n.a.
1969	77	99	110	90	121	−3.2	1.0	22	n.a.
1970	88	93	111	94	119	−0.7	2.0	30	8
1971	96	99	106	96	111	—	2.9	27	9
1972	100	100	100	100	100	0.1	4.0	26	9
1973	108	94	146	129	113	5.0	5.6	22	9
1974	96	110	242	212	115	−1.2	n.a.	19	8
1975	102	116	193	220	88	−5.6	3.7	24	9
1976	131	123	169	217	78	−5.8	4.1	30	13
1977	157	119	171	241	71	−3.6	3.5	32	17
1978	153	141	194	246	79	−4.9	3.6	34	23
1979	165	153	236	270	87	−5.4	3.7	33	21
1980	201	156	246	359	69	−5.4	2.9	36	25

n.a., not available; —, not applicable.

[a] Net of imports consigned as inputs for export production.

Source: Alburo and Shepherd, 1988 (columns 1–5, appendix table E.7.3; column 6, appendix table E.7.1; columns 7 and 8, appendix table E.7.2; column 9, appendix table E.7.11)

The growth of exports, the restraint on imports, and a relatively favorable position on invisibles led to a clear improvement in the current account of the balance of payments for 1970–3, in spite of the terms of trade. Indeed, the 1973 current account surplus, equivalent to 5 percent of GDP (table 5.3), was unprecedented. In 1974, the position reverted to a deficit as a result of the poor growth of exports. The improved trade performance allowed a reconstruction of foreign exchange reserves after their severe depletion in the last balance-of-payments crisis: equivalent to one month's imports in 1969, they covered almost six months by 1973 (table 5.3). There was also a notable improvement in the overhang of foreign debt from the crisis (and external debt as a proportion of GDP was reduced from 30 percent in 1970 to 16 percent in 1974; see table 5.3). This improvement may partly have reflected the effect of inflation on the level of debt, but the structure of debt improved as well through the virtual elimination of its short-term component (Alburo and Shepherd, 1988, appendix table E.7.2).

Prices, Real Effective Exchange Rates, and Real Wages

Even in the late 1960s inflation did not exceed 6 percent a year, but the domestic price level accelerated to an average of 16 percent in 1969–73, and then jumped by 31 percent in 1974 (calculated from table 5.4). These were levels of inflation previously unknown in the Philippines. To an extent, this inflation was pushed by the effects of natural disasters and disease on food production in 1970–2, as well as by the effect of the 1970 devaluation on the peso price of imports. However, the inflation rate was considerably lower than the peso price rise of imports and exports.

Relative international and domestic price movements can be compared through the REER. Given the extreme divergence of world prices for different product groups, it is unwise to rely on any single REER after the early 1970s, but instead we compare REERs for different representative product groups.[1] Table 5.4 gives REERs for exports, imports, rice, and (import-substituting) manufactures. For each product group except rice there was a sharp rise (depreciation) in the REER, following devaluation in 1970, of around 24–8 percent. The improved REER was generally

---

[1] During the 1970s there are also key divergences between alternative domestic and international price indices, such that the choice of price index affects the direction of the REER. From around 1969 the Philippine general WPI began to grow at a greater rate than either the CPI or the GDP implicit price deflator (which evolved comparably with each other). Thus the use of the WPI in preference to the other two indices as the denominator of the REER, other things being equal, would make for a slower rise or faster fall of the REER. Naturally, there are many international price series from which to choose a numerator for the REER. For instance, from 1960 to 1983 the US producer price index grew by 12 percent, while the OECD export index shrank by 9 percent (World Bank, 1985a, table 20).

Table 5.4 Price and wage indices, 1967–1980 (1972 = 100)

Year	1 GDP implicit price deflator	2 WPI general	3 All exports	4 All imports	5 Rice	6 Manufacturing	7 Agriculture laborers	8 Wage earners
			Real effective exchange rates				Real wage costs[a]	
1967	64	61	94	75	122	78	134	122
1968	67	63	95	78	119	68	137	119
1969	71	64	90	75	109	65	128	113
1970	82	79	117	100	112	92	104	107
1971	94	91	107	99	83	97	93	100
1972	100	100	100	100	100	100	100	100
1973	118	124	125	112	209	107	93	82
1974	155	183	159	140	307	102	80	61
1975	167	193	125	144	185	114	92	65
1976	183	210	102	134	132	110	101	68
1977	197	231	96	183	120	110	110	64
1978	215	247	99	128	154	118	107	69
1979	247	292	105	122	125	114	94	73
1980	286	346	96	143	143	109	81	74

[a] Deflated by the General WPI.
Source: Alburo and Shepherd, 1988 (columns 1 and 2, appendix table E.5.1; column 3, appendix table E.6.5; columns 4 to 6, appendix table E.6.4; columns 7 and 8, appendix table E.5.7)

maintained for these groups until 1973 or 1974 (with the exception of exports in 1972), and sometimes much longer.

In other words, the 1970 devaluation, in the 1970–4 period, was dissipated neither by domestic inflation nor by the adverse movement of the terms of trade. After the period around 1974 the trend to rising REERs (if at times ambiguous) was over.

Whether deflated by the WPI or the CPI, the real wage showed a clear and remarkable decline in the year of devaluation and was more or less halved in the period 1969–74 (table 5.4 reports on real wage costs deflated by the WPI). This was true for both agricultural and nonagricultural wages. The fact that wage inflation was far less than domestic inflation overall has implications both for income distribution and the pattern of comparative advantage in the Philippines. We return to the issue of real wages in our discussion below of the growth of manufactured exports after 1974.

Production

The successful external stabilization of the economy had no obvious counterpart in the growth of the economy (table 5.5). Overall GNP growth rates in 1969–72 picked up a little from those of the late 1960s. In agriculture, growth remained generally low, in spite of strong export growth, because of natural disasters and crop disease. There was no

Table 5.5 Growth and structure of the economy, 1967–1980 (percent)

| | Growth rates of GDP (in 1972 prices) | | | | Share in total GDP (in 1972 prices) | | |
Year	Total	Agriculture	Mining	Manufacturing	Agriculture	Mining	Manufacturing
1967	5.4[a]	3.0[a]	11.2[a]	9.3[a]	30.1	1.5	23.6
1968	5.6	7.1	20.8	6.4	30.5	1.7	23.8
1969	4.9	3.1	15.5	4.0	29.9	1.9	23.6
1970	4.8	2.2	18.0	8.5	29.2	2.2	24.4
1971	5.7	4.9	17.4	6.7	29.0	2.4	24.6
1972	5.2	3.8	4.9	6.2	28.6	2.4	24.8
1973	8.5	6.2	4.0	14.0	28.0	2.3	26.1
1974	5.0	2.3	0.2	4.7	27.3	2.2	26.0
1975	6.6	4.3	3.0	3.5	26.7	2.1	25.3
1976	7.9	8.0	3.2	5.7	26.8	2.0	24.8
1977	6.2	5.0	16.8	7.5	23.5	2.2	25.1
1978	5.5	4.2	3.9	7.3	26.1	2.2	25.5
1979	6.3	4.5	18.0	5.4	25.7	2.4	25.3
1980	5.3	5.0	4.8	4.2	25.6	2.4	25.0

[a]NDP.
Source: data supplied by NEDA, January 1985 estimates

obvious change in the growth trend for manufacturing. The year 1973 was a high-growth year across all sectors. It was led by the commodity boom and the demand thus generated by the export sectors for industrial goods and for services. In the period 1970–4 there was little discernible change in the structure of the economy.

Labor and Unemployment

The employment shares of the major sectors changed little in the first part of the 1970s (table 2.4), but the statistics indicate an important break in unemployment trends. In an economy like that of the Philippines the true level of unemployment is difficult to measure, but a reasonably consistent set of figures for 1967–74 suggests a definite fall in open unemployment rates from the late 1960s until about 1974. According to table 5.6 this rate averaged 8 percent in the four years 1967–70 and under 6 percent in the four years 1971–4. This trend is corroborated by a large fall over the same period in the share of the employed labor force seeking additional work – an indicator of underemployment. This share fell from one quarter in 1968 to one tenth in 1974.

There is a clear pattern to the fall in open unemployment (see table 5.7 on the changing structure of unemployment). First, female unemployment fell faster than male. Second, it was inexperienced labor, rather than experienced, that benefited from improved employment prospects; the

Table 5.6 Unemployment and underemployment, 1967–1979 (percent)

Year	1 Unemployed as percentage of labor force	2 Share in total employment of those wanting additional work
1967	8.2[a]	26.3
1968	9.4[a]	27.6
1969	6.9[a]	n.a.
1970	8.1[b]	n.a.
1971	5.2[a]	15.6
1972	7.9[a]	13.1
1973	4.7[a]	12.9
1974	5.0[a]	10.5
1975	4.5[c]	12.0
1976	{ 4.5[c] { 4.0[d]	n.a.
1977	4.5[d]	n.a.
1978	4.0[d]	n.a.
1979	4.0[d]	n.a.

n.a., not available.
[a] May survey (reference period, one week).
[b] Census.
[c] August survey (reference period, one week).
[d] Third quarter (reference period, one quarter).
Sources: column 1, Department of Labor, Yearbook of Labor Statistics, various issues; column 2, Domingo and Feranil, 1984, table 6.12

inexperienced unemployed constituted 6.4 percent of the labor force in 1968 and 1.9 percent in 1975. Third, it was the age group 10–19 whose unemployment rate fell most. Fourth, the unemployment rate in agriculture fell faster than in services, while it did not fall at all in industry.

These indicators of changes in the level of underemployment are likely to be closely linked with the fall in real wages over roughly the same period. A widening of the wage differentials may be implied between skilled labor (predominantly male, older, and urban) and unskilled labor (predominantly female, younger, and rural). There is no obvious evidence, however, that real wages in agriculture fell more than in industry; nor is there any direct evidence that wage differentials between the skilled and unskilled were growing.

Foreign Investment

An important strand of the policy to promote nontraditional exports – and even a part of the justification for declaring martial law – was the

Table 5.7 Structure of unemployment, 1967, 1970, and 1974 (percentage distribution of total unemployed)

Category	1967	1970	1974
Total	100	100	100
Male	51	51	61
Female	49	49	39
Experienced	35	44	60
Inexperienced	65	56	40
Aged 10–19	54	32	34
Aged 20–44	40	50	59
Aged 45–64	6	14	7
Aged 65 and over	–	4	–
Agriculture	49	56	35
Industry	18	17	29
Services	33	27	36

–, nil.
Sources: Department of Labor, *Yearbook of Labor Statistics*, various years; data supplied by Ministry of Labor and Employment

encouragement of export-oriented foreign investment. There are general indicators that foreign direct investment, low in the early 1970s, grew significantly after 1972. According to balance-of-payments data assembled by Lindsey and Valencia (1982, table 2), gross direct investment inflows averaged US$3 million a year in 1970–2, shooting to an average of over US$100 million a year for the rest of the decade (though with no consistent growth trend after 1972). According to figures on the amount of investments approved under incentives legislation, the share of foreign investment – this is synonymous with foreign inflows into the Philippines – grew from 33 percent in 1970 to over 50 percent in 1974 and 1975, but fell back thereafter (NEDA, 1984, table 6.14).

1970–1974: a Summary

The 1970–4 devaluation episode saw a stabilization of the external sector through an improved situation for balance of payments, reserves, and foreign debt. While export performance was aided by 1960s investment coming on stream, it was not helped by the terms of trade. Macroeconomic restraint helped make devaluation effective until 1973. The gradual loss of effectiveness from then on can be ascribed to more expansionary macroeconomic policy, but above all to the terms-of-trade shock after 1974 which was insufficiently offset by exchange rate adjustment. The failure of the economy to grow faster reflects not only the cost of external stabilization but also the disasters affecting food supply in 1970–2.

Devaluation most directly affected the existing export sectors (including the newer "traditional" exports such as bananas, which had grown out of investment in the 1960s). The direct impact on manufacturing was notably small: the improved REER for manufacturing, instead of stimulating import substitution, may well have merely increased the level of tariff redundancy for a sector that had already exploited most import substitution possibilities (including backward linkages). Nonetheless, manufactured exports became more attractive relative to import substitution and, even if they had less obvious impact in 1970–4 than later, they nonetheless grew in this period.

Martial Law: the Impact on Trade Policy

The authoritarian rule of President Marcos lasted from 1972 to 1986. Much has been written on the political and economic excesses that developed in this period, but the dust has yet to settle, and with the end of the regime it can be expected that more complete analyses will be forthcoming. This section relies particularly on two papers, both written between the assassination of Benigno Aquino (August 1983) and the end of the Marcos presidency. The first, by economists from the School of Economics of the University of the Philippines, analyzes the antecedents to the 1983 economic crisis (De Dios, 1984). It heavily emphasizes the role of politics in the development of the 1983 economic crisis. The other paper by an academic who until 1980 was in the Marcos government characterizes the damage to the economy of politically inspired economic regulation (Sicat, 1984).

Martial law was declared in September 1972. It found its immediate political justification in the civil unrest of 1970–2, some of which was sparked off by the 1969 presidential election, the costliest – and many say the most corrupt – election in the first quarter century of Philippine independence. Of course, it was also the case that the constitution limited any one president to two terms in office, and President Marcos's second term expired at the end of 1973.

Martial Law

Martial law also had an important economic justification – that of "constitutional authoritarianism" which the government could defend in that "it eliminated many of the costs of decision making and transactions associated with checks and balances" (De Dios, 1984, p. 59). This economic rationalization, drawing much of its inspiration from the example of the Asian newly industrialized countries, was by no means regarded at the time as a pretext: it provided the implicit condition under which some key technocrats participated in government; it was also part of the basis for the strong support that the government received in the 1970s from the international aid and banking communities.

The economic justification may also have been, initially at least, an important part of the populist political strategy of the government. The goal of this strategy was to gain support for the authoritarian regime through economic development and also, apparently, to break the power of some entrenched elites, notably the sugar bloc. To begin with, the regime had popular support.

A spate of reforms, indeed, took place in the early days of martial law, including government reorganization, a new rural development push, and – though less important – the industrial incentives and tariff reform discussed above.

In place of the diffuseness permitted by the old congressional system, martial law effectually centralized political and economic power. This centralization was on the President, rather than on the broader machinery of government as represented by the cabinet. Indeed, collective decision making appears to have become progressively less important. The President ruled by edict – mainly the Presidential Decree – and such edicts were not always published. Changes in the regime, such as the establishment of a parliament (the Batasan Pambansa) in 1978 and the lifting of martial law in 1981, tended to be cosmetic.

Around the middle of the decade, after the first flush of martial law, the political system began to deteriorate. The dominant objective of building up political power and wealth among a small circle of privileged associates of the President – "crony capitalism" – increasingly superseded the efforts of the technocrats to manage the economy in pursuit of broader more conventional goals such as growth, stability, and equity.

This is not to say that there was complete unity of purpose even among the technocrats. Indeed, the technocrats came from different corners of the economic debate. In very broad terms, the planning and economic coordination function within the government centered on NEDA which has remained somewhat weak politically. Industrial promotion was first centered on the BOI, and then on the Ministry of Trade and Industry which was created in 1974 (and shares its minister with BOI). BOI and the Ministry have generally been more protectionist than NEDA, though this protectionism does not extend to inward investment (and cannot therefore be characterized as completely "economic-nationalist"). The Ministry of

Finance, economically the most powerful ministry, has stood somewhere in the middle. In sum, the technocrats were themselves far from being a body of public servants favoring liberal policies and disfavoring intervention.

Martial law politics from the mid-1970s onwards had several economic effects. Most important was the considerably increased intervention in the economy. Much of this was *ad hoc* and discriminatory (and did not rely on any corpus of economic theory). This intervention led to the development of public and private monopolies, or created market-distorting privileges for specific individuals or firms. Another not very productive outcome was a large growth in public and publicly guaranteed investment. This development was a principal cause of the external debt crisis of 1983. It also led to an *ad hoc* extension of the public sector when some of the publicly guaranteed investment projects failed. The corollary to such politically motivated intervention was a growing incoherence in public economic management: "constitutional authoritarianism" eventually proved less capable of rational economic government than the congressional system it replaced.

The Growth of Public and Private Monopolies

A great many government measures had the objective of granting public and private monopolies and economic privileges. These included exclusive rights to importing, exporting, and domestic trade, tax and tariff concessions to individual firms and institutions, and the collection of large funds under private control (De Dios, 1984, pp. 40–1; see also his appendix 1 which lists many of the relevant decrees by the sector to which they apply). Political and personal gain were not the exclusive goal of these measures. Some of them, such as import controls for the car manufacturing program, were originally justified in the context of an import substitution industrialization strategy. The full impact of all these measures is still to be assessed, but some examples can be given.

The best-known monopolies were in sugar and coconuts. In 1974, the government created a monopoly in the domestic marketing and export of sugar which proved extremely costly to cane producers, provided windfall gains to politically favored sugar distributors, and led to foreign exchange losses (De Dios, 1984, pp. 42–9).

A levy introduced on coconut farmers in 1973 was intended to be used for replanting and other developmental programs. Instead it mainly went to financing the purchase of a bank through which a private milling and marketing company (UNICOM) was established. This company in turn captured three quarters of the country's coconut-milling capacity and used its purchasing power further to depress producer prices (De Dios, 1984, pp. 49–51). Thus the coconut farmers financed the very monopsony that was to tax them further.

The government's international trade monopoly on rice and corn was extended in 1975 to wheat. In 1981 this monopoly was extended to domestic trade, and the government's direct involvement in wheat supply appears to have disrupted the flour market considerably (Sicat, 1984, pp. 37–8).

Monopolies were also accorded to specific private firms. Sicat (1984, pp. 44–8) quotes the monopoly on the import of meat from Australia and New Zealand (a private firm in conjunction with the Bureau of Animal Husbandry), an import monopoly on black and white televisions for one firm, a monopoly to produce newsprint, and a monopoly on satellite communications transmissions (see also De Dios, 1984, p. 41). In addition, specific firms received duty-free privileges that gave them advantages over competing firms, for instance in the cigarette and soft drinks industries (Sicat, 1984, pp. 45–6).

Government bodies outside agriculture also got their share of newly created monopolies. One better-documented example is a majority-government-owned corporation, PAGCOR, which was created to operate a public monopoly in gaming (Collas-Monsod, 1985). In another case the government-owned Experimental Cinema of the Philippines was exempted from censorship (under Executive Order 770 which created it) for the purpose of fostering artistic creativity. This enabled it to acquire a *de facto* monopoly for showing pornographic movies.

Generally, those wishing to import products for which BOI-registered capacity already existed had to get permission from BOI, which then consulted the local producers. This occurred, for instance, with synthetic fibers, newsprint, and a number of "progressive" programs where the small number of firms selected to participate were required to increase the degree of local content over time; in turn, the import of kits for assembly was only permitted for the participating firms and the import of assembled products was more or less banned. Such programs were introduced for cars, trucks, motorcycles, consumer electronic goods, and diesel engines.

An important element of intervention and monopolization in the economy has been the growing role of government in financial markets (De Dios, 1984, pp. 36–40). The publicly owned Philippine National Bank (PNB) and the DBP acquired an increasing share of banks (called "political banks" in De Dios). These developed close political connections with the government, and added to the real degree of concentration in the financial system.

One of the first acts of martial law (General Order 5) was to ban strikes in "vital industries," broadly defined to include exporting industries, among others. More generally, labor legislation in the period 1972–6 sought to revamp the collective bargaining system along corporatist lines.

Whatever the motivation for intervention, the various measures of the type discussed above added up to a significant move toward the concentration of economic power in public hands, and in a limited number of private hands, in the modern sector of the Philippine economy, particularly from the mid-1970s. Doherty (1982), in a study of interlocking directorates, traced the apparent interrelationships of prominent individuals and families through the major banks and other financial institutions. He concluded that "about 81 families spread through 10 banking groups are identified as controlling the Philippine economy" (p. 25). These 81 families covered not only a new elite that, since the onset of martial law, had gained power through its closeness to the presidential family (largely through family ties), but also survivors of the old elite which had either allied themselves to the President or managed to survive in spite of some hostility; the latter group included the sugar bloc in general (Doherty, 1982, p. 30).

The Growth of Investment and Foreign Debt

Since the mid-1950s the ratio of gross domestic capital formation to GDP had been slowly rising (figure 4.2). It was 16 percent (in 1972 prices) in 1955 and 20 percent in 1973 (though it had been higher in the period 1964–8). After 1973 it rose quite remarkably to 29 percent by 1976, remaining above 25 percent till 1983. Rising durable equipment and private and public construction expenditures all contributed to this, but the strongest growth was in public construction whose ratio to GDP rose from under 2 percent in 1973 to over 5 percent in 1976 and stayed there till 1982. Moreover, an important part of private investment was publicly guaranteed.

The increase in investment may have been partly countercyclical in intent. Whether or not this is so, much of the public and publicly guaranteed investment appears to have been of very dubious quality and politically inspired. There was a surge of public investment in prestigious showcase buildings for instance (De Dios, 1984, p. 34; Sicat, 1984, pp. 53–4). Politically connected private individuals were able to invest at low rates of interest in poor projects. For instance, the PNB guaranteed the foreign exchange debts of a number of new sugar mills, ultimately merely adding to excess capacity in the sugar-milling industry (De Dios, 1984, p. 48). A rising incremental capital-to-output ratio (ICOR) over time is one indicator of inefficient investment. According to De Dios (1984, p. 15), the ICOR rose from 4.2 in the 1960s to 5.0 in the 1970s and to 9.0 by the 1980s.

Several private sector projects have since gone bankrupt, and the government or its financial institutions have taken over the defaulting investments: thus the public sector has grown surreptitiously. For instance, the government has come to own several of Manila's underoccupied luxury hotels.

The rise in the level of investment was financed in two principal ways. First, an increase in the budget deficit partly financed the increase in public investment after 1974. The average budget deficit was 1.1 percent of GDP in 1975–80 compared with an average deficit of 0.1 percent in 1967–74 (calculated from table 5.2). Second, both public and private investment were increasingly financed by foreign borrowing. The ratio of external debt to GDP, having fallen from 30 percent in 1970 to 19 percent in 1974, began a steady rise after 1974, reaching 36 percent by 1980 (table 5.3).

The international economic climate between the two oil crises was ripe for greater foreign borrowing since real interest rates were low. In addition, the Philippines had cultivated its relations with the international financial community since the early 1970s, a strategy served by the sense of discipline and progress in the early days of martial law (Sicat, 1984, pp. 51–2). The Philippines had a good international credit rating.

The acceleration of investment, which has a large import component, and the use of foreign loans to pay for it are reflected in the structure of the balance of payments. From 1970 to 1974 there was on average a surplus in the current account representing 0.6 percent of the level of GDP (partly due to an exceptional surplus in 1973), while there was an average deficit of 5.1 percent in the next five years (calculated from table 5.3). The deficit was partly financed by the drawing down of foreign reserves, which went from 4.5 months' worth of imports in 1974 to 3.7 months' worth in 1980 (and continued to fall thereafter).

In summary, public and publicly guaranteed investment grew remarkably in the martial law period. Much of this investment proved rather unproductive. The budget deficits that partly financed the investment had an inflationary effect, while the growth in foreign indebtedness laid up problems that came to a head in the early 1980s.

The Loss of Coherence in Economic Policymaking

The result of *ad hoc* and highly discriminatory interventions in favor of certain groups, and of a public investment policy that often had similar political ends, was a certain loss in the coherence of economic policymaking within the government. Public economic decisions became less answerable to any review process within government (and in the cabinet) and more amenable to the ability of different ministries and factions to further their particular interests. Sicat (1984, p. 43) describes how, in some situations, "the institutional process of advice and coordination was left with situations of *fait accompli*."

Coherence (in terms of the rational making of economic policy at least) sometimes suffered because information on new public activities was not always available to the government. This information gap might occur either because provisions for accountability in new public activities were simply insufficient or because some transactions involving public money did not go through the budget.

Increasing Intervention and the Development of Trade Policy

The 1973 tariff reform had sought to reestablish a certain coherence in tariff protection, in part by removing many of the previously permitted tariff exemptions. Statistics from the Tariff Commission show these exemptions creeping back in the middle of the decade. The ratio of estimated duty exemptions to actual duty paid on all imports rose from 9 percent in 1973 to 31 percent in 1976, and remained above 20 percent for the rest of the decade (Tariff Commission of the Philippines, 1976, 1983). This massive return of exemptions was not primarily due to investment and export incentives legislation, and must largely reflect the kind of *ad hoc* privileges outlined above.

At the beginning of the 1970s, direct import controls operated solely through the Central Bank. New controls were introduced on an *ad hoc* basis during the 1970s, either as measures of protection in connection with government development programs – for example, the BOI's local-content programs for cars, trucks, and so on – or as measures to favor political associates of the regime. Most of the new restrictions seem to have been imposed from the mid-1970s onwards; not only was this the period from which the government became more active in dispensing specific industrial favors, but also the growth in the deficit of the current account of the balance of payments encouraged the authorities to be more circum-spect about imports.

In 1984 the government put together a list of all the items for which import permission had to be sought (Central Bank, 1984). This list gives a sense of the way in which import controls have grown since 1970. In addition to those nonessential and unclassified consumer goods controlled since 1969 and not liberalized in 1981–2, this list covers a broad variety of products for which import permission had to be sought from specific government departments. Thus, not only had import controls grown, but the responsibility for administering them had become very decentralized.

The growth of import monopolies, exemptions, and import controls from the mid-1970s variously benefited the government, individual produc-ing firms, producing sectors, and consuming firms and institutions. It is difficult to draw firm conclusions about the direction of the effect on levels of protection. At very least, since many of the measures were designed to favor specific firms or institutions, they further distorted domestic competi-tion and introduced greater uncertainty.

1974–1980: the Changing Structure of Foreign Trade and Payments

The External Sector

Export volume grew impressively from 1974, and faster than in the preceding years at 8 percent a year in 1975–82. Traditional exports – coconut oil, pineapples, bananas, and lumber – showed sustained growth in the second half of the 1970s. Prices, however, were very unstable and continued to fall relative to import prices (table 5.3). Between 1974 and 1980 the structure of exports changed fundamentally: the share of the top four export groups (coconut, sugar, wood, and copper concentrates) fell from 1977 to 43 percent, while the share of manufactured exports rose from 12 to 44 percent (table 2.5).

Imports grew substantially in volume (5 percent a year in 1975–82), but not as much as exports; import prices, however, rose far more steeply. Part of this import growth was directly related to export growth in the form of imported industrial inputs. After a 34 percent decline in 1975, the terms of trade continued to decline with scarcely a rally, at 6 percent a year on average in 1975–82 (see figure 2.1).

Invisible exports and imports grew relative to merchandise trade in the 1970s. Some of the growth of invisible exports was from the remittances of contract workers (which, from negligible levels in 1970, had come to account for a quarter of such exports by 1982). However, invisibles accounted for only one third of the large current account deficit of the balance of payments by 1982; the principal source of this deficit was the steady rise in interest payments on foreign loans (see below). The current account of the balance of payments went from unprecedentedly large surplus in 1973 (+ 5 percent of GDP) to unprecedentedly large deficit in 1975 (– 6 percent of GDP). This level of deficit, in terms of GDP, was maintained for the rest of the 1970s (table 5.3). To begin with, in 1975 the current account deficit was partly financed by drawing down international reserves, but from then on (until 1983) reserves were maintained at a higher level and the current account deficit was financed by increased external borrowing. In all, the post-1974 policy of accommodating a semipermanent current account deficit with foreign borrowing represents a remarkable turnaround from the policies of external balance pursued in 1970–4.

The Growth of the Economy

In spite of the generally depressed nature of international markets after the turbulence of 1973–4, the growth record of the Philippine economy after

Table 5.8 Average annual growth rates of gross
domestic product, 1969–1974 and 1974–1980
(percent)

	GDP	Agriculture	Manufacturing
1969–74	5.7	3.9	8.0
1974–80	6.6	4.4	6.4

Source: calculated from Alburo and Shepherd, 1988,
appendix table E.1.1

1974 appeared to be a little better than in the period preceding it, as the
average real annual growth rates indicate (table 5.8).

The improvement in agricultural growth may partly have reflected the
impact of the government food program from 1973. In particular, it was
only after the natural disasters of the early 1970s that rice could realize the
full potential of the green revolution. The apparent fall in manufacturing
output growth may in part reflect the effects of foreign exchange shortages
after 1974: the two best years of growth, 1976 and 1977, were the years
when the current account deficit was smallest. Manufacturing growth
would also have been smaller without the growth of nontraditional exports
which we estimate to have increased manufacturing GDP growth by
around half a percentage point a year for 1974–80.

From 1975, rates of GDP growth in construction were high. This
reflected the 1973–5 acceleration in the pace of investment.

Real Effective Exchange Rates

While there was an undeniable deterioration in the balance of payments
after 1974, the evidence on the realignment of REERs – which might be
expected to accompany such a deterioration – is difficult to interpret. One
conventional form of REER compares the movement of these domestic
price levels with the movement of those of major foreign trade partners
(the foreign price levels being weighted by domestic imports or exports).
Such measures for the Philippines clearly indicate a marked deterioration
after 1974. Several commentators have used this kind of measure to
indicate an apparent fall in Philippine competitiveness, and to link it to
overvaluation of the exchange rate (see Pante, 1982; Bautista et al., 1979,
p. 29).

Yet the REERs used earlier in this chapter comparing the Philippine
GDP to world price indicators for specific tradeables commodity groups
(table 5.4) do not tell quite the same story: either there is no obvious
deterioration in REERs after 1974 or the deterioration is not as severe as

Table 5.9 Different measures of average real effective exchange rates, 1970–1973 and 1974–1980

	Average for 1970–3	Average for 1974–80
1 Import-weighted producer price of major trading partners divided by WPI	100	77
2 Unit price of imports divided by GDP deflator	100	132
3 Unit price of exports divided by GDP deflator	100	100
4 World price of rice divided by GDP deflator	100	132
5 World price of manufactures divided by GDP deflator	100	112

Source: calculated from Alburo and Shepherd, 1988, appendix tables E.6.4 and E.6.5

indicated by the REER discussed in the preceding paragraph. This can be seen in table 5.9 in which the average REER for 1970–3 (= 100) is compared with that for 1974–80.

Rows 2–5 show a stationary REER for exports and an improved REER for manufactures, imports, and rice in the second period. By comparison, the REER using the weighted index of producers' prices in major trading partners (row 1) shows a significant deterioration in the second half of the 1970s.

Why the difference? First, there was an important divergence in 1972–4 between the GDP deflator and the WPI. Over this two-year period the WPI rose by 83 percent, the GDP inflator by only 55 percent. The gap has since been maintained more or less. Since the GDP is a reasonable proxy for prices of nontradeables, while the WPI is largely composed of domestic and imported tradeable goods, it can be argued that the process of rapid world inflation in 1972–4 permanently affected the ratio of prices of nontradeables to tradeables. (In this sense rapid external inflation unmatched by internal inflation is exactly the same as a domestic devaluation.)

The second source of divergence in REERs relates to the "world price" series. It appears that the (weighted) producer prices of the Philippines' major trading partners behaved differently from their export prices, inflation being greater in the mid-1970s in their export prices than their producer prices.

In summary, even though the period 1975–80 is characterized by large trade deficits, there is not unambiguous evidence of falling REERs to explain this. Instead it is plausible to attribute much, if not all, of the trade deficit to the import requirements of the higher investment ratio. In order for the tradeables-producing sector to accommodate this rising import requirement without a current account deficit, the peso would have needed to devalue further and the REER also to have risen.

The Growth of Nontraditional Manufactured Exports in the 1970s

Nontraditional manufactured exports (NTMEs) grew from 10 percent of total exports in 1974 to 32 percent by 1980 (table 5.10). They reached 51 percent by 1983. This is a remarkable change in the structure of exports, particularly, if, as argued in this chapter, the incentive system did not fundamentally change in favor of NTMEs.

These exports are dominated by labor-intensive assembly-type activities. In 1980, footwear and clothing and electronic assembly accounted for 59 percent of total NTMEs, while food products, handicrafts, and furniture were important among the remainder (NEDA, 1984, table 7.5). Much of the footwear and clothing and electronic assembly activity is highly import intensive and takes place in physical enclaves. For the most part, these enclaves are bonded warehouses, but there are also a handful of

Table 5.10 Growth of nontraditional manufactured exports, 1967–1984 (percent)

	1	2	3	4	5	6
		Share of consignment NTME in total exports		Value added in CNTME		Share of gross NTME in total manufacturing output
Year	Share of gross NTME in total exports	Gross CNTME	Net CNTME	Footwear and apparel	Electrical goods	
1967	n.a.	3.9	0.6	15.6	a	2.7
1968	n.a.	4.0	1.2	28.3	a	2.3
1969	n.a.	4.1	0.9	21.7	a	2.8
1970	10.0	3.1	0.3	8.1	a	3.5
1971	9.3	2.9	0.1	2.4	a	3.7
1972	10.6	3.1	0.4	14.1	a	4.1
1973	9.9	3.1	0.2	23.6	18.5	6.4
1974	9.9	3.5	0.4	11.9	5.1	5.2
1975	15.6	5.2	1.0	25.0	8.6	6.6
1976	22.9	7.0	− 0.9	− 5.9	− 19.4	8.3
1977	22.9	7.4	1.0	29.4	− 11.0	7.7
1978	29.5	11.1	1.2	26.6	− 3.0	8.9
1979	31.8	12.2	1.9	33.1	4.6	11.5
1980	38.0	14.0	2.3	35.7	6.4	11.7
1981	42.9	17.3	4.7	29.9	21.4	n.a.
1982	48.8	22.2	8.0	35.9	29.1	n.a.
1983	51.7	n.a.	n.a.	n.a.	n.a.	n.a.
1984	54.4	n.a.	n.a.	n.a.	n.a.	n.a.

n.a., not available.
Column 2, gross value of consignment NTME; column 3, net value of consignment NTME, that is, consignment exports *less* imports; columns 4 and 5, consignment exports *less* consignment imports expressed as a ratio to consignment exports.
[a] No recorded trade.
Source: Alburo and Shepherd, 1988, appendix table E.7.10 and E.7.11

export-processing zones. Much of the labor employed in labor-intensive exporting is female.

The entrepreneurs are a mixture of local and foreign and tend to be "nontraditional" in the sense that they are not largely recruited from the domestic or foreign entrepreneurial cadres of the Philippine import-substituting sector.

There are thus positive features to the new exports – labor intensity and, possibly, a seed-bed for some kinds of entrepreneurs. Net export earnings are a good deal less, however, than gross export earnings. A large amount of nontraditional exporting takes place under consignment conditions – imports enter duty free under the specific condition that they be incorporated in export goods. The major products involved are footwear and clothing, electrical goods (mainly semiconductor assembly), and the beneficiation of iron ore pellets (which we do not consider further here).

Assuming that consignment imports and exports correspond, in the sense that materials imported are (eventually) exported, the "value added" in consignment trade – that is, the net foreign exchange earned – can be calculated. According to the trade statistics, the ratio of value added in consignment trade has been variable and often low (see table 5.10, columns 4 and 5, for these ratios in footwear and clothing and electrical goods). For footwear and clothing the value added ratio averaged 21 percent for the period 1967–82, lower for the period to 1976 and higher and less variable from 1977. For electrical goods, trade only started in 1973, and for the period 1973–82 the ratio averaged only 6 percent and was highly variable. It is difficult to conceive of a margin of value added that is really this small.

If we net out consignment import from total NTMEs – that is, if we consider only value added in consignment exports – the share of NTMEs in total exports is reduced to 8 percent in 1974, 25 percent in 1980, and 38 percent in 1983 (table 5.10, column 3). Since many of the NTMEs outside consignment trade are similarly import intensive (notably nonconsignment footwear and clothing), it becomes apparent that the growth in NTMEs was less dramatic than might at first appear. Nevertheless, it still seems correct to talk of a fundamental change in the structure of exports.

Activities characteristic of most NTMEs may have few economic linkages with the rest of the economy. However, as long as even narrow margins of value added are not overly subsidized, they are not undesirable in themselves. There are few direct indicators of the economic efficiency of NTMEs in general. The analysis of export incentives earlier in this chapter would suggest that activities with such low value added were unlikely to have been very highly subsidized. This may not be so where the government has provided infrastructure. A study by Warr (1984) of the first Philippine export-processing zone, in Bataan, concluded that, partly because of the infrastructural costs, this had proven a very expensive way of promoting exports. In fact, the export-processing zones have not become the major conduit for the NTMEs; bonded warehouses have been considerably more important.

There are several reasons for the growth of NTMEs. First, the REER for manufactures rose from 1960. In other words, domestic costs rose more slowly than world prices. Both the REER for imports and the REER for import-substituting manufactures – the best proxies we have for a REER for NTMEs – record a large rise during the 1960–2 decontrol and a smaller, but substantial, rise following the 1970 devaluation. Thus the liberalization episode of the early 1960s and the "quasi-episode" of the early 1970s laid the basis for NTME growth.

Second, from 1969 to 1974 real manufacturing wage costs fell dramatically. The real unskilled wage appears to have been halved (see above). The real wage recovered sightly by 1980, but remained well below its pre-1970 level (table 5.4 and figure 2.1).

We have argued that the incentives to NTMEs introduced in the early 1970s actually provided a quite modest counterweight to peso overvaluation and protection in the import-substituting sector. On the other hand, these incentives were important in providing effectively for exporters to acquire imported inputs at world prices.

Finally, there was a surge of foreign investment receiving BOI incentives in 1973 and 1974. This can be associated with the stable investment climate that early martial law provided in the eyes of foreign investors. No doubt a part of this investment went into nontraditional export capacity.

The long-term fall in the real wage has emerged as crucial to the changing structure of exports in the 1970s, not only supporting the growth of NTMEs but also turning the Philippines into an important direct exporter of labor (mainly to the Middle East). A real wage fall of the magnitude apparent in the period 1969–74 is difficult to explain, however.

Lal (1986) examines this fall in real wages in the Philippines in terms of the Stolper–Samuelson theorem that protection raises the relative price of the scarce factor. In the Philippines land was abundant and labor scarce, and the devaluations of 1960–2 and the early 1970s reduced the protection to labor, and hence its price. Lal also argues that the devaluation after 1969 was larger than that needed to eliminate the trade deficit of 1969, and actually generated a temporary payments surplus; this overly large devaluation led to a larger than necessary fall in real wages, and the effective devaluation that was maintained in the early years of the 1970s kept the real wage low.

Post-martial-law interventions in the labor market, such as the ban on strikes in "vital" industries in 1972, also perhaps affected the wage level. Much of the fall in real wages had occurred before martial law, but the new labor market conditions may have helped prevent a faster return towards the real wage levels of the 1960s.

We have already suggested that the fall in real wages from 1969 is likely to be associated with a fall in unemployment and underemployment from the same time. Nevertheless, the fall in real wages, in an economy where average per capita incomes were nonetheless growing, clearly implies an increasing maldistribution of income. A review of the evidence in De Dios (1984, pp. 20–4) shows how income distribution has generally worsened since the early 1970s, but does not illuminate the particular episode of declining real wages.

In conclusion, the 1970s was a mixed decade for trade liberalization. First, the government on the whole increased the taxation of the traditional sector. These taxes – whether in the form of export or domestic taxes – hit farmers more than processors. Second, the degree of monopoly in the import-substituting sector of the economy sharply increased in the second half of the decade and there was a partial return towards the kind of distorted economy of the control era of the 1950s. In spite of these developments, exports in the 1970s – both traditional and nontraditional – fared surprisingly well. The difference from the 1950s was that REERS and real wages were considerably lower.

6

1980–1983: the Tariff Reform Program

The program to reduce tariffs and remove residual import controls which began in 1981 did not follow a balance-of-payments crisis (as in 1970), nor was it the result of clamor for better terms to exporters (as in 1960). Yet this episode promised the most fundamental trade liberalization since 1960, or possibly even since independence. In the event, a broader economic crisis derailed the episode in 1983. The trade liberalization process was resumed in 1986, albeit under different political circumstances. In this chapter we describe the policy reforms of 1981–3 (and the circumstances in which they occurred), measure – to the extent data and the limited nature of the reforms permit – their economic impact, and analyze the circumstances which led to the reversal of reforms in 1983.

The Background to Trade Liberalization

The Political Background

Trade policy reforms came about as a consequence of the evolving views of a number of "technocrats" in government, their alliance with the World Bank, and authoritarian political conditions. An increasing number of policymakers became convinced that a more open trading system was imperative for economic efficiency and rational industrial development (Bautista, 1985). By the late 1970s, the intellectual ferment from both academia and parts of government coalesced into pressure for basic policy reforms in industrial and trade incentives. The major government-funded study of industrial incentives undertaken by Bautista et al. (1979) was an important expression of the need for these reforms.

It is not clear that the "technocrats" in favor of trade policy reform were in a majority in government, but they found an ally in the World Bank, which was pursuing a new policy of lending in return for specific policy reforms. The Philippines was one of the first countries to use a structural adjustment loan (SAL) in pursuit of trade liberalization and industrial restructuring. Negotiations for a SAL began in 1979.

Another factor conducive to the trade liberalization was the political environment. This was generally stable in the period leading up to the 1981 trade liberalization policy and during its early implementation. (Growing dissent, more activist media, and stronger political opposition played a role only after the turmoil of 1983.) There was a certain convenience in promulgating a liberalization program under these conditions in two respects. First, any opposition was likely to be ineffective in the face of a strong and monolithic regime. Indeed, in comparison with the protracted and heated arguments surrounding decontrol, the floating of the exchange rate in 1970, and the new tariff code of 1973, public discussion of these reforms, with their potentially far-reaching consequences, was remarkably little. Second, there was a growing loss of coherence in economic policy-making in the later 1970s (Sicat, 1984). In the absence of proper cabinet discussion, for instance, minority views might easily prevail.

In addition – though no doubt less important – the Philippines joined the General Agreement on Tariffs and Trade (GATT) in 1980. This carried a commitment to reduce tariff and nontariff barriers to trade, and in fact, during the months following the country's official membership in January, a number of import duties were reduced and commodity-specific import restrictions removed.[1]

The regime that sponsored the liberalization policy had been in power since 1966. Why did such a fundamental reform come so late? In fact, the same political regime was in power when the exchange rate was floated in 1970. The big difference was the centralization of power as a result of the 1972 declaration of martial law, the abolition of the legislature, and the use of Presidential Decrees to substitute for the formulation of laws.

Economic Conditions before the Liberalization

In the three years preceding the 1981 trade liberalization, exports grew (in current dollars) at 17 percent a year and imports at 16 percent (Alburo and Shepherd, 1988, appendix table E.7.3). In real terms, however, exports had been growing substantially faster than imports as the terms of trade continued to deteriorate. The balance-of-payments current account further deteriorated from a deficit equivalent to − 4.9 percent of GDP in 1978 to

---

[1] In *Memorandum to Authorized Agent Banks* 2 (Central Bank of the Philippines, 1980a), 66 tariff headings were removed from the restricted import category and made fully importable. In February (Central Bank of the Philippines, 1980b), 13 tariff lines were reduced. In May, another 29 lines from restricted categories were lifted (Central Bank of the Philippines, 1980c).

– 5.4 percent in 1980 (table 5.3). The current account deficit had remained very high – typically 5 percent of GDP – since 1975 and continued to be largely funded by increasing foreign debt.

Overall, Philippine GDP grew at real annual rates of 5.8 percent in 1978–80 (Alburo and Shepherd, 1988, appendix table E.1.1). Both the United States and Japan, the country's major trading partners, had real growth rates below this average. In fact, these two countries experienced real declines in the face of the second oil shock and the recession that followed.

Protection in the economy as a whole in the years before the 1981 trade liberalization seems in general to have become slightly more restrictive. For instance the ratio of the black-market to the official exchange rate increased slightly in 1977–9 (table 3.2). Similarly, the IIIP (the ratio of the WPI for imports to the f.o.b. import price index in pesos) increased in 1979 before easing up again in 1980.

The inflation rate, as measured by the GDP deflator, increased by 9.2 percent in 1978, 15.2 percent in 1979, and 15.5 percent in 1980 (table 5.4).

The Tariff Reform Program and Related Policies

The Policy Targets

The 1981 trade liberalization has two components (Tariff Commission of the Philippines, 1983): (a) the liberalization of nontariff restrictions on imports, the so-called "import liberalization program," and (b) the reduction of tariff protection – the Tariff Reform Program proper.

The import liberalization program aimed to eliminate the need for seeking prior approval from the Central Bank for the import of nonessential consumer (NEC) and unclassified consumer (UC) items. At this time, some 1,304 items belonged to the NEC–UC category. The aim was to liberalize all these items completely by 1985.

The broad targets of the tariff reform included a reduction in maximum nominal tariffs from 100 to 50 percent, a reduction in the degree of tariff escalation, and the lowering of the average rate of tax- and tariff-based effective protection from 45 to 28 percent by 1985. The tariff reform was to be pursued in four stages covering 14 major industries and ten residual sectors over the course of a five-year period from 1981 to 1985.

Although the tariff program *per se* did not explicitly encourage exports, the narrowing of effective protection rates (EPRs) across sectors implied raising the EPR for some exports from negative to positive values, or at least reducing the penalty these sectors faced. Export encouragement played a role in the associated changes in policy that affected the incentive system (see the section below on fiscal policy).

Table 6.1 Phasing of the Tariff Reform Program, 1981–1985

	Phases of tariff reductions			
	I	II	III	IV
Items/sectors covered	Peak tariff rates	Food processing Textiles and garments Leather and footwear Pulp and paper	Cement Iron and steel Automotive Wood and wood product Glass and ceramics Furniture Domestic appliances Machinery and capital equipment Electrical goods	Agriculture and forestry products Basic chemical and petroleum Basic nonferrous
Number of tariff lines covered	177	272	396	480
For modification	All	184	229	149
For reduction	–	167	129	128
For increase	–	14	86	13
Others	–	3	15	8

–, nil.
Source: Tariff Commission of the Philippines, 1983

The four phases of the tariff reform program are shown in table 6.1. Most of the tariff modifications were for reductions in rates; the rate increases mostly covered commodities or industries where nominal rates were below 10 percent. Reducing the range of nominal tariffs from 0–100 percent to 10–50 percent would lead to a range of EPRs estimated to be 10–80 percent, compared with a range before the reform from negative EPRs to over 200 percent for some consumer goods. The revised tariff schedules were incorporated in the new Tariff and Customs Code of 1982, which specified the annual tariff changes from 1981 to 1985.

The Timetable for Liberalization

The Tariff Reform Program was to be carried out over five years to allow sufficient time for affected industries to adjust (table 6.1). The reduction of peak tariff rates was to be executed over two years (phase 1): in 1981, the ceiling rates were to be reduced to 70 percent *ad valorem*, and then further reduced to 50 percent in 1982. The five-year program of tariff adjustment started in 1981: the adjustment program was announced in three groups of industries, constituting three further phases of the reform. Phases 2 and 3 were carried out in January 1981 (Executive Orders 609 and 632-A), while phase 4 became operative in August 1981 (Executive Order 706).

For the import liberalization part of the program, 263 items were to be liberalized in January 1981. Another 610 were to be taken off the list in

January 1982, 87 in 1983, and the remainder (around 200) by 1984; 145 items were to continue restricted for reasons of health, defense, or safety. The 960 items scheduled to be liberalized in 1981, 1982, and 1983 were mostly in the NEC–UC category. They belonged to the food, chemical, cosmetic, pharmaceutical, wood, leather, rubber and plastic products, textiles and garments, furniture and travel goods, footwear and headgear, and electrical and electronic appliances industries. Beyond this, plans for which item would be liberalized when were vague. Only in the case of 12 classes of goods in the area of basic raw materials and semifinished goods (together covering some 1,200 items) were specific dates given for liberalization: caustic soda, basic iron and steel products, tires (except used tires), gasoline and kerosene engines (by January 1982); fabric and textiles, vinyl-asbestos tiles and sheets, and hydrogen peroxide (by January 1984); newsprint, portland cement, and sheet glass (by January 1985).

Related Policies

Exchange Rate Policy
When the liberalization program got under way in 1981, the exchange rate policy was one of a floating rate with margins established by "guiding rates" on dollar trading floors of the Bankers' Association of the Philippines (BAP). Except for some marginal exchange regulations (such as increased foreign exchange allowance for travel, export prohibition of foreign exchange without Central Bank approval, and so on), there were no new forms of exchange control in 1981 (see Central Bank of the Philippines, 1981; IMF, 1981). The prevailing average rate in 1981 was 8.2 per US dollar.

In early 1982, exchange controls were further relaxed. Certain documentary requirements for "no-dollar imports" were eliminated (Central Bank Circular 849) and there was a reduction in reserve requirements for import letters of credit from 100 to 50 percent in July 1982. By the second half of the year, however, controls started to increase. By October the net foreign exchange position of commercial banks was not permitted to exceed 20 percent of outstanding letters of credit, and all excess exchange holdings were to be sold to the Central Bank (Central Bank of the Philippines, 1982a). By December, an import surcharge of 3 percent for all import transactions was imposed.

In 1983, exchange controls became even more stringent, culminating in the suspension of exchange transactions in November. In January 1984, restrictions were placed on imports under documents against acceptance (D/A) and open accounts (O/A) (Central Bank of the Philippines, 1983). Duties were made payable at the time of opening letters of credit. Required reserves were raised to 100 percent for importers' letters of credit. In April an import surcharge of 5 percent was introduced (IMF, 1984).

The guiding rates for 1982 and 1983 were ₱ 9.171 and ₱ 14.001 respectively per US dollar. The REER for imports rose (appreciated) slightly by 4 percent in 1981 and then fell by 15 percent in 1982 before rising by 17 percent in 1983 as a result of the exchange rate adjustments of June and October (table 3.2).

Monetary Policy

Monetary policy in 1981 was moderately tight to counteract the growing deficits in the external accounts (table 6.2). A financial crisis in early 1981 reversed this trend, and monetary policy moved toward moderate expansion for the rest of the year as the Central Bank bailed out financial institutions to restore confidence.

Monetary policy was likewise moderately expansionary in 1982 to accommodate expected recovery (and stimulate the economy) from the 1979 recession. Reserve requirements were reduced during the year.

Table 6.2 Monetary policy indicators, 1981–1984

Indicators	Dec 1981	Dec 1982	Dec 1983	Mar 1984
Central Bank				
Net domestic assets (billion pesos)	20.658	33.617	52.731	59.331
Reserve money M_1 (billion pesos)	17.798	18.644	27.723	24.843
M_3 (billion pesos)	82.100	95.300	113.000	n.a.
Required reserves for commercial bank (%)	19.9	18.0	23.0	24.0
Manila reference rate (90 days) (%)	n.a.	16.7	16.9	16.1
Money market rates (interbank) (%)	14.9	16.0	n.a.	n.a.
Central Bank interest rate (%)				
Nontraditional exports	3.0	3.0	7	MRR90–9
Traditional exports	8.0	8.0	MRR90–6	6
Commercial bank rate (%)				
Savings deposits	(1.0)	9.8	9.7	9.7
Time deposits	(1.0)	17.4	22.5	15.5
Lending	18.0	14.4	16.2	21.5
Real interest rate (%)				
CPI (1978 = 100)	157.1	177.6	223.9	238.2
Savings	[a]	5.5	4.3	4.1
Time	[a]	9.8	10.0	6.5
Lending	11.4	8.1	7.2	9.0

n.a., not available.
MRR90–9, Manila reference rate (90 days) minus 9 percent; MRR90–6, Manila reference rate (90 days) minus 6 percent.
[a] No ceiling as of July 1, 1981.
Source: IMF, 1984

Growth in Central Bank net domestic assets was rapid at 63 percent between December 1981 and December 1982. A 62 percent rise in net credits to the public sector was mainly responsible, reflecting expansion in the budget.

By 1983, policy became less expansionary to reduce the balance-of-payments deficit. Growth in Central Bank net credit to the public sector declined as the budget deficit was cut, particularly between the end of December 1982 and March and June 1983. Towards the latter part of the year, however, reserve money expanded again to provide large overdrafts and emergency lending to financial institutions that were experiencing substantial withdrawals.

A financial reform in 1980 included interest rate deregulation for borrowing and lending, fiscal incentives to increase equity investments in financial institutions, and legislation encouraging broader banking services, all of which were meant to improve savings and the intermediation process.

Fiscal Policy

Since the recession of 1979, the government had adopted a countercyclical policy (through deficit financing) in the expectation of a recovery a year or two later. The recovery did not materialize. Given that the deficits were financed ultimately from foreign borrowings, they helped precipitate an eventual exchange crisis.

The rapid deterioration of the government accounts is reflected in the increasing ratio of the aggregate deficit to GNP from 0.2 percent in 1979 to 4.3 percent in 1982 (table 6.3). This fell sharply in 1983 to 1.6 percent of GNP. The domestic-based deficit did not deteriorate as rapidly, since expenditures exclude repayments less lending.

The ratio of government consumption expenditure to total government expenditure declined from 1979 to 1982 or 1983, indicating an increase in the share of investment expenditures. When the deficits had to be scaled down, however, capital investment suffered, thus raising again the share of government consumption in all government expenditures.

In addition to general fiscal policy, there were specific fiscal reforms designed to accompany the 1981 trade liberalization. The fiscal discrimination against imports through different definitional bases for imported and locally produced goods, as well as through the imposition of an advance sales tax on imports, was alleviated. Most of the fiscal realignments took place in 1983. For instance, there was a uniform 25 percent imposition of the advance sales tax on imports (March 1983), a reduction in the number of tax brackets for cigarettes from eight to ten and a reduction in tax differentials on imported and domestically produced spirits, wines, and cinematographic films.

Table 6.3 Government revenues and expenditures, 1979–1983

Item	1979	1980	1981	1982	1983
1 Total revenue[a] (billion pesos)	29.3	34.4	35.7	38.0	45.3
2 Domestic revenue (billion pesos)	39.1	34.1	35.5	37.7	45.0
3 Total expenditure[b] (billion pesos)	29.7	37.7	47.9	52.4	51.5
4 Domestic expenditure (billion pesos)	25.4	32.6	38.9	40.8	43.4
5 Surplus or (deficit), row 1 – row 3 (billion pesos)	(0.4)	(0.7)	(12.2)	(14.4)	(6.2)
6 Current GNP (billion pesos)	221.0	265.1	303.6	336.1	377.4
7 Current national income (billion pesos)	200.4	240.5	273.0	301.4	338.2
8 Ratio of surplus or (deficit) to GNP, row 5 divided by row 6 (%)	(0.2)	(0.3)	(4.0)	(4.3)	(1.6)
9 Ratio of surplus or (deficit) to national income, row 5 divided by row 7 (%)	(0.2)	(0.3)	(4.5)	(4.8)	(1.8)
10 Government consumption expenditure (billion pesos)	18.3	21.2	24.8	29.2	31.4
11 Ratio of government consumption expenditure to total expenditure, row 10 divided by row 3 (%)	61.6	56.2	51.8	55.7	61.0

[a] Includes grants received.
[b] Includes lending minus repayments.
Sources: IMF, International Financial Statistics, various issues; NEDA, Philippine Statistical Yearbook, various issues

Finally, in a new Omnibus Investment Code in April 1983 (Parliamentary Law 391) incentives to nontraditional exports were increased. Calculations for hypothetical cost structures made earlier (table 5.1) suggest that the 1983 legislation raised the value of export incentives compared with what the previous legislation of 1973 offered.

Restrictions of International Capital Movements

Capital movements are partly controlled through regulating foreign exchange transactions in the banking system. In this context, as early as 1972 inward and outward capital movements, with the exception of certain transactions related to the financing of international trade, required prior and specific approval of the Central Bank (see IMF, 1982b, p. 354). The flexibility given to agent banks in balancing foreign exchange holdings also partly dictates the degree of restriction or relaxation of the acquisition of invisible instruments. Policy has ranged from requiring banks to have full foreign exchange cover for their foreign currency liabilities to requiring that the banks hold no more than a certain fraction of their net foreign exchange position (for example, 20 percent of outstanding letters of credit).

As a general rule, however, restrictions have been placed on outflows of capital rather than inflows (which are generally encouraged). There were only minor changes in these policies after the 1981 trade liberalization and until the 1983 exchange crisis.

Implementation of the Liberalization Policy until 1983

The various phases of the Tariff Reform Program were implemented according to schedule (until their completion in 1985). During the implementation, the distribution and average values of nominal tariffs gradually changed. By the end of 1983, the average nominal tariff fell to 29 percent, from 43 percent in 1980 (table 6.4).

Table 6.4 Dispersion of tariff rates, 1980–1983

Tariff rates (%)	Number of tariff lines			
	1980[a]	1981	1982	1983
10	322	671	660	650
20	197	420	429	452
30	211	284	341	344
50	186	252	525	366
70	128	182	83	134
100	327	2	–	–
Total number[a]	1,283	2,300	2,300	2,300
Average nominal rate (%)	43	34	30	29

–, nil.
[a] Does not sum to column items because of other tariff rates.
Source: Tariff Commission of the Philippines, 1983, using data from PD 1464

This was not so for the import liberalization program. The number of controlled items scheduled for removal in 1983 was reduced from 87 to 48 in response to hearings conducted by the Ministry of Trade and Industry. The major setback to the import liberalization, however, came with the exchange crisis in October 1983. First, this resulted in a substantial redundancy of tariff protection since all exchange transactions were effectively controlled. Second, new quantitative restrictions were being imposed on specific items in 1982 and 1983 (these were consolidated by October 1984, under Central Bank Circular 1029). Finally, priorities were established for the use of foreign exchange upon partial resumption of trading transactions.

Political stability was shaken in the latter part of 1983 by the assassination of Benigno Aquino and its consequences. This was the immediate trigger to the economic crisis of October 1983 which delayed the impact of import liberalization. Apart from this, objections to the liberalization program were fragmented, and the government maintained that serious objections to the reforms should be considered in an integrated manner and as part of the broader sweep of economic policy.

Economic Performance Following the Trade Policy Reforms

Given that the 1983 reimposition of import controls put the trade liberalization in abeyance, it is unlikely that much can be learned about the 1981–3 liberalization experience from the post-1981 performance of the economy.

Major Price Developments

From 1980 onwards inflation was well in excess of 10 percent a year according to the CPI (table 6.5), but domestic price changes were also more or less offset, for the external sector, by nominal devaluations. As a result REERs did not vary consistently in 1980–2. There was some real depreciation during 1980 and real appreciation in 1982. A sharp real depreciation began at the end of 1982 after the onset of the economic crisis.

The real (daily) wages of nonagricultural workers in Metro Manila declined sharply until 1982 before recovering their 1980 levels in 1983. There was also a drastic deterioration in the terms of trade. By the first quarter of 1983 these were 63 percent of their level in the first quarter of 1980, but by the last quarter of 1983 they had recovered to 87 percent of this level.

What is most noticeable in real interest rate movements is their stickiness in spite of the deregulation of the rate beginning with the 1980 financial reforms (table 6.2).

External Transactions

It is difficult to discern any liberalization-related pattern to the movement of aggregate imports, even on a quarterly basis (table 6.6), since the liberalization was staggered across different sectors, new restrictions emerged towards the end of 1982 and in 1983, and there were adverse exchange rate movements in 1983. A separate estimate for imports in NEC and UC categories reveals that these accounted for 1.2 percent of total imports in 1981 compared with 0.9 percent in 1980, reflecting a 33 percent increase.

Any pattern for exports is also difficult to discern. There was a decline in exports in the last three quarters of 1981. The share of the ten principal exports declined while manufactured exports continued to increase. Trade balances remained negative, worsening after the first quarter of 1981.

The size of the current account deficit of the balance of payments became alarming in 1982 and 1983, averaging over 7.7 percent of GDP in these two years, compared with the already large deficits – typically of 5–6 percent – that had been the rule since 1975 (table 5.3). The growing

Table 6.5 Quarterly price movements, 1980–1983

Item	1980				1981				1982				1983			
	I	II	III	IV	I	II	III	IV	I	II	III	IV	I	II	III	IV
CPI (percentage change)	–	3.2	3.6	3.1	2.1	1.7	5.1	4.1	3.4	0.7	3.4	10.0	1.7	1.5	5.3	12.3
Nominal exchange rate (per US$)	7.42	7.49	7.55	7.58	7.68	7.96	8.10	8.29	8.29	8.41	8.66	8.90	9.45	10.10	11.00	13.90
REER (1980 = 100)	94	103	103	100	101	96	98	101	95	93	91	102	105	115	n.a.	n.a.
Terms of trade (1972 = 100)	76	70	67	63	67	58	58	59	59	58	61	58	49	58	64	67
Real wages (1980 = 100)	n.a.	100	n.a.	n.a.	n.a.	94	n.a.	n.a.	n.a.	95	n.a.	n.a.	n.a.	101	n.a.	67

–, nil; n.a., not available.
Sources: IMF, International Financial Statistics, various issues; data supplied by Asian Development Bank

Table 6.6 The external sector, 1981–1983 (percentage change by quarter, in current prices)

Item	1981				1982				1983		
	I	II	III	IV	I	II	III	IV	I	II	III
Imports f.o.b.	-1.4	7.2	2.9	-8.1	3.3	2.8	-5.3	-4.5	0.5	2.0	-0.1
Exports f.o.b.	4.5	-8.9	-7.2	-1.0	-4.8	6.0	-12.0	2.5	-4.0	7.0	-2.0
SITC 0–4	8.6	-18.7	-18.2	-0.2	-3.6	12.5	-24.1	17.9	-5.1	-0.8	-6.3
SITC 5–9	-1.4	6.0	5.9	-2.0	-5.7	-0.3	1.2	-10.0	-2.9	11.6	5.2
Ten principal exports	7.8	-23.8	-9.0	1.2	-3.2	8.2	-15.0	6.2	-2.1	1.7	n.a.
Current account balance	-35.8	111.7	43.7	-26.7	27.7	2.7	9.4	-19.9	4.3	-12.1	n.a.
Foreign debt	7.4	4.3	11.9	7.0	5.6	6.4	6.8	n.a.	n.a.	n.a.	n.a.

n.a., not available.
Source: Central Bank of the Philippines, 1982b; Asian Development Bank, 1984

deficit was accommodated both by running down reserves and by increasing foreign debt. Central Bank foreign exchange reserves declined from the equivalent of 8.9 percent of GDP in 1980 to 2.6 percent in 1983 (Alburo and Shepherd, 1988, appendix tables E.1.1 and E.7.2), with the decline particularly steep in the first three quarters of 1981. External debt grew from a ratio of 36 percent of GDP in 1980 to 44 percent in 1982, and leapt to 55 percent in 1983.

While it is possible that the partial trade liberalization itself may have played a part in this disastrous evolution of the Philippines' external situation after 1981, world economic conditions can hardly be said to have been conducive. The Philippine terms of trade continued to decline until 1982, while the early 1980s saw a substantial recession in OECD markets, constraining the penetration of Philippine nontraditional exports and leading to declines in traditional exports.

The Growth of Output

From 1980 to 1983 real GDP grew by 2.6 percent a year (table 4.8), an average that was brought down by the growth rate of only 1 percent in the crisis year of 1983 (Alburo and Shepherd, 1988, appendix table E.1.1). In fact, real per capita output and incomes were slightly lower in 1983 than 1980 (NEDA estimates). The growth slowdown affected all sectors, but growth in agricultural output in 1980–3 was lower than that of manufacturing which in turn was well below that of services (Alburo and Shepherd, 1988, appendix table E.1.1).

Table 6.7 presents the shares of imports in total supply for selected manufacturing industries from 1980 to 1983. Chemical and chemical product industries show an increase in the share of imports in supply along with paper and paper products, textile manufactures, and metal products. Transport equipment, however, shows a marked decline in imports over the period.

Unemployment, Business Failures, and Worker Layoffs

Data from employment surveys have become sparser since around 1980; however, new series have become available in recent years on business failures and worker layoffs.

Unemployment
There is some slight evidence that open unemployment rates increased from 1981 to 1982 (5.3–6.0 percent, according to the third-quarter figures of table 6.8), but the peculiar fall in the figure in 1983 (4.6 percent in the third quarter) is not easy to explain in view of the economic crisis of that year.

Table 6.7 Shares of imports in total supply of manufactures, 1980–1983[a] (percent)

Industry	1980	1981	1982	1983
Food manufactures	15.6	15.8	16.8	16.0
Beverages and tobacco	6.5	6.9	8.5	10.3
Petroleum and coal products	63.9	64.2	60.9	62.6
Chemical and chemical products	48.4	50.1	50.8	54.8
Rubber products	30.8	25.7	30.0	25.6
Paper and paper products	35.2	32.4	38.3	37.6
Textile manufactures	19.0	19.3	19.4	26.6
Nonmetallic mineral products	24.8	15.6	14.5	12.6
Basic metal	57.1	53.6	57.9	54.6
Metal products	47.6	48.2	50.6	50.5
Machinery except electrical	84.0	81.3	81.2	82.0
Electrical machinery	57.6	55.2	52.3	52.3
Transport equipment	72.3	61.0	57.7	65.6
Miscellaneous manufactures	63.7	59.7	55.6	57.3

[a] Imports at c.i.f. values (in pesos) are divided by the sum of imports and domestic value added.
Sources: National Census and Statistics Office (NCSO), *Foreign Trade Statistics of the Philippines*, 1980, 1983; NEDA, *Philippine Statistical Yearbook*, 1984

Table 6.8 Labor force and unemployment, 1980–1983

	1980		1981		1982		1983	
Category	III	IV	III	IV	III	IV	III	IV
Population of working age (thousands)[a]	28,835	29,072	29,781	30,023	30,074	30,978	31,676	31,907
Labor force (thousands)	17,705	18,634	18,421	19,005	18,488	19,980	20,465	20,521
Participation rate (%)	61.4	64.2	61.7	62.6	60.1	63.6	64.6	64.3
Unemployment rate (%)	5.4	4.3	5.3	5.4	6.0	5.5	4.6	4.1
Underemployment rate (%)	n.a.	n.a.	n.a.	n.a.	n.a.	n.a.	30.1	31.8

n.a., not available.
[a] 15 years and older.
Source: data supplied by National Census and Statistics Office

Business Failures

The frequency of business failures might be expected to increase in the short run as liberalization proceeds. In the Philippines dissolutions of domestic corporations have been reported since 1980 and include the amount of paid-up capital withdrawn from business (table 6.9). However, since many businesses are organized informally as single proprietorships or partnerships, the dissolution variable does not capture the incidence of

Table 6.9 Business dissolutions, 1980–1983 (by quarter)

	1980				1981				1982				1983			
	I	II	III	IV	I	II	III	IV	I	II	III	IV	I	II	III	IV
Number																
Manufacturing	4	5	10	4	11	6	12	7	6	6	6	6	8	6	8	13
All sectors	18	13	36	26	26	22	30	38	26	28	20	13	24	30	24	32
Value of paid-up capital in million pesos																
Manufacturing	0.2	2.4	1.1	0.9	3.3	0.8	3.1	1.0	9.8	0.8	1.1	0.7	64.1	3.1	117.1	4.0
All sectors	4.0	2.7	7.4	6.6	8.1	5.6	4.4	10.6	18.7	4.0	4.9	1.4	106.4	8.9	121.6	334.3

Source: data supplied by Securities and Exchange Commission

failures accurately. Nevertheless, since exposure to foreign trade is probably greater in more formal businesses, their frequency of failure would suggest some response to trade liberalization.

There is little evidence of sharp departures from past movements in the number of dissolutions of domestic corporations that may be associated with the 1981 liberalization, whether the measure is the number of corporations seeking dissolution, the value of paid-up capital withdrawn, or the share of the manufacturing sector in total dissolutions or paid-up capital withdrawals. It is true, however, that the absolute value of capital withdrawn from business has been rising over the period 1981–3, more acutely in 1983.

Worker Layoffs

One indicator of possible unemployment and a measure of factor turnover is the number of workers terminated by industry. This information has been available in the Philippines since 1978 in the aggregate and by major sectors, although the coverage of (voluntary) reporting by firms is not widespread (table 6.10). The share of manufacturing workers in the total number of workers terminated did not really increase substantially in 1983 and 1984. Whereas in 1981 81 percent of all workers terminated (as reported by firms) came from the manufacturing sector, the ratio fell to 70 percent in 1982, 74 percent in 1983, and 62 percent in 1984.

Relating layoffs in manufacturing to the REER may add to our knowledge about the transitory employment effects of trade liberalization. The REER is the best proxy we have for overall trade policy trends during

Table 6.10 Workers laid off, by industry, 1981–1984

Industry	1981	1982	1983	1984
Agriculture, fishery, and forestry	3,399	1,347	7,218	3,888
Mining and quarrying	3,420	6,175	1,685	6,574
Manufacturing	63,648	34,436	55,613	58,283
Electricity, gas, and water	0	0	0	0
Construction	1,055	1,373	2,814	6,621
Wholesale and retail trade	2,351	1,629	3,545	6,412
Transport, storage, and communication	1,743	2,638	1,745	4,140
Others	2,850	1,914	2,792	7,318
Total workers laid off	78,466	49,512	75,428	93,386
Number of reporting establishments	n.a.	638	1,267	2,212

n.a., not available
Source: data supplied by Labor Statistics Division, Ministry of Labor and Employment

the 1980s.[2] Figure 6.1 tracks worker layoffs (total and in manufacturing) against the reciprocal of the REER as we have defined it (we use the reciprocal for diagrammatic presentation, since the expected relationship is a positive one between layoffs and a price level that is rising in the Philippines relative to world price levels).

Manufacturing layoffs declined when the REER depreciated in the second quarter of 1981 and did not respond to the appreciation in the second and third quarters of 1981. In the subsequent quarters continued depreciation was accompanied by a further reduction in layoffs (fourth quarter of 1981 until third quarter of 1982), but the reaction to the severe

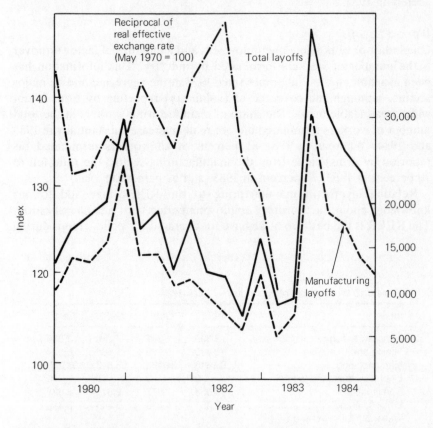

Figure 6.1 Real effective exchange rates (left-hand scale) and worker layoffs (right-hand scale), 1980–1984

Sources: real effective exchange rates, Asian Development Bank; layoffs, table 6.10

[2] The REER we use is one calculated by the Asian Development Bank which compares the ratio of import-weighted producer prices for the Philippines' major trading partners to the Philippine WPI. (The original source gives the REER in the reciprocal form to the convention followed in this study.) This REER is used because it is the only REER series for the Philippines that we have that is calculated monthly.

appreciation of June 1983 did not really result in massive layoffs. Indeed the large numbers of terminations seem to have occurred in early 1980 and not during the episode *per se*.

The crude exercise based on figure 6.1 must be recognized for its particular limitations. The coverage of layoff data is incomplete and varies, and there are factors other than the REER, such as wages and profitability, that influence layoffs. A more formal analysis of industrial layoffs by industries, separating import-substituting and export-oriented industries (Alburo, 1985), has revealed behavior that follows expectations about sectoral responses to trade liberalization. The import-substituting industries examined included textiles, chemicals, and paper and printing, while clothing, furniture and wood, and footwear represent export-oriented industries. Although both types of industry have different lag structures in their reactions to changes in the REER, in general export-oriented industries reduce, and import-substituting industries increase, their layoffs with real depreciation.

This analysis suggests that, in the Philippines trade environment, import-substituting industries have a different expectation from export-oriented industries as to the movement of REERs. In particular, it is postulated that the former seek to influence exchange rates in order to keep expected rates close to the past rate, while the latter give more weight to the current REER and behave accordingly.

These sectoral responses are best illustrated by the clothing and textile industries. The clothing sector, which is export oriented, increases its layoffs once the REER appreciates. The textile industry, an import-substituting sector, does the reverse, reducing layoffs in response to real appreciation of exchange rates. If the major object of a trade liberalization policy is to affect the REERs, these responses would be expected.

Imports and Worker Layoffs

An increase in real imports might normally be expected to follow a trade liberalization episode, although the consequent movements of the exchange rate and relevant elasticities could have opposite effects. Figure 6.2 shows, for 1980–3, the value of aggregate imports (c.i.f.), the value of manufactured imports (SITC 5–9, 1981–3 only), and the numbers of workers terminated or laid off in the manufacturing sector. There is very little perceptible connection between aggregate imports and workers terminated by industry during liberalization.

However, changes in manufactured imports have a slight interaction with layoffs, especially when a one-quarter lag is considered, but the results are curious (Alburo, 1985). During this period of trade liberalization imports increased (as too did the ratio of manufactured to total imports), but import-substituting industries reduced their layoffs. This result might be explained by what went wrong in the trade liberalization:

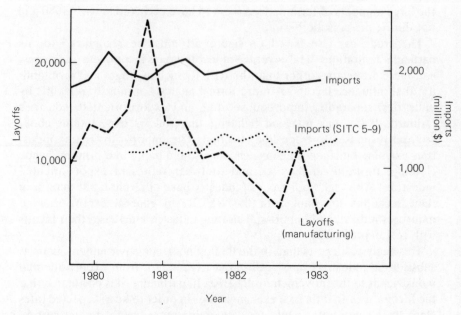

Figure 6.2 Imports and worker layoffs, 1980–1983

Sources: imports, data supplied by NEDA; layoffs, data supplied by Labor Statistics Division, Ministry of Labor and Employment

tariff reductions may have improved the access of industry to the imported inputs on which it traditionally relied, while the reversal of the liberalization of nontariff barriers early in the episode maintained the protection to the industry's output.

An Evaluation of Trade Policy from 1980 to 1983

An Implicit Rationale for the Sequencing of Trade Liberalization

There is no direct evidence that an explicit rationale existed for sequencing the third episode in gradual stages over five years. The first phase of reducing the highest tariffs appears to be consistent with a broad liberalization drive. Thereafter, it might be assumed that the first industries to be liberalized would be those thought to have smaller adjustment costs relative to others in later phases. However, the ability of industries to resist trade liberalization may depend on their political influence in policy decisions. In the same vein, those which initially enjoyed less protection may have less initial influence and thus would be the first to be subjected to liberalization.

Table 6.11 Some characteristics of industries in the Tariff Reform Program

Phases	Industry	EPR 1979 (%)	FA/L,[a] 1980	Concentration ratio[b] 1980
Phase 2	Food processing	− 13	76.9	34.1
	Textile and garments	77	61.6	23.0
	Leather and footwear[c]	− 18	17.2	17.2
	Pulp and paper	102	125.2	57.6
Phase 3	Cement	30	n.a.	59.1
	Iron and steel	n.a.	102.7	57.5
	Automotive[d]	3,715	56.4	53.0
	Wood and wood products	0	35.8	24.2
	Glass and ceramics	n.a.	62.7	37.1
	Furniture	− 3	10.6	17.1
	Machinery	45	38.0	11.2
	Electrical and electronic products	90	22.8	55.7
Phase 4	Agriculture and forest products	0	n.a.	n.a.
	Basic chemical[e]	n.a.	164.4	29.3
	Basic nonferrous	n.a.	39.8	n.a.
	Plastic and rubber products	56	36.7	54.9
	Cosmetics, perfumery	n.a.	45.2	147.0[f]

n.a., not available.
[a] Book value of fixed assets divided by number of production workers, in thousand pesos.
[b] Percentage ratio of net sales of all firms in a given industry that fall in *Business Day's* list of the top 1,000 corporations to the total sales of the same industry as measured by the 1980 *Annual Survey of Manufactures*.
[c] For EPR, wearing apparel and footwear.
[d] For FA/L and concentration ratio, transport equipment.
[e] For FA/L and concentration ratio, industrial chemicals.
[f] Exceeds 100 percent owing to varying classifications.
Sources: data supplied by Tariff Commission of the Philippines; Hooley, 1985; *Business Day*, various issues; NCSO, *Annual Survey of Establishments*, various issues

To see the magnitudes surrounding these dimensions, table 6.11 presents the industrial sectors programmed for tariff reform and some of their economic characteristics – relative factor proportions, EPRs for 1979, and concentration ratios in 1980. In many instances there is no neat matching between industry characteristics and products subject to tariff reform. Thus caution must be exercised for these cases.

The concentration ratio is measured as the sales of all the firms in a given industry that fall in the list of the top 1,000 corporations divided by the total sales of the same industry as measured by the *Annual Survey of Establishments*. The ratio is meant to provide a proxy for political influence rather than economic concentration. The greater the number of firms in a given industry that belong to this base, the greater, it is postulated, is that industry's potential political power. Conversely it is possible that firms may account for say 90 percent of an industry's output. Yet if those firms do not belong to the top 1,000 corporations it may simply mean that the industry itself has little potential political influence.

Although the evidence is at best meager, the industries liberalized in phase 2 had, on average, lower levels of effective protection initially (1979) than those affected in phases 3 or 4. Moreover, concentration ratios were likewise lower among them than for phase 4 industries. However, there was a wide degree of variation in the factor proportions (measured by the value of fixed assets per employee) of the industries by phases.

An implication from this is that the phasing of the third episode may have been dictated more by considerations of economic and political influence than by the economic calculus of adjustment costs. It suggests that those sectors that were less protected to begin with would be the first to be exposed to liberalization. All this is of course consistent with the broad context of the reform, that is, to allow those most affected sufficient time to adjust to a new trade regime. Notable exceptions to this implied sequencing are wood and wood products, furniture, and agriculture and forestry products. In the case of pulp and paper, restrictions were reimposed on the import of final goods even before this phase was implemented.

Partial Liberalization and the Level of Protection

Once the program removing quantitative import controls had begun, the reimposition of many controls happened for clear and specific reasons. There is evidence that many reimpositions were to protect particular firms or industries, that the items removed from the schedule for liberalization were more important in consumption than those that were pursued, and that subsequent policy changes effectively eroded the strength of the episode.

Reimposition of quantitative restrictions in the face of tariff reform for the same item usually made the latter irrelevant. What is to be noted in the episode is that more than 80 percent of the items affected by the tariff reform were producer goods, whereas the import liberalization mostly affected consumer goods. However, phase 1 of the tariff reform – reducing peak rates – reinforced the import liberalization since the items affected were mostly NEC and UC items.

Since the tariff reform was completed on schedule in 1985, but import restrictions were reimposed, there were serious consequences for the effective protection enjoyed by domestic import-substituting industries. The tariff reform tended to reduce the cost of inputs (though this was not always so, given that reform involved raising as well as lowering tariffs). However, the reimposition of import controls tended to restore the levels of nominal protection enjoyed by consumer goods before the Tariff

Reform Program. It is quite possible that average effective protection on consumer goods even increased.

Thus, if the sequencing of the tariff reform and import liberalization components falls out of step, the consequences for effective protection can be perverse. Ironically, therefore, the net effects of trade policy in 1981–3 resembled the decontrol process of the 1960s in reverse.

The Failure of Trade Policy Reform in the Early 1980s

The trade liberalization attempted in the early 1980s became completely derailed in 1983 when full control of foreign exchange was introduced as a consequence of the economic crisis that had developed.

In spite of the growing commitment to reform of the more "technocratic" parts of the government, the trade liberalization movement in the early 1980s was politically fragile. After all, it was conducted by the same government that had introduced a considerable degree of distortion and monopoly into the economy in the preceding years. Indeed, partial reversals were quick to follow some of the moves to decontrol imports in 1982. In spite of this political fragility, it was undoubtedly the broader circumstances of the economy that aborted the liberalization by 1983. These circumstances did not develop after the trade liberalization measures were introduced, but for the most part preceded them. They were partly internal circumstances that were in the government's control, partly external circumstances that were not. The government's failure to tackle those internal problems that were in its control probably doomed the liberalization from the start.

The external conditions related on the one hand to the Philippines' terms of trade, on the other to the effects of recession in the OECD countries after 1979. The period from 1974 to 1981 marked the sharpest sustained decline that the country had experienced in its terms of trade since World War II (in spite of a partial recovery in 1977–9). The 1981 terms of trade stood at a mere 53 percent of the 1974 level. The rising price of oil after 1979 played its part in the external shock to the Philippine economy, but so too did the way the OECD countries reacted to the second oil price rise. Instead of seeking to reflate their economies and "grow out of" recession – as they did after 1973 – these countries put a primary emphasis on combating inflation through more deflationary policies. On the one hand this meant low growth and severely affected the markets for developing-country exports. On the other hand, it meant high real interest rates which made it more expensive not only to borrow but also to service existing debt. One calculation (supplied by the World Bank) is that three quarters of the Philippine external debt accumulated between 1978 and 1982 is explained by increasing interest rates and oil prices.

The magnitude of these external shocks predicated a very sizable adjustment in exchange rates and government expenditure, but this simply did not occur until the partial collapse of the economy from 1983.

From 1975 onwards the Philippines sustained a current account deficit – equivalent to around 5 percent of GDP – that was extremely high by historical standards. This deficit was related to the enormous increase in the level of investment that occurred in the mid-1970s, from 20 percent of GDP (in 1972 prices) in 1973 to 27 percent in 1975, remaining above 25 percent until 1984. Much of the increased investment was either public or based on publicly guaranteed foreign loans. Such an increase in investment financed by increased foreign debt might have been justified in the period of low real interest rates that prevailed until 1979, had such investments proven sufficiently productive to repay the debts. However, much of this investment was of very dubious quality (and there was a dramatic rise in ICORs), largely for political reasons.

By the early 1980s there were some important failures among these investments and the government, as the guarantor of the foreign debt that had financed many of them, found itself taking them over and seeking to refinance them. At the same time the government was also having to refinance many of its own poorly performing corporations. These financial requirements led to large government deficits and to an increase in foreign borrowing at a time when this made far less financial sense. From 1981 government macroeconomic policy became very expansionary: in 1981 and 1982 the national government budget deficit reached a record of 4 percent of GDP. Even in the profligate election year of 1969 this figure had not reached 3 percent.

From the mid-1970s onwards exchange rate policy appears to have been little more than one of accommodation: the nominal exchange rate crept slowly up, more or less offsetting the more rapid inflation in the Philippines than in world markets (though the precise direction of change of the REER depends on the particular price series chosen). Nominal exchange rates certainly did not devalue sufficiently to maintain Philippine comparative advantage in its traditional exports which suffered particularly from falling relative prices. In 1982, for instance, the REER for exports was only 70 percent of its 1979 level. It was not really until 1983–4 that the peso was devalued by a sufficient margin to make a significant improvement in REERs.

The REER had arguably been too high ever since the mid-1970s, given the existence since this time of a large trade deficit and a level of foreign borrowing that was not justified by the productivity of the investments it was financing. (Of course it was really the investment ratio that was too high.) Moreover, the reduction in tariffs and the liberalization of import controls from 1981 was likely to put even more pressure, in the short term at least, on the exchange rate. Clearly, insufficient emphasis was placed by policymakers on the relationship of the exchange rate to trade liberalization.

It is possible that the limited trade liberalization from 1981, without any significant exchange rate adjustment, contributed to the developing balance-of-payments crisis. If it did, its contribution must certainly have been minor. In fact, the very shortness of the life of this liberalization episode testifies to the imminence of the balance-of-payments crisis that had been building up independently. By the first half of the 1980s the current account deficit had reached unmanageable proportions and it only remained for a political event, the assassination of Benigno Aquino in August 1983, fully to trigger the economic crisis.

7

The Economy's Response to Changes in Trade Policy

In this chapter we look at the way the tradeables-producing sectors of the economy – agriculture, mining, and manufacturing – have reacted to changing trade policies over the post-war period (or over as much of this as the statistics allow). The recentness of the Tariff Reform Program and several important discontinuities in statistical series in 1980 mean that this long-term view almost completely excludes the years of implementation of the last episode. In fact, the coincidence of this episode with a deep economic crisis would probably make interpretation of even up-to-date figures very difficult; to the extent that interpretation is possible, this has already been undertaken in chapter 6.

Agriculture

In the following paragraphs seven product groups in agriculture, fisheries, and forestry are discussed: two food crops (rice and corn) and five export product groups (coconuts, sugar, bananas, pineapples, and forest products) now account for about half of agricultural output. Livestock and poultry and fishing are the major remaining sectors not covered for lack of data. For the seven product groups covered, we report REERs, real output, volume of trade, area harvested, and mean yield.

Coconut products (figure 7.1) – copra (the unprocessed oil-bearing flesh of the coconut), desiccated coconut, coconut oil, and its byproduct coconut meal – remained the dominant group of agricultural export products in the 1970s. The Philippines is the major world supplier of these products (whose prices have moved closely together), but competition between coconuts and other edible-oil products restricts the Philippines' ability to manipulate world prices. Since the late 1950s oil exports, and to a lesser extent desiccated coconut exports, have grown while copra exports have tended to decline. This substitution has largely occurred for technological reasons (the falling cost of transporting bulk oil) and, because of preferential Philippine access to the US market, Philippine trade policy itself has

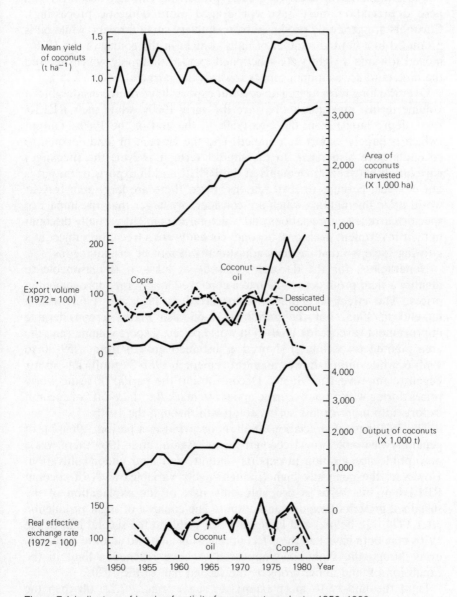

Figure 7.1 Indicators of levels of activity for coconut products, 1950–1983

Sources: mean yield and area harvested, NEDA, *Philippine Statistical Yearbook*, 1976, table 5.2, and 1984, table 5.2; export volume, Alburo and Shepherd, 1988, appendix table E.7.5; output, NEDA, *Philippine Statistical Yearbook*, 1976, table 5.1, and 1984, table 5.1; real effective exchange rate, Alburo and Shepherd, 1988, appendix table E.6.5

not discriminated in favor of greater processing (though decontrol and peso depreciation must have encouraged more domestic processing). Coconuts are generally produced by many very small farmers, while oil is produced in a limited number of mills (which, in the course of the 1970s, moved towards a tight state-sanctioned export monopoly which allowed the millers to act as monopsonists towards the farmers).

Over the long term aggregate coconut exports have risen considerably in volume terms, most markedly since the early 1960s, while their REERs rose (depreciated) from the late 1950s to the end of the 1960s. Output (which is largely export determined) and the amount of land devoted to coconuts have also risen. In the shorter term, however, the (negative) correlation between movements in the REER and in exports or output is not obvious, perhaps for two reasons. First, there are large year-to-year world price fluctuations which are considerably larger than the impact of specific currency depreciations and which farmers might partially discount in their investment decisions. Second, coconuts are a tree crop subject to a growing cycle, so that capacity adjustments cannot be instantaneous.

Nonetheless, for the decontrol episode at least, it is reasonable to identify a clear producer reaction to a perceived long-term improvement in prices. The effective depreciation occurred in 1961 and 1962, with a tail-end in 1965, but the period 1957–65 also marks a considerable improvement (except for 1960–1) in world prices. Export volume (and the area planted to coconuts) showed a sustained growth from 1959–60 to 1965–6, while output showed an improvement in 1961–3 (unofficial exports began to improve from 1959). Decontrol and the period of rising world prices during which this occurred appear to mark the "take-off" of coconut exports into more or less sustained growth through the 1970s.

The 1970 peso depreciation similarly occurred in a period, 1969–74, of generally favorable world coconut prices. Again, after 1969 there was a perceptible acceleration in exports, output, and land under cultivation. However, the generally high (though highly variable) level of coconut REERs in the 1970s is probably only part of the explanation of the sustained growth of exports and output. The collapse of sugar production after 1974 (see below) and increasing rice yields in the second half of the 1970s may both have had the effect of releasing land and labor to coconuts, even though the Philippines appeared to have reached a limit to the expansion of land under crops by the second half of the 1970s.

Until the mid-1970s most exports of sugar (figure 7.2), till then the second most important export product group, went to the United States under quota. Since quotas were generally filled, changes in REERs indicate changes in profitability rather than in incentives to produce. Export volume was boosted in the 1960s by increases in the US quota. The end to the US quota arrangements in the mid-1970s and the fall in Philippines' export prices led to a substantial decline in output, exports, and area under cultivation from the mid-1970s which in turn, we have

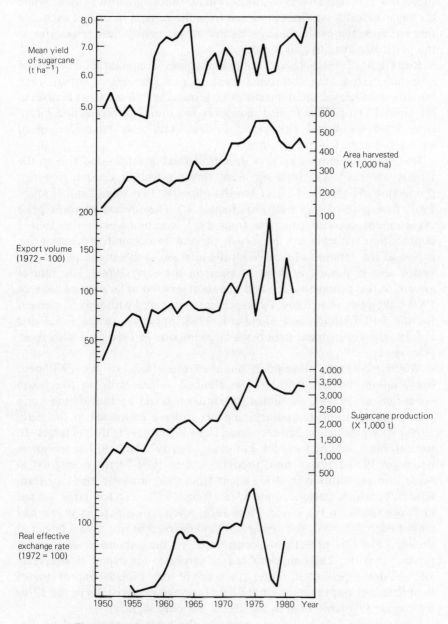

Figure 7.2 Indicators of levels of activity for sugar, 1950–1983

Sources: as for figure 7.1

suggested, released factors of production for other agricultural uses. While the sugar industry was thus insulated from the general impact of exchange rate changes, the evidence suggests that it was nonetheless responsive to the particular incentives it faced.

Rice (figure 7.3) has remained the Philippines' dominant food crop. The government has long controlled trade in rice (as well as corn), using imports to influence the domestic price level, a key element, of course, in the cost of living. This import monopoly has insulated production incentives from the world rice price, at least until the establishment of substantial export surpluses after 1977.

It is thus not surprising that decontrol (and a substantial rise in the REER for rice) had little apparent direct effect in encouraging rice production. The indirect effect was the opposite. (Treadgold and Hooley, 1967, first pointed this out; see chapter 4.) The favorable world price evolution of coconut products from 1957, combined with the 1961–2 depreciation, encouraged the switch of land to coconut production for export at the expense of rice. With the increase in US sugar quotas, this switch also continued in favor of sugar in the early 1960s. The rate of growth of rice production fell and rice shortages led to large price rises: in 1960–6 the price of rice rose by 86 percent, compared with only 37 percent for the CPI (Alburo and Shepherd, 1988, appendix tables E.5.3 and E.5.1). The government undertook large imports in 1964–7 to allay these price rises.

World rice price movements annulled the effects of the 1970 peso depreciation, though world prices climbed substantially in the boom conditions of 1971–4. A similar substitution effect to that of the early 1960s, though more temporary, appears to have happened in the early 1970s. Rice production had recovered from 1968 to 1971, thanks largely to the new high-yielding varieties, but plunged in 1972 and 1973 as an export boom (in 1970–2 for coconut products and in 1969–74 for sugar) led to some land substitution in 1973. Apart from this, however, the long-term tendency, which became quite clear from 1974, was for large output increases thanks to HYV rice. From 1976, when self-sufficiency in rice had almost been achieved, the amount of land devoted to rice in fact began to decline, and this presumably contributed to the expansion of coconut product exports. The considerable rice surpluses for export in the years 1977–81 developed, then, rather as a result of technological improvements than from any improvement in REERs (average rice REERs in the 1970s were more favorable than in the 1960s, but only slightly).

Corn (figure 7.4) is a major input to the large livestock and poultry sectors and is the Philippines' second food crop for domestic consumption. The country has remained largely self-sufficient in corn, with marginal imports and no exports. The story for corn is much like that for rice. The growth of corn production in 1960–6 was very low, notwithstanding the substantial 1960–2 rise (depreciation) in the REER for corn, while the

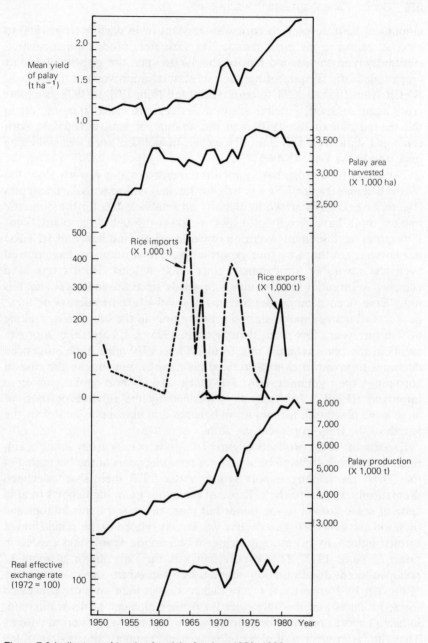

Figure 7.3 Indicators of levels of activity for rice, 1950–1983

Sources: mean yield and area harvested, NEDA, *Philippine Statistical Yearbook*, 1976, table 5.2, and 1984, table 5.2; trade volume, United Nations *Yearbook of International Trade Statistics*, various years; output, NEDA, *Philippine Statistical Yearbook*, 1976, table 5.1, and 1984, table 5.1; real effective exchange rate, Alburo and Shepherd, 1988, appendix table E.6.4

amount of land devoted to corn was stagnant or in decline from 1960 to 1965 as export crops grew rapidly. As with rice, production recovered substantially in the second half of the 1960s when the growth of export crops tailed off. In spite of another substantial improvement in the corn REER from 1969 to 1974–5, corn output fell from 1970 to 1973 as export crops again took off. Finally, as too with rice, corn yields grew rapidly in the second half of the 1970s and the amount of land devoted to corn remained static from this time. (However, unlike rice, corn was still being imported in the later 1970s.)

Two other food crops have joined the ranks of major exports since the 1950s: bananas (figure 7.5) – mostly for Japan – and processed pineapples (figure 7.6). Though grown in quantity on smallholdings for the domestic market, both have developed export markets through large plantations. Pineapples have seen an evolution of world prices (and hence of REERs) not untypical of that for other export crops, but world prices have moved even less favorably for bananas, since 1960 at least. Both crops have achieved substantial improvements in yields since around 1960 and this must have been a major feature in the relative export success of these products. Banana exports started growing only in the late 1960s, "taking off" in one year, 1968, and then again in 1975–9. Clearly, the improvements in the real exchange rate from 1961 to 1970 must have influenced decisions to invest in export-oriented plantations, but, unlike the case of coconuts, export volumes showed no quick, that is, short-term, reaction to improved REERs. This may be explained by the relative newness of large-scale plantation techniques in bananas and pineapples and/or by the length of the tree–crop cycle, or both.

Exports of forest products (figure 7.7) grew rapidly from small beginnings in the early 1950s to become for a few brief years at the beginning of the 1970s the leading export group. After 1973 their share declined dramatically, thanks to the collapse of the major item, log exports (and in spite of some growth in the minor but more processed items lumber and plywood and veneers). This decline was largely related to the exhaustion of forests; indeed an increasingly stringent ban on log exports has existed in principle since 1975. This export ban was the only major element of policy-induced discrimination among forest product exports until the 1980s. (In 1981 export taxes were higher on logs than on more processed forest products and this introduced a further element of discrimination; hitherto export taxes had been intermittent and not very discriminatory.) Thus the faster growth of plywood/veneer and lumber exports than of log exports before the 1975 ban must presumably be explained by the growth of processing capabilities and the effect of currency depreciation on the incentive for local processing.

While export prices for the different forest products have experienced broadly similar cycles, the precise timing of these cycles, as well as the size

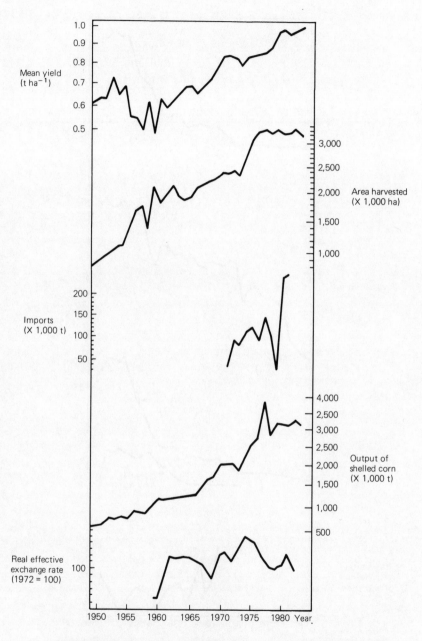

Figure 7.4 Indicators of levels of activity for corn, 1949–1983

Sources: as for figure 7.3

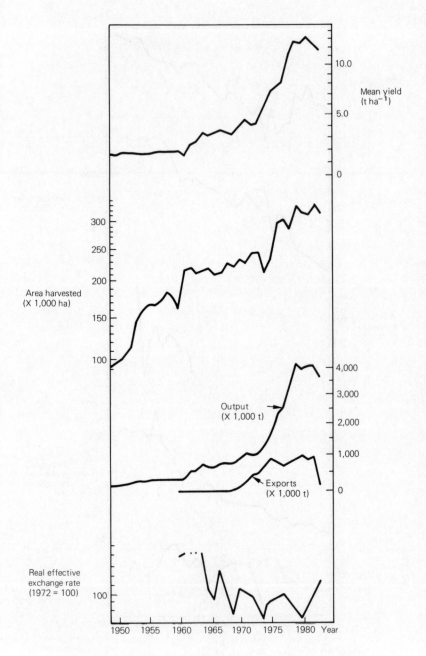

Figure 7.5 Indicators of levels of activity for bananas, 1949–1983

Sources: as for figure 7.1

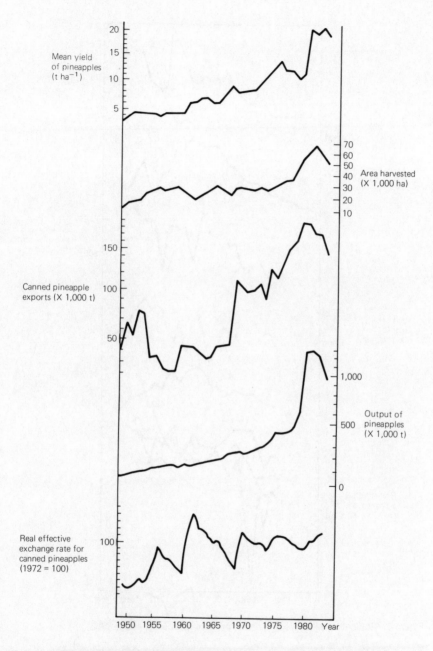

Figure 7.6 Indicators of levels of activity for pineapples, 1949–1983

Sources: as for figure 7.1

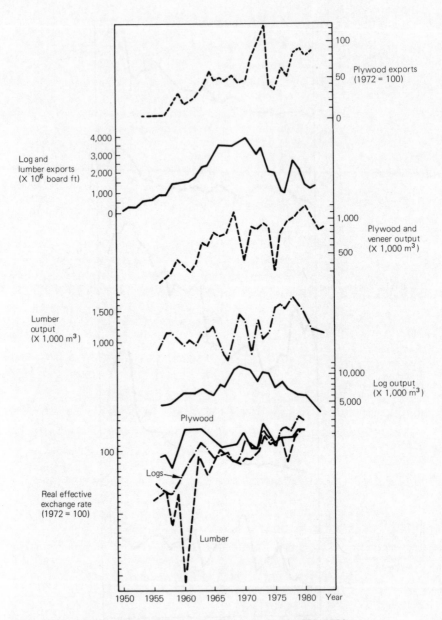

Figure 7.7 Indicators of levels of activity for forest products, 1950–1983

Sources: exports, Alburo and Shepherd, 1988, appendix table E.7.5; output, NEDA, *Philippine Statistical Yearbook*, 1976, table 6.12, and 1984, table 4.11; real effective exchange rate, Alburo and Shepherd, 1988, appendix table E.6.5

of their peaks and troughs, has differed between products (unlike coconut products). A combination of rising world prices from the end of rhe 1950s and peso depreciation in 1960–1 meant generally rising (depreciating) REERs around the decontrol episode: the REER for logs rose in 1958–63, that for lumber in 1960–6, and that for plywood in 1958–60. It is not clear whether there was an immediate response to this, but if there was, it was the growth in volume of plywood and veneer exports in 1960–4 rather than any change in log and lumber exports. Similarly, forest product REERs generally rose from 1968–9 to 1973; plywood and veneer exports, having stagnated from 1964 to 1969 (in a period of a falling REER), again took off in 1969–73, while log and lumber exports actually declined. Thus a case can be made, from the evidence of the first two liberalization episodes, for a possible rapid reaction of plywood exports to price incentives, but this is not the case for logs.

Evidence from data at the aggregate level of agriculture, forestry, and fishery (figure 7.8) reinforces some of the subsectoral evidence to suggest that the agricultural sector reacted clearly and promptly to the improved export prices of the early 1960s and early 1970s. The REER for all exports is the best available proxy for an REER for export agriculture (89 percent of exports were agricultural in 1960, 68 percent in 1970, and 42 percent in 1980; manufactured exports, which substituted for agricultural exports in the 1970s, are probably underrepresented in the export price index). This REER rose continuously in 1957–62, fell less rapidly until 1969, and then rose discontinuously in 1969–74. In the absence of a measure of agricultural exports in constant prices, we have taken the ratio of exports to domestic agricultural product, both in current prices, as a measure of export performance. This ratio will change when the REER changes, even if real export and real output volumes stay constant. Even so, it is remarkable that from 1959 to 1963 this ratio for agriculture jumps from 26 to 45 percent, falls by a similar magnitude by 1969, and then rises by a similar magnitude from 1969 to 1974.

The ratio of agricultural imports to agricultural domestic product (also at current prices) shows a similar evolution (though the ratio is far smaller). The evidence from these two ratios reflects the evidence from the individual agricultural products: that the two liberalization episodes – more precisely, the two episodes of depreciation combined with rising world prices – increased the share of exports in agricultural activity and displaced some import-substituting activity, which accounts for an increase in imports to make good this shortfall. In addition, a distinct slowdown in the secular decline in the share of agriculture in domestic product (this time in real terms) is also evident for the period 1957–68. This slowdown, which is not evident for the early 1970s, is the counterpart of the slowdown in the growth of the manufacturing sector at roughly the same time (see below).

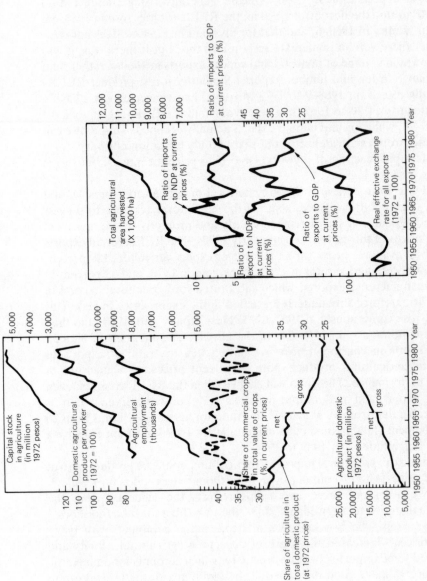

Figure 7.8 Indicators of levels of activity for agriculture, forestry, and fishery, 1949–1984

Sources: capital stock, data supplied by Philippine Institute of Development Studies; domestic product per worker, and employment, Alburo and Shepherd, 1988, appendix tables E.3.1 and E.2.1; share of commercial crops, NEDA, *Philippine Statistical Yearbook,* 1985, table 5.1; share of agriculture in domestic product, and agricultural domestic product, Alburo and Shepherd, 1988, appendix table E.1.1; total area harvested, NEDA, *Philippine Statistical Yearbook,* 1975, table 5.2 and 1984, table 5.2; real effective exchange rate for all exports, Alburo and Shepherd, 1988, appendix table E.6.5

Mining

The mining and quarrying sector is dominated by export-oriented mining, copper concentrates alone having continued to account for over 60 percent of domestic product. Figure 7.9 provides REERs, real output, and export volumes for copper concentrates, and real output, employment, and labor productivity data for mining as a whole. Copper export prices were marked by a large sustained improvement from 1958 to 1970, and this provided a far more substantial impetus to the large 1958–70 rise in the REER than the peso depreciations of 1961–2 and 1970. From 1974 to 1982 deteriorating export prices meant a loss of part of this improvement in the REER.

Copper output (which has moved very closely with mining and quarrying domestic product throughout the period), copper exports, and total mining employment showed a marked acceleration in growth in the second half of the 1960s. Growth dropped off in the first half of the 1970s, but took off again in the second half of the decade. Finally, output and exports shrank considerably from the beginning of the 1980s.

The stepwise progression of mining activity reflects the lumpiness and long lead times of investment. The acceleration of growth during the second half of the 1960s came almost a decade later than the beginning of the export price improvements which presumably triggered the investments of the 1960s. Similarly, the partial collapse of copper mining in the 1980s occurred some few years after the REER for copper had been at its most favorable.

Manufacturing: Decontrol and Import Substitution

Analysis of the impact of trade policy on different manufacturing activities is hampered by the absence of quantitative indicators of changing protection (or REERs) at the subsectoral level, questionable census and survey statistics on levels of economic activity (in spite of the brave cleaning-up job performed by Hooley, 1985, on the 1956–80 series), and a lack of information on real levels of imports and exports. As an imperfect proxy for the latter, we have constructed a series of import ratios (imports as a percentage of production plus imports minus exports) and export ratios (exports as a percentage of production) for 20 manufacturing subsectors for 1956–80 (Alburo and Shepherd, 1988, appendix tables E.7.8 and E.7.9). These are of necessity in current prices; thus the ratio changes when the REER changes, even when relative volumes stay constant. The evidence of the import ratios is the best indicator, if imperfect, of when and in which subsectors import liberalization has had an impact.

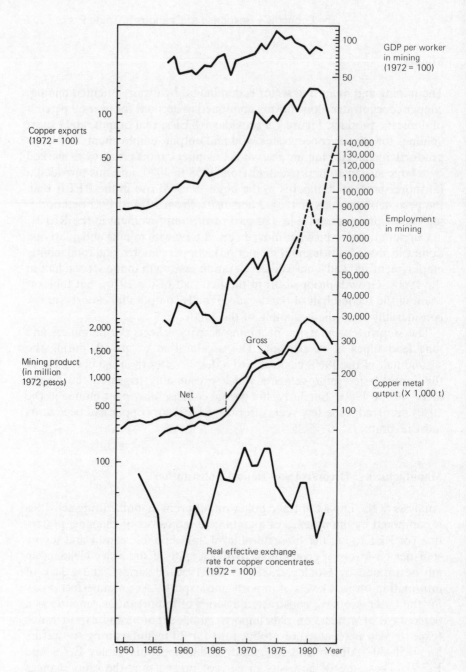

Figure 7.9 Indicators of levels of activity for mining, 1950–1983

Sources: GDP per worker, exports, employment, and mining product, Alburo and Shepherd, 1988, appendix tables E.3.1, E.7.5, E.2.1, and E.1.1; copper metal output, NEDA, *Philippine Statistical Yearbook*, 1976, table 8.7, and 1984, table 6.8; real effective exchange rate, Alburo and Shepherd, 1988, appendix table E.6.5

For manufacturing as a whole the import ratio is available in real prices (figure 7.10). This ratio indicates unequivocally that manufacturing has experienced a long-term import-replacement trend, to 1973 at least, interrupted by a clear reversal of the trend during 1963 to 1968–9. Growth rates of manufacturing domestic product in the first half of the 1960s were the lowest for the whole post-war period until the late 1970s. Survey and census data generally support national accounts and employment survey data in suggesting that growth of manufacturing output and employment in 1960–5 was lower than in most of the other five-year periods since the 1950s (figure 7.10 and table 7.1). However, low growth had already set in by 1960, as import substitution possibilities progressively declined in the 1950s, while decontrol only became effective from 1962.

Table 7.1 Periodic growth rate in manufacturing, 1956–1980 (percent per annum)

Indicators	1956–6	1960–5	1965–70	1970–5	1975–80
Output					
1 Domestic product at 1972 prices					
(National Accounts)	6.3	5.4	6.9	7.0	6.0
2 Survey/census value added at 1972					
prices[a]	12.6	5.2	9.7	4.1	− 0.1
3 Central Bank index	6.9	6.0	4.9	10.3[b]	n.a.
Employment					
4 Total manufacturing (labor force survey)	1.4[c]	2.0	3.8	2.0	4.6[d]
5 Survey/census[a]	7.2	6.6	4.0	7.5	10.1
6 Central Bank index	2.8[c]	2.0	4.4	3.0[b]	n.a.
Assets (survey/census at 1972 prices)					
7 Fixed assets[a]	11.8	26.1	8.4	4.7	7.2
Value added per employee (1972 prices)					
8 Whole of manufacturing	5.0[c]	2.5	3.0	4.8	2.3
9 Survey/census[a]	5.1	− 1.3	5.4	− 3.2	− 10.1
Total factor productivity					
10 Survey/census[a]	0.1	− 0.1	0.3	− 0.1	− 0.2

n.a., not available.
[a] Establishments employing 20 or more workers.
[b] 1970–3.
[c] 1957–60.
[d] 1975–8.
Sources: row 1, calculated from Alburo and Shepherd, 1988, appendix table E.1.1; rows 2, 5, 7, 9, and 10, Richard Hooley unpublished data; rows 3 and 6, Central Bank, 1974, tables 124 and 127, row 4, Alburo and Shepherd, 1988, appendix table E.2.1; row 8, Alburo and Shepherd, 1988, appendix table E.3.1.

There is also evidence of a low growth in average labor productivity and a fall in total factor productivity in the first half of the 1960s. If the statistics are correct, the growth of capital-to-output ratios through to the end of the 1960s may help to explain the poor productivity. Yet it is curious that fixed assets continued to grow in the early to middle 1960s when output growth had been checked (figure 7.10).

It is difficult to discern obvious subsectoral patterns in the 1960s. Table 7.2 classifies subsectors by their import substitution behavior in the 1960s, and records whether trends in output and employment or total factor productivity coincide with these. Note that, for what the statistics are worth, there are as many cases of productivity rising with increasing imports as falling.

Several general points can be made about the sectoral impact of the decontrol episode. First, the effect of increased import penetration was felt across most sectors (Alburo and Shepherd, 1988, appendix table E.7.8). Footwear, chemicals, and basic metals were the only clear examples among the major subsectors producing import-substituting tradeables of no apparent adverse break in the import substitution trend. Second, the break in the trend of the import ratio seemed to occur in almost all cases in 1963 (1962 in a few cases) – one full year after the January 1962 decontrol. The synchronized nature of the increase in the import ratio (in spite of generally restrictive macroeconomic policy, in 1962 at least) suggests that the impact of decontrol policies was general.

Third, according to the available evidence, the negative impact of increased import penetration on domestic industrial activity was often temporary; levels of activity recorded by the second half of the 1960s, admittedly in a period when macroeconomic policy was more conducive to demand growth but before import controls were reimposed. Fourth, there seem to be few convincing cases of outright decline in levels of output or employment: if liberalization lowered the growth rate, adjustments could still be made in most industries in a context of overall growth.

Finally, if decontrol had a broad liberalizing effect across the majority of industries, there may well have been different effects within these industries: all industries consisted of a mix of activities, each of which was affected in different ways by decontrol, depreciation, and tariff changes such that the outcome for any one industry would itself be mixed and difficult to predict. Perhaps the best examples of this are industries such as textiles, paper, electrical machinery, and transport equipment, which combine both the production of intermediate goods and the assembly of these into final goods. If the statistics could separate yarns from cloth or paper production from paper bags, a good deal more turbulence might be discovered in the adjustment of industry to decontrol.

Manufacturing: Trade Liberalization and Export Promotion

If import liberalization largely relates to the decontrol episode (before the 1980s at least), the growth of nontraditional exports might be expected to

Table 7.2 Directions of change in manufacturing activity following the 1960–1962 decontrol

Industries	Evidence of interruption in import substitution trends	Evidence of interruption in total factor productivity (TFP) trends		Evidence of interruption in output and/or employment trends
		TFP falls	TFP rises	
Industries where an interruption of a long-term (1956–80) import substitution trend occurs during the period 1962–9				
Food processing	1963–70	1965–75	—	1964–70[a] (employment fall in 1966)
Textiles	1963–8	—	1963–72	1963–5 (employment fall in 1965)
Paper	1963–5	1962 to 1964–5	—	(slight employment fall in 1965)
Nonmetallic mineral products	1963–6	—	1962–7	1958–64
Nonelectrical machinery	1963–71	1961–70	—	1960–71 (employment falls in 1962–5)
Petroleum products	1962–6	—	—	—
Industries where an import substitution trend in the 1950s is no longer evident in the 1960s and 1970s				
Rubber products	1963–7	—	1964–8	1961–4
Metal products	1963–9	—	1964–8	(employment falls 1965–9)
Electrical machinery	1963 onwards	1963–5	1965–9	—
Industries with no obvious import substitution trend during the period 1956–80				
Clothing	1962–4	—	1963–72	— (employment falls 1964–71)
Furniture	1963–8 (very slight)	1964–7	—	— (employment falls 1964–71)
Transport equipment	1963–70	1963 to 1965–6	—	1964–9
Beverages	1965–9	—	—	—
Industries where a long-term import substitution trend was not clearly interrupted				
Footwear				
Chemicals				
Basic metals				

—, not applicable.

[a] Traditional exports fell in the second half of the 1960s.

Source: Alburo and Shepherd, 1988 (import substitution, appendix table E.7.8; total factor productivity, appendix table E.3.2; output, appendix table E.1.2, deflated by table E.5.2; employment, appendix table E.2.2)

be a consequence both of decontrol and of the export promotion of the early 1970s. The ratio of nontraditional manufactured exports to total output, whether expressed in current or constant prices, has grown, slowly at first, since 1962, having declined in the 1950s (figure 7.10 and table 5.8). This ratio began to accelerate – albeit from a low level – from 1969 onwards, before the 1970 depreciation. Since the 1960s, then, the growth of these exports has been steady but far from impressive compared with that of the Philippines' southeast Asian neighbors. This slow and steady growth trajectory is consistent either with the idea that nontraditional (and hence infant) export activities need time to develop, or with the idea that the incentive to develop them has remained too small, or with both these hypotheses.

Two further points can be made. First, exports have developed across a broad range of industrial sectors, even though export levels in many of these remain modest and exports have overall become dominated by clothing, shoes, and electronics (and by a consignment/subcontracting mode). Second, different product groups appear to have "taken off" into exports, in the sense of achieving a sustained growth, at different times. There is little obvious pattern to this, though the traditional labor-intensive products – clothing, footwear, furniture – were among the first of these, while labor-intensive electronics assembly had to await the growth of demand for subcontracting in advanced countries. Three intermediate-good exports that started developing in the 1970s – petroleum products, nonmetallic mineral products, and metal products – experienced declining export levels in the mid-1970s, possibly as a result of import substitution in the Philippines' southeast Asian export markets. The broad chronological pattern of export "take-off" is more or less as follows:

1950s	embroidery
1962	petroleum products
1967	footwear, furniture
1969	clothing, nonmetallic minerals, metals, machinery
1970	textiles, metal products, paper
1972	electronics
1973	chemicals, transport equipment
mid-1970s	food

There is one indicator of nontraditional manufactured export growth after 1980 in the series on export volume in figure 7.10. This series (which may well overstate the real rate of export growth because of the nature of the price series used to deflate export value) clearly indicates a stagnation in exports from 1981. This may in turn reflect the fall (appreciation) in the REER for manufacturing since 1978 and the rise in real wages since 1974.

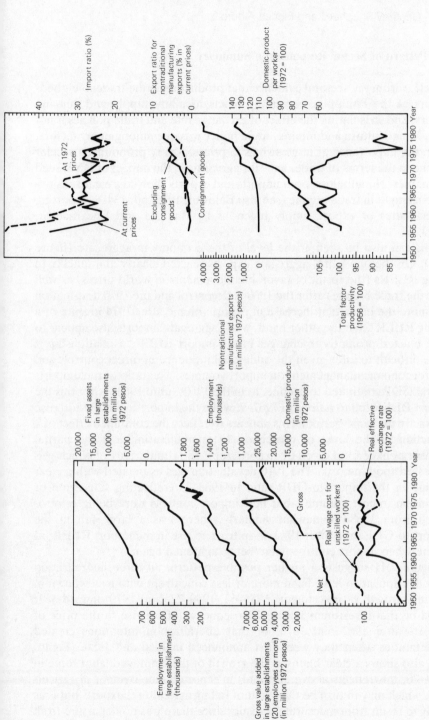

Figure 7.10 Indicators of levels of activity for manufacturing, 1950–1984

Sources: fixed assets in large establishments, Richard Hooley, unpublished data; employment in large establishments, and employment, Alburo and Shepherd, 1988, appendix tables E.2.2 and E.2.1; gross value added in large establishments, Richard Hooley, unpublished data; domestic product, real wage costs, real effective exchange rate, import ratio at current prices, export and nontraditional manufactured exports, domestic product per worker, and total factor productivity, Alburo and Shepherd, 1988, appendix tables E.1.1, E.5.7, E.6.4, E.7.8, E.7.11, E.3.1, and E.3.2

The Pattern of Sector Responses: a Summary

It is clear from the sectoral evidence that production in the tradeable-goods sectors of the Philippines economy reacts to many supply and demand factors, and so isolating the effect of exchange rate and trade policies is not easy. In agriculture and mining, trade policy was one among many factors, given the importance of large swings in prices, a very pronounced secular decline in the terms of trade, and, for agriculture, the impact of HYV seed techniques. Nonetheless, both imports and exports showed a clear sensitivity to changes in trade regime (see also Baldwin, 1975, pp. 134–8, reporting on estimates of export supply functions by Bautista and Encarnacion, 1971).

This can also be seen at the level of the economy in aggregate (figure 7.11). On the one hand, aggregate exports reacted clearly and quickly to rising REERs (the result of favorable movements in world prices, as well as in the trade regime) after the 1960–2 decontrol and the 1970 devaluation (but note the important increase in export volume after 1974 in spite of a falling REER). On the other hand, while aggregate imports also appear to have reacted promptly to changes in the import REER, a relationship is more difficult to infer given the additional influence of direct controls and macroeconomic management on import volumes. The ratio of real imports to real GDP continued to decline, as in the 1950s, until 1963. After this the import REER fell to a floor in 1967–9, while the import-to-GDP ratio rose in exactly the same period. This appears to reflect the combined effect of a reduction in the level of protection to manufacturing and the partial displacement of food crops by export crops, the counterpart of which was increased food imports. The 1970 devaluation was associated with a clear decline in the import-to-GDP ratio in 1968–73 (reflecting stagnation or decline in import volume), but new import controls were being reintroduced from 1968. Somewhat similarly, there was a large fall in the import-to-GDP ratio after 1980, in spite of no rise in the import REER, at a time when import controls were being tightened again.

Figure 7.11 suggests a further possible pattern: all three liberalization episodes appear to have been more or less concurrent with a slowdown in the real growth of investment (1959–62, 1969–72, and 1979 onwards). It could be that investment fell as a consequence of the rise in the price of imports after 1962 and 1970, or that liberalization intentions created uncertainties when they were first announced in 1960 and 1980. (Figure 7.11 also shows a clear hiatus in the growth of the employed labor force in 1964–70; this reflects above all trends in reported employment in agriculture, which may in turn be the result of falling agricultural exports but is as likely to result from inaccurate statistics since there was no departure from

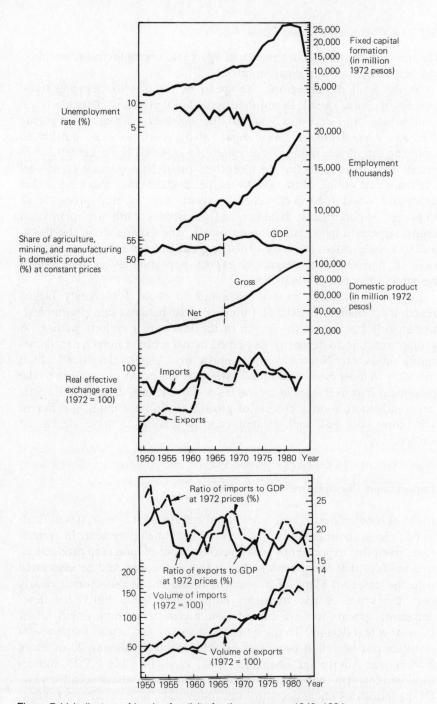

Figure 7.11 Indicators of levels of activity for the economy, 1949–1984

Sources: fixed capital formation, data supplied by NEDA; unemployment, data supplied by Ministry of Labor and Employment; employment, Alburo and Shepherd, 1988, appendix table E.2.1; share of agriculture, mining, and manufacturing in domestic product, data supplied by NEDA; domestic product, real effective exchange rates, and volume of trade, Alburo and Shepherd, 1988, appendix tables E.1.1, E.6.4, E.6.5, and E.7.3

the trend at this time in the growth of aggregate unemployment, working-age population, or participation rates.)

At the level of subsectors, the speed of reaction to changing trade policies of course varied. Established agricultural products, particularly the smallholder crop coconuts, showed the quickest reaction to changing REERs. The plantation crop, sugar, also proved to react quickly to changing incentives, though its reliance on a captive US market until 1973 meant that it was reacting to incentives other than general trade and exchange rate policy. More tentatively, the evidence may also suggest that processed wood (plywood, veneer) exports also reacted promptly to improved export prices. Bananas and pineapples, both new plantation crops, appear to have reacted more slowly. The experience of the 1960s, and to a lesser extent the early 1970s, suggests that the general responsiveness of agriculture to improved export opportunities in turn pulled resources out of food production.

Copper concentrate exports appeared to show a markedly lagged reaction to changes in REER (more so than bananas and pineapples), presumably because of the length of the investment cycle in mining. A prompt reaction to decontrol was noted across a broad range of manufacturing subsectors. Nontraditional manufactured exports developed, albeit modestly in most cases, in a broad variety of subsectors in response to the piecemeal improvements in incentives to export since decontrol. Exports apparently started on a process of growth at different times in different subsectors, the less sophisticated exports tending to have developed earlier.

Imports and Unemployment

In the absence of dependable subsectoral employment figures, it is difficult to be precise about the impact of decontrol on unemployment. In agriculture, given that export crops pulled resources out of food crop production, it is unlikely that the growth hiatus in rice and corn could be associated with the enforced idling of productive resources. Manufacturing clearly bore the brunt of any transitory employment losses but, even here, decontrol appears to have caused slower growth in employment rather than an actual decline. To the extent that survey and census employment statistics can be relied upon (for establishments employing 20 or more workers see Alburo and Shepherd, 1988, appendix table E.2.1), subsectoral employment did not tend to fall in more than one consecutive year. Of the industries where decontrol was followed by increased import ratios, only one, nonelectrical machinery (a very small employer at the time), experienced falling employment for more than one year which could plausibly be associated with increased imports.

For the economy as a whole there is no obvious relationship of unemployment with the ratio of imports to domestic product (see figure 7.11). Indeed, in the years of 1963–8 when the real import-to-GDP ratio rose from 28 to 34 percent in manufacturing, unemployment was not above average; for 1963–6 it was distinctly below the average for the 1960s (although the industrial sector and unskilled workers did take an enlarged share of total unemployment in 1964, 1965, and 1966 compared with the other years for which data are available; see Department of Labor, various years).

Conclusions

When there are so many other influences on economic behavior, it is of course difficult to discern clear patterns in the economy's response to changes in trade and exchange rate policies. The impressions gained from the descriptive approach adopted in this chapter are preliminary (indeed, the post-war statistical series available for the Philippines are rich enough to promise good prospects for further econometric study). Yet it has become apparent that trade and exchange rate policies have played an important role in influencing the pattern of output. Trade liberalization has been seen to raise the level of both exports and imports (though policies have taken a longer or shorter time to work through according to the particular product). Surprisingly, perhaps, the import liberalization of the 1960s – admittedly a less thoroughgoing liberalization than has occurred in many other countries – did not seem to have any long-lasting adverse impact on levels of employment.

8
The Long-term Experience of Trade Liberalization in the Philippines

In this concluding chapter we review the long-term pattern of trade liberalization in the Philippines with particular reference to the apparent success and failure of each episode and the nature of the political commitment to trade liberalization. We also seek to draw some conclusions on the sequencing and timing of Philippine trade liberalization that might be relevant to trade liberalization elsewhere.

The essential features of the three post-war trade liberalization episodes in the Philippines up to 1983 are as follows.

Decontrol, 1960–1965

Import controls were removed in two distinct phases: in 1960–1 a partial peso depreciation was achieved through the introduction and subsequent modification of a multiple exchange rate system; in January 1962, import controls were completely and immediately removed and a reunified exchange rate (except for an export tax element) was allowed to float down. A full liberalization had not been intended and there was some compensation for the removal of import controls through selected tariff increases. The residual export tax element was removed in 1965.

This reform was gradually eroded by domestic inflation, and by the effect of export expansion in agriculture, which took resources away from food production for the domestic market. Then a more expansionary economic policy from 1966 led to a series of balance-of-payments crises which resulted in the partial reintroduction of controls in 1969 and a subsequent devaluation.

Export Promotion in the 1970s

A peso depreciation in 1970 was followed by export incentives later in the year and the strengthening of these in subsequent years, especially 1973.

This was a weak liberalization episode: on the one hand, the import controls partially reintroduced in 1969 stayed in place; on the other, the relatively rapid growth of nontraditional exports from the mid-1970s was as much due to stagnating or falling real wages as to trade policy *per se*.

While nontraditional exports came to play a more important role in foreign exchange earnings, the current account went into long-term deficit from the mid-1970s as a result of an acceleration in investment, particularly public investment, and a continued steep deterioration in the terms of trade. This deficit was funded by heavy foreign borrowing, and in the early 1980s a major economic crisis developed around the balance-of-payments problem.

The Tariff Reform Program of the Early 1980s

The Tariff Reform Program had two components: a tariff reform (chopping off the highest rates and reducing tariff escalation) undertaken from 1981 to 1985, and the elimination of import controls on a large number of items (broadly those that had been recontrolled in 1969) in a number of stages by 1985. After the economic crisis of 1983 foreign exchange controls were reimposed.

The long-term sequence of replacing import controls by a tariff (1960–5), promoting manufactured exports (1970–3), and liberalizing the manufacturing import substitution sector (1981–5, but temporarily aborted in 1983) was not preplanned; each stage has been at least partly reversed. For the period that we have reviewed in this study it is difficult to perceive any long-term commitment to, or, indeed, very substantial achievements of, trade liberalization in the Philippines. This lack of commitment and consequently of achievement provides a lesson in itself, but limits the inferences that can be drawn about how liberalization might have been better achieved.

The 1962 decontrol represents the most substantial liberalization achievement of the three episodes, both promoting exports and leading to a more market-oriented system of resource allocation within the still-protected import substitution sector, but it did not arise from a commitment to the idea that the economy should become more fundamentally open. The April 1960 decontrol program was reluctantly undertaken by a government that continued to believe in the virtues of nurturing an infant industrial sector with protection. The decontrol decision was part of a political bargain: in 1959 the government wanted to get Congress to legislate stabilization measures (the 1959 import margin fee that was eventually legislated), in return for which Congress sought the government's commitment to decontrol. Congress's own interest in decontrol reflected the dominance of the export bloc, particularly the powerful sugar interests. Initially, at least, decontrol was to prove politically popular – in spite of the unpopularity of the export bloc – because of increasing public outrage at the corruption associated with import controls. When the new Macapagal administration replaced the gradualist approach to decontrol with complete and immediate decontrol in 1962, the motivation again seemed as much political – based on equity and corruption issues – as economic.

From the beginning the policy objective had been to maintain protection, once decontrol was achieved, through higher tariffs. It was through poor planning that these tariffs were not high enough to do this, but neither were they low enough to shake out the inefficient firms. The balance-of-payments crisis of the early 1960s was largely solved by the prompt reaction of primary product exporters to decontrol. Decontrol did, it is true, stimulate manufactured exports, but continuing high protection to industry limited the effects of this. Thus the relative strength of the import substitution lobby remained large and, after the crisis of the early 1960s was solved, the lobby was able to reassert itself and contribute to the erosion of liberalization from the later 1960s.

The second episode, export promotion in the 1970s, did not represent nearly as fundamental a commitment to new exports as in the most successful exporting developing countries. Incentives to the import substitution sector had been increased by the reintroduction of import controls in 1969, while the export incentives to counter this domestic market were not very great. If new export growth did appear to be impressive in the 1970s, this was to an important extent for reasons other than direct export promotion measures (see below). There has been a tendency to ascribe more success to these policies than they warrant – *post hoc ergo propter hoc*.

In fact, the set of industrial incentives that emerged in the early 1970s arose from the compromise reached in the late 1960s between stronger forces wanting to increase intervention, planning, and protection and weaker forces wanting a more open economy. Undoubtedly the hand of the pro-interventionist lobby was strengthened by generally negative perceptions of decontrol: the 1960s had come to be viewed as a lean decade for manufacturing industry. The poor record of industrial growth in this decade was partly the result of declining opportunities for import substitution, but decontrol came to be seen as the major culprit. This negative view of decontrol partly reflected a genuine sense of apparently wasted resources (the development of overcapacity, for instance), but it also reflected a very large loss of rents for some industrialists when direct import controls were removed. (More generally, trade liberalization may have earned an unjustifiably bad reputation in the Philippines because policies of stabilization in the early 1960s and early 1970s had to pay for the excesses of the immediately preceding period.)

As for the third episode, the Tariff Reform Program (with its associated liberalization of import controls), it is difficult to see any initial build-up of pressure to a point where the major part of the government favored such a potentially thoroughgoing reform. Indeed it may be appropriate to see the Tariff Reform Program decision as a kind of "palace coup" brought about by a minority in government (the so-called "technocrats") in alliance with the World Bank, which was offering structural adjustment lending in return for policy reform.

In the context of feeble political commitment to trade policy reform in the Philippines, liberalization episodes have occurred every now and then, either to correct external disequilibria or to bow in the direction of the solutions prescribed by the Western community: US government support for the election of President Macapagal in 1961 was not unconnected with his intentions to accelerate decontrol; the IMF played a major role in the 1970 peso devaluation; the World Bank played a crucial role in the Tariff Reform Program.

To say that there has been little sustained commitment to trade liberalization in the Philippines raises other questions. Many subsequently liberalizing countries had little initial commitment, but something occurred along the way to change this. What was different about the Philippines? This question can best be answered in a more rigorous comparison of experience across countries, but a plausible hypothesis about the Philippines can be suggested. The country's rich resource base – the backbone of its development since the middle of the nineteenth century – is central. This resource base provided the surplus on which a high-cost import-substituting manufacturing sector could be built from the 1950s onwards. By the same token the primary-product-exporting sector was sufficiently resilient (until the later 1970s at least) to respond rapidly to balance-of-payments crises (in the early 1960s and early 1970s). There was never any pressure on manufacturing to become more efficient. Resource-poor countries, however, have little choice but to overcome crises through creating an efficient industrial sector that can export.

Since the beginning of the 1970s the Philippine economy *has* responded to its progressive loss of comparative advantage in primary product exports by exporting manufactures; but, given the inherited strength of the protectionist lobby, these exporters have largely developed in the enclaves of bonded warehouses and export-processing zones without much undermining the lobby. Nonetheless, the logic of the Philippines' changing comparative advantage is that primary exports can no longer solve external crises, that manufactured exports must increasingly do so, and that trade policies must change accordingly.

Two further explanations of the lack of commitment to more liberal policies may reflect factors more specific to Philippine history. First, public hostility toward traditional agricultural exporters, a consequence of the politics of the 1950s, meant hostility toward the more liberal trade policies that these exporters espoused. Second, the country's "love–hate" relationship with its ex-colonial power, the United States, has helped to breed an autarkic brand of nationalism that continues to fuel protectionist sentiment.

The Episodes: Success and Failure

The 1960–2 import decontrol was undoubtedly a significant achievement (even though tariffs were deliberately raised from 1962 to compensate producers for their loss of nontariff protection). Yet decontrol changed the economy curiously little. Certainly it immediately encouraged traditional exports, as well as small amounts of nontraditional manufactured exports. However, while the import-substituting manufacturing sector was visibly hit by imports in the early to middle 1960s, it neither contracted (indeed, it recovered in the second half of the decade), nor did its structure change in any obvious way.

At the very least, the 1960s decontrol and the 1970 devaluation succeeded in the medium term as instruments of external stabilization, but in both cases the gains were overtaken by the reintroduction of expansionary macroeconomic policies. In addition, the long-term deterioration in the Philippine terms of trade continually threatened these gains.

The direct measures of export promotion adopted in the early 1970s played a necessary role in the rapid growth of nontraditional manufactured exports from this time: these exports would not have taken off without effective provisions for exporters to acquire imported inputs at world prices. Beyond this, however, these measures were limited: the subsidies they provided to offset the anti-export bias of other trade policies were modest. Instead, the restructuring of exports away from traditional primary sector products towards nontraditional manufactures were largely the result of the progressively more favorable exchange rate achieved by decontrol and the 1970 devaluation, the collapse of parts of the traditional export sector from the mid-1970s as a result of world price developments (but also helped on its way by a growing commercial policy bias against these exports), and a quite remarkable fall in the real wage in the period 1969–74. The realized comparative advantage of the Philippines seems to have shifted quite dramatically from agriculture to unskilled labor, whether this labor was in the form of domestic value added to imported clothing and electronic components or of direct exports of labor to the Middle East.

The third episode, the Tariff Reform Program of the early 1980s, is noteworthy for its decisive derailment in 1983, and two specific points are worth making. First, compared with the other two episodes, and by any standards, the timing was wrong, though some of this may be considered bad luck rather than bad judgment. The wrong external conditions were constituted on the one hand by the more rapidly deteriorating terms of trade at the beginning of the 1980s than in the early 1960s or 1970s, and on the other hand by the severe recession in the OECD countries, which limited market opportunities and led to a rise in real interest rates. The wrong internal conditions, where bad judgment was more evident, were the growing precariousness of external debt and the rundown of foreign reserves after six to seven years of uninterrupted and large current account deficits. These deficits in turn reflected high levels of investment (particularly public) and a drop in public savings. Moreover there was no attempt – until after 1980 at least – to tackle the trade deficit through devaluation. (It may be that trade liberalization contributed to the balance-of-payments crisis of 1983, though this must have been quite a marginal effect.) Second, it appears that this potentially major reform was carried out with some disregard for its macroeconomic consequences, specifically the need for devaluation to accommodate the effects of liberalizing manufactured imports.

Timing and Sequencing Issues

The issue of one-stage versus gradual multistage liberalization (see the preface to the volume) can be taken up both within episodes and between them, that is, over the longer term. Both decontrol and the Tariff Reform Program were internally sequenced episodes. The original decontrol plan was to remove controls (and by implication depreciate the peso) within four years. This kind of gradual, but vague, approach ran a risk of reversal because it created uncertainty about where the exchange rate would finally end up and also because the government, particularly in view of the electoral cycle, would find it expedient to retain the import control system in order to dispense favors. This is why the decontrol episode had to be saved by an acceleration in 1962. The alternative would probably have been a reversion to full controls.

The Tariff Reform Program was more clearly sequenced than the first part of decontrol. In fact, this episode was planned precisely to remove quantitative restrictions and aim for a more uniform structure of nominal and effective protection. The phasing and sequencing of the program, however, were not really clear-cut and, after a first phase, there were simultaneous tariff reductions for industries across the remaining three phases, with the final objective of specific tariff rates to be achieved by 1985.

One danger confronting this type of liberalization, involving the replacement of import controls by tariffs, is a subsequent policy reversal in which restrictions may be reimposed even though tariff reform may be proceeding on schedule. In the Philippines, an important part of the tariff reform was to reduce the duties on many imported inputs. When combined with the reimposition of direct import controls, this must have led to increased rates of effective protection in many cases.

The phasing of tariff reform appears to have been partly dictated by the initial protection levels enjoyed by an industry, as well as by the political influence of an industry (as proxied by the presence of large firms in the industry). The underlying rationale for this phasing is presumably to allow a longer period for highly protected (or influential) industries to adjust.

Because liberalization in the longer term was not supported by any sustained commitment of policymakers, it is easy to argue that the process, starting in 1960 and still incomplete today, was too gradual: there was enough time for opponents to organize reversals of policy, as happened at the end of the 1960s. Long-term liberalization processes may make sense – preannounced tariff cuts have underlain a long-term liberalization process in the OECD countries, for instance – but under the specific post-war circumstances of the Philippines, where there are strong interests vested in continued protection, rapid liberalization may have made more political sense.

Until about the mid-1970s the beneficial effects of liberalization were sustained by agricultural exports, if only because liberalization in import-substituting manufacturing had been limited in amount (and even reversed over time). Over the long term the ability of agricultural exports to sustain this leading role has become limited for several reasons. The first is the persistent and large secular decline in the terms of trade of agricultural (and mining) exports. A second reason is the substitution effect: increases in agricultural exports appear to have reduced the protection of food crops for domestic consumption in the mid-1960s, and probably also in the early 1970s. This in turn necessitated increased food imports. Partly for this reason the first Marcos administration put considerable emphasis on rural development policies in the late 1960s as a necessary condition for successful export growth. Finally, since about 1977 there has been no growth in the total area of land harvested: land may have become an increasingly scarce resource.

Given both the terms of trade and the resource limitations on agriculture, a successful long-term liberalization of the economy has to mean the growth of nontraditional manufactured exports. In spite of the large change of export composition in their favor in the 1970s, manufactured exports have not become the new motor of the economy (as elsewhere in southeast Asia): nontraditional manufactured exports (including consignment exports net of consignment imports) rose from 2 to 8 percent of manufacturing output from 1970 to 1979, but it is doubtful that this figure has grown much since.

Moreover, it is difficult to see how Philippine-style export promotion policies have played a useful role in the sequencing of trade liberalization in economic terms. Such exports took place largely as an enclave activity – often in the physical enclaves of bonded warehouses and free-trade zones – using few local material inputs and consisting principally in the export of Philippine labor. There is nothing wrong with this if unskilled labor is what the country has in abundance and such activities are not subsidized, but it is difficult to argue, where there is so little obvious impact on the import-substituting sector (either in terms of demand for its products or competition with its outputs), that this style of exporting forms part of the adjustment or learning process that presumably justifies its place in a sequence. However, from a political point of view, the growth of the export sector may yet promote an effective constituency of industrialists favoring a more open trade regime.

A Postscript on Trade Policy Developments since 1986

The Aquino government that came to power in 1986, under political circumstances different from those prevailing earlier, has made considerable efforts to renew the process of trade policy reform. The tariff reform had already been completed by 1985, as too had a number of measures (from 1983 onwards) that eliminated most of the protective impact of domestic indirect taxation.

The key post-1985 liberalization has occurred with the dismantling between 1986 and 1988 of a large number of the nontariff import controls that had not been eliminated by 1983, or had been reintroduced by that year. (In fact, the plans for this liberalization were drawn up at the end of 1985.) Of almost 2,000 items still controlled in early 1986, few more than 500 were to remain controlled by 1988. These remaining controls were largely for protecting various progressive manufacturing programs (in vehicles, engines, and consumer electronics) and for reasons of health, safety, and national security. Thus the ground lost in 1983 appears to have been largely regained. What is more, the considerable reversal since 1984 in economic policies – the greater emphasis on monetary and fiscal discipline – should provide a far more supportive environment for trade reform than in the early 1980s.

The government's evident commitment to reform provides grounds for optimism that this new openness of the Philippine economy can be sustained. Yet the forces for greater protection – particularly the producers who fear they will suffer from liberalization, and who are now freer than before 1986 to organize politically – should not be underestimated either. In this study it has been argued that over the long term the low level of commitment to a more open economy has partly been sustained by the existence of politically powerful but economically inefficient import substitution interest. Perhaps those interests still need to be convinced of the case for reform.

Appendix 1 A Summary of the Three Liberalization Episodes

First Episode: Decontrol, 1960–1965

Policy Characteristics

Nature	Dismantling of import controls, accompanied by effective devaluation and offset by *ad hoc* tariff rises
Size	Major liberalization, though somewhat offset by tariff rises
Duration, stages	Partial progress in 1960–1 through staged reform via multiple exchange rates; complete import control and downward float of exchange rate in early 1962

Economic Circumstances before Liberalization

Balance of payments	Stable from 1957 onwards, but at a low level of reserves after a 1953–7 deterioration
Prices of major exports	Favorable, rising in 1957–9
Prices of imports	Favorable, falling slightly
Inflation rate	No inflation in the 1950s
Growth of GDP	Respectable in 1958 and 1959 (note the long-term decline in rates through the 1950s)
Currency overvaluation	High for the 1950s and growing from 1955

Political Circumstances before Liberalization

Government	Stable US-style democracy; mainly a vehicle for sectional interests
Public debate	Decontrol as part of a broader public debate in which pro-Keynesian and pro-decontrol (landowner) interests allied against economic conservatives and the import substitution lobby; the government decontrolled reluctantly as a *quid pro quo* for congressional support for conservative economic measures

Ideology	No ideological shift; the key public issue was corruption and the equity effect, not the resource allocation effect, of decontrol
Administrative arm of government	Central Bank
International influence	Little, except some US influence on 1962 acceleration of decontrol
Accompany Policies	
Exchange rate	1960–1, managed depreciation; 1962, float at first (completely eliminating black-market premium), then managed
Export promotion	None
Export taxes	Export tax through multiple exchange rate 1962–5
Monetary policy	1960–1 relaxation; 1962–4 tightening
Fiscal policy	Largely dictated by two-year political (election) cycle; deficit in 1961
Implementation of decontrols	
Stage departure	Successful acceleration, that is, complete achievement of import decontrol, in 1962
End of episode	Partial reintroduction of import controls in 1967–9 as a consequence of expansionary economic policies without depreciation
Economic Performance Following Decontrol	
GNP growth	5%–6% a year
Inflation	Price rise – apparently induced by export sector – evident from mid-1959; 1960–5 fairly stable inflation around 5%
Real wages	Significant fall 1959–64
Imports and exports	Export improvement from 1959–61 and improved balance of payments in 1961–6

Second Episode: Devaluation and Export Promotion, 1970–1973

Policy Characteristics

Nature	1970 devaluation (with some foreign exchange controls retained); incentives to nontraditional exports (subsidies, export-processing zones, bonded warehouses, foreign investment incentives); a modest tariff rationalization in 1973

Size	Modest export promotion
Duration, stages	*Ad hoc* strengthening of export incentives 1970–3)
Economic circumstances before devaluation	
Balance of payments	Big deficits 1968 and 1969
Terms of trade	Continuing marked deterioration
Inflation rate	Around 3% a year in 1967–9
Growth of GDP	Low – around 3.5% a year in 1965–9
Currency value	Modestly growing overvaluation 1962–7, then more rapid 1967–9
Monetary and fiscal policy	Expansionary from 1966, especially prior to 1969 presidential election
Political Circumstances before Devaluation	
Government	Generally continued stability until the 1969 election, then some growth in unrest
Public debate, ideology	In the wake of the business sector's and Congress's disappointment with post-decontrol growth, the weight of debate favored a return to intervention/planning, but non-traditional export promotion was an easily agreed compromise with the weaker free-trade lobby
Administrative arm of government	The BOI played a key role in developing export incentives
International influence	The IMF and the international banks were important in the 1970s devaluation; more generally, in the early 1970s the government was very active in aligning itself with aid donors
Accompanying Policies	
Exchange rate	Slow managed devaluation in the 1970s
Export taxes	Introduction of (*de facto* permanent) taxes on traditional exports from 1970
Agricultural policy	End of preferential access to US sugar market in 1973; growing interventions in other sectors (e.g., marketing monopolies, levies) from 1972
Fiscal and monetary policy	Tight 1970–2, expansionary in 1973 and 1974
Controls	Strengthening of investment (1967) and price (1970) controls

Factors Affecting Policy Implementation

Political change	Martial law (1972) at first introduces economic reform with a liberal tendency; thereafter a growing intervention and lack of policy coordination and "crony capitalism"
Shocks	National disasters and disease affected food production 1970–2; oil crisis in 1973; commodity boom in 1973–4 interrupts serious secular deterioration in terms of trade
Balance of payments	The 1975 terms-of-trade shock and the post-1973 boost to investment (mainly public) leads to a "permanent" balance-of-trade deficit, met through higher foreign borrowing

Economic Performance

Growth	Dip in 1969–74 growth; recovery in 1974–80
Unemployment	Apparently falling trend from 1968 to late 1970s
Inflation	Big rise after 1969 (16% a year in 1969–73)
Real wages	Unprecedentedly large fall in real wage in 1969–74; slow rise thereafter
Balance of payments	Balance of trade reestablished in 1970–4 through export growth and import standstill, reserves and foreign debt stabilized; significant shift of export structure toward nontraditionals becomes apparent from 1974; from 1974 large trade deficit is financed by growing foreign debts

Third Episode: Tariff Reform Program, 1981 to June 1984

Policy Characteristics

Nature	Removals of quantitative restrictions to import for 1,304 items; general tariff reforms to reduce peaks and dispersions of tariff rates
Size	Substantial reform of tariff code
Duration	5 years, 1981–5
Stages	Four phases covering different industries

Economic Circumstances before Tariff Reform Program

Balance of payments	Further deterioration between 1978 and 1980 in the current account
Prices of major exports	Mixed, recovering for logs, lumber, plywood, falling for sugar, copra, coconut oils; general export price index increasing between 1977 and 1980
Prices of imports	Increasing between 1977 and 1980 (more than movement of export price index)
Inflation rate	Increased between 1978 and 1980
GNP growth rate	Fluctuating but 5-year average (1975–80) high by historical standards
Shocks	Second oil crisis 1978–9
Agricultural output	Recovering

Political Circumstances before Tariff Reform Program

Government	Stable, little opposition
Public debate	Very thin on tariff and trade policies
International influence	Substantial, from multilateral institutions

Accompanying Policies

Exchange rate	Floating 1981–3; suspension of exchange transactions in 1983–4
Monetary policy	Tight at the start of 1981; easy thereafter till 1983; financial reforms and deregulation in 1980–1
Fiscal policy	Large deficits initially as counter-cyclical policy, eventually tightening; neutralization of indirect taxes for goods irrespective of domestic or imported origin
Capital movement	No change – easy for inflows, restricted for outflows

Implementation of Tariff Reform Program

Departures	Import liberalization aborted in 1983; tariff program continued but not binding due to unavailability of exchange resources

Economic Performance

Prices	CPI slow increase until third quarter of 1983: real effective exchange rates depreciated at end 1981; appreciated in 1982 before sharp decline in late 1982 and 1983; real wages declined

Balance of payments

Growth

Unclear, though deficits continued

Real GDP growth declining in 1981 and 1982; zero growth in 1983

Appendix 2 A Chronology of Major Changes in Trade Policy and Related Policies, 1946 to June 1984

Date	Policy Changes
1946–1959	
Apr 1946	The Philippine Trade Act of the US Congress establishes mutual Philippine–US preferences, to be phased out by 1974, and limits Philippine freedom to change exchange rate (₱ 2 per US$)
1949–53	Establishment and improvement of foreign exchange control system
Mar 1951	17% tax on sales of foreign exchange
Dec 1954	US–Philippine (Laurel–Langley) Agreement accelerates the elimination of Philippine preference to US imports (90% of full tariff by 1965) and gives the Philippines control of its exchange rate
Sep 1955	Foreign exchange tax of 17% (reducing by 1.7 percentage points per annum to zero by 1965) replaces 1951 foreign exchange tax
Sep 1955	Barter law (RA 1410) provides some export incentives
June 1957	Tariff reform (RA 1937) generally raises tariffs
Jul 1959	RA 2609 legislates foreign exchange tax (subsequently fixed at 25%) and stipulates decontrol
Decontrol 1960–1965	
Apr 1960	Establishment of multiple exchange rate system, allowing some uncontrolled purchases of foreign exchange at a depreciated rate, at the start of an envisaged multistage program of import decontrol by 1964
Sep 1960	Small modification of multiple rates representing a slight revaluation for imports
Nov 1960	Modification of multiple exchange rate, in a second stage, to extend the percentage of transactions covered by the free rate
Mar 1961	Further extension, in a third stage, of transactions covered by the free rate

Jan 1962   Elimination of almost all exchange controls (except for a 20%
                    penalty retention of export proceeds at the official rate);
                    the peso is allowed to float freely (but is managed from
                    mid-1962); import duties raised on many items; special
                    time deposit required on imports
1962–4   Some relaxation of special time deposit requirements
Nov 1965   Elimination of penalty exchange rate for exporters and
                    formal move to unified exchange rate of ₱ 3.9 per US$
1966–1969
1967   Investment Incentives Act (RA 5186) contains the first
                    (modest) incentives for nontraditional exports
1967–8   Reimposition of some measures to discourage imports (cash
                    margin deposits, ceilings on commercial bank foreign
                    exchange transactions)
Jun 1969   Reintroduction of import controls on less "essential" imports

Devaluation and Export Promotion, 1970–1973
Feb 1970   The peso is floated (and is fixed at ₱ 6.4 per US$ by the end
                    of the year) and a penalty export rate is introduced (80% of
                    export earnings converted at the old rate); some, but
                    incomplete, removal of June 1969 controls
May 1970   Export duties of 8%–10% replace penalty export rate
Aug 1970   Export Incentives Act (RA 6135) improves incentives to
                    nontraditional exports
Nov 1972   Legislation to create the first export-processing zone
1972   Government monopoly on foreign trade in rice and corn
                    extended to all grains
Jan 1973   Further improvements to incentives on nontraditional exports
                    (PD 32)
Jan 1973   Tariff reform rationalizes tariff structure (for instance, getting
                    rid of many exemptions) without significantly reducing
                    protection
1973   Legislation to encourage the use of bonded warehouses for
                    exporters
1973   Sugar agreement with the United States ends
1973   Levy introduced on coconut farmers

1974–1979
Feb 1974   Additional premium duty on traditional exports (to apply
                    when export prices are high)
1975   Ban on log exports
1974–5   Moderate managed devaluation (from about ₱ 6.8 to ₱ 7.4
                    per US$)
1974–6   Reintroduction of many tariff exemptions
1978   Minor tariff reform
1979   Marginal measures to strengthen nontraditional exports
                    (bonded warehouses, export-processing zones, export trad-
                    ing)

1980	More flexible exchange rate policy introduced (peso moves from around ₱ 7.4 per US$ dollar in early 1980 to around ₱ 9 at the end of 1982)

The Tariff Reform Program, 1981–1985

Jan 1981	First stage of tariff reform: first reduction of peak tariffs (to 70%) for 177 tariff lines and first rate reforms for 14 industries – 668 tariff lines – to be completed by 1985 Liberalization of imports of 264 items (of 960 to be liberalized by 1983, out of a total of 1,304 imports still restricted)
August 1981	First tariff rate reforms for a further three industries – 480 tariff lines – to be completed by 1985
Jan 1982	Second stage of tariff reform: second and final reduction of peak tariffs (to 50%)
Feb 1982	Liberalization of imports of a further 610 items. This was quickly followed, especially in Feb–Sep of 1982, by a reimposition of import controls on many of the items
Dec 1982	Surcharge of 3% imposed on all import transactions
1983	Liberalization of imports of a further 48 items
Apr 1983	Import surcharge raised from 3% to 5%
Apr 1983	New Omnibus Investment Code, Parliamentary Law 391 (export incentives tend to increase)
Jun 1983	Exchange rate devalued from ₱ 9.2 to ₱ 11 per US$
Oct–Nov 1983	Exchange rate further devalued to ₱ 14, all foreign exchange comes under Central Bank control, suspension of foreign debt repayments, and some export taxation is increased
Mar 1984	Import surcharge raised from 5% to 8%
Jun 1984	Exchange rate devalued from ₱ 14 to ₱ 18 per US$, import surcharge raised to 10% additional 10% excise tax on foreign exchange sales introduced, and export stabilization tax introduced.

References

Agoncillo, Teodoro A. (1969) *A Short History of the Philippines*. New York and Toronto: New American Library.

Alano, Bienvenido P. (1984) "Import smuggling in the Philippines: an economic analysis." *Journal of Philippine Development*, no. 20, vol. XI(2), 157–90.

Alburo, Florian (1985) "Import liberalization and industrial lay-offs." University of the Philippines School of Economics, Discussion Paper no. 8511.

Alburo, Florian A. and Geoffrey Shepherd (1988) *"The timing and sequencing of a trade liberalization policy: unpublished appendices."* Available from the Brazil Department, World Bank, Washington, DC.

ADB (Asian Development Bank) (1984) *Key Indicators of Developing Member Countries of ADB*, April. Manila: ADB.

Baldwin, Robert E. (1975) *Foreign Trade Regimes and Economic Development: The Philippines*. New York: Columbia University Press.

Bautista, Romeo M. (1981) "The 1981–85 tariff changes and effective protection of manufacturing industries." *Journal of Philippine Development*, no. 15, vol. VIII (1 and 2).

Bautista, Romeo M. (1985) "Trade liberalization in the Philippines." Mimeo. London: Trade Policy Research Centre.

Bautista, Romeo M. and Jose Encarnacion, Jr (1971) "A foreign trade sub-model of the Philippine economy, 1950–69." University of the Philippines School of Economics, Discussion Paper no. 7178.

Bautista, Romeo M. and John H. Power and Associates (1979) *Industrial Promotion Policies in the Philippines*. Manila: Philippine Institute for Development Studies.

Business Day, various issues.

Castro, Amado (1969) "Philippine export development, 1950–65." In T. Morgan and N. Spoelstra, eds, *Economic Interdependence in South-east Asia*. Madison, WI: University of Wisconsin Press.

Central Bank News Digest, April 12, 1966, p. 8.

Central Bank of the Philippines (1980a) *Memorandum to Authorized Agent Banks*, 2, January 28.

Central Bank of the Philippines (1980b) *Memorandum to Authorized Agent Banks*, 578, February.

Central Bank of the Philippines (1980c) *Memorandum to Authorized Agent Banks*, 10, May.

Central Bank of the Philippines (1981) *Memorandum to Authorized Agent Banks*, 7.

Central Bank of the Philippines (1982a) *Memorandum to Authorized Agent Banks*, 39.

Central Bank of the Philippines (1982b) *Philippine Financial Statistics*, March. Manila.

Central Bank of the Philippines (1983) *Memorandum to Authorized Agent Banks*, 1.

Central Bank of the Philippines, *Annual Reports*, various years, Manila.

Collas-Monsod, Solita (1985) "Power and privilege: the Philippine amusement and gaming corporation." University of the Philippines School of Economics, Discussion Paper no. 8501.

David, Cristina C. (1983) "Economic policies and Philippine agriculture." Manila: Philippine Institute for Development Studies, Working Paper no. 83–102.

De Dios, Emmanuel S., ed. (1984) *An Analysis of the Philippine Economic Crisis.* Quezon City: University of the Philippines Press.

Department of Labor, *Yearbook of Labor Statistics*, annual, Manila.

Doherty, John F. (1982) "Who controls the Philippine economy: some need not try as hard as others." In Belinda A. Aquino, ed., *Cronies and Enemies: the Current Philippine Scene.* Honolulu, HI: Philippine Studies Program, Center for Asian and Pacific Studies, University of Hawaii, Philippine Studies Occasional Paper no. 5.

Domingo, Lita J. and Imelda Z. Feranil (1984) "Changing labor force in the Philippines." Diliman, Quezon City: Council for Asian Manpower Studies, Discussion Paper.

Fabella, Armand (1964) "Some aspects of the strategy of development planning." In Gerardo P. Sicat, ed., *The Philippine Economy in the 1960s.* Institute of Economic Development and Research, University of the Philippines.

Friend, Theodore (1986) "Philippine–American tensions in history." In John Bresnan, ed., *Crisis in the Philippines: The Marcos Era and Beyond.* Princeton, NJ: Princeton University Press.

Golay, Frank H. (1961) *The Philippines: Public Policy and National Economic Development.* Ithaca, NY: Cornell University Press.

Hartendorp, A. V. H. (1961) *History of Industry and Trade of the Philippines*, vol. 2, *The Magsaysay Administration.* Manila: Philippine Education Co.

Hooley, Richard (1985) *Productivity Growth in Philippine Manufacturing: Retrospect and Future Prospects.* Manila: Philippine Institute for Development Studies.

ILO (International Labor Office) (1974) *Sharing in Development: A Programme of Employment, Equity and Growth for the Philippines.* Geneva: ILO.

IMF (International Monetary Fund) (1981) *Annual Report on Exchange Arrangements and Exchange Restrictions.* Washington, DC: IMF.

IMF (1982a) *International Financial Statistics Supplement on Trade Statistics.* Washington, DC: IMF, Supplement Series no. 4.

IMF (1982b) *Twenty-third Annual Report on Exchange Restrictions.* Washington, DC: IMF.

IMF (1984) *Annual Report on Exchange Arrangements and Exchange Restrictions.* Washington, DC: IMF.

IMF, *International Financial Statistics*, various years. Washington, DC: IMF.

Lal, Deepak (1986)"Stolper–Samuelson–Rybczynski in the Pacific: real wages and real exchange rates in the Philippines, 1956–1978." *Journal of Development Economics*, 21 (1), April, 181–204.

Lindsey, Charles W. and Ernesto M. Valencia (1982) "Foreign direct investment in the Philippines: a review of the literature." In *Survey of Philippine Development Research II.* Manila: Philippine Institute for Development Studies.

NCSO (National Census and Statistics Office), *Annual Survey of Establishments: Manufactures* (replaced *Annual Survey of Manufactures* from 1975). Manila: NCSO.

NCSO, *Foreign Trade Statistics of the Philippines*, various years. Manila: NCSO.

NEDA (National Economic and Development Authority) (1978) *The National Income Accounts, CY 1946–1975.* Manila: NEDA, Philippine National Income Series no. 5.

NEDA, *Philippine Statistical Yearbook*, various years. Manila: NEDA.

Pante, Filologo, Jr (1982) "Exchange rate flexibility and intervention policy in the Philippines, 1973–1981." *Philippine Economic Journal*, no. 49, vol. XXXI (1 and 2).

Payer, Cheryl (1974) *The Debt Trap: The IMF and the Third World*, Harmondsworth: Penguin.

Power, John H. (1971) "The structure of protection in the Philippines." In Bela Balassa and Associates, *The Structure of Protection in Developing Countries*. Baltimore, MD: The Johns Hopkins University Press.

Power, John H. and Gerardo P. Sicat (1971) *The Philippines: Industrialization and Trade Policies*. London: Oxford University Press.

Power, John H. and Tessie D. Tumaneng (1983) *"Comparative advantage and government price intervention policies in forestry."* Manila: Philippine Institute for Development Studies, Working Paper no. 83–05

Roxas, Sixto K. (1968) "Policies for the private sector." *Philippine Economic Journal*, no. 15, 1st semester, vol. VIII (1).

Senga, Junio (1983) "A note on industrial policies and incentives structures in the Philippines: 1949–1980." *Philippine Review of Economics and Business*, 20 (3 and 4), September–December.

Sicat, Gerardo P. (1974) *New Economic Directions in the Philippines*. Manila: NEDA.

Sicat, Gerardo P. (1984) "A historical and current perspective of Philippine economic problems." Mimeo. Address delivered before the 21st Annual Meeting of the Philippine Economic Society, December 8, at the Philippine International Convention Center, Manila.

Steinberg, David (1986) "Tradition and response." In John Bresnan, ed., *Crisis in the Philippines: The Marcos Era and Beyond*. Princeton, NJ: Princeton University Press.

Tan, Norma (1979) "The structure of protection and resource flows in the Philippines." In Romeo M. Bautista and John H. Power and Associates, *Industrial Promotion Policies in the Philippines*. Manila: Philippine Institute for Development Studies.

Tariff Commission of the Philippines (1976) *Annual Report 1975*. Quezon City.

Tariff Commission of the Philippines (1983) *Annual Report 1982*. Quezon City.

Treadgold, Malcolm and Richard W. Hooley (1967) "Decontrol and the reduction of the income flows: a second look." *Philippine Economic Journal*, no. 12, 2nd semester, vol. VI (2), 109–28.

United Nations, *Yearbook of International Trade Statistics*. vol. 1, annual. New York: United Nations.

Valdepeñas, Vicente B., Jr (1970) *The Protection and Development of Philippine Manufacturing*. Manila: Ateneo University Press.

Warr, Peter G. (1984) *"Export promotion via industrial enclaves: the Philippines' export processing zone."* University of the Philippines School of Economics, Discussion paper no. 8407.

World Bank (1982) *World Development Report 1982*. New York: Oxford University Press.

World Bank (1985a) *Commodity Trade and Price Trends*, 1985 edition. Baltimore, MD: The Johns Hopkins University Press.

World Bank (1985b) *World Development Report 1985*. New York: Oxford University Press.

World Bank (1986) *World Development Report 1986*. New York: Oxford University Press.

World Bank (1987) *World Development Report 1987*. New York: Oxford University Press.

Part III

Singapore

Bee-Yan Aw
Pennsylvania State University

Contents

List of Figures and Tables

Acknowledgments

I wish to thank Ms Chow Kit Boey for supervising the data and information collection as well as for insightful comments on preliminary drafts. I am grateful for helpful comments from Stephen Guisinger, Oli Havrylyshyn, Michael Michaely, Demetris Papageorgiou, Richard Snape, and Martin Wolf. Thanks are also due to the staff of the Trade and Development Board for their assistance. Special thanks are due to Timothy Dunne for the data synthesis and computer work for this country study.

1

The Singapore Economy

Introduction

The historical heritage of Singapore as an entrepôt port between the West and its southeast Asian neighbors has led to the development of an economy based on a relatively open and liberalized trade regime. Its apparent uniqueness as a city state with heavy reliance on multinationals may, however, be misleading: like many other developing countries, its market-based economy embodies considerable government policy intervention. Moreover, a key aspect of Singapore's trade policy is the shift from trade to fiscal incentives, not unlike many of the other countries studied in the project. In-depth study of Singapore's experience with trade liberalization and the economic success associated with it consequently yields important lessons and insights for other developing countries.

The focus of this study is the liberalization episode of 1968–73. While the main policies encouraging exports were officially announced in 1967, they became fully effective only in 1968 which also marked the beginning of significant and continuous reductions in the degree of import protection via tariffs and quotas. By 1973, not only were all quotas abolished but a large number of tariffs had been removed. The remaining duties were few, with half of them retained for revenue rather than protective purposes. Some of the remaining duties also served the purpose of giving Singapore some leverage in its trade negotiations with its partners in the Association of South East Asian Nations (ASEAN).

Thus, while liberalization efforts continued through the early 1980s, the process had slowed down considerably compared with the period 1968–73. Given the government's strong commitment to an open-trade policy, not only were reversals nonexistent but adjustments were often made in domestic policies in order to bring them into line with the country's free-trade stand.

The present study comprises eight chapters. An overview and descriptive background of the economy is provided in this chapter. A review of the long-term pattern of trade policy in chapter 2 is followed in chapter 3 by an exposition of the extent of trade liberalization and the ways in which the episode was carried out. The policies that accompanied trade liberalization are outlined in chapter 4, while in chapter 5 the economic performance following liberalization is examined at the economy-wide and sector-specific levels. In chapters 6 and 7 an attempt is made to evaluate the link between investment incentives and trade incentives respectively and the performance of selected industries. Finally, the conclusions of Singapore's experience with trade liberalization and the inferences that can be drawn from it are summarized in chapter 8.

Overview

Singapore is an island city state with an area of 618 km^2 and a population of 2.5 million in 1983. It is strategically located in the center of southeast Asia and on the crossroads between east and west Asia. It is flanked by Malaysia to the north and east, Indonesia to the south and west, and the Philippines to the northeast. Unlike its neighbors, Singapore possesses no natural resources except a deep natural harbor and a strategic location. However, before the 1960s these two features together with its free port policy were sufficient to establish Singapore's lucrative role as an entrepôt for China and southeast Asia. By 1960, however, increased direct trading by its neighbors forced the restructure of the economy toward one based on the manufacturing sector.

Singapore obtained full internal self-rule from Britain in 1959 and became part of the Federation of Malaysia between 1963 and 1965. In the expectation of forming a common market with Malaysia, Singapore followed an import-substituting industrialization policy from 1963 to 1965. Since its separation from Malaysia, however, it has vigorously pursued an export-oriented strategy.

In response to acute unemployment in the 1960s, labor-intensive manufacturing was encouraged from 1965. Import duties and quotas were increased to protect industries as appropriate; these trade restrictions were gradually liberalized as the emphasis changed to export-oriented trade strategy. By 1973, domestic labor shortages and the increasing threat of protectionism in markets in industrialized countries led to restructuring into an economy based on skill-intensive activities.

Political Background

The People's Action Party (PAP) came into power in 1959 and has remained the ruling party ever since. The period 1959–65 was dominated by political events. The earlier years were characterized by political instability as the government, which consisted of the so-called democratic socialists, contended for political supremacy with a pro-communist faction, the Communist United Front (CUF). The political infighting resulted in numerous strikes called by the CUF as part of its attempt to coerce the government. The CUF were defeated again in the referendum of 1962 and the government managed to restore a measure of industrial peace and stability. In 1964, strikes accounted for the loss of only 35,908 mandays, down from the yearly average of 279,013 mandays for 1960–3.

In September 1963, Singapore officially became a member of the Federation of Malaysia. During this period Indonesia embarked on a policy of confrontation toward Malaysia; the consequent loss of official trade with Indonesia, her second largest trading partner, had a serious effect on Singapore's economy. In August 1965 Singapore was separated from Malaysia, and with the separation all hopes for a Malaysian common market vanished.

The establishment of Singapore as an independent republic did not signal an end to its problems. The republic needed to attain official recognition as a sovereign state by the international community, and a defense force had to be built from scratch. In addition, in July 1967, the British announced their intention of ending their military presence in Singapore. This was expected to erode the confidence of investors and exacerbate the already serious problem of unemployment.

Thus the political front, at least for the first decade of Singapore's independent existence, was characterized by incessant confrontation: domestically, between the communists and the social democrats; within Malaysia, between state and central governments; internationally, between Malaysia and Indonesia. According to Goh (1977a):

> The outcome turned out, in every instance, to be favorable to Singapore and her democratic socialist leadership, but it was no pushover . . . a more mundane explanation is that Singaporeans had the grit and stamina to persevere in adversity. When the lucky breaks came, we were able to take advantage of them.

On the positive side, popular support was behind the Singapore leaders during the difficult years. To many Singaporeans, the PAP leaders had demonstrated their ability to defend and enhance the economy's interest.

Moreover, despite political preoccupations the government rapidly built up industrial infrastructure and cheap housing for a young and growing population. The Economic Development Board (EDB), created in 1961 to spearhead the government's industrialization drive, effectively and quickly established low-cost industrial estates furnished with all the facilities required of modern industries – power, water, gas, transportation – as well as assisting prospective investors with loan finance, market studies, and labor recruitment. Overseas offices were established to help producers find markets for their products. The Export Promotion Center was established in 1965 to disseminate information on tariff structures of export markets, standards and specifications, and quota restrictions. The Center also made available export financing and export credit insurance to exporters. The government was particularly concerned to foster the confidence of investors through predictable policies:

> It is therefore necessary for government policy and practice to be consistent, predictable and rational. Further, governments must develop a repute for keeping their word, of honoring their commitments and discharging their expected obligations. Anything less than this would seriously dampen investor enthusiasm. (Goh, 1973b)

Goh (1977a) attributed the success of Singapore's performance to the thoroughness and high standard of integrity with which government policies were implemented.

In the 1963 general election, the PAP won 47 percent of the total votes cast. Five years later, this percentage shot up to 84 percent. The continuity of the one political leadership undoubtedly contributed towards the ability of the government to respond positively to the rapid changes of the 1960s and thus to maintain political stability. That the government had achieved its goal of encouraging investor confidence is evident by the increased role played by private investment. Total investment, as measured by gross domestic capital formation increased rapidly throughout the 1960s not only in absolute terms but also as a proportion of gross domestic product (GDP). Total investment as a percentage of GDP increased from about 22 percent in 1966 to about 29 percent in 1969 (table 1.1). Of this increase, the most rapidly growing component was the private sector. Between 1966 and 1969 private sector investment increased from S$234 million (Singapore dollars) to S$596 million, an increase of 156 percent, compared with an increase from S$239 million to S$323 million in the public sector over the same period.

Table 1.1 Public and private investment (million Singapore dollars)

Year	Public sector	Private sector
1966	239.6	233.7
1967	224.9	293.4
1968	300.9	435.0
1969	322.4	596.1

Source: Goh, 1970

In the post-independence period efforts were concentrated primarily on the economic front. In general, decision making was and is highly centralized, with policy measures typically initiated by the senior political leaders and the bureaucracy rather than by parliament. As the realization grew that export expansion was the only way to sustain the economy, accelerate industrial expansion, and absorb manpower, policy measures were swiftly undertaken to switch industrial policy from the domestic market to export promotion. Various fiscal incentives were liberally granted to firms that specialized in production for export. The government also established new organizations to seek export markets, to foster sound industrial relations, and to promote productivity consciousness among management and labor. The Employment Act of 1968 introduced measures to reduce the scope of collective bargaining and give new powers to employers, while trimming the rights and benefits of labor. Supporting changes were made in labor and educational policies to improve Singapore's competitiveness in the international markets. The National Wages Council, with representation from the unions, employers, and government, was formed in 1972 firstly to advise the government on general wage guidelines and wage adjustments with a view to developing a coherent wage system consistent with long-term economic and social development, and secondly to advise on incentive systems to promote efficiency and productivity in various enterprises (Tan, 1984). The policy switch was perceived by both the government and the public as an urgently needed practical solution to the problems encountered by the republic in the post-independence era:

> The government was very successful in conveying this sense of urgency to the general public. This would explain why measures to promote a stable industrial relations environment, e.g., the amendments to the Employment Act and the Industrial Relations Act, would be introduced in 1968 without major sectoral protests. The growing availability of goods and services such as public housing, and the success of wooing foreign investment showed in no uncertain terms the commitment of the PAP to the national cause. As the country prospered, this sense of urgency was converted to a sense of pride. (Seah, 1984)

The government's success in overcoming the crises of the 1950s and 1960s, as well as its commitment to the welfare of the general public, has contributed significantly to public support for its policies and programs in subsequent years. For instance, according to two informed observers of public housing (Yeh and Pang, 1973):

> There is no doubt that the relatively successful public housing program, affecting a large segment of the middle and lower classes, has further enhanced their national pride, political stability and support for the govern-

ment. Public housing is probably the most visible and demonstrative project. Its success has assured support for many other government policies . . .

The ability of the government to mobilize massive resources toward its economic goals without any manifest resistance has also, in part, been attributed (Hassan, 1976) to the so-called "transition syndrome," that is, a predisposition in the populace to consider change and progress highly desirable objectives. This syndrome can be ascribed firstly to the migrant character of the population and secondly to the urban nature of the economy. The migrants to Singapore generally set a premium on hard work, thrift, readiness to change, and social mobility, while the highly urbanized area is conducive to "the development of impersonal commodity markets, market mentality and rational bureaucratic organization, factors which are crucial in the economic and industrial development within the framework of a free enterprise market system" (Hassan, 1976).

Economic Background

Growth Rates

Since its separation from Malaysia, Singapore has made remarkable economic progress (table 1.2). GDP grew at an impressive rate of 13.2 percent a year in 1968–73 relative to the corresponding rate of 6.8 percent in 1960–7. Growth rates in gross domestic fixed capital formation (GDFKF) were also remarkable, averaging over 20 percent a year during the period 1960–73. Given the sharp fall in population growth over the decades of the 1960s and 1970s, per capita real GDP rose significantly (table 1.3).

Table 1.2 Gross domestic product and gross domestic fixed capital formation (percent)

| Year | Average annual growth rates | |
	GDP	GDFKF
1960–7	6.8	22.9
1968–73	13.2	23.5
1974–82	8.5	10.8

Source: Department of Statistics, 1983

Structural Change

Aw (1988, appendix table 1) shows how the contribution of the major sectors of the economy has changed since 1960.

Table 1.3 Per capita gross
domestic product (constant 1968
Singapore dollars)

Year	GDP
1960	1,298
1965	1,473
1970	2,466
1975	3,634
1980	5,180

Source: Department of Statistics,
Yearbook of Statistics, 1960–82

The share of the primary sector (agriculture and fishing) in GDP declined from 4.3 percent in 1960 to 1.5 percent in 1980.

The tertiary sector remains a significant contributor to GDP, although its share has slowly declined from 76.6 percent in 1960 to 68.8 percent by 1980. The greatest decline within this sector is in trade, comprising domestic and entrepôt trade, which contributed 33 percent of GDP in 1960 but only 24 percent in 1980. The decline in the role of entrepôt trade in the economy, however, is partially offset by the growing importance of the financial and business service sector whose share in GDP rose from 11.5 percent in 1960 to 16.6 percent in 1980.

In contrast, the share of the industrial sector has risen consistently from 19.1 percent in 1960 to almost 30 percent in 1980. The bulk of the increase was taken up by the manufacturing sector, whose share in GDP rose steadily from 13 percent in 1960 to 19.3 percent in 1970. This share rose further to 22.3 percent of GDP by 1980. The construction sector has also increased its share over the years (from 3.7 percent in 1960 to more than 6 percent in the 1970s), helping to boost the performance of the overall industrial sector.

Population and Labor Force

From the early 1930s through the late 1960s, Singapore recorded live births of 41–8 per 1,000 population, one of the highest birth rates in the world. Between the census years of 1947 and 1957 the annual rate of population increase stood at 4.3 percent and subsequently exceeded 3.1 percent annually until 1961. The decreasing trend in the rate of natural increase beginning in the mid-1950s was due to a steeper decline in the crude birth rate relative to that of the crude death rate. Table 1.4 summarizes the information on population growth since 1947. Unemployment was a serious problem during the 1960s with a large population of young people

Table 1.4 Population growth

Year	Population (thousands)	Average annual population growth rate (%)	Average annual crude birth rate (%)	Average annual rate of natural increase[a]
1947–57	1,445.9 (1957)	4.4	4.5	3.5
1957–66	1,934.4 (1966)	3.2	3.5	2.9
1966–70	2,074.5 (1970)	1.8	2.4	1.9
1971–80	2,413.9 (1980)	1.5	1.9	1.4

[a] Per 100 population.
Source: Department of Statistics, 1973, 1981, 1983

entering the labor force. Through the 1960s, more than 50 percent of the total population was under 20 years of age. The population growth rate slowed down to 2 percent by 1967 and has stabilized at around 1.2 percent since 1980, largely owing to a successful family planning program.

A closer examination of table 1.4 reveals the changing role of net migration in determining the population growth rate over the different period. Between 1947 and 1957, net migration into the city state of Singapore, particularly from Peninsular Malaysia, was responsible for almost 23 percent of the total increase in population during that period. Net migration was less significant during the period 1957–66, so that the annual rate of population growth exceeded the annual rate of natural increase by only a small margin. After that period the inflow of Malaysian migrants into Singapore declined significantly as Malaysians drifted to their own expanding urban centers with growing job prospects, and as migration between the two territories came under strict immigration control after the separation of Singapore from Malaysia in 1965. Although migration into Singapore was still under tight control during the 1970s, short-term guest workers were selectively admitted to overcome the shortage of local labor. In 1980, 7.3 percent of the total increase in population was contributed by net migration.

The age structure of the population changed from a broad-based pyramid in 1957 to a spindle-shaped structure with the broadest section at age group 15–19 years in the late 1970s. Consequently, the dependence ratio, defined as the ratio of the population aged under 15 and over 59 to the population aged between 15 and 59, fell from 87 in 1957 to 60 in 1977 and 52 in 1980.

Table 1.5 summarizes the changes in the labor force. During the period 1965–70 the labor force was between 30 and 35 percent of the total population. In the 1970s an average of 38.4 percent of the total population was in the labor force. By 1980 this figure had risen to 45 percent. The

Table 1.5 Labor force and unemployment

Year	Mid-year population (thousands)	Labor force (thousands)	Labor force participation rate (%)		Unemployment rate (%)
			Male	Female	
1957	1,455.9	472	88	22	4.9
1965	1,886.9	557	n.a.	n.a.	8.7
1970	2,074.5	723	84	30	6.0
1975	2,262.6	852	82	37	4.6
1980	2,413.9	1,093	85	47	3.5

n.a., not available.
Source: Ministry of Trade and Industry, 1974

increase in the labor force in the 1970s was due primarily to the increase in the rate of female participation, particularly among the younger age groups.

The age structure of the labor force was very similar to that of the total population. Relative to 1957, the workforce in 1970 and 1980 was younger. In 1970, of the economically active persons aged ten years and over, about 40 percent were under 25 while only about 3 percent were over 60. These proportions remained fairly stable throughout the 1970s.

The rapid population growth in earlier decades and the consequent labor force explosion in the late 1950s created growing unemployment. The unemployed as a percentage of the total labor force increased from 4.9 percent in 1957 to a peak of 15.3 percent in 1962. After 1962 this rate gradually declined, reaching 8.7 percent in 1965 (see table 1.5). The acceleration in the pace of industrialization and, in particular, the change in the mid-1960s to industrial policy emphasizing labor-intensive and export-oriented industries coincided with significant declines in the unemployment rate to 4.7 percent by 1972 and later to 3.5 percent by 1980. In fact, by 1970 there were signs of labor shortages in the economy.

As employment expanded, its structure changed (Aw, 1988, appendix table 2). Since 1957, the proportion of the total work force employed in the primary and tertiary sectors of the economy has fallen while that employed in the secondary sector has increased. The manufacturing sector contributed the most dramatic increase in employment, increasing almost fivefold between 1957 and 1982 to become the largest employer in the economy and accounting for 30 percent of total employment by 1980. The second-largest employer in the economy is the trade sector, followed by other services and transport and communications. A rapidly growing employer is the finance, insurance, and business services sector.

Education and the Labor Market

Concerted efforts began in the mid-1960s, in connection with the push toward industrialization, to gear the educational system toward providing the skills needed for an industrial society, with the emphasis shifting from academic to technical and vocational training in broad basic skills. Given the long gestation period of such a restructuring process, heavy reliance was placed on the expansion of informal on-the-job training as well as on the ability of firms to adjust to the availability of different kinds of workers. The latter is particularly important in Singapore where the bulk of new industry is connected with international firms. There is evidence that such firms located in Singapore are relatively flexible in their factor requirements, given their ability to decide the type of operation to initiate. The importation of foreign workers with appropriate skills was actively encouraged in some instances, particularly as full employment had been achieved since the early 1970s. By 1973 more than 100,000 or an eighth of the local labor force were reportedly foreign. Most of them were from neighboring West Malaysia.

The movement of foreign workers is regulated by government immigration policy, which has tended to follow market forces by restricting entry during recessions and encouraging entry during booms. A study of the characteristics of foreign workers revealed their overrepresentation at the highest (professional, administrative and managerial occupations) and lowest (production jobs in construction and manufacturing sectors) ends of the skill spectrum (Lim and Pang, 1984). In general, the unskilled foreign workers are often given only temporary employment permits while the professionals and entrepreneurs are encouraged to settle permanently in Singapore.

From the 1950s through the early 1960s the Singapore labor market was characterized by a strong and militant trade union movement that was often more concerned with political than with industrial goals. This movement was brought under control by 1964 when the PAP succeeded in establishing the National Trade Union Congress (NTUC) which became the national umbrella organization of a "moderate" labor movement. The government's success in bringing the labor movement under its control is reflected in the small number of days lost in industrial disputes from 1964 onward (table 1.6). The number of mandays lost declined from 388,219 in 1963 to only 1,011 in 1977. Union membership fell steadily from 1964 through 1970 and has increased since then to reach a peak of almost 250,000 (or 24 percent of the workforce) in 1979 (Aw, 1988, appendix table 3). More than 90 percent of total union membership, however, is affiliated with the NTUC.

Table 1.6 Industrial stoppages and trade disputes

	Industrial stoppages			
Year	Number	Workers involved	Mandays lost	Trade disputes (number)
1960	45	5,939	152,005	804
1965	30	3,374	45,800	801
1970	5	1,749	2,514	486
1975	7	1,865	4,853	709
1980	–	–	–	484

–, nil.
Source: Department of Statistics, 1983

The industrial climate further improved when the government passed the Employment Act and the Industrial Relations Amendment Act in 1968. In line with its belief that the economy's success in industrialization hinged on attracting foreign investments with low wages and labor discipline, the former act standardized terms and conditions of employment, defining the maximum and minimum limits of fringe benefits, while the latter removed from collective negotiations such issues as recruitment, retrenchment, and dismissal. In terms of achieving industrial peace, these political and legal moves were highly successful. Since 1968, the number of mandays lost through strikes and other labor disputes has been negligible. The ultimate goals of the two acts were to reduce labor costs by raising labor productivity and stabilizing wages.

Indeed, average wages have remained relatively stable throughout the periods of rapid growth in the manufacturing sector. On average, between 1965 and 1972 the rate of growth in average annual earnings per worker in the manufacturing sector increased by less than 10 percent a year. The figure for the period between 1972 and 1982 was slightly higher, with an average increase of 11 percent a year. In real terms the figures are 8.7 percent and 3.5 percent respectively.

Investment and Foreign Ownership

Associated with the growth in GDP has been a much faster rate of capital investment. In general, total investment increased at more than twice the rate of increase of the GDP between 1960 and 1973 (see table 1.2). Investment amounted to 10 percent on GDP in 1960 and increased to more than one third of GDP from 1970 onwards.

Table 1.7 indicates the financing of GDFKF. Gross investment is financed either by gross national savings (GNS) or net borrowing from abroad (NBA). Not only has GNS been the major source of GDFKF, it

Table 1.7 The financing of gross domestic fixed capital formation (current market prices)

Year	GDFKF	GNS	NBA
1960	244.5	− 52.3	296.8
1965	647.7	341.0	306.7
1970	2,244.5	1,129.7	1,114.8
1975	5,236.1	3,850.9	1,385.2
1980	10,991.1	7,641.8	3,349.3

Source: Department of Statistics, 1983

has also grown in importance over the years. About 50 percent of GDFKF was financed by GNS between 1965 and 1971. From 1972 onwards, on average about 73 percent of GDFKF has been financed by GNS.

Foreign enterprises in Singapore, originally concentrated in the trade and services sectors, have greatly increased their role in manufacturing since 1960. Although the contribution of foreign capital to capital formation fell from 70 percent in the early 1960s to around 30 percent in the late 1970s, foreign capital inflow has increased significantly in absolute terms. By 1982 it was S$2.7 billion (a billion is a thousand million throughout) compared with S$1.1 billion in 1970. In the manufacturing sector, the share of foreign investment in gross fixed assets has increased from 45 percent in 1966 to 81 percent in 1979. Foreign manufacturing investments in terms of gross fixed assets are largest in the petroleum industry, followed by the electrical and electronics industries, metal and engineering industries, and chemicals industry. These four industries together accounted for three fourths of all foreign manufacturing assets in Singapore in 1981.

Monetary and Fiscal Policies

Given the extreme openness of the economy, the scope of monetary policy is limited. The attitude of the Monetary Authority of Singapore (MAS) toward its monetary policy can be summarized as follows:

> The policy direction was aimed largely at maintaining a strong exchange rate for the Singapore dollar, while ensuring sufficient liquidity to accommodate real economic growth. Underlying this shift in emphasis away from targets for interest rates and money supply growth in the conduct of monetary policy is the view that the exchange rate is a relatiely more important anti-inflation instrument in the context of the small and open Singapore economy. Price stability then, continued to be the prime objective. The emphasis given to a strong exchange rate policy also facilitated the policy of upgrading and restructuring the domestic economy. (MAS, *Annual Report*, 1981–82)

During the liberalization period there were strong links, not just between monetary and exchange rate policies, but between both these policies and the fiscal policy. The Singapore dollar tended to appreciate over the period as a consequence of the country's persistent balance-of-payments surplus since the 1960s together with growing inflow of foreign capital and high real growth rates of GDP. To prevent overappreciation, the MAS sold Singapore dollars, expanding the money supply. The continuing monetary expansion from 1966 to 1975 helped to counter the deflationary impact of government surplus as well as the liquidity drain in the financial system caused by the large and increasing contributions of employees and employers to the Central Provident Fund (CPF).[1] The liquidity shortage since 1969 has been partially relieved by the large inflow of foreign funds.

Aw (1988, appendix table 12) shows the trend and cyclical movement of money, income, and prices in Singapore in the period 1968–83. The picture is one of continuing monetary expansion, although in general monetary growth did not exceed income growth. Prices were stable, except in 1973 and 1974 when Singapore had imported double-digit inflation because of the abrupt rise in oil and food prices.

During the bulk of the liberalization period the economy was essentially operating under a system of fixed exchange rates. While it is often appropriate for countries to adjust exchange rates in conjunction with trade liberalization to counteract the deflationary effects on domestic prices, the need for exchange rate adjustment was minimal: Singapore's history of relatively stable prices, as well as the fact that the import liberalization was relatively minor, meant that only modest devaluation would be required to offset deflationary effects. Moreover, since the liberalization took the form of transforming quantitative restrictions (QRs) to their tariff equivalents for most commodities, nominal prices of import substitutes were not significantly depressed.

The link between monetary policy and international commercial policies during the liberalization period was at best indirect. The expansionary monetary policy was responding not to the need to counter the deflationary effects of liberalization but, as described above, to overappreciation of the Singapore dollar, the government budget surplus, and the need to insure adequate liquidity to meet nominal growth objectives. However, it may

---

[1] The CPF is a system of forced savings out of wage income. During the 1970s the rate of contribution to the CPF from employers and employees was raised to fairly high levels. In 1984, the rate was 25 percent from each side, subject to certain floor and ceiling limits. Most of these funds were invested in local government securities. Thus public sector deposits with the banking system, which include the advance deposits by the CPF transferred in anticipation of the purchase of government bonds, have been a consistent and large net withdrawal of money from the system.

Table 1.8 Government budget[a] (million Singapore dollars)

Year	Revenue	Expenditure	Surplus/deficit (−)
1964	432.9	325.8	107.1
1965	507.6	391.8	115.8
1966	585.2	530.3	54.9
1967	663.0	592.1	70.9
1968	803.0	702.0	101.0
1969[b]	1,261.2	1,101.5	159.7
1970	1,266.5	1,206.5	60.0
1971	1,468.5	1,437.7	30.8
1972	1,749.3	1,579.2	170.1
1973	2,219.2	2,107.4	111.8
1974	2,556.9	2,492.6	64.3
1975	3,092.2	2,984.4	107.8

[a] Pertaining to the Consolidated Revenue Account only.
[b] Refers to the period from January 1, 1969, to March 31, 1970.
From 1970, the financial year is from April 1 to March 31.
Sources: Department of Statistics, *Yearbook of Statistics*, 1983–4; Department of Statistics, 1983

also have offset any short-run contraction of economic activity arising from the liberalization policy.

The strain on the government budget associated with the short-run effects of trade liberalization was insignificant for several reasons. The consistent budget surplus since 1964 (table 1.8) put the government in a strong fiscal position before, during, and immediately after the trade liberalization episode so that any temporary strains of liberalization on its budget could be absorbed without resorting to extraordinary measures.

Government revenue in Singapore comes from three sources: (a) taxes, (b) disposal of goods and services, and (c) income from property, investments, and financial claims. The changes that have taken place in the structure of taxation since 1966 are shown in table 1.9. Reliance on taxes on income and profits has increased, while it has declined significantly for taxes on international trade (in this instance, import duties). Reliance on taxes on property declined while that on taxes on payrolls and on goods and services increased.

The above trends are remarkable because, during this period, no major changes occurred in personal income tax rates or deductions while generous fiscal incentives were provided to businesses which reduced the company income tax base. In particular, one of the major provisions under the Economic Expansion Incentives Bill of 1967 was the application of a concessionary tax rate of 4 percent of profit from exports instead of the normal company tax rate of 40 percent. In general, the government's revenue policy consisted largely of relying on economic growth to expand

Table 1.9 Tax reliance ratios by broad categories (percent)

Year	Income and profit tax	Property tax	Payroll tax	Tax on goods and services	Tax on international trade
1966	26.0	18.5	2.2	19.4	33.9
1967	27.0	18.7	2.2	26.6	25.5
1968	29.4	18.0	2.1	28.0	22.5
1969–70	29.5	19.7	2.1	30.4	18.3
1970–1	32.1	15.3	2.2	29.3	21.2
1971–2	34.1	16.5	2.4	30.0	17.0
1972–3	35.9	15.6	2.4	29.8	16.3
1973–4	38.4	15.5	2.4	28.1	15.6
1974–5	46.5	15.8	2.4	23.7	11.5
1975–6	51.3	13.9	2.6	21.9	10.5

These ratios are defined as revenue from a particular category divided by total tax revenue.
Source: Asher, 1984

the tax bases and thereby to generate additional revenue without large discretionary changes, except with respect to vehicle taxes.

Whereas 60–70 percent of total government revenue comes from taxes, revenue from tariffs constituted no more than 4 percent during the period 1965–75 and therefore cannot be considered an important source of government funds. Moreover, the replacement of QRs on imports with tariffs in the initial stages of the trade liberalization episode actually had a positive impact on government revenue. More specifically, tariff revenues increased significantly, following the imposition of tariffs on 180 items in 1965 and new duties on perfumes, cosmetics, motor vehicles and parts, and clothing in 1969.

In the latter half of the 1960s concerted efforts were made to encourage selected industries to expand and export their products. Thus an increasing share of the government's development expenditure was channeled toward such industries as the electrical and electronic, engineering, and metal fabrication industries, which were expected to play an increasingly important role.

The insignificant contribution of tariffs to total government revenue and the strong fiscal position of the government budget, coupled with the absence of any system of adjustment assistance or benefits paid to distressed workers in the import-competing sectors, mean that there is no direct link between fiscal policy and the liberalization policy. Changes in the government's tax and expenditure policies were related more to general development goals than to the need to compensate for expected decline in revenue from tariffs and other commercial policies. For instance, restrictive fiscal policy on car ownership could have a negative impact on tariff revenue, as was the case in 1975. The various schemes introduced in 1974 and 1975 to discourage ownership and use of private passenger cars resulted in sharp declines in new car registrations and imports of motor vehicles and parts. Since motor vehicles and rubber tires and tubes were major sources of fiscal revenue, decreased tariff revenue from these items resulted in a fall in total tariff revenue in 1975, a year when the protective tariff scheule remained unchanged.

The government's fiscal strength, which allowed it to spend more money on development, was due to several major factors (Tsao, 1984a). The government's basic philosophy with respect to provision of public goods and services has been to charge for them at full cost, with the exception of such pure public goods as defense, internal security, education, and housing. Secondly, the ability of the government to acquire low-cost land for general and industrial development under the Land Acquisitions Act and the Controlled Premises Act meant that the cost of such development was low and that any land sold to private developers earned the government capital revenue.

In sum, the strong fiscal position of the government during the liberalization period was the result of rapid economic growth, careful fiscal management, and successful official efforts to maintain a balanced budget in the context of the country's drive toward rapid industrialization. An official statement in this vein noted:

> In Singapore, we have found that the old-fashioned conservative policy of balancing the government budget – in fact of budgeting for a substantial surplus on current account to finance development expenditure – produces the best results in the long run. (Goh, 1973b)

Trade

The external trade of Singapore is made up of entrepôt and non-entrepôt trade. The former refers to imports that are meant for reexport either in their original form or in a more processed form. Over the years significant structural changes have occurred in the role of entrepôt trade in Singapore's export as well as import trade.

Table 1.10 shows the changing shares of domestic exports, reexports, and manufactured exports in total exports for the periods 1960–7, 1968–73, and 1974–82. The share of domestic exports in total exports has increased rapidly during the periods under review, rising from an average of 14.4 percent in 1960–7 to 60.6 percent in 1974–82. In contrast, the share of reexports in total exports has declined continuously from a high of 85.6 percent in 1960–7 to 39.4 percent in 1973–82, although in absolute terms reexports have increased significantly. The ratio of manufactured exports to total exports has risen from 8.9 percent in the early 1960s to an

Table 1.10 Composition of total exports (percent)

Year	Domestic exports	Reexports	Manufactured exports
1960–7	14.4	85.6	8.1
1968–73	46.6	53.4	30.9
1974–82	60.6	39.4	53.4

Source: Department of Statistics, *Singapore External Trade Statistics*, various issues

average of 34.3 percent during the subperiod 1968–73 and further to 53.4 percent for 1974–82. In fact, manufactures account for almost all Singapore's domestic exports.

Over the 1960–7 period, manufactured exports increased at an average annual rate of 17.7 percent. The rate of increase rose to 46.8 percent over the 1968–73 period and declined to 22.2 percent over the 1974–82 period (table 1.11). Of the key industries, petroleum products, nonelectrical machinery, and transport equipment led the high-growth industries, while beverages, tobacco, leather products, rubber products, and nonmetallic products exhibited the lowest growth rates. Consequently, the relative shares of traditional exports such as food, beverages, wood and cork products, paper and paper products, printing and publishing, footwear and leather products, rubber products, and nonmetallic products have fallen over the years, while those of petroleum products, nonelectrical machinery, and plastic products have risen.

The changing structure of total imports also reflects changes in the relative importance of entrepôt and non-entrepôt trade. The increase in total imports over the period 1960–74 originated entirely from non-entrepôt imports or what are often referred to as retained imports.[2] Retained imports grew by an annual average rate of 12 percent from 1960

Table 1.11 Growth rates of total exports, domestic exports, and manufactured exports (percent)

Year	Average annual growth rates		
	Total exports	Domestic exports	Manufactured exports
1960–7	0	25.3	17.7
1968–73	18.0	29.2	46.8
1974–82	21.2	24.6	22.2

Source: Department of Statistics, *Singapore External Trade Statistics*, various issues

[2] Data on retained imports have been estimated by Nyaw (1979).

to 1967, and 33 percent from 1968 to 1973 (table 1.12). The structure of retained imports reflects the economy's dependence on imports to supply domestic demand for consumption as well as investment goods, although the emphasis has changed significantly during the period under review to reflect the importance of the manufacturing sector. In 1960, next to food, manufactured goods were the largest component of retained imports. By 1980, the largest component of retained imports was mineral fuels, the input for the export-oriented petroleum refining industry, followed by machinery and equipment, much of which consists of equipment and input for other manufacturing industries.

Table 1.12 Real export and import values (thousand Singapore dollars)

Year	Total imports	Retained imports	Total exports	Domestic exports
1960	3,748	1,190	3,196	199
1961	3,642	1,303	3,041	214
1963	3,933	1,658	3,199	314
1965	3,464	1,700	2,733	386
1967	4,161	2,200	3,297	1,049
1968	5,084	2,948	3,891	1,592
1969	5,992	3,414	4,549	2,073
1971	7,833	6,001	4,861	2,186
1973	9,954	7,755	7,086	3,811
1974	11,667	n.a.	7,979	5,017

n.a., not available.
These figures were deflated by GDP export and import deflators at constant 1968 prices.
Source: Nyaw, 1979

Balance of Payments

Singapore's overall performance in its balance of payments[3] is measured by the balance on current account, the balance on capital account (excluding official foreign reserves transactions), and the balance of unrecorded flows as shown in the balancing items.[4] The changes in the official foreign reserves show how the overall surplus or deficit was being financed.

Since independence, this overall balance figure has been in surplus. The surplus of S$1.4 billion (nominal Singapore dollars) in 1980 is ten times the

[3] Aw (1988, appendix table A.2) shows the components of Singapore's balance-of-payments accounts for selected years.
[4] The large and increasing balancing item represents errors and omissions associated with the general lack of comprehensive data on foreign transactions.

surplus in 1960. During the period 1960–80 the current account deficit has widened, reflecting the country's dependence on imports for both its consumption and its industrialization program, which required large and increasing imports of intermediate and capital goods (over 84 percent of total retained imports in the 1970s). The deficits in current account were offset by increased net service earnings from the expansion of transport and tourism (averaging S$2.8 billion annually in the 1970s compared with S$580 million annually in the 1960s) and by net foreign capital inflow from long-term foreign investments and Singapore's growth as a financial center. Net capital inflow in the 1970s totaled S$14.3 billion compared with only S$1 billion in the 1960s.

2
The Long-term Pattern of Trade Policy

Brief Review

From its founding in 1819 through the 1950s, the very existence and prosperity of Singapore depended on entrepôt trade. Thus, before 1960, consistent with its free port status, the only tariffs on imports were for revenue purposes and were limited to duties on liquor, tobacco, and petroleum products. The limited scope for expansion of entrepôt trade together with the serious problem of unemployment in the late 1950s led to concerted efforts at industrialization.

The initial strategy of industrialization as laid out in the First Development Plan (1961–4) emphasized import substitution via the use of tariff and quota protective devices. Additional import items came under protection when Singapore joined Malaysia (1963–5); many of these were introduced and became part of the Malaysian common market tariff. This import substitution strategy, already in place before the merger with Malaysia, was simply reinforced during the merger.[1] In general it was felt that, as a traditionally export-oriented economy, Singapore's high import ratio provided the government with substantial opportunities to select the kinds of manufacturing industries which can be established through the use of import restrictions. The establishment of the common market with Malaysia was the key precondition for pursuing such an import substitution industrial strategy. It was expected that the new industries initiated in Singapore after its independence in 1959 would greatly benefit from the availability of a larger protected Malaysian market. Other incentives introduced during this time included a five-year tax holiday and accelerated depreciation allowances for potential investors under the Pioneer Industries Ordinance of 1959.

---

[1] The architect of Singapore's industrialization program and economic policies throughout the 1960s and 1970s was Keng Swee Goh, an economist who held the position of Finance Minister during 1959–65 and 1967–70. He was the Republic's first Defense Minister (1965–7) when Singapore separated from Malaysia and again from 1970 until his recent retirement.

Singapore's membership of the Federation of Malaysia (1963–5) proved to be short lived as a combination of political and racial differences between Singapore and Malaysia plagued the union. Differences in the negotiations on financial arrangements and over the structure of the common market resurfaced. Indonesia, in protest over the establishment of the Federation, suspended trade relations with Malaysia with immediate and adverse effects on the economy of Singapore.

After independence, as excess capacities loomed with the loss of the potential Malaysian hinterland and hence of a larger domestic market, the government's immediate response was to increase protective duties. At the same time, however, QRs were gradually removed or replaced with tariffs.

Imports were liberalized simultaneously with a gradual shift in industrial policy from import substitution to export promotion. Initially, labor-intensive manufacturing activities were encouraged because of the high unemployment in the 1960s. Quotas were either gradually abolished or replaced by tariff protection for those industries that were expected to develop export markets as well as serve the domestic market. Both tariff duties and import quotas were closely monitored by government agencies; the smallness of the economy made it administratively feasible to keep both tariff and quota items under constant review.

In addition to import restrictions, several ordinances were passed to provide foreign and local entrepreneurs with incentives to invest in industrial activities. One ordinance specifically aimed at encouraging exports was the Economic Expansion Incentive Act of 1967. Under this Act, 90 percent of export profits is exempt from taxes. The period of relief is three years for pioneer companies and five years for nonpioneer companies. Tax exemptions were also allowed on interest on foreign loans, royalties, technical expertise, and technical assistance fees. The government increasingly encouraged the participation of foreign investments and foreign entrepreneurship. New specialized institutions were set up to assist the manufacturing sector in the search for export markets, to foster sound industrial relations, to promote productivity consciousness among labor and management, to establishment quality standards, and to train labor in the required industrial skills.

Thus the trade policy in Singapore is characterized by a very liberal regime before 1960, followed by increasing restrictiveness in the early 1960s which reached a peak in the mid-1960s before a return to gradual liberalization from 1968 to 1973. Table 2.1 gives a chronological summary of the various measures and policies introduced during the liberalization episode. While efforts at liberalization were concentrated during this period, the economy continued to liberalize throughout the 1970s.

Table 2.1 Singapore: liberalization episode, 1968–1973

Year	Policy change
1967 (passed) 1968 (fully effective)	Economic Expansion Incentives (Relief from Income Tax) Act that favored large export-oriented enterprises with tax concessions
1968	Very significant reductions in the number and restrictive level of quotas, and replacement of quotas with tariffs; tariff escalation on numerous items due to fear of recession brought about by British military withdrawal Functions of EDB parceled out to specialized institutions to aid foreign investors producing for export market Employment Act and Industrial Relations Amendment Act to secure and maintain industrial peace and wage stability
1970	Rapid dismantling of tariffs and quotas as protective devices Economic Expansion Incentives (Relief from Income Tax) (Amendment) Act that encouraged investments on an even larger scale geared toward the export market Increased government loan commitments at preferential rates and government equity participation in selected exporting enterprises.
1973	All quotas abolished; record number of tariff removals in any single year as well as substantial downward revisions of existing tariffs Removal of infant industry protection

The Context of Liberalization

The Singapore economy was relatively healthy in 1968. Table 2.2 displays the key economic indicators of the economy from 1966 to 1968. Singapore's balance of payments continued in surplus during that year, and the real growth in GDP was 14 percent over the previous year. Trade, the mainstay of the economy, was buoyant and exports continued to increase rapidly. Domestic exports increased by 43 percent over 1967, thus increasing their share in GDP from 32 percent in 1967 to 40 percent in 1968. The commodity terms of trade showed a slight improvement from 95.2 in 1967 to 95.5 in 1968 (Choi, 1979–80). The unemployment rate fell from 8.1 percent in 1967 to 7.3 percent in 1968. The intensity of inflation as

Table 2.2 Key economic indicators

Indicator	1966	1967	1968
GDP at 1968 factor cost (million S$)	3,127.1	3,537.4	4,042.1
Annual change (%)	10.53	13.12	14.27
Domestic exports (DX) (million S$)	965.0	1,111.0	1,592.0
Annual change (%)	127.6	15.1	43.3
DX as percentage of GDP	31.8	32.2	40.1
Commodity terms of trade (1964 base year)	101.3	95.16	95.5
Unemployment rate (%)	8.7	8.1	7.3
Inflation: annual change (%)			
CPI	2.0	3.3	0.7
GDP deflator	1.3	0.6	1.1
GDFKF (million S$)	658.7	751.4	996.8
GDFKF at 1968 prices: annual change (%)	3.00	14.07	32.66
GDFKF as percentage of GDP	21.06	21.24	24.66
GNS (million S$)	540.0	611.3	865.3
As percentage of GNP	15.7	15.9	19.7
Balance of payments (million S$)	153.0	304.0	664.0

Source: Department of Statistics, 1983

measured by the consumer price index (CPI) was low throughout the 1960s: in 1968, it was 0.7 percent. Similarly, the rise in the GDP deflator was only 1.1 percent in 1967. GDFKF increased by 32.7 percent in 1968, a large jump from the previous year's figure of only 14.1 percent.

The buoyancy of the economy during 1968 stemmed from several favorable external sources. What undoubtedly helped most was the boom in the economies of the United States, Europe, and Japan, Singapore's principal trading partners. Moreover, the separation from Malaysia in 1965 had ended confrontation with Indonesia, bringing a resumption of trade with that country. According to the Budget Speech of 1967, exports to Indonesia in that year were around S$335 million. Finally, the availability of foreign investment capital increased as tight labor conditions in Hong Kong forced a great many Hong Kong industrialists to establish manufacturing facilities in Singapore to take advantage of Singapore's wage and political stability (Hughes and You, 1969).

On the domestic front, a principal contributor to rapid growth, particularly in the manufacturing sector, was the efficient infrastructure in the form of essential services like power, water, gas, port facilities, transport and communications. Singapore's infrastructure was, in fact, generally on a par with that of developed countries. This achievement was largely the work of the EDB, the government's agency for promoting industrial growth.

Between 1965 and 1967 the number of items subject to tariffs increased substantially. Some of the new tariffs were in retaliation against the increased protectionist stand assumed by the Malaysian government after separation from Singapore in 1965. Others, together with quotas, were imposed on imports to protect the small domestic market from foreign competition and to give domestic producers a breathing space to overcome problems associated with infant industries. Concerted efforts to reorient the manufacturing sector toward production for export were made only in late 1967.

The increased urgency and rigor with which the export-oriented strategy was pursued was directly a result of two external developments:

1 the announcement in 1967 by the British government of its intention to accelerate the withdrawal of its military forces from its base in Singapore to 1971 instead of 1975;
2 the announcement by Malaysia of its intention to terminate participation in the joint currency board arrangement for the issue of currency; it had also, in late 1965, imposed tariffs on numerous items, thereby closing the Malaysian market to goods made in Singapore.

The British announcement of accelerated withdrawal of troops had severe economic implications for Singapore. In 1966 British military expenditure accounted for more than 14 percent of Singapore's GDP, and military spending was directly and indirectly responsible for about 20 percent of employment in Singapore. It was therefore envisioned not only that unemployment would increase but also that local expenditure, which the base facilities generated, would fall. Moreover, there were fears that the British announcement might undermine the confidence of investors.

It therefore became evident by 1967 that the Singapore government had to decide rapidly and effectively on a strategy and tactics to achieve the following different things simultaneously (Soo Ann Lee, 1973):

1 maintain confidence in the new Singapore dollar to be issued from June 1967;
2 build up a military capability;
3 look for new export markets for industrial goods to replace the Malaysian market;
4 raise the level of technical education to meet the needs of industry;
5 expand government development expenditure to offset the economic effects of the British military rundown.

3
Implementation of the Liberalization Policy

The liberalization that effectively began in 1968 was a continuous gradual process. By the end of 1973, all import quotas were abolished and only 91 items – six-digit Standard Industrial Trade Classification (SITC) commodities – were still subject to relatively low levels of import duties, as opposed to 217 in 1967.

Tan and Ow (1982) define 1965–7 as the import substitution phase, followed by the export orientation phase between 1967 and 1969. There is evidence, however, that some moves toward export orientation had already started by late 1965. In his Annual Budget Speech of 1965, the Minister of Finance stated the government's intent to build up the industrial base largely with export markets in view, and to attract manufacturers with established foreign markets. The EDB in its 1965 Annual Report revealed that:

> Shortly after independence (from Malaysia in 1965) the government announced a number of new investment and export incentives, including the provision of double deduction for market development expenditures . . . the Board welcomes the Government's action, taken shortly after August 1965, in initiating world-wide trade promotion and developing economic cooperation with all friendly countries.

Tariffs and Quantitative Restrictions

The first protective tariffs and quotas (QRs) had been introduced in 1960 and 1963 respectively. Table 3.1 shows the changes in quota and tariff restrictions from 1965 through 1975. The number of protected items increased somewhat with Singapore's initial strategy of industrialization via import substitution. Numerous items had come under protection from 1963–5 when Singapore was part of Malaysia. The number of protected

Table 3.1 Quota and tariff changes

| | Import quotas | | Protective duties | | | |
| | | | New duties | | | |
Year	Number[a]	Level[b] (%)	Number imposed	Number replacing quotas	Net change in total number	Average nominal rate (%)
1965	230[c]	51	175	68	175	0.63
1966	88	42	16	5	16	3.72
1967	72	41	20	7	16	3.59
1968	31	71	65	22	65	3.02
1969	26	78	24	7	17	3.78
1970	12	74	1	0	-11	3.28
1971	7	72	3	0	-36	3.04
1972	5	50	2	1	-7	3.66
1973	0	0	0	0	-153	4.14
1974	0	0	1	0	-8	1.99
1975	0	0	1	0	1	2.84

[a] End-of-year number of six-digit SITC commodities that had quota restrictions; therefore quotas that were imposed and removed within the same year are excluded.
[b] Quota level as a percentage of a given year's import level (between 1962 and 1966) averaged over the three-digit categories that were restricted by the quota; the higher the percentage, the less restrictive the quota.
[c] As of May 1965.
Sources: Department of Imports and Exports Control and Registration, 1964–73; Customs and Excise Department, Singapore, Annual Report, various years

items, which was only eight in the pre-Malaysia era, increased to 183 by the end of 1965.

Immediately after independence in 1965, two major changes were made in the use of tariffs and quotas. The first was the replacement of all but 88 commodity quotas by tariffs, and the second was the increasing reliance on protective duties.

Singapore's levels of protection were low compared with those of other countries. Nominal protection rates (NPRs) for the import-competing industries averaged slightly over 3 percent each year during the period from 1965 to 1978. Year-to-year variation during that period was small, with the largest increase occurring between 1965 and 1966 when the NPR jumped from 0.6 to 3.7 percent.

Quota restrictions were first instituted in 1963 and increased in coverage and intensity through 1966. After 1967, both the number of items and the intensity declined. From 1966 to 1969, about one third of all new duties each year went to replace import quotas. By the end of 1973, all import quotas were abolished. Over time, these quotas have been imposed on and

Table 3.2 Degree of trade liberalization

Year	Major changes in quotas and tariffs	Overall change in trade policy	Index of liberalization
1964	Over 200 quotas imposed	Beginning of restrictive policy	18[a]
1965	74 quotas abolished 68 quotas replaced by tariffs 107 new tariffs (nrq)	More restrictive	11
1966	11 new tariffs (nrq) 5 quota-replacing tariffs t_n increasing rapidly	Slightly more restrictive	10
1967	Peak tariff year for industries 13 new tariffs (nrq) 7 quota-replacing tariffs t_n decreasing	Almost no change	10
1968	19 quotas abolished Less restrictive quotas 43 new tariffs (nrq) 22 quota-replacing tariffs t_n decreasing	Less restrictive (beginning of liberalization)	12
1969	Quota liberalization for many industries 17 new tariffs (nrq) 7 quota-replacing tariffs t_n increasing 7 tariffs abolished	Slightly less restrictive	13
1970	14 quotas abolished 12 tariffs abolished t_n decreasing	Much less restrictive	15
1971	5 quotas abolished 39 tariffs abolished t_n decreasing	Less restrictive	16
1972	2 quotas abolished 9 tariffs abolished t_n increasing	Marginally more restrictive	15
1973	All quotas abolished 153 tariffs abolished t_n increasing	Less restrictive (end of liberalization)	17
1974	9 tariffs abolished t_n decreasing	Less restrictive	18
1975	t_n increasing 1 new tariff	Slightly more restrictive	17

nrq, not replacing quota; t_n, overall nominal tariff rate.
[a] Index for 1963 = 19.

removed from imports ranging from final consumer goods (for example, processed food, electric light bulbs, refrigerators, clothing) to intermediate goods (wood products, steel rods and bars, wires). In some cases the removal of quotas was complete, while in others they were replaced by tariffs, relaxed to a higher quantitative limit, or subjected to specific licensing whereby the importer had to apply for permission to import the licensed product.

The government's attitude to the use of both QRs and tariffs left no doubt that they were to be temporary. QRs were reviewed every six months from the date that each was first enforced. Tariff protection, either in place of QRs or in the form of new tariffs, was often contingent on the growth and export potential of the industry and emphasized protection of infant industries in general. The emphasis on export potential is perhaps one of the most distinctive features of official policy toward import protection.

Table 3.2 indicates the degree of trade liberalization overall. This is expressed as an index which is arrived at by taking into account the major changes in quota and tariff restrictiveness only. As mentioned above, efforts to encourage exports occurred simultaneously with the liberalization of imports. Unfortunately the quantification of the former policy is not possible and the index is restricted entirely to the import side. However, the relevance and importance of export incentives will be examined in chapter 6.

The Index of Liberalization

The effects of tariffs and quotas are given equal weights in the construction of the index for 1965–7. Thereafter, the effects of tariffs tend to dominate the index because the share of total items restricted by quotas became rather insignificant (0.5 percent of total six-digit SITC items). Modifications in the index for 1968–75, while influenced by changes in the economy-wide nominal tariff measures, depend on both the magnitude of the replacement of quotas by tariffs and the degrees of quota restrictiveness. (The methodology involved in the estimation of the economy-wide nominal tariff is described in detail in appendix 1.)

The index of liberalization, which ranges from 1 to 20 with 1 representing the most highly controlled trade regime and 20 the most free, is presented in figure 3.1 and the last column of table 3.2. Before 1965, both tariffs and quotas were insignificant. Thus the pre-1965 index is set at 18 for 1964. In 1965 many items were under quotas and tariffs. The nominal tariff for that year was low because many duties were imposed at the end of the year. The abolition of quotas and their replacement with tariffs for a large number of items also occurred at the end of the year. The index for 1965

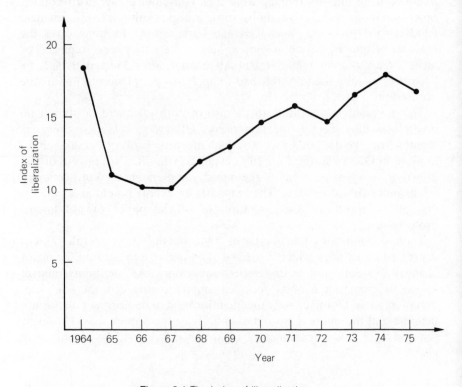

Figure 3.1 The index of liberalization

thus falls to 11. The phenomenal increase of the nominal tariffs in 1966 (by 490 percent over the previous year) meant only a slightly more restrictive trade policy (index of 10) given the moderating effects of the loosening of quotas over a broad front, as mentioned before. The index remains fairly constant in 1967 relative to 1966 since only negligible changes in tariff and quota were observed. The increase in the index to 12 in 1968 is due to the moderate fall in the nominal tariff, reinforced by a reduction of more than 50 percent in the number of items subjected to quotas as well as to the reduced restrictiveness of the quotas. In 1969 dramatic changes in the level of restrictiveness of the quotas were partially offset by the relatively large increase in the nominal tariff. The years 1970 and 1971 represent increased degrees of liberalization with lower nominal tariffs and active abolition of the few existing quotas as well as a net reduction in the total number of tariffs. The year 1973 saw the removal of tariffs for a great many items as well as the total abolition of all quotas. Despite a 0.5 percent rise in the overall nominal tariff rate over 1972, tariff rates went down for a wide variety of commodities. The index thus increases to 17. The index for 1974–5 remains relatively stable with increases in the economy-wide tariffs in general offset by reductions in the number of items subject to tariffs.

Sectoral Breakdown

The breakdown of industry nominal tariffs as well as the industry share of total manufacturing output is shown in appendix 1, table A1.1.

The industries that were most heavily protected by tariffs throughout the period 1968–73 were furniture and fixtures, footwear, and rubber products. However, the share of these industries in total manufacturing was relatively insignificant or declining during the period. On average, over half the industries received zero or negligible tariff protection; the most important of these (in terms of share of manufacturing output) were wood products, electrical and nonelectrical machinery, and the iron and steel industries. Over the period 1965–75, the higher levels of tariff protection afforded in the late 1960s to the food, metal grills and other fabricated products, and other manufacturing industries shifted to transportation equipment and oil rigs and clothing by the early 1970s. In fact, by 1975, of the 19 industries that received tariff protection at some point during the period under consideration, only five retained significant tariff rates. These were the transportation, furniture and fixtures, clothing, paints and pharmaceuticals, and rubber products industries.

Thus the low nominal rates of tariff protection throughout the period from 1968 to 1973 result from two features: (a) in the first half of the period, high tariff rates were granted to industries with smaller shares of total manufacturing output; (b) in the latter half, conversely, the more important industries were granted high levels of protection, but these were offset by the large number of industries that had negligible rates of tariff protection by that time.

The restrictiveness of QRs across sectors is indicated in table 3.3. Of the 25 industries under consideration, QRs were nonexistent for nine. However, of these nine, only textiles is significant in terms of its share in total manufacturing output. In general, QRs appeared to be most restrictive from 1967 to 1968 for the remaining industries, particularly for the food, clothing, rubber products, iron and steel, electrical machinery, and transport equipment industries. By 1970, the QRs for these industries were either removed (clothing, rubber products) or became much less restrictive, in terms of both increased percentages of permitted imports of the products of these industries and reduced coverage of the number of items within the industries. As mentioned before, all QRs were abolished by the end of 1973.

Table 3.3 Degrees of quota restrictiveness across sectors, 1967–1973

Food	1967–9	T	Brick, tiles, clay products	1967–73	N
	1970–3	L	Cement and concrete	1967–73	N
Textiles	1967–73	N	Asbestos, stone, nonmetallic	1967–73	N
Clothing	1967–8	T	Iron and steel	1967–8	T
	1969–73	N		1969–73	L
Leather and products	1967–73	N	Nonferrous metals	1967–73	N
Footwear	1967–73	N	Fabricated metal products	1967–8	L
Wood products	1967–8	L		1969–73	N
	1969–73	N	Nonelectrical machinery	1967	L
Furniture and fixtures	1967–73	N		1968–73	N
Paper and products	1967	N	Electrical machinery/	1967–8	T
	1968–72	L	electronics	1969–72	L
	1973	N		1973	N
Printing and publishing	1967–8	L	Transport equipment	1967–8	T
	1969–73	N		1969–71	L
Industrial chemicals	1967–8	L		1972–3	N
	1969–73	N	Professional/scientific	1967	N
Paints and pharmaceuticals	1967–9	L	equipment	1968	L
	1970–3	N		1968–73	N
Rubber products	1967	T	Other manufacturing	1967–8	L
	1968–73	N		1969–73	N
Plastic products	1967–73	N			
Pottery, china, and glass	1967–8	N			
products	1969–70	L			
	1971–3	N			

T, tight quota; L, loose quota; N, no quota.
Sources: Customs and Excise Department, Singapore, *Annual Report*, various years; Department of Imports and Exports Control and Registration, 1964–73

Features of the Policy

It is important to note that, unlike many of the other countries in the project, the trade liberalization policy in Singapore was characterized by the following features.

1 There was no long history of protection granted to industries before the period of liberalization. In fact, the only tariffs that existed then were for revenue purposes and were very limited in scope.
2 Even with the introduction of tariffs and quotas as protective devices, they were relatively low in level and degree of restrictiveness – there were no prohibitive tariffs and quotas.
3 Protected industries understood that any tariffs or QRs granted were subject to frequent review and were temporary.
4 The industries granted protection were identified as the "growth" industries capable, at some point in the future, of catering to the export market.

4

Accompanying Policies

Exchange Rate Policy

Before 1972 Singapore was a member of the Sterling Area, with its dollar pegged to the pound sterling within the prescribed margin of 1 percent. The bulk of its foreign exchange reserves were held in sterling for use as the intervention currency as well as for international payments.

However, concern over the growing weakness of the pound sterling led to disassociation from the Sterling Area in June 1972 when the pound sterling was floated. The gold parity of the Singapore dollar at 0.290299 gram of fine gold was maintained. The floating prompted Singapore to switch its intervention currency to the stronger and more stable US dollar and to establish an exchange rate of S$2.8196 per US$1. The same gold parity was maintained despite US dollar devaluations in 1971 and 1973 which had increased the price of gold.

Underlying Singapore's exchange rate policy was the objective of maintaining price stability. The government held strongly to the belief that this objective was attainable if a strong exchange rate for the Singapore dollar was maintained through prudent and careful management of its domestic policies. The disassociation from the Sterling Area in 1972 when the pound sterling was floated was a deliberate attempt to avoid increases in import prices, cost of living, and wages. Moreover, there was some concern that a devaluation of the Singapore dollar would run the risk of instability in labor–management relations, an outcome that might well outweigh the export opportunities created by the devaluation of the currency.

In 1973 the Singapore dollar joined the floating system in an effort to contain imported inflation as well as the massive amounts of speculative funds moving into the Asian Currency Units (ACUs) in Singapore.[1] The

---

[1] ACUs are banks which are authorized to deal only in foreign currencies; they are free from reserve requirements or lending restrictions, and are the institutional basis for the rapidly growing Asian currency market that is mainly denominated in US dollars to serve nonresidents.

decision to float was also seen as a means of stimulating a more active foreign exchange market, in line with the government's desire to encourage Singapore's development as a financial center. The float, however, is managed by the MAS, the government body that, with the exception of currency issue, performs all the functions of a central bank.

Aw (1988, appendix table 4) shows the official exchange rates for 1966–75. The rates were rather steady, fluctuating around S$3.08 per US dollar up to 1970. After that, the Singapore dollar displayed an appreciating trend, reaching a rate of S$2.37 per US dollar in 1975. The effective rates (available only for imports and reported by Aw, 1988, appendix table 5) differ only slightly from the official rates because of the low levels of nominal protection. The real effective rates of exchange, derived by deflating the effective rates by the GDP deflator and inflating by the import price index, show steady rates between 1967 and 1970 and a gradual appreciation from 1971 to 1973, owing primarily to lower inflation rates in Singapore compared with its trading partners. After 1973, the effects of the oil crisis led to rapid rises in domestic prices and thus a weaker Singapore dollar.

Figure 4.1 shows both the nominal and real effective exchange rates of the Singapore dollar calculated using trade weights as reported by Rana (1981). In his paper, the indices NER_i and RER_i of the nominal and real effective exchange rates respectively of country i are defined as follows:

$$NER_i = \frac{\Sigma_{j \neq i}(m_{ij}/m_i)r_j}{r_i}$$

$$RER_i = \frac{\Sigma_{j \neq i}(m_{ij}/m_i)r_j/p_j}{r_i/p_i}$$

where r_k for $k = i, j$ is the price of the US dollar in terms of the currency of country i or j, m_{ij}/m_i is the value of country i's imports from country j as a proportion of country i's total imports, and p_k for $k = i, j$ is the wholesale price index in local currency for country i or j with May 1970 as the base year. Rana also constructs the index of relative prices at home and abroad which is defined as

$$RP_i = \frac{P_i}{\Sigma_{j \neq i}(m_{ij}/m_i)/p_j}$$

Figure 4.1 shows that the NER and RER for Singapore were quite stable until about 1972, after which they underwent significant changes. Since 1971, the Singapore dollar has shown an appreciating trend with respect to its trading partners, indicating perhaps a loss of competitiveness in world markets exacerbated by expansionary fiscal and monetary policies and high energy costs. Since 1975, however, the index of relative prices has been

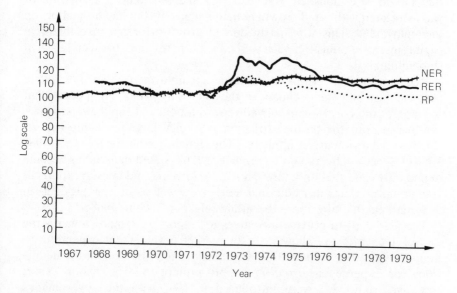

Figure 4.1 Movements of nominal and real effective exchange rates and relative prices (May 1970 = 100)

falling steadily, indicating that Singapore has been inflating at a slower rate than its partners. The falling relative price index was sufficient to offset completely the effect of the appreciating currency, so that in real terms the effective exchange rate in January 1979 was the same as that in March 1970.

Thus, for most of the liberalization period, the exchange rate, both in nominal and real terms, remained stable, except for the last two years when it displayed an appreciating trend.

Investment Incentives and Export Promotion

Investment incentives were granted to industries as early as 1959 with the enactment of the Pioneer Industries (Relief from Income Tax) Ordinance, which reduced the tax rate from 40 percent to only 4 percent for a five-year period for companies that qualified as "pioneer industries." A second ordinance, the Industrial Expansion (Relief from Income Tax) Ordinance, reduced taxes for firms that expanded in order to produce approved products. The major goal of these ordinances was to encourage all kinds of manufacturing industry, and, since great reliance was placed on new foreign capital coming in, it was difficult to specify the types of industries that should be established. Between 1961 and 1965 industrial investment was associated with rapid growth in national income but had little effect on unemployment. This was partly due to growing foreign investment in capital-intensive industries such as chemicals, petroleum, basic metals, and shipbuilding.

Recognizing that serious and chronic unemployment might precipitate political instability and endanger the very survival of an independent Singapore, the government moved toward a policy of rapid industrialization based primarily on the attraction of foreign investment into export-oriented labor-intensive industry. The Finance Minister, in his 1968 Budget Speech delivered on December 5, 1967, stated that "it has become abundantly clear that only through a rapid increase in domestic exports of traditional products in traditional markets as well as of new products in new markets that Singapore can attain salvation" (Goh, 1968).

The first steps to provide incentives for export were made towards the end of 1965 with tax allowances for market development expenditures, granted under the Income Tax Amendment Act, and double tax deductions for expenses incurred in export promotion. The major export incentives, however, were introduced in 1967 with the government's proclamation of the Economic Expansion Incentives (Relief from Income Tax) Act. Its aim was to amend and consolidate the existing laws providing incentives for establishing pioneer industries and expanding established industries, and to introduce new inducements to encourage export production and the application of science and technology to industrial operations.

Under this bill, profits of approved manufactured goods and additions to exports were to be taxed at only 4 percent instead of the usual company income tax of 40 percent. In fact, this provision was even more generous than it appeared because, in order to simplify accounting procedures for the firms and the government, markets to which a firm had exported regularly for five years were considered to be "established" and profits on exports were to be regarded as the same as profits on domestic sales. Total profits were therefore to be simply apportioned between exports and total sales by the share of exports in total sales. Since profits on exports were usually lower than on domestic sales, this meant that the actual value of the tax concession was greater than its face value. Firms enjoying these privileges, however, were no longer able to use double deduction for expenses incurred in opening up new export markets.

In order to qualify for export tax concession, the enterprise had to fulfill two conditions:

1 free on board (f.o.b.) export sales must be at least S$100,000 in the operating year in which the incentives commenced;
2 these sales must be at least 20 percent of the value of the enterprise's total sales.

The tax concessions were for a period of 15 years for nonpioneer firms but ten years for pioneer firms which had already enjoyed a five-year tax holiday under the 1959 Pioneer Industries (Relief from Income Tax) Ordinance.[2] In fact, when the decisions were initially made on tax incentives for the export industries, the tax privilege for export profits at the concessionary 4 percent was for a 20-year period (Goh, 1977b).

By 1970, it was found that some of these benefits were "over generous," in the sense that by then the economy had achieved a vastly improved political and economic climate so that it was felt that reducing these incentives would not diminish foreign investment. Moreover, an amendment was necessary to encourage larger-scale investments. Thus the liberal tax incentives contained in the 1967 Economic Expansion Incentives Act were reduced with the passage of the Amendment Act of 1970. From 1970 onwards, the tax privilege for qualified export industries was reduced to five years for nonpioneer enterprises. Where the export enterprise is also a pioneer firm, the combined tax relief is a total of eight years. However, the tax relief period for both pioneer and nonpioneer export enterprises can be extended to a maximum of 15 years, provided that

1 the enterprise incurs a fixed capital expenditure of at least S$1 billion, or at least S$150 million with 50 percent of its paid-up capital held by permanent residents of Singapore, and
2 the Ministry of Finance decides that the enterprise will help promote or enhance economic and technological development.

It is noted that, if annual export sales fall below the S$100,000 level, tax relief will be terminated even before the end of the previously approved period.

By the early 1970s, some labor-intensive industries which had previously obtained pioneer status were no longer eligible. This applied particularly to some of the products from the food processing, pharmaceutical, and textile industries. Moreover, by the mid-1970s, pioneer status was no longer granted to companies producing exclusively for the local market. Industries with a high degree of technology are particularly encouraged,[3] since these industries (a) are more productive and can generate greater output, and (b) can stimulate other industries through "linkage effects."

---

[2] Under the Economic Expansion Act 1967, an industry can be declared a pioneer industry if the industry is one which "is not being carried out in Singapore on a scale adequate to the economic needs of Singapore" and for which there appear to be favorable prospects for development.

[3] According to Nyaw (1979), the new industries and products declared eligible are aircraft components and accessories, compressors, transformers, diesel and petrol engines, electrical and portable tools, telephone exchange equipment, microwave equipment, magnets and magnetic materials, typewriters, cameras, watches and clocks, miniature lamps, and a range of plastic raw materials.

The Economic Expansion Incentives Act of 1967 included other incentives not offered exclusively to exporters but to investors in general, although exporters appear to be the primary beneficiaries. These incentives included a reduction in income tax from 40 to 20 percent on earnings from approved royalties, technical assistance fees, and contributions to research and development, complete tax exemption on such income or contributions if it is invested in the equity capital of the company and complete tax exemption on interest received by overseas enterprises or individuals on approved loans to Singapore enterprises for the purchase of capital equipment.

The export industries targeted as the main beneficiaries of the incentives were clearly spelled out in an official statement in the 1967 Annual Report of the EDB:

> The development strategy should be now more oriented towards industries in which Singapore has great competitive advantages. This means firstly, the development of industries such as ship-building, ship-repairing and aircraft engineering for which the strategic location and infrastructure facilities offer special advantages. Secondly, having regard to the comparatively good education background of Singapore's labor force, it would be only logical to concentrate on industries with a high skill-content. This consideration led to special emphasis during the past two years on the development of metal and engineering industries and electrical/electronics enterprises. A wide range of these products are now already being manufactured in the Republic. It is considered that, for future development, the investment opportunities in these industries should be especially explored.

In addition to the incentives provided in the Economic Expansion Incentives Act, preferential loans and equity participation were made available to selected domestic industries. These government loans were made initially through the EDB (from 1962 to 1968) and after 1968 through the Development Bank of Singapore (DBS).

Before 1968, the industrial financing function of the EDB grew very slowly, and much of the government money provided for this purpose was invested in income-bearing securities and deposits. The amount of loans disbursed by mid-1968 amounted to S$66.3 million, equivalent to 15.3 percent of capital expenditure in the manufacturing sector (excluding new investments) in the period 1960–8. However, loan commitments increased very rapidly from 1968 onwards.

Table 4.1 shows the share of total loan commitments in various categories of industries. From 1966 to 1969 the share of the cumulative total loan commitments to the traditional industries (primarily the food, textile, wood, and paper industries) averaged around 33.6 percent. The large share for these highly labor-intensive industries was consistent with the urgent need to generate employment opportunities during that period.

Table 4.1 Share of total loan commitments in manufacturing (percent)

Year	Traditional industries[a]	"Targeted" nontraditional industries[b]	Others[c]
1966	31.0	43.3	25.7
1967	27.3	49.8	22.9
1968	35.2	33.2	31.6
1969	41.0	49.4	9.6
1970	36.5	51.0	11.5
1971	29.5	51.0	19.5
1972	21.5	52.7	25.8
1973	19.5	61.6	18.9
1974	19.9	61.1	19.0
1975	17.5	65.0	17.5

[a] These industries include food, textiles, textile products and footwear; wood and paper products; printing and publishing; leather and leather products; and rubber and rubber products.
[b] This category comprises basic metal and metal products; electrical and nonelectrical machinery, apparatus, appliances, and supplies; and transport equipment.
[c] This category comprises chemical and chemical products; petroleum and petroleum products; nonmetallic mineral products; and miscellaneous.
Sources: for 1965–8, EDB, 1964–8; for 1969–75, DBS, 1969–75

However, this share gradually fell between 1970 and 1972 to an average annual share of 29.2 percent and declined further in the next three years to an average for the whole period of just below 19 percent.

The "targeted" nontraditional industries, which includes the metal and engineering as well as the shipbuilding industries, had an average share of about 44 percent of the total cumulative loan commitments to manufacturing during the period 1966–9. This share increased to an average of 51.6 percent over the period 1970–2 and jumped to 62.6 percent over the period 1973–5. New loan commitments to the shipbuilding and repair industries accounted for the bulk of the increase during 1973–5, while those to the metal and engineering industries were responsible for the large increase during 1970–2.

Table 4.2 indicates the share of new loan commitments made each year in the different categories of industries. The average annual share of new loans committed from 1966 to 1968 in the traditional industries (38 percent) was much higher than the 11 percent average for 1971–5. However, the average share for the "targeted" nontraditional industries increased from an annual average share of 38 percent during the period 1966–8 to 64 percent for 1971–5. That is, during the 1970s consistently more than half of new loans committed each year went to the "targeted" nontraditional industries.

Table 4.2 Share of new loan commitments in manufacturing (percent)

Year	Traditional industries	"Targeted" nontraditional industries	Others
1966	46.7	35.3	18
1967	9.6	79.7	10.7
1968	58.6	0	41.4
1969	n.a.	n.a.	n.a.
1970	n.a.	n.a.	n.a.
1971	12.4	48.6	39.0
1972	2.0	48.2	49.8
1973	11.9	85.3	2.8
1974	21.4	57.7	20.9
1975	7.3	82.2	10.5

n.a., not available.
Sources: for 1966–8, EDB, 1964–8; for 1969–75, DBS, 1969–75

In general, therefore, as far as investment incentives in the form of subsidized loans are concerned, the nontraditional industries were granted an equal or larger share of total loans relative to the traditional industries in the period 1966–9. However, during the first half of the 1970s this share, particularly for new loans, increased significantly for the nontraditional industries and plunged for the traditional ones.

The interest rate on these loans was only marginally below the market interest rate (about 0.5 percent). It was initially fixed at 7 percent in order to serve as an incentive to the private sector to set up industries. In 1963 the interest was reduced to 6 percent a year and remained at that rate until August 1965 when it was raised by 2 percent a year, a rate at which it remained until the financing functions of the EDB were transferred to the DBS in August 1968.

As a further attraction, applicant companies could borrow up to 50 percent of their fixed capital requirement from the EDB on medium- or long-term loans of up to ten years, provided that the sum borrowed did not exceed the paid-up capital. To avoid competing with the usual functions of commercial banks, no loans were normally granted for working capital.

EDB equity participation was smaller than its loan commitments and was given to provide the necessary capital for key industries, or to ensure sound and rapid development. Government equity participation was relatively insignificant in the earlier period between 1966 and 1969 with funds evenly spread out among the textile, food, metal and engineering, shipbuilding, and chemical industries. From 1970 onward, however, equity participation increased significantly in the petroleum as well as the shipbuilding industries (Soo Ann Lee, 1973).

Restrictions on International Capital Movements

From 1965 to the early 1970s, the regulations in Singapore for international capital movements were characterized by the following features:

1 Capital transfers to and from other countries in the Sterling Area were not restricted. Inward and outward transfers between Singapore and countries outside the Sterling Area required exchange control approval. Capital inflow, however, was freely permitted but usually authorization was subsequently required for investing such capital in Singapore (MAS *Annual Report*, 1971).

2 Singapore nationals could make investments in countries outside the Sterling Area only upon approval of the exchange control authorities; this was given only when such investments were considered to serve the economic interest of the country.

3 Investment by residents of countries outside the Sterling Area, other than Rhodesia, in quoted stock and bonds was freely permitted if transactions were made through a recognized stock exchange with funds from an external account or transferred in a specified currency. Investments in new industrial development projects were not restricted.

Overall, apart from minor regulations regarding safety, pollution, employment, and industrial relations, there were no controls on private investment. In principle, the government made no distinction between local and foreign capital. Legislation offering incentives for private industrial development is open to both sources equally. There were no restrictions against foreign ownership of business entities in Singapore; businesses which are completely foreign owned may operate. However, there was a tendency, although not reflected in written legislation, to encourage joint ventures emphasizing foreign expertise and the participation of local capital (Nyaw, 1979).

Foreign investment could bring unlimited amounts of capital into Singapore. There were no antimonopoly laws, no licensing process for foreign or local private investments, no controls on technology transfers or required registration of contracts or licenses, and no limitations on profit remittances, technology payments, or capital repatriation overseas.

Since the early 1960s, the government industrial policy has actively welcomed foreign investment. An official statement by the Singapore Prime Minister (Kuan Yew Lee, 1978) stated:

> . . . the rate of development necessary if we were to generate the jobs to mop up unemployment, running at 10 percent of the workforce in 1960, could never be achieved at the pace at which Chinese and Indian Singaporean

enterprise was slowly moving from traditional retail and entrepôt trade into new manufacturing or servicing industries . . . (there is) far greater potential in the expanding subsidiaries of American, European, and Japanese corporations.

Thus, even without precise estimates of its extent, the total contribution of direct foreign investment to investment, output, and employment in manufacturing in the early 1960s was regarded as crucial to industrial development. To the Singapore government, it seemed that whatever costs foreign investment imposed, the benefits it brought were greater. Foreign investment was desired not so much for the capital itself, given the high rates of domestic savings, but for the associated technological expertise and ready markets.

Although controls on private foreign investment were few, the government influenced the sectoral allocation of resources over time by varying the degree and distribution of various investment incentive schemes, ranging from tax exemptions and write-offs to direct subsidies and allowances.

In the early to mid-1960s, confronted with high unemployment, the government liberally granted fiscal incentives, protective duties, and subsidized loans (as outlined above) to both local and foreign investors in labor-intensive industries such as textiles, clothing, footwear, and electronics.

By 1967, the emphasis changed from labor-intensive industries to those that were both capital and skilled labor intensive, such as the metal and engineering as well as the shipbuilding industries. The package of investment incentives was gradually directed to these new industries.

The change of emphasis reflected the government's intention of encouraging foreign investment in industries which would have not only higher value added but also high export potential. Simultaneously, import duties were gradually replacing existing quotas, and the levels and coverage of both import duties and quotas were reduced.

A 1966 survey of 119 firms with direct capital investment from the six principal investing countries concluded that the foreign investors, almost without exception, stated that taxation concessions and pioneer status had not played a significant role in bringing them to Singapore (Hughes and You, 1969). Most firms claimed that they would have established their manufacturing operations without them. The main factors which they claimed attracted them to Singapore were the government's welcoming attitude, expressed in positive assistance mainly through the EDB and other government departments, and the efficiency of the public services and utilities. The availability of industrial estates at very low cost was also important.

In addition to the above incentives, the MAS has been progressively liberalizing its exchange controls in a number of discrete steps throughout the 1970s. The liberalization was applied particularly to the ACUs, which were specifically authorized to deal only in foreign currencies. As distinct from "domestic" banks, there were no reserve requirements on ACU deposits and the liquidity ratio (initially 20 percent) was abolished in 1972. In the same year, Singapore resident companies were given the authority to receive and hold foreign exchange from "scheduled territories." Other relaxations followed (MAS, *Annual Reports*, 1973–7):

1 From July 1973, Singapore residents and resident companies were permitted to invest in specified currencies up to a limit of S$100,000 and S$3 million respectively in portfolio investments or in deposits with the ACUs; approved unit and investment trusts were allowed to invest in specified currencies up to S$5 million or 15 percent of their funds in portfolio investments including deposits in ACUs and to borrow from the ACUs; Singapore residents were allowed to buy and sell gold in the Singapore gold market, which was formerly restricted to nonresidents, and to export gold freely.
2 From February 1976 the ceiling for investments in specified currencies and securities was raised from S$100,000 to S$250,000 for individuals and from S$3 million to S$5 million for corporations; the definition of "scheduled territories" was extended to include Indonesia, the Philippines, and Thailand; restrictions of movements of currency notes and transactions with nonscheduled territories were also relaxed.
3 Finally, formal exchange controls were completely liberalized on June 1, 1978. As of that date, Singapore residents could freely make deposits with or accept loans from the ACUs.

All in all, the Asian dollar market represents a relatively free external market in foreign currencies, where the institutions concerned operate with tax and other concessions not available to their domestic counterparts. The liberalization of exchange control is in line with the government's goal of internationalizing Singapore's financial center, although every effort has been made to maintain some separations for Singapore dollar transactions.

Domestic Controls

Singapore has a long record of internal price stability. For the six years before 1967, the CPI rose by only 9.1 percent or at an annual rate of only about 1.5 percent. Although this annual rate rose to 2.7 percent during

1967–72, prices rose little relative to many countries. Thus the Singapore economy is characterized by an absence of price controls. Instead,

> the government has opted for improving the market mechanism to ensure that higher import prices and higher domestic production costs do not lead to unwarranted increases in consumer prices. Information on prices of basic food items are disseminated through the mass media. Consumer co-operatives are established to overcome monopolistic pricing and reduce distribution margins. Profiteers are subject to public sanctions. (Chia, 1974)

Before 1968, there was no formal wage policy in Singapore. The Employment Act of 1968 embodied some elements of wage control. Under this Act, annual paid leave, retirement benefits, and overtime work were restricted. Bonus payments are negotiable only up to one month's salary. Any bonus or *ex gratia* payment over and above one month's salary is tied to labor productivity.[4] Before 1968

> practically all workers in the private sector have been receiving annual bonuses ranging from 2 weeks' wages to 23 months' wages and these bonuses were regarded by workers as part of their wages rather than as an incentive payment for higher productivity. (Ow and Goh, 1974)

Pioneer industries which began operations on or after January 1968 had to comply wholly with all the terms and conditions of employment as detailed in the Employment Act for five years from the data of commencement of operations in Singapore. It was hoped that the successful implementation of this Act would attract employment-creating foreign investment into the country by guaranteeing the prospective employer considerable wage stability as well as minimizing the possibility of labor unrest (Industrial Relations Act, 1970).

Data on average real hourly earnings distinguished by import-competing activities and export industries are not available. However, the evidence that exists suggests that, despite government intervention in wage determination via the Employment Act, it is generally true that, given the domestic price stability, the economy overall was not subject to any significant wage pressures during 1965–70. Average hourly earnings for all industries grew at an average annual rate of 3.8 percent during 1967–73.

The end of 1971, however, marked the economy's gradual movement from the chronic high unemployment of the 1960s to an era of full employment. Indeed, by 1970, sectoral labor shortages were experienced, and immigration controls were relaxed in that year. In 1972 the government set up a tripartite National Wages Council (NWC) to provide general

---

[4] It is not clear in the literature how this is actually implemented. What is clear is that employers, with the passing of the Act, have much more discretion over employees' wages.

wage guidelines for the economy. These wage guidelines are the outcome of bargaining within the NWC, but factors such as labor productivity, cost of living, and wages in other countries which are Singapore's major competitors are also taken into account. In general, the recommendations cover all industries and corporations. The government normally accepts the recommendations for the public sector in full, but they are not binding in the private sector; instead they are guidelines, to be implemented fully only if companies can afford to do so.

Since 1972, the NWC has made the following recommendations for wage increases: (a) 8 percent annual wage increases and an additional one-month payment in 1972; (b) a 9 percent annual wage increase in 1973; (c) a 6 percent increase in 1974 plus an extra S$40 for those earning less than S$1,000 per month; (d) a 2 percent annual increase in 1975. During and in the few years immediately after the world recession of the mid-1970s, the NWC recommended modest wage increases to insure the competitiveness of the labor-intensive export industries. The government's endorsement has given the NWC such credibility and authority that its recommendations are widely implemented. Thus wage increases were heavily influenced by NWC recommendations. Real weekly earnings fell in 1973 and barely increased in 1974 in all industries. Given full employment in 1971 and the adverse movement in the terms of trade owing to rising food and energy prices in 1973 and 1974, the moderation of increases in the nominal wage could be directly attributed to the effectiveness of the wage restraint policy of the NWC as well as the increasing reliance on foreign labor, both unskilled and skilled.

The government's intervention in the labor market is most significant in the system of forced public savings in the form of CPF contributions. The CPF, established in 1955, was intended to provide income security for its members in old age. Since then, it has become a major institutional feature of the Singapore economy because of the enormous increase in both the rates of contribution and the proportion of contributors. From 1955 to 1968 the rate of contribution by both the employer and the employee was constant at 5 percent. Since 1968 both rates have been steadily increasing (table 4.3). In 1968 the rate was increased to 6 percent for each side, and by 1976 the combined rate of contribution stood at 30 percent. Simultaneously, the number of contributors as a proportion of the labor force has increased from about 45 percent in the late 1960s to around 80 percent by the beginning of the 1970s.

In siphoning off increasing proportions of purchasing power through CPF contributions and restraining wage increases through the NWC wage guidelines, the government has managed to maintain an inflation rate below the world level throughout the 1970s.

Until recently, government interventionism had no apparent adverse impact on economic growth. In fact, the interventionist approach, at least

Table 4.3 Rates of Central Provident Fund contributions (percent)

	Rate per year					
	1955	1968	1970	1972	1974	1976
Payable by employer	5.0	6.5	8.0	14.0	15.0	15.0
Payable by employee	5.0	6.5	8.0	10.0	15.0	15.0

Source: Department of Statistics, Yearbook of Statistics, various years

in some areas, was seen as important in Singapore's economic success. However, the interventionist role has come under intense scrutiny in the context of the current recession. In particular, it has been suggested that the recession is probably the product of the government's real wage policy as well as the forced savings policy of the CPF. The commitment to an open frontier that Singapore has worked toward and maintained in the last decade should be an advantage, since distortionary effects of domestic policy tend to become quickly apparent, making the necessary adjustments more obvious and imperative.

5

Economic Performance Following Liberalization

Economy-wide Performance

Price Levels

During all but the last year of the liberalization episode major prices remained relatively stable.

During 1967–72, the CPI rose by an average annual rate of only 1.3 percent while the GDP deflator increased by an average annual rate of 2.4 percent (table 5.1). Several reasons have been given in the literature for the low rate of inflation during this period. Chia (1974) cites the limited, low, and decreasing role of tariff protection for manufacturing industries, a phenomenon which enabled the economy to avoid the inflationary pressures generated by domestic physical constraints and monopolistic elements. Other reasons cited for the low rates of inflation include domestic policies, the most important of which were the importation of both skilled and unskilled foreign workers and the effective

Table 5.1 Rates of change in price indices (percent)

Year	CPI	Annual average of CPI	GDP	Annual average of GDP
1967	3.0		0.5	
1968	0.6		1.0	
1969	− 0.1		2.0	
1970	0.3		1.5	2.4 (1967–72)
1971	1.9		4.1	
1972	2.0	1.3 (1967–72)	5.1	
1973	19.5		12.1	
1974	26.8		17.5	14.2 (1973–5)
1975	3.7	16.7 (1973–5)	13.1	

1972 = 100.
Source: Department of Statistics, 1983

implementation of wage guidelines which kept the lid on wage increases when the excess supply of domestic labor was rapidly diminishing.

In 1973 and 1974 inflation in Singapore rose to record levels. The CPI rose by 19.5 percent in 1973 and 26.8 percent in 1974 before slowing down to 3.7 percent in 1975. The increases in the GDP deflator were not as dramatic as, though significantly higher than, the earlier period. The GDP deflator rose by an average annual rate of 14.2 percent during the period 1973–5. The primary reason for the high rates of inflation in 1973 was the rapid rise in prices of imported food (particularly rice and other cereals). The high rates of inflation in 1974 were mainly due to the inflation in imported foods and energy; the latter caused inflation in the prices of such commodities as domestic transport, fuel, and electricity.

Real Rate of Exchange

Effective rates of foreign exchange for 1967–75 were calculated only for imports. The relevant data required to estimate the level of subsidies for exports are not available except for the 1967 study by Tan and Ow (1982). (The results on the degree of industry export subsidies found by Tan and Ow will be reported in the industry performance section, and their time trend will be inferred from information on the level of loans committed to various sectors.)

The economy-wide effective foreign exchange rate and its components are shown in table 5.2. The industrial sectors, classified according to the Standard Industrial Classification (SIC) categories, are disaggregated into large groups following Nyaw (1979) as shown in appendix 2. These groups are as follows: consumer goods industries, intermediate goods industries,

Table 5.2 Effective exchange rate for imports by broad categories (Singapore dollars per US dollar)

Year	Economy-wide	Consumer goods	Intermediate goods	Capital goods
1966	3.142	3.214	3.126	3.102
1967	3.136	3.190	3.116	3.127
1968	3.128	3.181	3.113	3.123
1969	3.143	3.205	3.123	3.144
1970	3.148	3.185	3.135	3.150
1971	3.081	3.108	3.061	3.091
1972	2.863	2.878	2.845	2.875
1973	2.507	2.503	2.472	2.541
1974	2.458	2.464	2.440	2.477
1975	2.394	2.407	2.382	2.406

Source: Department of Statistics, Singapore External Trade Statistics, various years; Table A1.2

and capital goods industries. The effective exchange rates (EERs) for each of these groups are calculated by computing the weighted average of the EER of the sectors in the group using the sector's import share as weights.

It can be seen in table 5.2 that the EERs for consumer goods are slightly higher than those for intermediate and capital goods for every year except 1973. In general, the EERs on consumer goods exhibit a gradual appreciation over time beginning in 1969, although at an annual average of about 2 percent above the economy-wide EERs over the period from 1966 to 1969. This difference narrowed in subsequent years to an annual average of slightly above 0.5 percent between 1970 and 1975.

While the EERs of both intermediate and capital goods categories, like the consumer goods category, also display a gradual appreciation over time beginning in 1970, each of these two categories differ significantly both from the consumer goods category and from each other. The EERs for the latter category are higher than those for intermediate goods for every year, but are only higher than those for capital goods from 1966 to 1972. The EERs of capital goods were above those for consumer goods in 1973 and 1974. The former are also higher than those for intermediate goods for every year except 1966.

Imports

Table 5.3 reports figures for total as well as retained imports. Given the importance of entrepôt trade activities in Singapore, retained imports represent a more accurate picture of the actual value of imported goods. The nominal values are deflated by the GDP deflator series to obtain the real values.

Table 5.3 Aggregate and retained imports

| Year | Real total imports (million S$) | Real RM[1] (million S$) | Growth rate | | Ratio of RM to GDP (%) |
			Real total imports (%)	Real RM (%)	
1966	4,127.4	1,734.6	—	—	0.45
1967	4,590.1	2,114.9	11.2	21.9	0.49
1968	5,537.9	2,879.0	20.6	36.1	0.58
1969	6,384.0	3,567.4	15.3	23.9	0.63
1970	7,474.0	4,722.7	17.1	32.4	0.74
1971	8,552.8	5,423.2	14.4	14.8	0.75
1972	9,538.0	6,191.3	11.5	14.2	0.76
1973	10,833.7	6,919.5	13.6	11.8	0.76
1974	11,539.2	8,634.2	− 5.8	− 1.2	0.85

—, not applicable.
[a]RM = retained imports = total imports − reexports.
Source: Department of Statistics, *Singapore External Trade Statistics*, various issues

Total and retained imports grew at an annual average rate of 12 percent and 20 percent respectively from 1966 to 1975. In general the annual growth rates were more rapid during the years immediately following liberalization and slowed down somewhat by the 1970s. The ratio of retained imports to GDP has been rising phenomenally over the decade from 0.45 in 1966 to 0.85 in 1974.

The rapid growth of retained imports taken as a whole masks the equally dramatic structural changes that the economy has experienced during the span of the decade under consideration. This can be seen by breaking down retained imports into three major categories: consumption goods, intermediate goods, and capital goods (table 5.4). Between 1966 and 1975, the composition of the import bundle has changed substantially. The share of consumption goods in total manufactured retained imports fell from 25.7 percent in 1966 to 14.5 percent in 1970 and 11.7 percent in 1975. However, the capital goods share rose from 23 percent in 1966 to over 40 percent by the early 1970s. The share of intermediate goods in total manufactured retained imports stayed fairly constant over the period, averaging around 53 percent yearly during 1966–9 and 45 percent during 1970–5.

Table 5.4 Retained imports in the manufacturing sector

Year	Consumption goods (million S$) (%)		Intermediate goods (million S$) (%)		Capital goods (million S$) (%)	
1966	388.8	(25.7)	773.4	(51.2)	347.8	(23.0)
1967	492.7	(24.1)	1,091.2	(53.4)	458.5	(22.4)
1968	525.2	(19.2)	1,518.3	(55.5)	690.1	(25.2)
1969	561.9	(15.9)	1,868.8	(53.0)	1,092.6	(31.0)
1970	683.3	(14.5)	2,190.5	(46.3)	1,854.0	(39.2)
1971	834.0	(14.9)	2,424.3	(43.3)	1,338.2	(41.8)
1972	891.9	(14.3)	2,577.0	(41.3)	2,767.9	(44.4)
1973	1,144.5	(14.6)	3,258.2	(41.5)	3,442.0	(43.9)
1974	1,555.5	(10.9)	6,910.5	(48.3)	5,835.4	(40.8)
1975	1,641.0	(11.7)	6,833.8	(48.9)	5,494.6	(39.3)

Source: Department of Statistics, Singapore External Trade Statistics, various issues

Exports

Table 5.5 reports information on total exports and domestic exports in real terms (using the GDP deflator). Domestic exports are derived by subtracting reexports from total exports.

Domestic exports grew very rapidly in real terms from 1967. Their share in total exports rose from 28 percent in 1967 to 42 percent in 1970 and

Table 5.5 Aggregate and domestic exports

Year	Real total exports	Real domestic exports	Growth rate Real total exports	Growth rate Real domestic exports	Ratio of domestic exports to GDP
1966	3,933.0	1,185.3	—	—	0.31
1967	4,044.7	1,291.3	2.8	8.9	0.30
1968	4,458.7	1,161.5	10.2	28.7	0.34
1969	5,310.7	2,224.8	19.1	33.9	0.40
1970	5,240.5	2,184.6	−1.3	−1.8	0.34
1971	5,662.8	2,320.5	8.1	6.2	0.32
1972	6,149.4	2,802.7	8.6	20.8	0.34
1973	7,943.3	3,911.5	29.2	39.6	0.43
1974	10,923.3	6,404.2	37.5	63.7	0.66
1975	9,216.5	5,957.2	−12.0	−7.0	0.58

—, not applicable.
Source: Department of Statistics, *Singapore External Trade Statistics*, various years

62 percent in 1975. Over the period from 1966 to 1975, exports of domestic origin increased at an average annual rate of 21.4 percent while total exports grew at an average annual rate of 11.4 percent.

If domestic exports are disaggregated into consumption goods, intermediate goods, and capital goods categories, a distinct pattern emerges (see table 5.6). From 1966 to 1969, the bulk of domestic exports consisted of intermediate goods, in particular petroleum products (average of 76 percent). In 1970, this share fell to 65 percent, and was replaced by increases in the share of capital goods which doubled from an annual

Table 5.6 Domestic exports in the manufacturing sector

Year	Consumption goods (million S$) (%)	Intermediate goods (million S$) (%)	Capital goods (million S$) (%)
1966	119.1 (19.0)	464.7 (74.2)	42.2 (6.7)
1967	116.8 (15.3)	591.8 (77.3)	57.1 (7.5)
1968	178.4 (16.7)	817.0 (76.6)	70.6 (6.6)
1969	209.7 (15.3)	1,046.5 (76.5)	111.4 (8.1)
1970	281.7 (19.1)	962.4 (65.3)	230.2 (15.6)
1971	354.6 (17.8)	1,238.7 (62.3)	394.4 (19.8)
1972	476.3 (18.3)	1,367.4 (52.4)	765.2 (29.3)
1973	699.1 (18.5)	1,881.9 (49.8)	1,200.8 (31.8)
1974	860.2 (12.3)	4,283.2 (61.0)	1,875.2 (26.7)
1975	981.3 (14.7)	3,868.2 (58.0)	1,817.6 (27.3)

Source: Department of Statistics, *Singapore External Trade Statistics*,
various years

average share of 7.2 percent during 1966–9 to 15.6 percent in 1970. Domestic exports of capital goods continued to replace intermediate goods thereafter, with their share in domestic exports rising to 31.8 percent in 1973. The share of intermediate goods in domestic exports fell to 49.8 percent in 1973. In 1974 and 1975 the latter share regained some importance owing to the rise in prices of petroleum products. The share of consumption goods has remained fairly constant at around 17.5 percent throughout the period 1966–73. This share fell to 12.3 percent in 1974 and 14.7 percent in 1975. Thus, over the decade under consideration, there has been a definite shift in Singapore's domestic exports away from intermediate goods and into capital goods with the share of consumption goods exports remaining fairly stable.

The level of export diversification can be measured using the Gini–Hirschman coefficients of commodity concentration (Hirschman, 1964). This was done by Nyaw (1979) for the period 1959–74; his methodology and results are summarized here.

The Gini–Hirschman coefficient $C_{jx,t}$ exports by country j in year t is defined as

$$C_{jx,t} = 100 \sum_{i=1}^{n} \left(\frac{X_{ij,t}}{X}^2 \right)$$

where $X_{ij,t}$ is the value of exports of commodity i by country j to the rest of the world in year t, $X = \Sigma\, X_{ij,t}$, that is, the total value of exports by country j to the rest of the world in year t, and n is the number of commodities. The commodity concentration coefficient is equal to 100 if only one commodity is exported. The larger is the number of goods exported (diversification of exports) and/or the more even distribution among these goods, the lower is the coefficient.

Table 5.7 shows the coefficients of commodity concentration for exports of all commodities and manufactured products for 1959–74. The commodity concentration index for total exports declined from 1959 to 1965, subsequently increased to 1969, and then fell again. The index for manufactured products also showed a declining trend from 1959 through 1968, but has remained relatively stable since then. This trend appears to be consistent with the switch in 1967 to an export-oriented policy based more on "upstream" manufactures than on the traditional exports to southeast Asia of processed raw materials imported from the region. Moreover, export manufacturing made possible scale economies and thus a broader-based industrial development.

Table 5.7 Coefficients of commodity concentration for exports of all commodities and manufactured products, 1959–1974

Year	All commodities[a]	Manufactured products[b] (SITC, three-digit level)
1959	47.61	32.41
1960	43.97	31.78
1961	38.10	31.98
1962	36.32	32.18
1963	33.15	31.56
1964	30.47	28.97
1965	30.47	29.41
1966	31.81	27.12
1967	32.60	24.48
1968	36.82	22.51
1969	39.61	23.46
1970	35.52	23.70
1971	33.54	24.91
1972	31.77	25.18
1973	31.43	25.37
1974	37.82	25.16

SITC, Standard International Trade Classification.
[a] Including reexports; SITC commodity groups amount to 40 items.
[b] Including reexports; based on SITC sections 5–8.
Source: Nyaw, 1979

Openness of the Economy

Table 5.8 records the openness of the economy over time using different measures. The first measure takes the ratio of total exports (TX) and total imports (TM) to the GDP. Given the importance of entrepôt trade in the Singapore economy, the ratio of retained imports (RM) plus domestic exports (DX) to GDP was calculated. The surplus of imports over exports in real terms is also reported in the table.

The ratio of total exports and imports to GDP remained fairly stable at around 2.0 over the entire period under consideration except for 1974 when it rose to nearly 2.4. However, the ratio of domestic exports plus retained imports to GDP rose gradually every year from 1966 through 1974. It increased from 0.75 in 1966 to 1.08 in 1970 and 1.56 in 1974, indicating that while the degree of openness has not changed much over time, the economy has become less dependent on regional entrepôt trade and more dependent on trade in manufactures with the rest of the world.

Therefore if this measure of openness is used, the economy was clearly more open, in terms of rapid growth rates in both imports and exports, during the liberalization period 1963–73. Since imports (total and retained)

Table 5.8 Measures of openness of the economy

Year	(TX + TM)[a] GDP (%)	(DX + RM)[b] GDP (%)	TM − TX[c] (million S$)	RM − DX[d] (million S$)
1966	2.08	0.75	194	549
1967	1.99	0.78	545	824
1968	2.02	0.92	1,079	1,218
1969	2.08	1.03	1,073	1,343
1970	1.99	1.08	2,234	2,538
1971	1.98	1.08	2,890	3,103
1972	1.92	1.10	3,389	3,389
1973	2.06	1.19	2,890	3,008
1974	2.39	1.56	1,332	2,334
1975	2.07	1.43	1,927	2,677

[a] Ratio of total exports and total imports to GDP.
[b] Ratio of domestic exports and retained imports to GDP.
[c] Surplus of imports over exports.
[d] Surplus of retained imports over domestic exports.
Source: Department of Statistics, Singapore External Trade Statistics, various issues

have grown at much faster rates than exports (total and domestic) over the period 1966–72, it is not surprising that the magnitude of import surplus has increased over this period.

While commodity trade, particularly in the manufacturing sector, is perhaps the most important and significant indicator of the degree of openness in the Singapore economy over time, the trade in labor services gained importance as early as 1968 when temporary foreign workers were allowed into the country to satisfy the labor requirements of the export manufacturing industries (Chow and Tyabji, 1980). This inflow of foreign workers, the majority of whom were from Peninsular Malaysia, gained momentum in the early 1970s as Singapore was confronted by an acute labor shortage in both the unskilled and skilled labor intensive industries. By 1973, foreign workers numbered over 100,000, or one eighth of the total Singapore labor force. The number of foreign workers was reduced with the onset of the 1973–4 recession and did not pick up again until 1978. Foreign workers were then critical for meeting the shortage of labor in the construction sector, which was undergoing boom conditions. Female foreign workers were encouraged to meet the needs in the export-oriented textiles, garment, wood products, and electronic products industries. These less skilled workers were given only temporary permits to stay, while skilled professional and entrepreneurial foreign workers were encouraged to take up permanent residence. Government policy controlled the supply of foreign workers, tightening supply during recessions and liberalizing it during booms.

Balance of Trade

Table 5.9 shows details of Singapore's trade balance on the goods and services account. It is clear from the table that over the period under consideration the merchandise trade account has been in persistent deficit with imports and exports of goods increasing at differential rates. Between 1966 and 1969, merchandise imports and exports grew at average annual rates of 15.5 percent and 12.6 percent respectively. These figures fell to 14.6 percent and 8.9 percent between 1969 and 1972. In the subsequent period, 1972–5, both imports and exports grew very rapidly, and the average annual rates reached 29.7 percent and 32.3 percent respectively. Overall, over the entire period under consideration, imports grew by an average annual rate of 18.8 percent, about 1.2 percent faster than exports each year.

The balance on the services account has been consistently in Singapore's favor, but only in 1966 was it large enough to offset the merchandise trade deficit. Offsetting the trade deficit are receipts from tourism, transportation (which includes mainly the earnings at the port and the airport from Singapore–foreign transactions), and foreign military services. There is also a positive balance on investment income which, apart from the transactions of the private sector, covers interest earned on foreign assets of the government and the statutory athorities. The large payment under services is for freight and insurance.

On the capital account, net inflow of long-term capital from private sources was large and increased steadily over the period under consideration.

It should be noted that it is very difficult to analyze Singapore's balance of payments with precision because of imperfect data, reflected in the large and increasing amounts shown in the item "balancing item" (that is, net errors and omissions). The magnitude of this item from 1967 to 1971 more than offsets the trade and services deficit.

Overall, the strong balance-of-payments record during the period under analysis provided the economy with a cushion against any adverse impact on the balance of payments arising from the liberalization of imports.

External Debt

Before 1966, the size of the government's external debt was minuscule. As can be seen from table 5.10, beginning in 1967, only one tenth of Singapore's debt is external; it rose from S$44.5 million in 1967 to S$173.8 million in 1970 and S$542.7 million by 1975. In 1972, of the total external debt of S$430.8 million, more than half was due to the UK Special Aid Fund, 3.2 percent to the World Bank, and 33.4 percent to the capital market.

Table 5.9 Balance of payments (million Singapore dollars)

	1966	1967	1968	1969	1970	1971	1972	1973	1974	1975
A Goods and services (net)	48	−170	−367	−546	−1,727	2,170	−1,400	−1,265	−2,395	−1,293
Exports	4,249	4,415	4,914	5,953	6,132	6,909	9,122	12,639	19,646	19,626
Merchandise	3,168	3,240	3,589	4,471	4,428	5,075	5,739	8,418	13,518	12,118
Services	1,081	1,176	1,325	1,482	1,704	1,834	3,383	4,221	6,128	7,508
Imports	4,201	4,586	5,281	6,499	7,860	9,079	10,521	13,904	22,040	20,919
Merchandise	3,825	4,148	4,759	5,863	7,048	8,091	8,796	11,636	18,920	17,810
Services	376	437	522	636	812	988	1,725	2,268	3,120	3,108
Trade balance	−657	−909	−1,170	−1,392	−2,619	−3,016	−3,057	−3,217	−5,402	−5,693
Balance of services	705	738	803	846	892	846	1,658	1,952	3,008	4,400
B Transfer payments (net)	−45	−39	−41	−39	−24	−36	6	−10	−95	−92
C Capital (net)	17	76	464	49	533	879	1,112	1,772	1,218	1,374
D Balancing item	133	438	608	829	1,783	2,302	1,225	508	1,990	977
E Overall balance (A + B + C + D)	153	304	664	292	565	975	945	1,005	718	966

Source Department of Statistics, 1983

Table 5.10 External public debt

Year	Total (million S$)	UK special fund (million S$) (%)	World Bank (million S$) (%)	Asian Development Bank (million S$) (%)	Capital market loan (million S$) (%)	Others (million S$) (%)
1966	62.8	–	–	–	–	62.8 (100.0)
1967	44.5	–	–	–	–	44.5 (100.0)
1968	71.7	10.8 (15.1)	–	–	–	60.9 (84.9)
1969	103.1	47.1 (45.7)	1.8 (1.7)	–	–	54.2 (52.6)
1970	173.8	119.5 (68.8)	5.4 (3.1)	–	–	48.9 (28.1)
1971	246.9	186.1 (75.4)	10.2 (4.1)	–	–	50.6 (20.5)
1972	430.8	231.2 (53.7)	13.8 (3.2)	1.8 (0.4)	143.9 (33.4)	40.1 (9.3)
1973	472.3	264.5 (56.0)	18.2 (3.9)	5.0 (1.1)	143.9 (30.5)	40.7 (8.6)
1974	493.9	270.1 (54.7)	27.6 (5.6)	6.3 (1.3)	143.9 (29.1)	46.0 (9.3)
1975	542.7	270.1 (49.8)	47.2 (8.7)	8.4 (1.5)	143.9 (26.5)	73.1 (13.5)

–, negligible.
Source: Department of Statistics, 1983

According to the World Bank's debt reporting system, Singapore's debt service ratio (ratio of sum of interest payments and repayments on the principal of external public and publicly guaranteed debt to the exports of goods and services) increased only slightly from 0.6 percent in 1970 to 0.8 percent in 1976. Over the same period, debt service as a percentage of gross national product (GNP) increased from 0.6 percent to 1.3 percent.

Aggregate Product

GDP and aggregate labor productivity figures are given in table 5.11. Estimates of total labor productivity are unavailable.

GDP grew by an average annual rate of 13.6 percent during 1966–9 and 10.7 percent during 1970–5. Aggregate labor productivity for a given year was obtained simply by taking the ratio of GDP at constant prices to total employment for that year. Productivity increased by an average annual rate of almost 8 percent during the three-year period from 1966 to 1969. Between 1969 and 1972, the average annual rate of increase held steady at 6.8 percent before falling to 3.2 percent during the period 1972–5. During the entire period under consideration from 1966 to 1975 the average annual rate of growth of labor productivity was nearly 6 percent. Thus the high growth period occurred from 1966 to 1972. This growth slowed significantly during the initial years of the oil crisis (1973–5).

Table 5.11 Aggregate labor productivity

Year	GDP at 1968 factor cost (million S$)	Employment (thousands)	Labor productivity (S$ per worker)	Rate of labor productivity growth (%)
1966	3,075	524	5,868	—
1967	3,475	552	6,296	7.3
1968	3,971	580	6,846	8.7
1969	4,502	610	7,380	7.8
1970	5,107	651	7,845	6.3
1971	5,747	691	8,318	6.0
1972	6,514	725	8,985	8.0
1973	7,247	781	9,283	3.3
1974	7,737	803	9,638	3.8
1975	8,044	813	9,889	2.6

—, not applicable.
Source: Tsao, 1984b

Aggregate Employment and Unemployment

In the early 1960s labor force growth had an important push effect in promoting rapid industrialization. Singapore faced an employment problem similar to that in many developing countries, namely, a rapid population growth with a less than adequate growth of employment opportunities.

It was not until after 1967 that earlier concerted efforts to promote industrialization began to have a significant impact on employment. While the net increase in 1967 was limited to some 5,000 new jobs, in 1969 over 14,500 new jobs were created compared with the previous year. In 1973 some 50,000 new jobs were created, twice the net increase in the labor force, bringing about a state of full employment in the economy.

The substantial increase in the working population in the 1970s was a direct result of increased female participation.

As a result of the above trends, the unemployment rate declined from 8.7 percent in 1966 to 6.9 percent in 1969 and 4.5 percent in 1973. Given that the unemployment figures are calculated from registrations with the employment bureau, it is conceivable that the 4.5 percent unemployment in 1973 reflected the high turnover rates consistent with a buoyant economy.

Aggregate Capital and Investment

The share of total investment in GDP has increased significantly over time from 22 percent in 1967 to more than a third of GDP in the 1970s (table 5.12). An important contributor to this high growth rate was the compulsory saving out of wage income through the CPF. In the 1970s the rate of contribution to the CPF from employer and employee was raised considerably. In 1968 the rate of contribution from each party was 6.5 percent. This increased gradually over the years to 10 percent in 1971 and then to 15 percent in 1975. In 1985 the contribution rate to the CPF was 25 percent each from the employer and the employee.

Table 5.12 Investment in Singapore

Year	Investment (million S$)	Percentage share of GDP
1966	729.4	21.9
1967	831.2	22.2
1968	1,075.2	24.9
1969	1,437.4	28.6
1970	2,244.5	38.6
1971	2,744.1	40.2
1972	3,354.4	41.1
1973	4,000.0	39.2
1974	5,592.0	44.6
1975	5,592.0	39.1

Source: Soo Ann Lee, 1984

An interesting feature of the growth of investment during 1966–9, apart from its size, is that the increase was fastest in the private sector. The figures for public and private sector investment are given in table 1.1.

The increase in private sector investment during the period from S$234 million to S$596 million, an increase of 156 percent, compares with an increase from S$239 million to S$323 million in the public sector, or a mere 35 percent growth in the public sector over three years. This changing composition of total investment reflects the massive inflow of private foreign investment during this period. Among the major reasons for this huge inflow are political stability, good infrastructure, wage stability, and a young educated workforce.

There is no existing measure of the ratio of capacity utilization in Singapore. Nyaw (1979) reports estimates of the rate of capacity utilization $\hat{U}_t$, roughly measured by the deviation from the exponential growth trend of industrial production. The fitted trend for total manufacturing including petroleum industries in Singapore is given by $\hat{Q}_m$, while Q_m denotes total manufacturing output. The rate of capacity utilization is smaller if $\hat{Q}_m - Q_m$ is positive and large. Since the deviation $\hat{Q}_{\hat{m}} - Q_m$ contains negative values, they are transformed into index form by adding a constant, that is $\hat{U}_t = \hat{Q}_m - Q_m +$ constant. Table 5.13 gives estimates of the rate of capacity utilization of total manufacturing industries.

Industry-specific Performance

Effective Exchange Rates

Industry EERs were calculated by adding the sectoral nominal tariff rates (appendix 1, table A1.1) to the official rates. These rates appear in appendix 1, table A1.2.

Table 5.13 Estimates of the rate of capacity utilization in total manufacturing industries

Year	$\hat{U}_t = \hat{Q}_m - Q_m$	$\hat{U}_t = \hat{Q}_m - \hat{Q}_m + 200$
1966	− 72.9	127.1
1967	− 70.5	129.5
1968	− 64.1	135.9
1969	62.7	262.7
1970	33.4	233.4
1971	40.3	240.3
1972	− 10.1	189.9
1973	277.7	477.7
1974	177.0	377.0

Source: Nyaw, 1979

In the early years of the liberalization period the industries with relatively high NPRs were the consumer goods industries of footwear, furniture, clothing, and food. During the same period NPRs on industries in the capital goods category were relatively insignificant, except for fabricated metals. Over the latter half of the period NPRs on the consumer goods industries fell. In the capital goods category, however, NPRs on the transportation equipment industry increased from 7.2 percent in 1972 to 21 percent the following year. These developments explain the relatively higher EERs in the consumer goods industries which subsequently declined over the liberalization period. EERs for the intermediate goods industries, like petroleum, industrial chemicals, and so on, were slightly lower than those for the other categories.

Subsidy rates for 1967 were calculated by Tan and Ow (1982). Their calculation account for the differences in tax and interest subsidies received by industries. These results are reproduced in table 5.14 along with the sectoral effective exchange rates which are obtained by accounting for the sectoral rate of subsidy in the 1967 official exchange rate of S$3.08 per US dollar. In their study, Tan and Ow conclude that, in Singapore, tax exemptions and concessional loans did not appreciably modify the pattern of effective protection. The table shows that in 1967 only five industries

Table 5.14 Effective exchange rates for exports, 1967

Industry	Subsidy (%)	EER (S$ per US$)
Food	0	3.080
Beverages	−5	2.926
Tobacco	−22	2.372
Textiles	12	3.450
Footwear	−2	3.018
Wood and cork	0	3.080
Furniture	−1	3.049
Paper products	−2	3.018
Printing and publishing	−6	2.895
Leather products	−8	2.834
Rubber products	5	3.234
Chemical products	1	3.111
Petroleum products	14	3.511
Nonmetal products	−3	2.957
Basic metals	2	3.142
Metal products	−2	3.018
Nonelectrical machinery	0	3.080
Electrical machinery	0	3.080
Transport	−2	3.018
Miscellaneous	−5	2.926

Source: Tan and Ow, 1982

received positive tax and/or interest subsidies: the petroleum products, textiles, rubber products, basic metals, and chemical products industries. Four other industries received zero subsidies (food, wood and cork, electrical machinery, and nonelectrical machinery) while the others were negatively subsidized, in particular the tobacco industry where the subsidy rate was − 23 percent.

Without more information on industry-specific tax and loan subsidies, it is impossible to quantify the differential degree to which industries were subsidized over time. The only information available in a time series form is the level of subsidized loans committed to different industries (table 5.15). Given the relative importance of tax incentives to industries, the level of government loans committed across industries may be a very misleading indicator of industry differences in the actual level of subsidy received. The information on such loans is nevertheless indicative of the general emphasis of government policy for industries targeted to receive special encouragement toward rapid growth.

Of the total subsidized loans committed to industries between 1968 and 1974, about 80 percent are long term (more than five years). A general inference that can be drawn from comparing table 5.14 with the table on yearly loans committed by the government to industries (table 5.15) is that after 1967, with the exception of the wood and paper industry, aid appears

Table 5.15 Loans committed each year in industrial enterprises (million Singapore dollars)

Industry	1966	1967	1968	1969	1970	1971	1972	1973	1974	1975
Food	–	–	1.3	n.a.	n.a.	–	1.0	–	5.5	2.3
Textiles	0.6	0.6	5.6	n.a.	n.a.	–	–	3.2	2.0	–
Textile	n.a.	n.a.	n.a.	n.a.	n.a.	–	–	3.2	2.0	–
Leather	n.a.	n.a.	n.a.	n.a.	n.a.	–	–	–	–	–
Wood and paper	2.2	0.7	3.3	n.a.	n.a.	8.3	0.8	10.0	9.6	5.4
Printing and publishing	–	–	–	n.a.	n.a.	–	0.2	–	5.0	1.0
Chemicals	1.1	–	1.0	n.a.	n.a.	–	6.0	0.8	5.3	4.4
Petroleum	–	–	–	n.a.	n.a.	9.5	39.2	–	–	2.6
Rubber products	–	–	0.5	n.a.	n.a.	–	–	0.4	–	–
Plastic products	–	–	–	n.a.	n.a.	–	4.7	1.2	4.4	2.4
Nonmetallic minerals	–	–	–	n.a.	n.a.	2.1	–	0.5	12.0	0.8
Metals and engineering	1.6	2.0	–	n.a.	n.a.	11.4	22.3	15.2	9.4	9.5
Metals	n.a.	n.a.	–	n.a.	n.a.	11.2	16.6	15.2	4.6	6.5
Nonelectrical machinery	n.a.	n.a.	–	n.a.	n.a.	0.2	5.7	–	4.8	3.0
Electrical products	0.5	0.2	–	n.a.	n.a.	8.6	6.3	–	3.5	1.0
Transportation	–	8.7	0.9	n.a.	n.a.	12.3	5.1	68.3	46.8	87.3
Optical and scientific goods	–	–	–	n.a.	n.a.	–	14.4	11.0	–	2.6
Miscellaneous manufactures	0.1	1.4	20.1	n.a.	n.a.	14.4	–	0.3	–	1.3
Total	6.1	13.6	32.7	–	–	66.6	100.0	110.9	103.5	120.4

–, negligible, n.a., not available.
Sources: for 1965–8, EDB, 1964–8; for 1969–75, DBS, 1969–75

to have moved away from the traditional rubber and textile products to some extent and toward even greater emphasis on metal products, electronic products, electrical and nonelectrical machinery, transport, and optical and scientific goods industries. The latter group of industries had zero or negative rates of tax and/or interest subsidy in 1967 according to the calculations by Tan and Ow. The data in table 5.15 show positive subsidized loans to two of these industries (metal products and transport industries) in 1967. Nevertheless, the change of emphasis was particularly evident in the early 1970s. In particular, from 1969 through the 1970s, the transportation industry, which consists primarily of shipbuilding, rig construction and fabrication, and equipment, received an increasing share of the total amount of subsidized loans. Beginning in the early 1970s, the service sector, primarily the financial institutions, was the recipient of a substantial proportion of new subsidized loans. The petroleum industry, and to a lesser extent the chemical products industry, continued to receive substantial loan subsidies during this period.

If the level of loan commitments to industry is indicative of the degree of industry subsidy, then the EERs of the metal products, electrical and nonelectrical machinery, transport, chemical, and petroleum industries in the post-1967 period are higher than the official foreign exchange rate for any given year in that period. Without more information on industry-specific tax subsidies and other forms of loan subsidies, stronger inferences are not possible on the actual changes in the EERs for exports.

Real Wages

Wage data by industry for the period 1966–74 are available in the form of annual earnings per worker. Since the wholesale price index series only started in 1974, real wages are obtained by deflating the annual earnings per worker by the CPI. During the period 1966–74, many industries have been reclassified to yield a more disaggregated industry breakdown. The wage data for 1966–9 follow the 1965 Census of Industrial Production (CIP) classification while the data for 1970–4 follow the more detailed 1970 CIP classification of industries.

The chemicals and petroleum industry had the highest wages in the manufacturing sector over the entire period, with the major contribution to the high wage coming from the petroleum industry. At the other end of the scale, clothing had the lowest wages in manufacturing. In 1970, the average annual earnings per worker in the petroleum industry were about 8.5 times those in the clothing industry. Industries on the higher end of the wage scale include industrial chemicals, transport equipment, nonmetal minerals, and iron and steel. Industries on the lower end of the wage scale include paper products, footwear, textiles, pottery, and plastic products.

Industries whose average wages grew significantly in 1968 were the transport equipment and basic metals industries, while real wages for industries such as paper products, nonelectrical machinery, and the chemical and petroleum industries fell substantially. In the following year, 1969, basic metals continued to reap large growth rates in wages, accompanied by chemical and petroleum products, paper products, and textiles. The large gains in the latter two industries are partially due to the extremely low base wage to begin with.

The average annual growth rates of wages computed for two different time periods are reported by Aw (1988, appendix table 6). The selected periods are 1966–9 and 1970–5. One reason for this particular breakdown is the change in industrial classification in 1970. As mentioned earlier the latter period contains more information because of the change in the level of disaggregation. More importantly, there were relatively high, though declining, rates of unemployment in the period 1966–9, while from 1970 onwards the Singapore economy started to encounter labor shortages.

Real wages rose substantially in only three industries during 1966–9: nonmetallic products (12 percent), textiles (12 percent), and the chemical and petroleum industries (9 percent). For the other industries, average wages rose little or even fell. Industries whose real wages fell substantially were electrical machinery, furniture, and fabricated metals.

The average annual growth rates of real wages in the period 1970–4 have a much smaller variance than those observed for the period 1966–9. They range from − 6 percent for the nonmetal minerals to 8.2 percent in the paper products industry. A possible reason is that in 1972 the government's NWC was set up to insure orderly and modest wage increases in the light of the tight labor market conditions. Since then, wage guidelines, though voluntary, have influenced wage increases in both the public and private sectors. The average annual growth rate of real wages during the period 1970–4 stood at 2 percent across all industries. Industries with relatively higher annual growth rates in real wages are paper products (8.2 percent), precision equipment (6.8 percent), paints and pharmaceutical products (6.7 percent), and leather products (6.4 percent).

Imports

On average, the industries with the most rapidly growing value of retained imports in the period 1967–70 are transport equipment, fabricated metals, nonelectrical machinery, and textiles (Aw, 1988, appendix table 7). Footwear imports increased by 85.5 percent in 1968, while there was an increase of 106.3 percent in transport equipment in the same year. Although retained imports grew more slowly across all sectors in the period 1970–5, the growth rates were still relatively higher, especially in plastic wear, fabricated metals, and footwear.

Industries with high ratios of retained imports to domestic output, primarily because of low levels of domestic production especially in the period 1966–9, include textiles, precision equipment, nonelectrical machinery, and industrial chemicals.

In general the ratios for the consumer goods industries fell steadily until 1973, when they started rising. The direction of change is more mixed for the capital goods industries: the ratios for electrical machinery follow the same downward trend as those for consumer goods, but the ratios for iron and steel, fabricated metals, and nonelectrical machinery rose between 1966 and 1973 before falling slightly in the 1970s.

An interesting observation is that the ratio of retained imports to production increased for 24 out of 28 industrial sectors in 1974, the first year of almost complete liberalization of import controls.

The major problem in determining the relationship between retained imports and EERs on both the aggregate and sectoral basis is statistical, given the small variation in EERs. Thus inferences drawn from elasticity estimates and correlations between retained imports and EERs are not very meaningful. Both Pearson and Spearman correlation coefficients between retained imports and EERs were computed, and as predicted these coefficients were extremely small.

However, some general inferences can be drawn from closer examination of the data on the growth rates of retained imports and EERs. Industries with relatively high EERs on imports (footwear, furniture, rubber products, and leather products), particularly during 1966–8, which underwent falling EERs subsequently, experienced moderate increases in retained imports over the period 1966–75. However, industries with near-constant EERs on imports in the period prior to the floating exchange rate (1966–72), as a result of zero or insignificant import tariffs, experienced both small and large increases in imports over the period.

It is clear from the data that, while the gradual removal of tariffs on imports may have been partially responsible for increases in retained imports in certain industries, other factors are significant in accounting for the observed changes in retained imports across industries. These factors include government fiscal and infrastructural policies aimed at encouraging selected industries and the growth in demand for particular imports from a rapidly growing economy.

Exports

As described earlier in the chapter, Singapore's domestic exports shifted over the decade from intermediate to capital goods leaving the share of consumption goods exports fairly stable. The trend reflects official policies in the late 1960s to early 1970s promoting industries which were higher value added, more skill intensive, and more technology intensive.

Exports grew considerably in most sectors in the period 1966–75 (Aw, 1988, appendix table 7). High growth is evident, particularly in the capital goods industries of transport equipment and nonelectrical and electrical machinery. The high rates for the electrical machinery, plastic products, and precision equipment industries were due partly to small or negligible exports in the base year. It is noteworthy that, out of 28 industry groups covering the manufacturing sector, only two (tobacco and leather products) achieved an average annual export growth of less than 10 percent.

The general upsurge of industrial exports is accompanied by a marked diversification of the export structure. The relative shares of traditional exports such as food, beverages, wood and cork products, paper and paper products, printing and publishing, footwear and leather products, rubber products, and nonmetallic mineral products have decreased over the years. At the same time, new industrial exports have increased in importance. These include electrical and nonelectrical machinery, transport equipment, plastic products, petroleum products, and precision equipment.

Trade Ratios

Aw (1988, appendix table 14) gives the trade ratios (defined as industry domestic exports plus retained imports divided by industry production) for the industries. A few features stand out. Of the 28 industries only two (beverages and nonelectrical machinery) showed a decline in trade ratios after 1973, the year of near-complete trade liberalization. In 1967, the first year of the liberalization episode, the trade ratio either remained stable or rose for most of the major industries (textiles, clothing, industrial chemicals, iron and steel, fabricated metals, nonelectrical machinery, transport equipment). The trade ratios for electrical machinery, paints and pharmaceuticals, and wood products fell slightly in the same year. Overall, trade ratios changed most dramatically over the period 1966–75 for industrial chemicals, fabricated metals, nonelectrical machinery, textiles, electrical machinery, and precision equipment industries. Trade ratios for the latter three industries declined sharply. However, large increases were recorded in industrial chemicals and fabricated metals, while the trade ratio for nonelectrical machinery rose very rapidly from 1966 and peaked in 1970 before declining gradually through 1975.

In 1967 industries with the highest trade ratios in absolute terms were textiles, industrial chemicals, and nonelectrical and electrical machinery. Industries with the lowest trade ratios in that year were tobacco, printing and publishing, nonmetal minerals, plastic products, and beverages. By 1970, the iron and steel industry joined the ranks of industries with the highest trade ratios.

Industry Output

The manufacturing sector has been the cornerstone of growth in Singapore since the mid-1960s. This growth is due not to natural resources or an agricultural base, since Singapore possesses neither, but rather to Singapore's ability to attract foreign investment and to provide these investors with a high quality physical infrastructure and a trained disciplined workforce. In the latter half of the 1960s, manufacturing growth surpassed GDP growth, generating about one third of the annual increment in GDP each year.

Total manufacturing output grew by an average annual rate of about 35 percent from 1967 to 1969. This rate slowed down to around 28 percent during the subsequent period 1970–5.

Relative to many other developing countries, Singapore's industrial pattern is characterized by a smaller consumer goods sector and correspondingly larger intermediate and capital goods sectors. For instance, the textiles and clothing industries play a much smaller role in Singapore's industrialization than in that of most other developing countries. The lack of emphasis on import substitution in the initial phase of its industrial development was partly responsible for this pattern. Other factors include the pattern of official promotion policies as well as the important role Singapore played as a leading centre for petroleum refining, shiprepairing, and shipbuilding, as well as electronics assembly and component manufacture.

The growth performance varied widely among industry groups. It is found (Aw, 1988, appendix table 8) that the major industries with rapid expansion rates in the years following 1967 were textiles, electrical machinery, transportation equipment (mainly shipbuilding and ship repair), plastic products, and chemical and petroleum products.

The main impetus in the electrical machinery industry is the electronics subsector, in which increased diversification has resulted in the manufacture of a wider range of domestic electric appliances and industrial equipment, for example, motor and electrical control devices, consumer audio and video products, and the more complex field of industrial electronics with products ranging from calculators to computer peripherals.

An industry of lesser importance in the late 1960s, but whose importance grew dramatically in 1970–5, was precision equipment. This industry manufactures precision engineering equipment such as specialized tools, dies, machine parts, cameras, lenses, and shutter systems.

The electrical machinery industry continued to grow quite quickly in the early 1970s. The nonelectrical machinery and iron and steel industries were among the few in that period whose growth rate exceeded that in the late

1960s, reaching average annual rates of 46.3 percent and 21.5 percent respectively during the period 1970–5.

The industries with the slowest growth during the entire period from 1966 to 1975 were beverages, tobacco, leather products, and glassware.

Problems similar to those encountered in the earlier section on imports arise here in determining the relationship between the change in sectoral output and the change in sectoral EER. In addition, since a quantitative measure of the effect of export subsidies over time on the official exchange rate is not available, it was not possible to relate changes in the total EER (on imports and exports) to changes in sectoral output. However, several observations can be made in the light of our qualitative assessment of the industrial bias in the granting of export subsidies by the government and the available EERs on imports.

The industries singled out by the government in 1967 for special incentives, fiscal and otherwise, were the engineering and metal-working industries; these include the electrical and nonelectrical machinery, iron and steel, and transportation equipment industries. Insofar as fiscal incentives and government-sponsored infrastructural facilities favor these over more traditional industries, the EER faced by these industries would in general be high relative to the other industries. The engineering and metal-working industries are among the group of industries with exceptionally high production growth in the period 1967–75. The output of electrical machinery and transportation equipment industries grew very rapidly, particularly in the period 1967–9, while growth rates for the nonelectrical, iron and steel, and precision equipment industries took off in the period 1970–5.

The industries not specifically singled out but which received a relatively large amount of subsidized government loans (textiles, petroleum, and chemicals products), particularly in the late 1960s, complete the above list of industries with exceptionally high production growth.

The above industries, with the exception of the textiles and electrical industries, are characterized by relatively high growth rates in value added per worker (Aw, 1988, appendix table 9). The textile industry was the least capital intensive, with the electrical machinery industry ranked among those with relatively low capital intensity. The high growth rates in output in these industries in the late 1960s were probably the result of the series of government incentives that encouraged the expansion of labor-intensive activities during the middle and late 1960s. As the economy approached full employment in the early 1970s and as focus shifted to the activities with higher value added, the output growth in the textiles industry in particular slowed down while the electrical machinery industry maintained its high growth by switching into more sophisticated high-technology products.

Industry efficiency is measured by labor productivity, defined as value added per worker. The sector with the highest labor productivity by far is the petroleum products industry. Other industries with relatively high productivity include industrial chemicals, paints and pharmaceuticals, tobacco products, iron and steel, and nonferrous metals. At the opposite end, industries with the lowest labor productivity are textiles, clothing, footwear, and leather products.

All industries, however, experienced an increase in labor productivity during the period 1966–75. Among the major industries, the average annual rate of growth in labor productivity was particularly marked in nonelectrical machinery, transport equipment, iron and steel, paints and pharmaceuticals, clothing, and textiles. A primary reason for rapid growth in the latter two industries is the very low base levels from which they started. The bulk of the major industries that registered impressive growth rates in labor productivity during the period 1971–5 were the capital goods industries such as iron and steel, nonferrous metals, nonelectrical machinery, transport equipment and precision equipment.

Industry Employment

Employment growth over time was concentrated in different sets of industries (Aw, 1988, appendix table 5.10): while the leading employers in 1967 were the food, wood products, printing and publishing, and nonmetallic mineral products industries, considerable shifts in the employment pattern had taken place by 1975. Increasingly, labor had moved into industries such as electrical machinery, transport equipment, textiles, clothing, and nonelectrical machinery. The total share of these industries in manufacturing employment increased substantially from 24.5 percent in 1967 to 40.1 percent in 1970 and 55.2 percent in 1975.

The electrical machinery industry was paramount in its contribution to employment creation, accounting for 26 percent of the new jobs created in manufacturing between 1967 and 1975. The industry's share of manufacturing employment increased from 3.1 percent in 1967 to 18.8 percent in 1975, to make it the largest single employer in the manufacturing sector. An even higher growth rate would have been achieved in the absence of the 1974–5 oil crisis.

The textile and clothing industries showed a higher rate of increase in employment between 1966 and 1969 than between 1970 and 1975. The higher rate in the former period was partially due to the small base and to the emphasis on labor-intensive activities. The share of these two industries in total manufacturing employment increased slightly from 11.1 percent in 1967 to 15 percent in 1975.

The chemicals and petroleum products industry is by far the least labor-intensive sector in manufacturing. Their share of total manufacturing remained stable at around 1–2 percent over the entire period from 1969 to 1975.

Capital and Investment

Capital stock, as measured by the net value of fixed assets, increased rapidly for the manufacturing sector as a whole, nearly doubling between 1966 (S$431 million) and 1969 (S$830 million). By 1974 and 1975 it had passed the S$3,000 million mark (see Department of Statistics, *Census of Industrial Production*, various years). However, expansion of capital stock was concentrated in certain industries.

Aw (1988, table 11) shows the growth rates of sectoral capital stock for the periods 1966–9 and 1970–5. The period averages, however, mask very rapid growth rates for certain sectors, particularly in the first two years after liberalization. Capital stock grew most rapidly in the textiles and clothing industries with a growth rate of 95 percent in 1968, slowing down to 35 percent in 1969. Although this was congruent with the labor-intensive industrialization program in the late 1960s, it was also the result of a small base. This growth slowed down even further in the period 1970–5 with the shift in emphasis from labor-intensive to capital-intensive industries. Despite the rapid growth in their capital stock, however, the contribution of textiles and clothing to the expansion in manufacturing capital stock was small, given the small base of the industry (which amounted to only 2.5 percent of total manufacturing fixed assets in 1967).

The largest contribution to growth in the manufacturing capital stock was made by petroleum and chemical products. Although its growth rate between 1966 and 1969 was less than that of the textiles industry for the same period, its contribution to the growth of total manufacturing capital stock was substantial because of its high capital intensity, particularly in petroleum refining.

Other major industries with very high growth rates in capital stock which made significant contributions to growth in manufacturing capital stock were transport equipment, electrical and nonelectrical machinery, miscellaneous manufacturing (mostly from precision equipment), and metal products.

The analysis in terms of changes in sectoral capital stock reflects the shift in government emphasis from labor-intensive industries to those with high capital and skill content. Under this policy, industries producing industrial machinery, petrochemicals, and sophisticated electronic components were actively promoted. Concomitant with this shift in emphasis, the beverages, tobacco, food, and printing and publishing industries experienced a decline in their share of total manufacturing fixed assets.

Estimates of capacity utilization are not available for Singapore. However, Nyaw (1979) calculated estimates of capacity utilization in Singapore's pioneer manufacturing firms for 1967 and 1968. This information is reproduced in appendix 1, table A1.3. There was a significant amount of underutilization of capacity in 1967 and 1968. In 1967, actual value of output by pioneer manufacturing firms was only about 60 percent of the estimated value of output at full production in 1967. This percentage fell to 50 percent in 1968. One of the reasons for the large underutilization of capacity in these years was the significant amounts of investment made in anticipation of the common market with Malaysia. The abolition of any hopes of such a market in 1965 led to the loss of the anticipated larger domestic market and thus the problem of excess capacity.

In Singapore, the extent of underutilization was especially serious in chemicals and chemical products, plastic products, food and beverages, textiles and garments, and electrical products. In all these industries, excess capacity was greater than 50 percent in 1967 and 1968. Many of these industries produce labor-intensive import substitutes and are restricted by export quotas in industrialized countries. Among the pioneer firms with greater capital intensity and higher productivity, the obstacle to further utilization of capacity has generally been a deficiency of skill.

In the 1970s, with the general upgrading of skills and relaxed immigration laws to relieve the skill bottleneck in the latter group of industries as well as increased incentives for industries to export their products, capacity utilization for these industries is likely to be much higher than in 1967 and 1968.

6

The Role of Investment Incentives

The System of Incentives

The constraints of a small domestic market and the traditional philosophy of free trade have disposed the government to use fiscal and associated domestic incentives rather than trade policy to foster investment. That is, the emphasis was on promotion rather than protection (Chia, 1984), with private enterprise and foreign investment playing an important part while the government set the pace and direction of resource flow through its various policy measures. Consequently, the system of protection via tariffs and quotas, as seen in chapter 3, was simple and moderate even during the short import substitution phase.

Economic incentives in the form of official ordinances and acts (detailed in the section on investment incentives and export promotion in chapter 3) make up only part of the package offered to attract investors. The entire system of investment incentives is quite complex in that the underlying industrial policy involves not just the use of fiscal incentives but also the provision of physical and institutional infrastructure, the enforcement of labor discipline and industrial peace, and accelerated manpower development. The government relied on the latter elements to create a favorable environment for investment by minimizing risks as well as maximizing economic returns. The nature of these incentives, however, make them difficult to quantify: hence the paucity of information on the degree to which industries have been implicitly aided.

The extent of economic incentives received by industries in the form of preferential loans and profit tax differentials was calculated by Tan and Ow (1982) for 1967 (see table 5.14). They conclude that the implicit subsidy to industries did not appreciably modify the pattern of effective protection. Another study by Chia (1976) estimated that in 1973 the interest subsidy implicit in the government loan used to develop the industrial estates amounted to only 0.11 percent of the value of gross output and 0.31 percent of value added of the firms located in industrial estates. Chia suggests that the value of the industrial estates to private enterprise lies not so much in lower rentals or capital requirements as in the ready availability of such sites.

While it may be true that each investment incentive taken in isolation provides only a small subsidy, it is quite likely that the entire system of incentives taken together contains a significant subsidy component that could in turn explain industry performance. Thus it may be useful to look at the group of industries that are the main beneficiaries of the government's system of investment incentives and compare their performance over time with that of the manufacturing sector as a whole. The following section does this for the group of "pioneer" industries, designed as such to receive not just the fiscal incentives under the Pioneer Industries Ordinance (1959) and the amended 1967 Economic Expansion Incentives Act but also the entire package of incentives offered to investors. It is important to keep in mind that most of the incentive measures are generally available to import-substituting and export industries alike. The export bias lies in the administrative discretion in the award of the various incentives (Chia, 1984). Another important qualification is that, given the many determinants of industrial performance, the analysis can, at best, only indicate whether the hypothesis that investment incentives are important in explaining industrial performance should be rejected.

Performance of Pioneer Industries

The percentage of pioneer establishments as a share of total manufacturing establishments increased gradually from 9 percent in 1965 to 16 percent by 1972.

Table 6.1 summarizes the more detailed data given by Aw (1988, appendix table 21) for the annual growth rates of the performance variables from 1965 to 1972. The growth rates of all the performance variables in the pioneer industries were impressive, particularly those of direct exports which were sustained into the later period. Employment growth rates, which were not as high as those of output, value added, or direct exports in the period 1965–8, performed much better in 1968–72 rising from 30 percent in 1965–8 to 41 percent in 1968–72. Although the growth rates of output and value added slowed down in the latter period, the average annual rate still exceeded 35 percent.

It is clear from the data in table 6.1 that, relative to overall manufacturing, the performance of the pioneer industries was superior by far. In general, annual growth rates were higher in the pioneer industries with respect to all the major statistics for almost every year under consideration. In fact, the gap in the growth rates between all manufacturing and pioneer industries of all except one performance indicator (value added) increased

Table 6.1 Period growth rates of major statistics of manufacturing and pioneer establishments in production, 1965–1972 (percent)

Economic variable	1965–8	1968–72
Establishments in production		
Manufacturing	17.1	5.1
Pioneer	29.2	11.5
Employment		
Manufacturing	17.2	22.5
Pioneer	30.3	40.7
Value of output		
Manufacturing	37.1	20.7
Pioneer	47.7	35.5
Value added		
Manufacturing	23.6	28.6
Pioneer	46.5	37.9
Direct exports		
Manufacturing	49.0	27.1
Pioneer	57.6	60.9

Source: Aw, 1988, appendix table 21

over time. Again, the largest gap between the growth rates of pioneer and manufacturing industries was in direct exports.

From the above evidence, investment incentives available to pioneer but not to nonpioneer industries appear to contribute to the superior performance of the former. However, several qualifications are necessary before any conclusive statement can be made.

First, it is important to look at the differences in the capital intensity of pioneer and manufacturing industries: this could be crucial to the discrepancy in performance. A crude indicator is the ratio of gross fixed assets to total employment as reported in table 6.2. It is clear that pioneer industries are more capital intensive than the manufacturing average. The higher capital investment could therefore account for their superior performance.

Second, the higher growth rates, particularly in export growth, of the pioneer relative to the nonpioneer firms could come from the type of industries that are attracted by the very nature of the incentives offered. Chia (1984) notes that export-oriented offshore-type investments, which are highly sensitive to the investment climate, tend to be attracted by the package of investment incentives since these to some extent demonstrate a country's favorable attitude toward the foreign investor.

Thirdly, most of the beneficiaries of the investment incentives are foreign investors whose operations tend to be larger, more likely to succeed (Goh, 1973), and export oriented. Thus it is possible that the

Table 6.2 The ratio of gross fixed assets to total employment in manufacturing and pioneer establishments in production, 1965–1972

Establishment	1965	1966	1967	1968	1969	1970	1971	1972
All manufacturing	5.5	6.4	6.4	6.6	9.4	8.7	10.2	10.5
Pioneer	24.3	30.0	24.5	21.3	19.9	23.4	23.9	25.4

Source: EDB, 1964–75

superior performance of the pioneer industries is due to the dominance of foreign corporations in these industries rather than the direct economic effect of the investment incentives.

Finally, it has been pointed out by many researchers that the awards of pioneer status were not very selective in the 1960s because of the urgent need to attract investments and improve the unemployment problem, but became more selective in the late 1960s and through the 1970s. To the extent that the industries targeted for the awards were more in line with the changing comparative advantage of Singapore, the higher growth rates of the pioneer industries relative to the nonpioneer industries may be only remotely related to the investment incentives available to the former group.

Thus, while the hypothesis that investment incentives explain the superior performance of pioneer industries compared with overall manufacturing cannot be rejected, this relationship is by no means unequivocal.

7

Trade Liberalization and Performance in Selected Industries

Of the 25 three-digit SITC industries, only eight appeared to have received significant levels of protection as well as to have experienced changes in the degree of that protection through tariffs, quotas, or subsidized loans. In this chapter we first report the time patterns of the responses for each of these eight industries separately, and then go on to attempt to link liberalization and industry performance in the industries taken together.

Performance of Selected Industries

Processed Food

In 1967 this category ranked first in terms of its contribution to employment (11 percent) and output (23 percent) in the manufacturing sector and second in terms of its share of total manufacturing value added (10 percent). However, by 1973, these shares had fallen to 4.5 percent, 9 percent, and 5 percent respectively, dropping its ranking to eighth in terms of employment, third in terms of output, and seventh in terms of manufacturing value added.

The levels of tariff protection of the food industry were generally low, ranging from around 5 percent between 1967 and 1969 to slightly above 1.5 percent by the end of the liberalization period. Some quotas were imposed on specific food items between 1965 and 1972. However, beginning in 1966 some of these quotas were either completely removed or replaced by tariffs. In general, the data on changes in quota restrictions in the food industry between 1967 and 1973 suggest that in 1967–9 quotas were relatively tight, while in 1970–3 they were looser.[1] Except for 1968,

---

[1] This judgment was made on the basis of the form (complete removal, replacement with tariff) of the liberalization effort and the degree of restrictiveness of the quota that was removed or replaced.

when the food industry received about 20 percent of total government loans committed in that year to industrial enterprises, tax and credit preferences are negligible in the category.[2]

In general, except for the value added per worker series, the absolute levels of production, employment, retained imports, and domestic export variables rose over time with a slight fall in 1972. However, the rate of growth declined over the same period for the production and employment series, while the growth rates of the remaining variables fluctuated.

While the lower growth rates in production and employment in the food industry during 1970–3 coincide with the period of almost complete liberalization in that sector, they continue the falling trend that began in the earlier period. This trend appears to be the result of official government policy to redirect the economy away from more traditional industries, like food and rubber products, to newer more skill-intensive industries.

Textiles

In 1967 the textiles industry was small, with a value added share of less than 1 percent. By 1973, it ranked fourth in terms of the share of manufacturing employment (7 percent) and its value added and output share in manufacturing rose to about 5 percent and 4 percent respectively.

The level of tariff protection in the textile industry (excluding clothing) has remained low and fairly constant over the period 1967–73, hovering around 2 percent. By 1975 all tariffs were eliminated. The most important form of government assistance in the late 1960s appears to have been concessional loans and taxes, which according to Tan and Ow (1982) amounted to 12 percent of value added in 1967. About 15 percent of total subsidized government loans in 1968 was granted to the industry. Quotas on textiles were insignificant, since they were completely removed by 1967.

The absolute levels of all the performance variables exhibit a smooth upward trend, with the largest jumps occurring between 1970 and 1973 for the output, employment, and domestic export series. In terms of growth rate, however, the output, employment, retained imports, and capital series exhibited a clear downward trend, with the largest decrease for all four variables occurring in 1969. The growth rate in domestic exports more than doubled between the periods 1967–9 and 1970–3. The average annual growth rate during 1967–9 was 17.9 percent. The largest jump in the later period occurred in 1971 when the growth rate in domestic exports reached 55.6 percent. This is not surprising, given that the textile firms were required to intensify their export drive in return for the relatively large concessional loans and taxes received (Tan and Ow, 1982). The share of

---

[2] Both the average effective rate of protection and effective rate of subsidy for the food industry was 5 percent in the Tan and Ow (1982) study.

exports in domestic textile output rose from two fifths in 1967 to two thirds by 1973.

Clothing

This category was one of the top three employers in the manufacturing sector, claiming between 7.5 and 10.5 percent of total manufacturing employment during 1967–73. Its contributions in terms of output and value added were much less significant, particularly between 1967 and 1970. In the early 1970s, its average share of total manufacturing output and value added reached between 3 and 4 percent annually.

In 1967 only undergarments were protected by tariffs. Quotas, however, were imposed on many items between 1965 and 1967. Most of these quotas were replaced by tariffs in late 1968, accounting for the higher nominal rates of protection in subsequent years. The nominal rate of protection jumped from 0.1 percent in 1967 to 13.5 percent in 1969, and remained relatively high through the 1970s. With the exception of the retained imports series, the absolute levels of all the remaining variables rose over time, with the largest absolute increase for output, employment, and domestic exports occurring from 1970 through 1973. Retained imports increased between 1966 and 1968 before falling in absolute terms during 1967–70. The levels slowly recovered between 1971 and 1973.

The growth rates for all the variables fell between 1967 and 1969 (or 1970) and rose in subsequent years.

Footwear

Footwear makes a very small contribution to manufacturing employment, output, or value added. It is, however, an industry that has undergone a significant amount of trade liberalization.

Quotas on footwear were completely removed by 1966. Protection was primarily through tariffs, particularly since independence (1965). A 40 percent duty was imposed on footwear imports following independence. The level of protection gradually fell between 1967 and 1975 from a high of 43.5 percent in 1967 to 16.4 percent in 1973 and finally to zero by 1975.

In terms of performance, except for the value added per worker series, the absolute levels for the other variables increased smoothly over 1967–72. The growth rates for output, employment, and domestic exports show a clear falling trend.

Rubber Products

Like the footwear industry, the rubber products industry is very small, contributing less than 2 percent each to total manufacturing output, employment, or value added in 1967. These shares fell to less than 1 percent by 1973.

This industry received both tariff and quota protection. The level of tariff protection reached its peak in 1967 at 10.9 percent and declined in subsequent years. Quotas were completely removed by 1968.

An upward trend for absolute levels is observed for all the performance variables (except capital), with the exception of the last two years of the liberalization episode. The downward trend after 1971 appears to continue after 1973. The growth rates for all the variables (again, except for capital) declined significantly if we compare the averages for the period 1970–3 with those for 1967–9. The growth rates for output and employment exhibit a continuous slide from 1970 through 1973.

Fabricated Metal Products

The importance of this industry in terms of its contribution to total manufacturing output, employment, and value added decreased slightly over the period under consideration. In 1973 its share in each of the three variables stood at around 5 percent, down from the 1967 figures of 8 percent for output and 6.5 percent for employment and value added.

Both tariff and quota protection were granted to the industry. The average tariff for the whole industry was about 6 percent in 1967 and declined gradually to zero by 1975. This average, however, hides a wide variation in the rate of protection granted to component industries. All the quotas imposed on the industry in 1964–5 were completely replaced by tariffs in 1968. The share of the total volume of subsidized loans to this industry was already significant in the middle to late 1960s, and became even more pronounced in the 1970s.

In general, although the absolute levels of all the performance variables exhibit upward trends, continuous downward trends are observed for the growth rates of employment and retained imports. While the domestic exports and capital investment growth rates were more variable over time, the average annual rates for the period 1970–3 also fell compared with those for the period 1967–9. The growth rate of output increased from 1967 to 1970, averaging 18.8 percent annually before plunging to − 2.3 percent in 1971 and recovering to 5 percent and 21 percent in 1972 and 1973 respectively.

Electrical Machinery

The contribution of the electrical machinery industry to the manufacturing sector was relatively small in 1967. However, the industry grew rapidly over the period under consideration. Its contribution in terms of its share in total manufacturing output, employment, and value added rose from

3 percent for each in 1967 to 15.5 percent, 22 percent, and 18.5 percent respectively by 1973. In 1973 this category ranked first in terms of its share of total manufacturing employment and value added and second in terms of its contribution to manufacturing output.

Tariff protection was low in this industry, ranging from a high of nearly 1.7 percent to below 1 percent throughout the 1970s. Quotas, however, were imposed on a wide selection of items, varying in severity and length of imposition. Quotas on items ranging from electric bulbs, batteries, and accumulators to electric refrigerators were restrictive from 1965 through mid-1968 (we will designate this the period of tight quotas). By the end of 1968, quotas on many items were removed while for some items they were replaced by tariffs. The period from 1969 to 1972 appears to be one when loose quotas were in place. Quotas were nonexistent in this industry by 1973. Government loans at concessional terms became important in the early 1970s.

Electrical machinery showed its most rapid and dramatic growth in output, employment, and domestic exports in 1969. The growth rate of output jumped from 25 percent in the period 1967–8 to 80.1 percent in 1969 before stabilizing at an average of around 50 percent in each of the subsequent years. Similarly, the employment growth rate rose from an average of 20 percent in the period 1967–8 to 107.3 percent in 1969, stabilizing at 46 percent from 1970 to 1973. The growth rate of domestic exports rose from − 23 percent in 1968 to 145 percent in 1969, falling off to an average annual rate of around 57 percent from 1970 to 1973. The growth rate of retained imports grew at an average yearly rate of 35 percent from 1967 to 1970, reaching a peak of 66.8 percent in 1970 before falling off to 22 percent in each of the subsequent years. The absolute levels of all the variables exhibited smoothly increasing trends over the entire period.

Thus, unlike other industries (with the exception of perhaps the textiles industry), the growth rates of output, employment, and domestic exports did not plunge dramatically in the latter half of the liberalization period. Instead, these variables appeared to maintain relatively high growth rates throughout, albeit at lower rates than the large growth spurts that occurred in the late 1960s.

Transport Equipment

The share of transport equipment in total manufacturing output, employment, and value added rose rapidly over the period 1967–73. Its share of output rose from from 4.7 percent in 1967 to 8 percent by 1973. Its contribution of 7 percent each to employment and value added in 1967 rose to 11 percent and 11.5 percent respectively by 1973.

The level of tariff protection increased from an average of 3.3 percent in 1967 to 7.2 percent in 1971. A huge jump in the level of tariff protection to

21 percent in 1973 was due primarily to higher tariffs imposed on imported passenger vehicles in 1972 as part of the government's policy of restricting car ownership. Quotas were imposed from 1965 through 1970 and were completely removed by 1971. Between 1968 and 1969, tariffs replaced quotas for several items. Data on quota restrictions indicate that these were relatively tight during 1967–8, looser in 1969–70, and nonexistent from 1971 to 1973.

High and increasing growth rates of both output and employment were achieved between 1966 and 1969. Growth rates for both variables plummeted during 1970–3. Retained imports grew at 111 percent in 1968 and fell to an average annual rate of 21 percent in subsequent years. The growth rates of domestic exports, labor productivity, and capital investment appeared to jump around from year to year without any clear pattern. The overall performance of the transportation industry masks the differences in performance of the main components of the industry, namely shipbuilding and repair and motor vehicle assembly.

Liberalization and Performance

The eight industries under consideration can be classified into those protected (in different degrees over time) by tariffs alone (footwear), by tariffs and quotas (rubber products, clothing), by tariffs, quotas, and subsidies (food, electrical machinery, transportation equipment, fabricated metals), and by tariffs and subsidies (textiles).

Tariff levels were among the highest in the footwear industry. Its NPR fell from almost 44 percent in 1967 to 16 percent in 1973, reflecting significant tariff liberalization. Tariffs and quotas were simultaneously liberalized in the food, rubber products, fabricated metals, and electrical machinery industries. Tariff levels declined in these four industries from an average of 6 percent in 1967 to almost zero by 1973. At the same time quotas in these industries were either completely removed by 1968 (rubber and fabricated metals industries) or replaced by tariffs (food and electrical machinery). The food industry was a major recipient of subsidized loans in the late 1960s, the electrical machinery industry in the early 1970s, and fabricated metals throughout the entire period 1967–73, with the share of total loans increasing over the period.

Levels of tariffs and quotas moved in the opposite direction in the clothing and transportation equipment industries. Over the period 1967–73, NPRs in both industries rose, partly because of the replacement of quotas with tariffs, beginning in 1968 for the clothing industry and 1969 for the transportation industry. In addition to the high NPRs (21 percent) the transportation industry received a high percentage of government-subsidized loans throughout the period 1967–73, but particularly in the early 1970s.

In contrast with all the above industries, all quotas in the textile industry were removed by 1967. This industry was characterized by an absence of quotas and low NPRs (2 percent) throughout the liberalization period. Subsidized loans were granted to the industries in the late 1960s. However, like the food industry, the share of total subsidized loans granted to the textile industry declined significantly in the early 1970s.

The eight industries examined above were the most significant in terms of their contribution to total manufacturing output, employment, or value added (at least 3 percent) in any given year, as well as experiencing significant liberalization. Aw (1988, appendix tables 15–20) shows the levels and growth rates of domestic production, employment, imports, exports, value added per worker, and net value of fixed assets. The levels of domestic output, employment, and exports increased for every year in the 1967–73 period for all eight industries. The beginning of the oil crisis (end of 1973) saw falls in the employment and output levels of the footwear, rubber products, and food industries, as well as declines in domestic export levels in the transportation equipment and rubber products industries.

The degree of trade restrictiveness (via tariffs, quotas, and subsidies) and the average annual rates of growth in the performance variables (output, employment, domestic exports, and retained imports), broken down into two subperiods 1967–9 and 1970–3, are shown in appendix 1, table A1.4. In the first five industries in the table the first subperiod was generally more restrictive with higher tariffs and tighter quotas, followed by the more liberal 1970–3 subperiod. However, except for the electrical and electronic machinery industry, the growth rates of all the performance variables declined, with the most drastic falls experienced in the footwear and rubber products industries. These trends, particularly for footwear and rubber, appear to be the result of restructuring away from the relatively more unskilled labor-intensive activities.

The electrical and electronics machinery industry displayed phenomenal growth in terms of output and employment over the liberalization period, averaging an annual rate of about 80 percent and 87 percent respectively during the period 1969–70. In the early 1970s, both growth rates stabilized at around a respectable 40 percent each year. The growth rate of domestic exports and retained imports grew from averages of 44 percent and 24 percent in the period 1967–9 to 57 percent and 33 percent respectively in the period 1970–3. Given the low levels of tariff protection granted (averaging below 1 percent during the entire period 1967–73) and the relaxation of quota restrictiveness only in the nonelectronic component of the industry, it is likely that the solid performance of the industry can more appropriately be ascribed to the facts that it is (a) an export industry based on cheap labor costs and benefits from massive inflow of foreign capital, technical expertise, and export markets in industrialized countries, as well as (b) one of the major recipients of concessional government loans in the early 1970s.

The next category of industries, clothing and transportation equipment, is characterized by rising tariff protection levels but easing quota restrictiveness over the period 1967–73. The contrast in performance of the two industries is clear from table A1.4. The clothing industry experienced rapid and rising growth rates in both employment and domestic exports, with the growth rates of production and retained imports remaining relatively stable from 1967–9 to 1970–3. In the early 1970s it had the second highest level of tariff protection, behind the footwear industry. A large hike in tariff rates in the industry occurred in 1969 in order to raise additional revenue to meet increased defense expenditure and to accumulate reserves in anticipation of the effects of the British withdrawal in 1971. However, the effect may have been to protect domestic production and employment from foreign competition. The industry, faced with rising production costs and labor shortages in 1970 as well as increasing protectionism in its traditional export markets, has sought to diversify its markets to combat the problem.

The high growth rates of the late 1960s in output and employment in the transport industry took a huge plunge in the early 1970s, despite rising rates of tariff protection granted primarily on motor vehicles. The motor assembly industry operated with an enormous excess capacity because the domestic market was so small. Despite tariff protection, the industry was rapidly losing market share to imports. As partial liberalization took effect in the early 1970s in the form of the replacement of quotas with tariffs, the overall growth rates of output and employment in the whole industry declined significantly despite the good performance of the shipbuilding and ship repair component. The latter industry boomed throughout the period 1967–73 with employment accounting for 10 percent of the total workforce in 1970 and output accounting for 20 percent of total manufacturing output in the same year. Rapid growth continued through 1976, supported only by government financing on internationally accepted terms. From 1972 to 1975 the output growth rate in current dollars was more than 35 percent per year. This good performance reflects in part oil exploration in the region, the successful exploitation of Singapore's natural comparative advantage of strategic location, and positive encouragement by the government in recruiting and training labor and in developing support activities.

Growth in the textile industry was explosive in the late 1960s, with output and employment growing at average annual rates of 48 percent and 42 percent respectively. Since 1970 the industry has become predominantly export oriented with domestic exports growing at a phenomenal 40 percent average annual rate from 1970 to 1973. The only significant form of government intervention in this industry was in the area of concessional loans and taxes in the late 1960s. According to Tan and Ow (1982), these concessions amounted to 12 percent of value added in 1967. In addition, the government, through the EDB, recruited the help of the International Executive Service Corps to provide the local industry with expert assistance in the development of synthetic textile products.

Overall, there is no clear or strong link between industry performance and the degree of protection provided by tariffs and quotas. The bulk of the decline in the performance variables of industries which had undergone significant liberalization can be explained by the restructuring of emphasis away from these industries (for example, footwear, rubber products, food) and toward others (for example, electrical and electronic machinery and fabricated metals). In industries with less significant liberalization efforts (clothing, textiles, and transportation) the contrast in performance appears to be related to the economy's underlying resource endowments, the export potential of the industries concerned, and important external factors such as the need to increase government revenue, upgrading to counteract foreign protectionism, and increased oil exploration.

In appendix 3 we report the results of a simple exercise conducted to find out whether the levels and growth rates of the performance variables of the various industries can be attributed to liberalization efforts during the period 1967–73.

The results indicate that tariff levels are insignificantly related to all the performance variables. This is to be expected since, as mentioned before, tariff levels were small and showed little variation over time. However, there is some evidence pointing to the desirability of using a strategy of gradually replacing quotas with tariffs over the liberalization period. QRs were shown always to have a negative effect on performance, with this effect becoming smaller as they are replaced by tariffs. These results may indicate the ineffectiveness of quotas in protecting domestic producers. Possible explanations rest with the creation of bottlenecks in the production process which are due directly to the implementation of the quotas as well as to long-run efficiency losses associated with QRs.

A weakness of the regression exercise is the exclusion of the effect of government subsidies on performance for the reasons mentioned before. Nevertheless, the broad implications of the regression results appear interesting.

It is difficult to postulate the importance of the role of the government in targeting industries for special treatment without more information on the magnitude of the entire package of investment incentives granted to these industries over time. The limited evidence on the role of investment incentives, presented in chapter 6, suggest that we cannot reject the hypothesis that investment incentives are instrumental in enhancing industry performance. Moreover, information gathered from the yearly growth rates of the performance variables across industries (Aw, 1988, appendix tables 15 and 16) is revealing. In particular, for the major sectors, the growth rates peaked earlier during the liberalization period for the traditional industries (footwear, rubber products, textiles, and food) and later for the nontraditional industries (electrical machinery, fabricated metals, transportation equipment). There were two output and employment growth peaks in the clothing industry, one in 1967 and the other in 1972. The distinctions in the growth peaks across industries appear to coincide with active government support of the traditional industries in the middle to late 1960s and the shift of such support to the nontraditional industries in the late 1960s to early 1970s. The effects of such government targeting also appeared, although not as dramatically, in the export performance of the sectors. While the bulk of the manufacturing sectors experienced not only increasing export levels but also high annual export growth rates, particularly high growth occurred in the capital goods industries of transport equipment and nonelectrical and electrical machinery.

Liberalization and Employment

Overall, the negative impact of liberalization on employment has been negligible for two main reasons. Firstly, the liberalization effort has been both modest and gradual. Secondly, it occurred during a period of very rapid general growth in GDP, aggregate employment, and investment commitments. The unemployment rate was halved in the period from 1967 to 1973 while GDP took off at an average annual rate of 12.8 percent during the same period. GDFKF was more than 22 percent on average each year from 1967 to 1973. In the context of such rapid growth, any negative impact on employment at the sectoral level becomes much less significant both politically and economically, given the increase in employment opportunities in the growing sectors.

Negative growth rates in employment were experienced in three sectors: paints and pharmaceuticals (1970–2), rubber products (1972–3), and footwear (1973). The degree of liberalization was highest in the footwear industry, with tariffs ranging from 44 percent in 1967 to 16 percent in 1973 and zero by 1975. Quotas were completely removed from this industry by 1966. The rubber products industry had an 11 percent rate of protection via tariffs in 1967, which declined in subsequent years. The paints and pharmaceuticals industry had only an average of 4–6 percent tariff protection between 1967 and 1973, with most of the liberalization occurring in the form of replacing quotas by tariffs. Despite the moderate degree of liberalization in these sectors, it is doubtful that the fall in employment was primarily the result of liberalization of imports into these sectors. The employment decline, particularly in the footwear and rubber products categories, can be attributed mainly to the general restructuring of the economy away from these industries. This is reflected partly in the fall in the level of government concessional loan commitments to industries like footwear and rubber products, and the simultaneous increase of such loans to metal and engineering and transportation equipment (see tables 4.1 and 5.15). The policy of restructuring did not take place overnight. In fact, almost immediately after independence from Malaysia in 1965, there were numerous official announcements of the government's intent to encourage the nontraditional activities and gradually deemphasize the more labor intensive traditional ones. Thus the industries had plenty of time to adjust their output and employment levels. The shift in focus from the rubber products and footwear industries is further reflected in negative growth rates not just in employment but in output, value added, and domestic exports.

Even if liberalization was perceived as the main factor for retrenchment in these three sectors, the small size of these industries meant that they gave less cause for concern to policymakers. The footwear and the rubber products industries contributed less than 2 percent each to total manufacturing output, employment, and value added in 1967. These shares fell to less than 1 percent by 1973. The paint and pharmaceuticals industry's share of output, employment, and value added was also small, ranging between 2 and 4 percent on average during the period 1968–73. In addition, the tight labor market of the early 1970s meant that ample job opportunities existed elsewhere. In particular, among the leading industries in the late 1960s to early 1970s were the textile and clothing industries, as well as the electrical and electronic industries whose factor and skill requirements are not dissimilar to those in footwear or the rubber products industries. These growth industries are not only labor intensive but also contribute a large and increasing share to the output, employment, and value added of the manufacturing sector. There is also some evidence that an increasing number of the labor force in the early 1970s was being absorbed into the service sectors (wholesale, retail, and other service activities).

In summary, the main reasons for the negligible adverse impact of liberalization on employment and thus adjustment costs are the simultaneous growth in other labor-intensive activities, the small size of the declining industries, and the modest and gradual liberalization effort that characterized the episode.

8

The Experience with Liberalization: Some Conclusions and Inferences

In this chapter we summarize some salient features of the economy, as well as of the liberalization episode, that distinguish it from other countries in the project as a prelude to drawing more general inferences about the timing and sequencing of liberalization. Table 8.1 provides a broad summary of the circumstances and consequences of the liberalization episode under consideration.

Political Commitment and the Choice of Export Promotion

Singapore is often viewed as a country characterized by open and liberal economic policies, whose economic performance has been among the most successful among developing countries. In general, growth has been rapid and sustained. Policies that continue to open up an already relatively open economy have proceeded at a moderate pace with occasional slowdowns due to political or international factors, but have rarely been reversed.

The transition to self-sustaining economic growth was far from smooth or easy. Internal and international conflict plagued the Republic throughout the first decade of its existence; the British announcement that their military presence was to end in Singapore further exacerbated the problems faced by the nascent state. Unemployment was massive and worsening and there was no agricultural sector for the unemployed to fall back on if the attempt to industrialize failed. Further, the prospects of entrepôt trade, the main sustenance of the economy, looked bleak as other countries began to bypass Singapore as a transit center and engage in direct trading with their terminal markets as well as with their import sources.

Difficult political and economic decisions had to be made. The political will to survive, and the willingness to embark on an economic strategy with little immediate payoff, ultimately transformed most of Singapore's problems into assets. Infrastructural facilities ranging from well-equipped

Table 8.1 Singapore summary table

Question	1968–73 episode
Broad nature	Continuous, gradual process; replacement of QRs with tariffs accompanied/followed by reduction or removal of QRs and tariff levels; promotion of exports; liberal use of foreign workers; strong multinational corporation involvement
Size, duration	Small, average
Ex ante economic circumstances	
Balance of payments – continuing surplus	Yes
Rate of growth	High (14%)
Growth of exports (domestic)	High (43%)
Commodity terms of trade	Improving
Unemployment	Falling (7%)
Rate of inflation	Very low (0.7%)
Rate of growth of GDFKF	High (33%)
Openness of economy	High
External factors	Favorable
Infrastructure	Efficient
Ex ante political circumstances	
Government	Stable ruling party since 1959; strong and stable
Ideological shift	No
Public support	Yes
International influence	Some; separation from Malaysia, British military withdrawal
Accompanying policies	
Exchange rate	Essentially fixed
Export promotion	Mainly tax concessions for export industries; preferential loans and equity participation for selected export industries
Monetary policy	Expansionary
Fiscal policy	Continuing surplus
Capital movements	High
Domestic controls	None on consumer prices but some in the labor market (wage control and forced public savings)
Implementation	
Stage departures	Unidirectional and continuous with no reversal
Economic performance	
Price levels	Very stable
Openness	High and increasing
Balance of trade	Widening deficits
GDP growth	Averaged more than 10% annually
Employment	Rising; reaching full employment by 1973
Wages	Stable

industrial estates to official institutional support were developed. An export-oriented strategy, initially instigated by the failure of the Malaysian common market, turned out to be the best long-run strategy to ensure sustained industrial expansion. With a domestic market of 2.2 million people too small to take advantage of economies of scale, a strong external reserves position, and very few natural resources, the switch to an export-oriented strategy was seen as a way of promoting greater competition and thus efficiency, of reaping economies of scale, and of earning foreign exchange to meet import requirements necessitated by population growth, rising standards of living, and the increasing need for material inputs to an expanding manufacturing sector.

Singapore's economic policies during the 1960s and 1970s were strongly influenced by the thinking of one man, Keng Swee Goh, who at various times held the post of Finance Minister of the Republic. An economist by profession, he believed that:

> If our experience can be used as a general guide to policy in other developing nations, the lesson is that the free enterprise system, correctly nurtured and adroitly handled, can serve as a powerful and versatile instrument of economic growth. (Goh, 1972)

This basic philosophy of free enterprise, however, is radically different from the *laissez-faire* policies of the colonial era. It was felt that the latter policies were responsible for little economic growth, massive unemployment, wretched housing, and inadequate education. Goh (1977a) writes:

> We had to try a more activist and interventionist approach. Democratic socialist economic policies ranged from direct participation in industry to the supply of infrastructure facilities by statutory authorities, and to laying down clear guidelines to the private sector as to what they could and should do. The successful implementation of these policies depended on their acceptance by the people, generally, and on the active cooperation of organized labor in particular. [In Singapore] all these conditions were fulfilled.

Government intervention in economic activities is considerable, ranging from numerous fiscal and other investment incentives to direct participation in industrial activities, some of which directly compete with activities of the private sector. It is claimed, however, that these activities of the government are not entirely inconsistent with the basic principle of free enterprise. Protection granted to industries whether via tariffs, quotas, or investment incentives was seen as a short-term measure to help infant industries produce for export. Government statements reflect general abhorrence of supporting inefficient or nonprofitable industries. With respect to government ownership of commercial and industrial undertakings:

Our guiding principle has been that these must operate on efficient business lines and compete with other firms on equal terms . . . They are expected to make profits and if they do not come up to expectations, they are allowed to go bankrupt as we do not throw good money after bad. (Goh, 1977c)

In fact, the degree of direct government participation in industrial activities through the creation of many public enterprises actually increased with the movement from the import substitution strategy of the 1965–7 era to the strategy of export promotion. This response was justified by the government on the grounds that few domestic entrepreneurs were willing to undertake production for the more risky international market while foreign entrepreneurs were restrained by the national wages policy that produced a higher price of labor in Singapore relative to its competitors in other developing countries.

The documented evidence suggests that public enterprises in Singapore, unlike those in many other countries, make money. Nevertheless, costs to society of such direct government intervention from the subtle crowding-out of domestic entrepreneurs, problems of direction and control, lack of initiative, and the consequence of business mistakes may be unavoidable, even in Singapore, as these public enterprises persist and expand over time.

Unlike many other countries that have similarly intervened in the country's economic activities, the Singapore government's interventionist activities in the context of a relatively open frontier and its willingness to put these activities to the test of international competition probably substantially reduce the costly distortions likely to arise from similar interventionism in a closed economy. In particular, government subsidies to export industries, while distortionary, are more self-limiting than the use of import restrictions as well as self-correcting given the high cost of continued subsidization and the government's open frontier commitment. It is this strong commitment to an open frontier that has, in fact, placed the government's interventionist role in the labor market in particular under intense scrutiny in the current recession. The high and rising rates of contributions to the CPF by employers and employees since the mid-1970s, coupled with the government's high wage policy mentioned before, have made Singapore much less attractive to multinational enterprises as well as rendered exports of existing enterprises less competitive in the international market. These developments and the government's unwavering commitment to a liberal trade regime have led to a closer examination of the relevant domestic policies so that appropriate adjustments can be made before large and prolonged economic costs are incurred.

The Importance of a Good Initial Position

In contrast with most of the other countries in the project, Singapore is a city-state with an economy based primarily on trade. As such, there has always been a plentiful supply of capital (Goh, 1972). Singapore's per capita income ever since it came into existence has been several times higher than that of other agriculture-based developing countries. The other advantage of a trade-based economy is that it provides not just a surplus for the creation of new modern industries but a ready pool of entrepreneurs with skills more apt to the business of establishing modern industries than those typical of a largely peasant-based economy. Thus it was not necessary to create an entirely new entrepreneurial class since one already existed, even though it was a class less skilled in industry than in trade.

Singapore was consequently in a favorable economic position right from the beginning of the liberalization episode, despite its turbulent political conditions, at least through the mid-1960s. Furthermore, the economy was not faced with any difficulties over foreign exchange since the government did not resort to deficit budgeting. The strength of the national currency in turn meant that it was not necessary to impose various government controls on trade and industry that are found in other developing countries. The balance of payments was healthy, conducive not only to the liberalization of import restrictions but also, in providing the financial backing for incentives, to active government encouragement of exports.

Perhaps more important than the internal conditions and policies was the generally favorable background of the world economy through the 1960s. The industrialized nations of the West and Japan experienced a long and sustained post-war boom almost to the end of the 1960s. The boom not only generated strong demand for a wide variety of imports into those countries, but also encouraged the rapid establishment of offshore manufacturing facilities in developing countries like Singapore, where government policies were considered credible and the political environment relatively stable, and which have a supply of disciplined and trainable labor and a good infrastructure.

The initial efforts at liberalization were sustained during a period of continued favorable internal and external economic circumstances. Unemployment continued to decline from 8.1 percent in 1967 to 6.0 percent in 1970 and 4.5 percent in 1973. This trend was a direct result of the accelerated pace of industrialization in general and the emphasis on labor-intensive export-oriented activities in particular. In fact, signs of labor shortages, first apparent in 1970, were met by the importation of foreign workers with appropriate skills. By 1973 reportedly more than 100,000 (one eighth) of the labor force were foreign. This external labor market provided a convenient safety valve, with entry restricted by government immigration policy during recessions and encouraged during booms.

Real growth rates in GDP rose rapidly, averaging over 13 percent a year during the period 1968–70. Not only was the balance of payments in surplus in every single year of the liberalization period, but the government budget also recorded surpluses during the same period.

The Importance of Foreign Entrepreneurship

A striking feature of Singapore's policy is the encouragement given to imported enterprise, as reflected by Goh (1977b):

> . . . this dependence (on foreign investment) is strongest in Singapore and [that] the participation of national enterpreneurs in promoting industrial development is smaller here than in any other country. Certainly the inducements offered to foreign investment are stronger and more varied in Singapore. [Moreover] . . . her position is probably unique in that she is now dependent on a continuing supply of foreign workers to sustain growth.

Foreign investment is attractive to Singapore not in its provision of physical capital but in its ability to help Singapore bridge the technological gap and to penetrate export markets. It was felt that the borrowing of foreign capital, expertise, managers, engineers, and marketing capabilities provided a shortcut to rapid industrial growth and export markets. This route was seen as an attractive alternative to relying on domestic sources, particularly through the late 1960s when the economy was plagued by massive unemployment. The rate at which local enterprise was moving from traditional retail and entrepôt trade into new manufacturing industries was too slow to generate enough jobs for the increasing number of unemployed (Kuan Yew Lee, 1978).

Consequently, government industrial policy, while not intending to do so, has in fact favored foreign over local investors. Major tax incentives were offered to designated pioneer enterprises with investments over S$1 million which clearly favored large foreign investors. In addition, government provision of infrastructural and institutional support concentrated primarily on attracting foreign investors at the expense of local enterprise (Deyo, 1981).

The high growth of exports from the manufacturing sector in the late 1960s through the early 1970s has been attributed by many authors to the export orientation of the multinational corporations that were based in Singapore rather than directly to the incentives provided by the government (Chia, 1984). By the early 1970s, more than 75 percent of total exports were from foreign- or foreign-majority-owned firms. In addition it was estimated that, by the early 1970s, over half the total investment stock in banking and manufacturing and 45 percent of manufacturing employment was accounted for by foreign firms (Deyo, 1981).

While the contribution of multinational corporations to Singapore's rapid growth is large, the continued heavy reliance on multinationals has had the effect not only of stagnating local private enterprise and thus preventing the development of local entrepreneurship but also of making the economy extremely vulnerable to world trading conditions. In the late 1970s the government became more aware of the lack of indigenous entrepreneurship and started actively encouraging the growth of local industries.

The Liberalization Episode

Industrial policy initially focused on the replacement of imports. However, the restrictiveness of tariffs and quotas, even at the height of the country's import substitution phase in the mid-1960s, was less than in other countries. Thus the efforts made toward liberalizing imports were not as intense or widely publicized. During the import substitution phase, the government was acutely aware of the constraints of vigorously pursuing an import substitution policy given the small domestic market and the possible distortion of resource allocation with high-cost domestic industries. In this context, tariffs and quotas were imposed very selectively and viewed as purely temporary measures to aid economically viable industries. Recipients of tariff or quota protection were therefore under constant pressure to become internationally competitive without government assistance. Tariff protection was generally granted only to those industries with the greatest potential for long-term growth. Continued protection was often contingent on the industries' potential ability to export without aid from the government. In the early to middle 1960s import-substituting efforts concentrated on selected labor-intensive and light industries.

Since protection was understood to be temporary, when policy shifted in 1967 toward a more outward-oriented strategy, it did not constitute a dramatic or major change in trade policy. More formally, trade liberalization in Singapore was characterized by a gradual multistage process beginning in 1968 and culminating in 1973. During this period, tariffs and quotas were gradually reduced on some items and quotas were replaced by tariffs on others. This replacement phenomenon was particularly active between 1968 and 1969 when about one third of all new tariffs imposed during that period replaced previous quotas. The separate stage of replacing QRs with tariffs was felt to be necessary to give protected industries time to reach full competitiveness with foreign imports. From 1970 to 1973 tariffs and quotas on many items were abolished, so that by

1973 quotas were nonexistent and only a few items continued to receive tariff protection.

Liberalization on the import side continued beyond 1973 to shrink the list of protected items, although at a much slower pace than in the period 1968–73. Reversals to the basic policy sustaining the open trade regime never took place. Often, in fact, domestic policies such as the government real wage and forced saving policies, had to be modified or changed to bring them into line with the economy's openness to international conditions and competitiveness.

Efforts at promoting exports took place simultaneously with import liberalization. This was not surprising given that the economy had a balance-of-payments surplus for every year of the liberalization period. These promotional efforts took the form of tax incentives and concessional loan commitments, as well as the provision of subsidized, modern, and efficient infrastructure primarily to attract foreign capital and technology. Industries were treated in a discriminatory manner with "growth industries" (textiles in the mid-1960s, and shipbuilding and repair, and electrical and electronics in the late 1960s) receiving additional incentives to export rather than higher tariff protection, with rare exceptions (for example, motor vehicle assembly).

The use of investment incentives to encourage the establishment of selected export-oriented industries was much more publicized than the liberalization of import restrictions. These incentives were not given to offset any anti-export bias created by the system of protection but to aid an infant exporting industry, an activity which presumably imposes high risks on the individual exporter and high costs of entering foreign markets (Chia, 1984). To the extent that these incentives were in fact important in providing the recipients with effective protection, the index of liberalization overstates the real extent of liberalization. Owing to data inadequacies and the nature of some of the incentives, the export subsidies cannot be quantified and the index is limited to the extent of liberalization on the import side. However, the role of investment incentives is examined in the context of the performance of a group of "pioneer" industries which are the primary beneficiaries of the incentives.

A casual comparison of the pioneer industries with the manufacturing sector as a whole indicates the overall superior performance of the former in terms of output, employment, direct exports, and value added. Given that these same pioneer industries are also more capital intensive and more likely to be multinational corporations (which are larger and tend to perform much better than the average manufacturing firm), the direct relationship between investment incentives and superior performance is equivocal. Nevertheless, we cannot reject the hypothesis that these incentives play a role, even if indirect, in the superior performance of the pioneer compared with the nonpioneer industries.

Liberalization and the Costs of Adjustment

The 1968–73 liberalization had no noticeable adverse effect in terms of unemployment. While employment declined in a couple of industrial sectors this was more the consequence of restructuring in general than of the liberalization *per se*. Moreover, the healthy economy minimized adjustment costs associated with trade liberalization. In fact it is not uncommon to find, during any given year of the period 1968–73, retained imports growing simultaneously with employment across the industries. This is not surprising given that rapid economic growth generates increased demand for domestic output (and thus employment) as well as imports. Moreover, increases in retained imports of the intra-industrial inputs will also serve to increase domestic output and employment.

General Inferences from the Singapore Experience

Single versus Multiple Stages

The liberalization episode was planned as a gradual process with two very simple stages: the first involved the removal or replacement of quotas with tariffs and the second the reduction in the level of tariffs and total abolition of all quotas. The replacement phenomenon indeed occurred most intensively at the beginning of the episode, between 1968 and 1969. Tariff protection also increased during that period. The period from 1970 to 1973 saw the gradual reduction of tariff levels and by the end of that period all quotas were abolished.

In the absence of a single-stage liberalization it is difficult to speculate which should be preferred. One obvious reason for favoring the multistage process is that the episode succeeded. It was seen as desirable by policymakers who were concerned about the adjustment costs that might follow a single-stage process. Nevertheless, the success of the multistage process was perhaps more a function of the consistency and thoroughness with which the liberalization policy was pursued and the strong political continuity and commitment to the issue of liberalization. Given relatively low protection levels to begin with and the virtual absence of adjustment costs associated with the actual liberalization, it could be argued that a single-stage process would have had the same success if pursued with the same intensity and commitment, and in the same circumstances.

The Length and Speed of the Liberalization Process

The liberalization episode took a total of six years. Given the general acceptance of the policy, this time period appeared desirable as there was little danger of policy reversal arising from pressure from lobby groups. The longer period thus perhaps avoided the adjustment costs associated with a single, short, and sweeping reform.

Separate Stage for Replacing Quotas with Tariffs

The separate stage involving the replacement of QRs with tariffs appeared to have occurred relatively smoothly in Singapore. It was felt that this separate stage was necessary to give protected industries time to reach full competitiveness with foreign imports. Results from a simple estimating model indicate the desirability of this strategy in terms of its effect on the economy's performance indexes. QRs are shown always to have a negative effect on performance, and this effect becomes smaller as they are replaced by tariffs. While the model is crude and simple, there is evidence to indicate the ineffectiveness of QRs in protecting domestic producers. A possible explanation is that QRs created bottlenecks in the production process.

A Separate Export Promotion Stage

Efforts at promoting exports took place simultaneously with import liberalization. The rapid growth rate in domestic exports meant that the economy was able to sustain the rapid growth in imports that followed liberalization. For an economy like Singapore which is highly dependent on imports, the simultaneous emphasis on export growth and import liberalization is important to avoid reversals of policy caused by the inability to finance the high import ratio. The strong balance-of-payments position as well as the strength and stability of the national currency during the entire liberalization episode made such a policy choice feasible.

Uniform versus Discriminatory Sectoral Treatment

In general, sectors were treated relatively uniformly until the very late 1960s and 1970s when government policies became a lot more selective with respect to the different investment incentives made available to industries. In terms of subsidized loans to industries, there appears to be some sectoral discrimination as early as the 1960s when the government wanted to promote labor-intensive industries like textiles and clothing, but, in general, a host of incentives other than subsidized loans was available to all industries. However, beginning in 1968–9, the government became more selective in granting investment incentives. The latter incentives include the ready and inexpensive provision of infrastructural facilities such as industrial estates, a containerized port, public utilities, and telecommunication services as well as technical support services and management training programs. In contrast with the mid-1960s, where such financial and service incentives were given after lengthy expert studies on the feasibility and viability of these industries, "identified industries" are given priority by the EDB, the government agency in charge of "putting the package (of incentives) together."[1] In general, the evidence is that the service incentives in the form of all the necessary support services involved in the implementation and start-up of an industry override the more objective financial incentives in importance.

The implication of the above is that government statements about which industries should expand most rapidly were the major incentive factor since they tend to create confidence on the part of private entrepreneurs that they could move into these industries with much lower risk than other industries given that these "identified industries" would be supplied with the service incentives more readily. As far as the government was able to decipher, they were in the business of supporting healthy industries. Any aid to selected industries was purely for infant industry reasons and thus was very temporary. Such enterprises were then expected to pay their way and earn enough surplus to finance future expansion without any government assistance. If they did not come up to expectations, they were allowed to fail.

The most prominent example is the motor vehicle assembly plant, first encouraged in 1963 to supply the anticipated Malaysian common market of 10 million people. After the separation from Malaysia, the Singapore government, in following the import substitution strategy, granted the industry tariff protection, the extent of which was raised over the years from 10 percent in 1966 to 45 percent by 1972. Despite this protection, production costs in the industry remained internationally uncompetitive and local assemblers were losing market share to imports. Moreover, linkages with local parts and components manufacturing failed to develop owing to the limited domestic market. The actual elimination of tariff protection, considered as early as 1973, was delayed by uncertainties over employment and economic growth resulting from the oil crisis of that year. All the local assembly plants were finally closed down by 1980 when the government removed all protection granted to the industry.

Of course, the problem with any industrial policy is the need for "very detailed data and a relatively complete understanding of how a particular industry competition is played out and about how the industry in question interrelates with other sectors of the economy" (Krugman, 1986). Given that these criteria for a successful policy of strategic export promotion are well beyond what policymakers possess in practice, great caution is necessary in the continuation of Singapore's policy of selective export promotion.

[1] This is clear from the *Annual Reports* (1967–9) of the EDB.

The benefits of Singapore's industrial policy is less clear than it appears. It is conceivable that the favored industries would have performed well without any direct government assistance and that all the investment incentives did was to hasten their good performance. It is clear, however, on the cost side that the willingness to subject supported industries (whether via tariff/quota or subsidy protection) to the test of international competition, and to gradually remove the support if they are found wanting, has enabled the economy to avoid the excessive costs often associated with the attempt to pick winners. Indeed, given the relatively open frontiers of the economy, the economic cost of supporting an inefficient industry is certainly more apparent and therefore less tolerable in view of the country's scarce resources.

Thus the important issue here appears to be not simply whether industries are treated uniformly or discriminatorily, but rather how the government structures the system of incentives in its discriminatory treatment of industries.

Appendix 1 Estimation of the Economy-wide Nominal Tariff

A time series of nominal and effective protection rates (NPRs and EPRs) is unavailable for Singapore. NPRs and EPRs have been calculated by Tan and Ow (1982) for the manufacturing sector for 1967, while Ting (1971–2) has calculated EPRs for a sample of pioneer industries in 1968.

Approximations of the level of nominal tariffs obtained for the period 1965–77 are reported in table A1.1. The average rates reported measure actual tariff levels (that is, net of tariff exemptions) rather than the average of the stated rates. The Customs and Excise Department publishes in its *Annual Reports* the Singapore dollar amount of protective duties collected during a given year at the three-digit SITC classification of commodities. The use of total import duties simplifies the calculation process significantly, given the multitude of specific and preferential tariff rates in existence. Given that a substantial proportion of total imports comprise reexports, the tariff rate of each of the three-digit SITC commodity groups can be approximated by taking the ratio of total protective duties to retained imports. However, retained imports are not published. The rate can be estimated from reexport values:

> total exports − domestic exports = reexports
> total imports − reexports − (value added on reexports) = retained imports

Since value added on reexports is not readily available, retained imports at export value are taken as a proxy of retained imports at import value.

To account for the relative importance of each of the three-digit SITC commodity groups, the tariff rates had to be weighted by production values. During the period under study, 1965–77, trade as well as industry categories have been redefined; accordingly, modifications had to be made to the commodity–industry correspondence table published in the *Singapore Input–Output Table*, 1973. Thus, the estimation process involves the following.

1 The industry level tariff rate is calculated by taking the ratio of total import duties (classified as protective duties by the Customs and Excise Department) to total retained imports at the three-digit SITC level.

Table A1.1 Nominal tariff and manufacturing output by industry (percent)

Industry	1965 NT	1965 Wt	1967 NT	1967 Wt	1969 NT	1969 Wt	1971 NT	1971 Wt	1973 NT	1973 Wt	1975 NT	1975 Wt	1977 NT	1977 Wt
Food	0.7	23.2	4.9	29.5	5.0	22.9	2.2	18.4	1.8	12.0	1.6	10.7	1.8	11.6
Beverages	0	5.5	0	4.2	0	2.9	0	2.2	0	1.3	0	1.7	0	1.6
Tobacco products	0	9.0	1.8	7.1	2.0	4.4	2.1	3.0	0	2.2	0	1.8	0	1.5
Textiles	0.7	1.2	1.8	1.2	2.0	2.7	2.1	4.1	2.2	5.3	0	3.3	0	3.3
Clothing	0	2.7	0.1	2.7	13.5	3.6	16.3	3.9	17.4	4.8	12.6	3.6	15.6	4.6
Leather and leather products	4.2	1.1	15.1	1.1	11.4	0.9	2.0	0.4	5.2	0.5	0	0.3	0	0.4
Footwear	5.9	0.6	43.5	0.7	18.2	0.8	25.7	0.8	16.4	0.4	0	0.4	0	0.3
Wood products	0	7.5	0	7.0	0	7.8	0	6.3	0	7.8	0	4.0	0	4.2
Furniture and fixtures	3.1	0.9	32.3	0.7	21.3	0.8	19.2	1.4	24.7	0.6	13.1	0.6	15.9	0.8
Paper and paper products	0.5	1.2	2.5	1.4	1.2	1.6	0.7	1.4	1.0	1.4	0	1.2	0	1.2
Printing and publishing	0	7.0	0	5.2	0	3.8	0	3.7	0	2.8	0	2.9	0	3.2
Industrial chemicals and cases	0.4	0.5	0.8	0.4	5.2	0.8	0.9	1.6	0	1.8	0.1	2.0	0	2.2
Paints and pharmaceuticals	2.9	2.0	3.6	3.6	6.2	3.3	4.8	2.8	3.8	3.1	9.4	3.5	8.8	3.3
Processing of jelutong and gum dawar	0	1.2	0	0.6	0	0.7	0	0.4	0	0.3	0	0.3	0	0.2
Rubber products	4.6	1.1	10.9	1.4	7.6	1.7	4.9	1.4	8.3	0.8	4.2	0.7	6.7	0.6
Plastic products	0.2	0.7	1.0	0.8	1.0	1.1	0.9	1.4	0.4	1.8	0	1.5	0	1.9
Pottery, china, glass products	1.1	1.1	3.8	1.0	3.4	0.8	3.7	0.5	3.0	0.4	0	0.4	0	0.4
Brick, tiles, clay products	0.1	0.8	0.2	0.4	0.1	0.4	3.7	0.4	3.9	0.3	0	0.2	0	0.2
Cement and concrete	0.1	1.8	0.4	2.0	0.3	1.9	0.2	1.7	0	1.6	0	2.7	0	2.2
Asbestos, stone, nonmetallic/mineral	0.1	2.1	0	1.1	0	0.5	1.1	1.1	0	1.0	0	1.1	0.1	0.9
Iron and steel	0.1	2.4	0.6	3.3	0.8	2.6	0.9	1.8	0.3	1.8	0	1.9	0.1	1.4
Nonferrous metals	0	0.7	0	0.4	0	0.9	0	0.7	0	0.6	0	0.5	0	0.5
Metal grills and fabricated products	1.5	11.0	5.9	8.2	3.5	8.0	2.0	7.1	1.1	5.7	0	6.5	0	5.7
Nonelectrical machines	0	2.3	0	2.3	0.6	2.4	0.5	4.4	0.5	5.7	0.1	9.6	0	6.7
Electrical machines and electronic products	0.3	2.9	1.7	3.3	1.2	6.2	0.7	12.6	0.4	20.7	0.7	20.9	0.6	25.5
Transportation equipment and oil rigs	0	5.9	3.3	6.0	6.1	11.6	7.2	12.2	20.9	10.7	12.0	13.5	17.8	11.9
Professional and scientific equipment	0	—	0	—	0.5	0.5	0.8	0.8	0	2.1	0	2.3	0	1.8
Other manufacturing	1.7	3.6	6.0	4.3	3.2	4.3	3.0	4.0	2.3	2.5	0.1	1.9	0	1.9
Total	0.63	100[a]	3.59	100	3.78	100	3.04	100	4.14	100	2.84	100	3.65	100

—, not applicable. NT, nominal tariff; Wt, weight.

[a] Weights may not add to 100 because of rounding errors.

Sources: Customs and Excise Department, Singapore, Annual Report, various years; Department of Statistics, Singapore External Trade Statistics, various years; Department of Statistics, 1978

Table A1.2 Sectoral effective exchange rate (Singapore dollars per US dollar)

	1966	1967	1968	1969	1970	1971	1972	1973	1974	1975
Food	3.183	3.231	3.242	3.233	3.182	3.093	2.863	2.489	2.445	2.410
Beverages	3.068	3.080	3.080	3.079	3.094	3.027	2.809	2.444	2.437	2.371
Tobacco products	3.068	3.080	3.080	3.079	3.094	3.027	2.809	2.444	2.437	2.371
Textiles	3.133	3.136	3.131	3.140	3.163	3.090	2.892	2.498	2.437	2.371
Clothing	3.070	3.082	3.097	3.496	3.572	3.519	3.296	2.869	2.733	2.670
Leather products	3.535	3.557	3.520	3.429	3.416	3.088	2.826	2.572	2.437	2.371
Footwear	4.670	4.420	3.558	3.638	3.914	3.805	3.469	2.844	2.439	2.371
Wood products	3.068	3.080	3.080	3.079	3.094	3.027	2.809	2.444	2.437	2.371
Furniture	4.166	4.074	3.798	3.735	3.762	3.609	3.407	3.048	2.952	2.681
Paper products	3.207	3.156	3.131	3.117	3.111	3.049	2.831	2.468	2.437	2.371
Printing and publishing	3.068	3.080	3.080	3.079	3.094	3.027	2.809	2.444	2.437	2.371
Industrial chemicals	3.126	3.103	3.117	3.238	3.138	3.054	2.837	2.467	2.438	2.375
Paints, pharmaceuticals, etc.	3.255	3.192	3.216	3.271	3.252	3.171	2.919	2.537	2.497	2.595
Petroleum products	3.068	3.080	3.080	3.079	3.094	3.027	2.809	2.444	2.437	2.371
Rubber products	3.598	3.417	3.417	3.313	3.261	3.175	3.064	2.647	2.537	2.472
Plastic products	3.097	3.111	3.102	3.108	3.124	3.053	2.833	2.454	2.437	2.371
Glassware	3.270	3.196	3.180	3.185	3.197	3.120	2.881	2.516	2.444	2.371
Clay products	3.081	3.085	3.084	3.084	3.094	3.140	2.908	2.540	2.460	2.371
Cement products	3.080	3.093	3.091	3.087	3.099	3.031	2.813	2.445	2.437	2.371
Nonmetal products	3.071	3.080	3.080	3.079	3.094	3.027	2.809	2.444	2.437	2.371
Iron and steel	3.078	3.097	3.104	3.105	3.120	3.054	2.832	2.450	2.437	2.371
Nonferrous metals	3.068	3.080	3.080	3.079	3.094	3.027	2.809	2.444	2.437	2.371
Fabricated metals	3.280	3.261	3.161	3.187	3.165	3.088	2.863	2.470	2.437	2.371
Nonelectrical machinery	3.068	3.080	3.085	3.097	3.112	3.042	2.821	2.456	2.442	2.373
Electrical machinery	3.134	3.132	3.132	3.116	3.117	3.047	2.820	2.453	2.450	2.387
Transport equipment	3.068	3.183	3.165	3.269	3.336	3.244	3.173	2.955	2.669	2.656
Precision equipment	3.068	3.080	3.080	3.079	3.094	3.027	2.809	2.444	2.437	2.371
Other manufactures	3.554	3.266	3.188	3.177	3.190	3.117	2.895	2.500	2.441	2.374

Source: calculated using table A1.1 and official exchange rates, from Nyaw, 1979

Table A1.3 Capacity utilization of pioneer manufacturing firms

Industrial	Output value (million S$)		Capacity utilized (%)		Excess capacity (%)	
	1967	1968	1967	1968	1967	1968
Food and beverages	112.6	155.5	35.6	38.1	64.4	61.9
Textiles and garments	28.8	59.0	28.1	34.8	61.9	65.2
Wood and paper products	22.5	35.6	74.2	42.2	25.8	57.8
Rubber and leather products	16.3	22.7	78.6	68.3	21.4	31.7
Chemicals and chemical products	14.1	29.0	34.1	18.9	65.9	81.1
Petroleum refinery and petroleum products	308.6	578.3	94.7	66.5	5.3	33.5
Nonmetallic mineral products	18.3	22.0	57.2	60.9	42.8	39.1
Metals and engineering	98.2	125.1	60.6	46.1	40.0	53.9
Electrical machinery, appliances, and components	21.4	25.0	46.6	43.8	53.4	56.2
Plastic products	3.1	6.5	32.5	26.5	67.5	73.5
Miscellaneous manufacturing	4.6	13.7	20.5	28.9	79.5	71.1
1 Total of "pioneer firms"	648.5	1,072.5				
2 Total of all firms	1,687.2	2,175.7				
3 Row 1 divided by row 2 (%)	38.5	49.3				

Source: Nyaw, 1979

2 A correspondence table that matches categories of commodities at the three-digit SITC level to their corresponding production categories at the three-digit SIC level over the period from 1965 to 1978 is constructed.

3 Production (output) values are then used as weights in deriving the overall nominal tariff.

The petroleum and rubber processing industries are noncompetitive importers because the natural resources required for their production are not available in Singapore. These two industries are therefore excluded from the estimation of the economy-wide nominal tariff.

Table A1.4 Trade restrictiveness and industry performance

Domestic industry	Retained imports (%) 1967-9	1970-3	Quotas[a] 1967-9	1970-3	Subsidies[b] 1967-9	1970-3	Output 1967-9	Output 1970-3	Employment 1967-9	Employment 1970-3	Exports 1967-9	1970-3	Imports 1967-9	1970-3
Footwear	31	21	N	N	X	X	28	5	24	3	16	13	22	9
Food	5	2	T	L	V	V(*)	22	5	13	2	14	9	7	7
Rubber products	9	7	T	N	X	X	23	3	19	3	31	4	22	10
Fabricated metals	5	2	L	N	X	V(†)	16	12	21	7	18	1	58	22
Electrical machinery	2	1	T	L/N	X	V	35	50	43	46	44	57	24	33
Clothing	7	17	T	N	X	X	31	29	16	24	26	36	5	4
Transport equipment	5	14	T	L/N	V	V(†)	42	19	49	9	55	38	64	22
Textiles	2	2	N	N	V	V(*)	48	38	42	30	18	40	38	4

[a] N, quota; T, tight quota; L, loose quota; L/N, change from loose to no quota; L/N, change from loose to no quota midway through period under consideration.

[b] Subsidies as measured by the level (X,V) and share (X,V) of total subsidized loans granted by the government (see table 5.15 for details); X, absence of subsidies; V, presence of subsidies; V(*), declining importance relative to previous period; V(†), increasing importance relative to previous period.

Sources: Customs and Excise Department, Singapore, Annual Report, various years; Department of Statistics, Singapore External Trade Statistics, various years; Department of Statistics, 1978, 1983; Department of Imports and Exports Control and Registration, 1964–73; Tan and Ow, 1982; EDB, 1964–8; DBS, 1969–75; Aw, 1988, appendix tables A.7–A.10

Appendix 2 Classification of Production and Trade Data

Industry	SIC code	SITC code
Consumer goods		
Food	311–2	012, 013, 022–4, 032, 046–8, 052, 053, 055, 061, 062, 073, 081, 091, 099, 411, 421, 422, 431
Beverages	313	111, 112
Tobacco	314	122
Wearing apparel	322	841, 842
Footwear	324	851
Furniture and fixtures	332	821
Printing and publishing	342	892
Scientific and precision equipment	385	281–6, 726, 861–4
Miscellaneous manufactures	390	891, 894–7, 899
Intermediate goods		
Textiles	321	266, 267, 651–7
Leather and leather products	323	211, 212, 611–3, 831
Wood and cork products	331	243, 631–3
Paper and paper products	341	251, 641–2
Industrial chemicals	351	512–5, 561, 571, 581, 599
Paints and pharmaceuticals, etc.	352	531–3, 541, 551, 553–4
Petroleum	353–4	321, 331–2, 521
Glassware	361–2	664–6, 812
Clay products	363	662–3
Cement and concrete products	364–5	661
Nonmetallic mineral products	369	274–6, 667
Capital goods		
Iron and steel	371	671–4
Nonferrous metals	372	681–9
Fabricated metals	381	675–9, 691–8
Nonelectrical machinery	382	711–2, 714–5, 717–9
Electrical machinery	383	722–5, 729
Transport equipment	384	731–5

Source: Department of Statistics, 1978

Appendix 3 An Estimation of the Effect of Liberalization on the Performance Indices

A cross-section time series regression of the various performance indices was run separately on the rates of nominal tariff and quota restrictions. The data for the tariff levels are those given in table A1.3 for 25 sectors during the period 1967–73. Dummy variables were used to represent the various degrees of restrictiveness imposed by quotas on the 25 sectors for 1967–73. Quotas were set at some percentage of the level of imports of a benchmark year, generally 1963. In some sectors, quotas were nonexistent throughout the entire period under consideration, while in others quotas were nonexistent for only part of the period. A sector is said to have a loose quota if, during the year under consideration, the bulk of quota levels range from 50 to 110 percent of the 1963 import levels or if quotas were replaced by tariffs. A few sectors had tight quotas, defined as years in which quotas were pervasive over the sector or when the majority of items in the sectors had quotas set at less than 50 percent of the 1963 import levels.

Table 3.3 (see chapter 3) shows the list of degrees of quota restrictiveness (T, tight; L, loose; N; none) that characterized the different years during the period 1967–73 across the 25 sectors under consideration.

The performance indices were represented separately by the levels and growth rates of output, employment, domestic exports, retained imports, and labor productivity for the 25 sectors over the time period under consideration.

In notation, the equation that was estimated can be represented by

$$Y_{it} = \beta_0 + \beta_1 D_1 + \beta_2 D_2 + \beta_3 T_{it} + \beta_4 D_1 T_{it} + \beta_5 D_2 T_{it} + u_{it}$$

where Y_{it} is the performance variable (output, employment, labor productivity, retained imports, or domestic exports) of sector i in year t, $i = 1, \ldots, 25$ and $t = 1967, \ldots, 1973$, $D_1 = 1$ if the quota is tight and zero otherwise, $D_2 = 1$ if the quota is loose and zero otherwise, and T_{it} is the rate of nominal tariff protection of sector i in year t.

D_1T_{it} and D_2T_{it} represent the interaction of the tariff rate in sector i and period t with the tight and loose quota regimes respectively. The coefficient for D_1T_{it} (β_4) is an estimate of the effect of changes in tariff rates on the performance variables during the tight quota regime. Conversely, the coefficient for D_2T_{it} (β_5) is an estimate of the effect of changes in tariff rates on the performance variables when the quota regime becomes loose.

Sector-specific dummies were also included in the regressions in order to account for the effect on the performance variables of sectoral differences that were constant over time. The coefficient estimates of these dummies appear very reasonable but are not reported here.

The equations are estimated using the fixed-effects estimation technique. The base year in each case is 1967 and the base sector is the food processing industry. Simultaneity in the system is ruled out since in general tariffs and quotas were based more on the export potential of the industries than on sector-specific unemployment of resource problems. In some industries the motivation for protection was for retaliation rather than protective purposes.

Table A3.1 reports the coefficient estimates of the effect of the different trade restrictions on the levels of output, employment, domestic exports, retained imports, and labor productivity. The effects of both the tight and loose quota regimes on all the performance variables are always negative and significant. More importantly, the coefficient for D_1 (tight quota regime) is always greater than that for D_2 (loose quota regime). That is, the falls in the levels of output, employment, retained imports, domestic exports, and labor productivity during the tight quota regime are always significantly larger than those during the loose quota regime. There are several possible reasons for these results. The first has to do with the inefficiency, in the broad sense, of the use of quotas. A related reason is the evidence that bottlenecks are created in the production process as a direct result of implementation of the quotas. Clearly, these bottlenecks would have a more severe impact on production the more restrictive were the quota levels.

In contrast, tariff levels are insignificantly related to all the performance variables. This is to be expected since, as mentioned before, tariff levels in general are low and show little variation over time. Similarly the effects on the performance variables of changes in tariff levels during the tight quota regime are positive but insignificant. However, when the regime switched to loose quotas, the effects of the tariff levels on all the performance variables, except labor productivity, became positive and significant.

Overall, the above results indicate that, while the performance variables are negligibly affected by changes in tariff levels, they are negatively and significantly related to quota restrictions. An interesting result is that, when the quota regime changes from tight to loose, the effect of the tariff levels on the performance variables changes from being positive and

Table A3.1 Coefficient estimates of the effect of tariffs and quota regimes on the performance variables[a]

Independent variable	Coefficient	t statistic
Dependent variable: output level		
Constant	712.4	18.4
D_1	−384.4	−7.3
D_2	−114.9	−4.3
Tariff	66.5	0.3
D_1T	555.4	0.8
D_2T	2,958.8	3.0
$R^2 = 0.79$		$F = 19.2$
Dependent variable: employment level		
Constant	14.6	9.0
D_1	−15.3	−7.0
D_2	−4.8	−4.3
Tariff	7.2	0.8
D_1T	38.1	1.2
D_2T	128.7	3.1
$R^2 = 0.74$		$F = 1.92$
Dependent variable: domestic exports level		
Constant	184.4	6.7
D_1	−181.3	−4.8
D_2	−65.9	−3.5
Tariff	−21.7	−0.2
D_1T	477.2	0.9
D_2T	1,609.8	2.3
$R^2 = 0.59$		$F = 7.13$
Dependent variable: retained imports level		
Constant	433.9	9.6
D_1	−399.0	−6.5
D_2	−105.7	−3.4
Tariff	−189.7	−0.8
D_1T	72.5	0.1
D_2T	3,597.7	3.1
$R^2 = 0.81$		$F = 21.8$
Dependent variable: labor productivity		
Constant	12.8	8.1
D_1	−5.5	−2.6
D_2	−1.7	−1.6
Tariff	−4.3	−0.5
D_1T	−15.1	−0.5
D_2T	42.2	1.1
$R^2 = 0.82$		$F = 22.7$

The base is the no-restriction regime: $D_1 = 1$ if quotas are tight; $D_2 = 1$ if quotas are loose; D_1T and D_2T are the interaction terms of tariffs with the respective quota regimes.

[a] Sector-specific dummies were included in the regressions although the coefficient estimates are not included in the table.

insignificant to being positive and significant. This result appears to point to the desirability of shifting from quotas to protection through tariffs (part of the definition used for determining the movement from tight to loose quota regimes).

In estimating the effects of the various trade restrictions on the growth rates of the performance variables it was also necessary to redefine the independent variables as changes in the levels. The following equation was estimated:

$$Y_{it} = \beta_0 + \beta_1 D_1 + \beta_2 D_2 + \beta_3 D_3 + \beta_4 D_4 + \beta_5 D_5 + \beta_6 T_{it} + \beta_7 D_1 T_{it} + \beta_8 D_2 T_{it} + \beta_9 D_3 T_{it} + \beta_{10} D_4 T_{it} + \beta_{11} D_5 T_{it} + u_{it}$$

Y_{it} and T_{it} are as defined before. The dummies D_1 through D_5 represent changes in the quota regimes as follows:

$$D_1 = \begin{array}{l} 1 \text{ if quota was tight in years } t \text{ and } t + 1 \\ 0 \text{ otherwise} \end{array}$$

$$D_2 = \begin{array}{l} 1 \text{ if quota was loose in years } t \text{ and } t + 1 \\ 0 \text{ otherwise} \end{array}$$

$$D_3 = \begin{array}{l} 1 \text{ if quota was tight in year } t \text{ and loose in year } t + 1 \\ 0 \text{ otherwise} \end{array}$$

$$D_4 = \begin{array}{l} 1 \text{ if quota was loose in year } t \text{ and there was no quota in year } t + 1 \\ 0 \text{ otherwise} \end{array}$$

$$D_5 = \begin{array}{l} 1 \text{ if there was no quota in year } t \text{ and loose quota in year } t + 1 \\ 0 \text{ otherwise} \end{array}$$

Table A3.2 Coefficient estimates of the effecct of tariffs and the changes in quota regimes on the performance variables[a]

Independent variable	Coefficient	t statistic
Dependent variable: growth rate of output		
Constant	−6.1	−0.4
D_1	−15.2	−0.7
D_2	5.9	0.6
D_3	17.8	0.7
D_4	27.8	2.5
D_5	−1.5	−0.1
T	36.8	0.5
$D_1 T$	776.6	1.2
$D_2 T$	−38.0	−0.2
$D_3 T$	451.2	0.6
$D_4 T$	−295.1	−1.7
$D_5 T$	682.8	0.6
$R^2 = 0.40$		$F = 2.65$

Dependent variable: growth rate of employment

Constant	−17.5	−1.4
D_1	−1.5	−0.1
D_2	9.4	1.2
D_3	16.4	0.8
D_4	19.9	2.3
D_5	53.5	3.4
T	48.9	0.9
D_1T	558.1	1.1
D_2T	78.3	0.5
D_3T	1,006.8	1.8
D_4T	−244.9	−1.8
D_5T	283.4	0.4
	$R^2 = 0.55$	$F = 4.9$

Dependent variable: growth rate of retained imports

Constant	−5.8	−0.4
D_1	19.6	0.9
D_2	17.9	2.0
D_3	43.4	1.8
D_4	13.4	1.3
D_5	−10.0	−0.6
T	−147.3	−2.2
D_1T	68.9	0.1
D_2T	−181.3	−0.9
D_3T	−1,134.4	−1.7
D_4T	−375.7	−2.4
D_5T	555.0	0.6
	$R^2 = 0.27$	$F = 1.47$

Dependent variable: growth rate of domestic exports

Constant	4.5	0.2
D_1	−27.0	−0.7
D_2	−10.3	−0.6
D_3	−36.0	−0.8
D_4	−18.3	−0.9
D_5	−12.7	−0.4
T	−14.6	−0.1
D_1T	754.7	0.6
D_2T	576.8	1.4
D_3T	1,648.5	1.3
D_4T	203.8	0.7
D_5T	1,752.0	0.9
	$R^2 = 0.2$	$F = 0.97$

$D_1 = 1$ if the quota was tight in years t and $t + 1$; $D_2 = 1$ if the quota was loose in years t and $t + 1$; $D_3 = 1$ if the quota was tight in year t and loose in year $t + 1$; $D_4 = 1$ if the quota was loose in year t and there was no quota in year $t + 1$; $D_5 = 1$ if there was no quota in year t and a loose quota in year $t + 1$; D_1T, D_2T, D_3T, D_4T, and D_5T are the interaction terms of tariffs with the respective quota regimes.

The tariff variable was entered in terms of levels rather than changes in the level given that many sectors had zero tariffs to begin with.

The interaction terms of each of the above dummies D_1 through D_5 with the levels of tariffs were included in the estimated model together with sector-specific dummies as in the previous exercise. Coefficient estimates of the latter are not reported.

Table A3.2 reports the coefficient estimates of the effect of tariff levels and the changes in the different quota regimes on the growth rates of output, employment, retained imports, and domestic exports.

The effect of the changing quota regimes on the growth rate of output had the expected signs although only the coefficient estimate on D_4 (when the quota changes from tight to loose) was significantly positive. The change either from a tight to a loose quota regime or from a loose to a no quota regime, or when loose quotas characterized two consecutive years, had a positive effect on the growth rate in output. In contrast, when quotas were tight in both years or when there was a change from a no quota to a loose quota regime, the effect on the growth rate in output was negative. The coefficient estimate for the tariff rates was positive but insignificant. Again, this is not surprising given the low and constant tariff rates across sectors over time. Likewise, the results for the effect of the interaction terms of tariffs with the different quota dummies were mixed and insignificant.

The effects on the growth rate in employment changes in quota regimes were similar to those on the growth rate of output except that for the coefficient estimate on D_5 (movement from no quota to loose quotas) which was positive and significant. As before, changes in tariff rates appear to have negligible and insignificant effect on the growth rate of employment. Of the interaction terms, only the coefficients on D_3T and D_4T are significant. That is, changes in tariff rates across sectors and time appear to affect the growth in employment positively when the quota regime changes from tight to loose, while the effect is negative when the quota regime changes from loose to no quotas.

The effect of changing quota regimes on the growth rates in retained imports generally carried expected signs. When quota regimes were tight or loose in both consecutive years as well as when quota regimes changed from tight to loose or loose to no quotas, the impact on the growth rate in retained imports was positive. This relationship was positive and significant in the case of D_2 (loose quotas in consecutive years) and D_3 (movement from tight to loose quotas). The effect on the independent variable or moving from a no quota to a loose quota regime was negative but insignificant. The coefficient estimate for the tariff variable was negative and significant. Of the interaction terms, only the coefficient estimate for D_4T (interpreted as the effect of changes in tariff rates during the movement from a loose to a no quota regime) was negative and significant.

The effects of all the changes in quota regimes (variables D_1 through D_5) and the tariff rates on the growth rates of domestic exports are always negative but insignificant. All interaction terms, in contrast, have a positive effect on the dependent variable but, again, the coefficient estimates are insignificant. As far as explaining the levels of performance in output, employment, retained imports, domestic exports, and labor productivity is concerned, the regression results show that the effects of the different quota regime are more significant than those of tariffs. Quotas in general tend to reduce the levels of all the performance variables, and the reduction is greater the tighter the quota restriction. In addition, the results indicate positive and significant effects on the performance variables of changes in tariff levels given a loose quota regime.

Although the results of changes in quota regimes and tariffs on the growth rate of the performance variables are not as significant as those on the levels of those variables, they reveal some interesting points. In general, a movement toward liberalization, whether it involves changes to a more liberal quota regime or lower tariffs, has a positive effect on the growth rates in output, employment, and retained imports. Conversely, a movement toward more restrictive quotas generally decreases output, employment, and retained imports. However, the majority of these coefficients are insignificant. The growth rate of domestic exports is negatively affected by changes in both quota regimes and tariffs, although insignificantly so.

References

Asher, Mukul G. (1984) "The fiscal system of Singapore." In Poh Seng You and Chong Yah Lim, eds, *Singapore: Twenty-five Years of Development*. Singapore: Nan Yang Zing Zhou Lianhe Zaobao.

Aw, Bee-Yan (1988) "The timing and sequencing of trade liberalization policies: Singapore, statistical appendices." Available from the Brazil Department, World Bank, Washington, DC.

Chia, Siow Yue (1974) "Inflation and growth: the case of Singapore." In V. Bhanoji Rao, ed., *Inflation and Growth*, Singapore: Stanford College Press.

Chia, Siow Yue (1976) "Introduction strategy and industrial performance in Singapore." Ph.D. dissertation, McGill University (unpublished).

Chia, Siow Yue (1984) "Export incentives, manufactured exports and employment in Singapore." In Pitou van Dijk and Harmen Verbruggen, eds, *Export-oriented industrialization and Employment: Policies and Responses with Special Reference to ASEAN Countries*, Amsterdam: Vrije Universitat.

Choi, S. C. (1979–80) *Consumer Prices in Singapore: 1935–78*. Singapore: Department of Economics and Statistics, University of Singapore (unpublished academic exercise).

Chow, Kit Boey and Amina Tyabji (1980) *External Linkages and Economic Development: the Singapore Experience*. Singapore: Chopmen, ERC Research Monograph Series 8.

Customs and Excise Department, Singapore, *Annual Report*, various years.

DBS (Development Bank of Singapore) (1969–75) *Annual Reports*, Singapore: Singapore National Printers.

Department of Imports and Exports Control and Registration (1964–73) *Notice to Singapore Importers*.

Department of Statistics (1973) *Report on the Census of Population 1970*, vol. I. Singapore: Singapore National Printers.

Department of Statistics (1978) *Singapore Input–Output Tables 1973*. Singapore: Singapore National Printers.

Department of Statistics (1981) *Census of Population 1980*. Singapore: Singapore National Printers.

Department of Statistics (1983) *Economic and Social Statistics, Singapore, 1960–82*. Singapore: Singapore National Printers.

Department of Statistics, *Census of Industrial Production*, various years. Singapore: Singapore National Printers.

Department of Statistics, *Singapore External Trade Statistics*, various years. Singapore: Singapore National Printers.

Department of Statistics, *Yearbook of Statistics*, various years. Singapore: Singapore National Printers.

Deyo, Frederic C. (1981) *Dependent Development and Industrial Order: an Asian Case Study*. New York: Praeger.

EDB (Economic Development Board) (1964–75) *Report and Accounts of the Economic Development Board*. Singapore: Singapore National Printers.

Goh, Keng Swee (1967) *Parliamentary Debates*, 26(8), col. 466. Singapore: Singapore Government Printer.

Goh, Keng Swee (1968) *Economic Survey of Singapore: Annual Budget Statement*. Singapore: Singapore National Printers.

Goh, Keng Swee (1970) *Economic Survey of Singapore: Annual Budget Statement*. Singapore: Singapore National Printers.

Goh, Keng Swee (1972) *The Economics of Modernization and Other Essays*. Singapore: Asia Pacific Press.

Goh, Keng Swee (1973a) *Economic Survey of Singapore: Annual Budget Statement*. Singapore: Singapore National Printers.

Goh, Keng Swee (1973b) "Investment for development: lessons and experience of Singapore, 1959 to 1971." Paper delivered at the Third Economic Development Seminar, Saigon, January 1973.

Goh, Keng Swee (1977a) "A socialist economy that works." In *The Practice of Economic Growth*, chapter 9. Singapore: Federal Publications.

Goh, Keng Swee (1977b) "Singapore in the international economy." In *The Practice of Economic Growth*, chapter 2. Singapore: Federal Publications.

Goh, Keng Swee (1977c) "Trade discrimination by the industrialized nations: some suggestions." In *The Practice of Economic Growth*, chapter 14. Singapore: Federal Publications.

Hassan, Riaz (1976) "Symptoms and syndrome of the development process." In Riaz Hasan, ed., *Singapore: Society in Transition*. Kuala Lumpur: Oxford University Press.

Hirschman, Albert O. (1964) "The paternity of an index." *American Economic Review*, 54(5), 761–2.

Hughes, Helen and Poh Seng You, eds (1969) *Foreign Investment and Industrialization in Singapore*. Madison, WI: University of Wisconsin Press.

Krugman, Paul R. (1986) *Strategic Trade Policy and the New International Economics*. Cambridge, MA: MIT Press.

Lee, Kuan Yew (1978) "Extrapolating from the Singapore experience." Special lecture at the 26th World Congress of the International Chamber of Commerce, Florida.

Lee, Soo Ann, ed. (1973) *Industrialization in Singapore*. Camberwell, Vic.: Longman Australia.

Lee, Soo Ann (1984) "Patterns of economic structure in Singapore." In Poh Seng You and Chong Yah Lim, eds, *Singapore: Twenty-five Years of Development*. Singapore: Nan Yan Xing Zhoi Lianhe Zaobao.

Lim, Linda and Eng Fong Pang (1984) *Trade, Employment and Industrialization in Singapore*. Geneva: ILO (International Labor Organization) World Employment Programme.

MAS (Monetary Authority of Singapore) (1971–3, 1973–9, 1981–2) *Annual Reports*.

Ministry of Trade and Industry (1974) *Economic Survey of Singapore*. Singapore: Singapore National Printers.

Ministry of Trade and Industry (1983) *Economic Survey of Singapore*. Singapore: Singapore National Printers.

Nyaw, Mee-Kau (1979) *Export Expansion and Industrial Growth in Singapore*. Hong Kong: Kingsway.

Ow, Chin Hock and C. M. Goh (1974) "Wages, productivity and prices." In V. Bhanoji Rao, ed., *Inflation and Growth*. Singapore: Stanford College Press.

Rana, Pradumna B. (1981) *ASEAN Exchange Rates: Policies and Trade Effects*. Singapore: Institute of Southeast Asian Studies.

Seah, Chee Meow (1984) "Political change and continuity in Singapore." In Poh Seng You and Chong Yah Lim, eds, *Singapore: Twenty-five Years of Development*. Singapore: Nan Yang Xing Zhou Lianhe Zaobao.

Tan, Augustine and Chin Hock Ow (1982) "Singapore." In Bela Balassa and Associates,

Development Strategies in Semi-industrial Economies. Baltimore, MD: Johns Hopkins Press for the IBRD and Inter-American Development Bank.

Tan, Chwee Huat (1984) "Towards better labor–management relations." In Poh Seng You and Chong Yah Lim, eds, *Singapore: Twenty-five Years of Development.* Singapore: Nan Yang Xing Zhou Lianhe Zaobao.

Ting, Grace Y. M. (1971–2) "Effective protection of pioneer industries in Singapore." Master's thesis, University of Singapore (unpublished).

Tsao, Yuan (1984a) *Policies for High Growth and Low Inflation: the Case of Singapore, 1965–83.* Singapore: National University of Singapore.

Tsao, Yuan (1984b) "Productivity trends in Singapore." In Poh Seng You and Chong Yah Lim, eds, *Singapore: Twenty-five Years of Development.* Singapore: Nan Yang Xing Zhou Lianhe Zaobao.

Yeh, Stephen and Eng Fong Pang (1973) "Housing, employment and national development: the Singapore experience." Paper presented at the SEADAG Seminar on Short-Term Employment Creating Projects in Southeast Asia, Baguio, Philippines, August 21–4, 1973.

Index